BRITAIN'S
FINAL
DEFENCE

BRITAIN'S
FINAL
DEFENCE

ARMING THE HOME GUARD,
1940–1944

DALE CLARKE

The
History
Press

Cover image: 'Members of the Post Office Home Guard receiving lessons on how to load the Spigot Mortar, 21st June 1943.' (Official photograph; author's collection)

First published 2016
This paperback edition published 2022

The History Press
97 St George's Place, Cheltenham,
Gloucestershire, GL50 3QB
www.thehistorypress.co.uk

British Library Cataloguing in Publication Data.
A catalogue record for this book is available from the British Library.

ISBN 978 0 7509 9895 6

Typesetting and origination by The History Press
Printed and bound in Great Britain by TJ Books Limited, Padstow, Cornwall.

Trees for LYfe

CONTENTS

INTRODUCTION

The organisation that became Britain's Home Guard was founded on 14 May 1940, and ordered to 'stand-down' in November 1944. It was never called on to fight; the invasion it stood by to repel might never have been a practical possibility or even a real intention; and the weapons it used are a byword for the obsolete, improvised, naive and whimsical. So why does it matter?

During the latter half of 1940, and well into 1941, a Nazi invasion of the United Kingdom was, for the British, a probability if not a certainty. The threat of invasion, and the need to guard against raids and sabotage, provoked popular, political and media demands that civilians be armed. 'Total Defence', as it became known, transformed the political, military, social and physical landscape of Britain. The population was more politicised than it had been during the First World War and war, as an extension of politics, rather than patriotic duty, became a matter for the citizen militant – raising important legal and ethical issues over the nature of 'combatants', and making the government answerable to a vociferous, demanding and engaged public. This resulted in the formation of the Local Defence Volunteers – subsequently renamed the 'Home Guard' – and thus the need for the British government to arm not only the rapidly expanding wartime British Army, but also a paramilitary militia, numbering well over 1.5 million men. In June 1940, that was entirely beyond the capacity of the British weapons manufacturing industry, state and private – although this could not possibly be admitted for obvious military and political reasons. The result was the importation of huge quantities of unfamiliar weapons from the United States, and investigation into the use of unconventional production techniques, and the use of non-strategic materials and innovative technologies. Indeed, the very definition of a 'weapon' was called into question – leading, for example, to the formation of the Petroleum Warfare Department – as was the matter of whether any limits could be, or should be, imposed on the means of fighting for the UK's national survival.

This book explores the weapons provided for the British Home Guard between 1940 and 1944, but will also examine the process through which a perception hardens into orthodoxy, which in turn can crystallise into an accepted 'historical fact'. The perception in question is that the wartime British Home Guard was poorly armed – in modern parlance, that it lacked combat power. For many years the prevailing view has been that the Home Guard represents a nadir of military effectiveness. We will explore the way that perception formed, in the first few months of the organisation's existence, as a result of a logistic crisis that the government could not possibly expose, was sustained through the period when the force actually flourished, and went on to become part of the post-war mythology of the Home Front. Most British families provided a member of the Home Guard, and the organisation is studied as part of the experience of the Home Front, as well as one of the manifestations of the 'citizen militant' that shaped post-war Britain. It is important, therefore, that some attempt is made to differentiate between fact and perception, and to point out the dangers of unthinkingly adhering to a largely illusory 'orthodox view'. There are real lessons to be learned about the way Britons reacted to the perceived threats of invasion and subversion, and the way that reaction was handled; also, the dangers of failing to meet public expectations where the provision of military equipment is concerned – something that became all too apparent during the recent British deployments to Iraq and Afghanistan.

References to the weaponry of the British Home Guard are characterised by misunderstanding and misrepresentation. Misunderstanding stems from the fact that very few Home Guards, or subsequent historians, have been 'weapons specialists', and as a consequence mistakes, soldiers' myths and old wives' tales have gained undeserved currency. Misrepresentation is a matter of context: terms such as 'old', 'ancient' or 'Great War' were associated with Home Guard weapons from the outset, for journalistic effect, ignoring the fact that a significant proportion of the small arms and artillery fielded by the British Army between 1940 and 1943 were of First World War or Edwardian vintage.[1] The wartime British public simply assumed that the weapons issued to the British Army were the best available. This, as we shall see, was not necessarily true. In terms of the study of military small arms and historical weapon systems the author is in an unusual position, being an army reservist with operational experience, a historian specialising in military technology and having been employed for several years as an armourer to the film and television industries. Much of that time was spent with Bapty & Co. Ltd, the UK's largest and oldest supplier of warlike stores to film, television and the theatre. During the Second World War the company's stock, and the collection of its owner, noted collector and authority the late Mr Mark Dineley, were placed at the disposal of the Home Guard. After the war, the company acquired additional stock, which included ex-Home Guard material. It was during the mid-1990s, while sorting, reassembling and restoring these items, that the author became convinced that the military potential of the Home Guard was being consistently underestimated. The Bapty collection represents a remarkable resource, further enhanced by a library/archive containing a wealth of period documents and illustrations.[2]

Since the 1970s, it has been impossible for any commentator to mention the Home Guard without reference to the BBC television situation comedy (also radio series, books, feature film and feature film reboot) *Dad's Army*. In the public mind *Dad's Army* was the Home Guard, and the Home Guard was *Dad's Army*. More than that, *Dad's Army* is seen to represent the armed aspect of the Home Front. In fact *Dad's Army* did *not* accurately represent the historical Home Guard – any more than its cousin *'Allo 'Allo!* can be said to accurately portray the French Resistance.[3] Although writers David Croft and Jimmy Perry drew on their own wartime experiences, as did the cast, considerable liberties were taken, and omissions made, for the comedy formula to work. Indeed, entire demographic groups are omitted – specifically, female auxiliaries, men of military age in reserved occupations and the political (left-wing) element that was so influential during the earlier part of the Home Guard's existence. One result of this was the need to create the portmanteau character 'Corporal Jones', an unlikely composite – simultaneously representing the 'traditionalist' and 'unconventional warfare' elements of the Home Guard – which only succeeds because of the skill of the writing and actor Clive Dunn's talent. As we shall see, the *actual* composition of the Home Guard directly affected its expectations of, and reaction to, the weapons that the authorities provided and the tactical role it was assigned.[4]

The Home Guard may be deeply embedded in British popular culture, but it has been largely ignored by the academic establishment – despite the fact that the formation of an armed 'people's militia', numbering, at its peak, almost 2 million men and some tens of thousands of women, and incorporating the framework of an organised, post-invasion resistance force, is among the UK's more dramatic responses to 'Total War'. A short popular history, Norman Longmate's *The Real Dad's Army*,[5] was published in 1974 to capitalise on the success of the BBC series, the author discreetly accentuating the first few months of the organisation's existence, when it most closely resembled the television portrayal. But despite, or perhaps because of the *Dad's Army* phenomenon, the Home Guard continued to occupy an academic vacuum. It was not until 1995 that S.P. MacKenzie, Assistant Professor of History at the University of Carolina, Columbia, published *The Home Guard*,[6] the first academic work wholly devoted to the subject, and still the most important. Professor MacKenzie's conclusion may be summarised in a sentence: 'National Morale, in short, determined the course of Home Guard development rather than strictly military considerations' (MacKenzie, 1996, p. 179):

> ... national morale was a key component in sustaining a viable war effort. And what the people in arms wanted badly enough, they either got or appeared to get. The LDV had been formed, after all, in order to control the burgeoning demand for civilian defence that manifested itself in the spring of 1940 rather than because there was an overwhelming military need for such a force. (MacKenzie, 1996, p. 176)

In other words, the Home Guard was never intended to be a serious fighting force, and its poor weapons are evidence of this – as MacKenzie puts it: 'weapons which in reality were of dubious fighting value, but which in all probability would never have to be fired in anger and could be presented as worthwhile' (MacKenzie, 1996, p. 177). Whether the Home Guard was an elaborate confidence trick to engage the British public in the war effort, or a crucial component of Home Defence, is for the reader to judge. What we will demonstrate, however, was that the efforts made to arm the Home Guard were very serious indeed, and even the most elderly and optimistic weapons in the Home Guard arsenal were shared with other fighting services.

Published twelve years after Professor MacKenzie examined the Home Guard from the political perspective, Professor Penny Summerfield and Dr Corina Peniston-Bird's *Contesting Home Defence* explored the organisation in its societal context.[7] The authors endeavour to tease out the social reality of the Home Guard from subsequent mythology and contemporary public relations, in order to determine whether it really served as a unifying focal point for national defensive spirit, or proved divisive, as the Left, the Right, traditionalists, modernists, and – most particularly – men and women pulled in their own directions. Summerfield and Peniston-Bird examine the extent to which the wartime Home Guard has been mythologised and, indeed, was *actively* mythologised during the four and a half years of its existence, and the effect of *Dad's Army* on perception of the Home Guard. The two academics also expose the difficulty of obtaining useful oral history from survivors of the Home Guard generation. The effect of *Dad's Army* can be likened to that of Shakespeare's depiction of Richard III, in that a portrayal has become so powerfully established that it insidiously alters reality:

> Whether they regarded *Dad's Army* as an accurate representation, were critical of its omissions, or … rather unwillingly accepted its judgements, men remembering their own Home Guard experiences could not escape *Dad's Army*. As the dominant representation of the Home Guard from the 1970s into at least the early years of the twenty-first century, it influenced the imaginative possibilities of their own recall and shaped personal memories. (Summerfield and Peniston-Bird, 2007, p. 232)

It is not just that, by repeated exposure, recollections have aligned with the depiction; there is a further factor that an audience will not admit an account that is at variance with the cherished orthodox view. It is important to record, from the perspective of folk, social and oral history, that this study was written with assistance from three former Home Guards, one of whom served in the Auxiliary Units (i.e. the 'British Resistance'), and none of whom had much time for *Dad's Army*. It was a privilege to share their memories, and their input was extremely valuable. Nevertheless, the greatest weight has been placed on contemporary wartime or near-contemporary accounts, and careful interpretation of period documents and artefacts.

The strength of the *Dad's Army* orthodoxy adds to the challenge of trying to determine to what extent the wartime Home Guard was appropriately and effectively armed. Indeed, until very recently, the whole topic was slightly embarrassing – almost unworthy of academic research. This self-consciousness is an inheritance from the earliest days of the Home Guard, and it is time to lay it to rest. It is perhaps more comfortable to examine the topic in broader terms, and the Home Guard does figure in studies of the English Volunteer tradition, such as Ian Beckett's *The Amateur Military Tradition*,[8] and Glen Steppler's *Britons, To Arms!*[9] It is also present as a component of the machinery of Home Defence in Peter Fleming's delightful *Invasion 1940*[10] and, more recently, the *Defence of Britain* project.[11] Fleming reflected the sardonic humour that was Britain's emotional shield against the terrifying prospect of unlimited technological war with an all-conquering fascist dictatorship. Although immensely entertaining, this does carry the inherent risk of subsequent generations laughing *at* the British of 1940–44, rather than *with* them, as they prepared, with whatever was at hand, to sell their lives and their freedom dearly. Fleming's counter-invasion theme was revisited by Arthur Ward in *Resisting the Nazi Invader*,[12] a popular history with a lively and informative text, particularly with respect to the Auxiliary Units. These Home Guard 'special forces' units appeal to modern taste and have attracted interest out of proportion to their size or military significance. David Carroll's short illustrated history *The Home Guard*[13] added to the popular end of the Home Guard oeuvre, which also includes local history, such as K.R. Gulvin's useful *Kent Home Guard: A History*.[14] For anyone interested in the topic, the internet provides an almost overwhelming Home Guard resource, particularly at the local level. It is an invaluable research tool, but needs to be approached with caution. Online material includes numerous educational synopses reflecting the 'orthodox' (i.e. *Dad's Army*) view of the Home Guard and its weapons, and, more interestingly, vast amounts of local unit histories and memoirs – admittedly of variable quality.[15]

Home Guard memorabilia, virtually worthless until the 1980s, is now eagerly sought by collectors and re-enactors, reflecting a general increase in interest in the Home Front. This interest has resulted in a market for niche publications such as *Vehicles of the Home Guard* and *Uniforms of the Home Guard* in the Historic Military Press 'Through the Lens' series,[16] as well as facsimile reprints of some of the commercially produced and official weapons training leaflets. Nevertheless, for a Second World War military topic, coverage of the Home Guard is thin. In terms of period sources, however, the researcher is faced with an embarrassment of riches, as the large and enthusiastic membership provided a lucrative market for opportunistic publishers. In the immediate absence of official support or infrastructure, a variety of manuals were produced – starting with Lieutenant Colonel J.A. Barlow's *The Elements of Rifle Shooting*, out of print after May 1938 but hastily republished in June 1940.[17] July 1940 saw the publication of *Rifle Training for War: A Textbook for Local Defence Volunteers*,[18] actually a revision of the manual produced for the First World War Home Guard equivalent, the Volunteer Training Corps (VTC). Capitalising on the organisation's change of name, *The Home Guard Pocket Manual* (October 1940)[19] was supported by the Ruberoid Company Ltd, and contained sound military advice from the RSM (regimental sergeant major) of the Sevenoaks Battalion Home Guard – as well as useful suggestions for the employment of Messrs Ruberoids' products in the construction of fieldworks and blackout precautions.

From 1941, specialist military publishers Gale & Polden, of Aldershot, produced training manuals for the American small arms used by the Home Guard. Their semi-official publications were joined by entirely unofficial efforts such as 'Bernards Pocket Books', which included in their 'Key to Victory' series the *Manual of Modern Automatic Guns* and *Commando and Guerrilla Tactics*, among volumes dedicated to cycling, photography and *'The Little Marvel' Reference Book for Vegetable Growers*.[20] The content of unofficial manuals frequently exceeded anything that could or would be found in an official publication, and at times verged on the frenzied, as in *The Home Guard Encyclopedia* (*c.* 1941),[21] which includes under its 'Sample Diagrams and Exercises' heading *'Fig. 3: Smashing Out of the Jaws of Death'*. The techniques for 'tying up securely', 'extraction of information' and 'holds, releases and silent killing' described in Bernard's *Manual of Commando and Guerrilla Warfare: Unarmed Combat*[22] (*'FOR H.G. & SERVICE USE'*) reflect the trend towards a 'people's war', and a willingness to set aside traditional conventions in order to prosecute a war of national survival. This was the ethos of those who had experience of fighting fascism, the veterans of the Spanish Civil War, including Hugh Slater, author of *Home Guard for Victory!*[23] (published in January 1941 and reprinted four times before the end of the month).

With the conventional military discredited and unable to lend much support, the Local Defence Volunteers looked to the Spanish Civil War and Finnish Winter War for lessons in what today would be termed asymmetric warfare – the means by which a small, ill-equipped, irregular force might defeat, or at least slow, a larger, better organised and technologically superior enemy. Self-appointed guiding spirits of the Home Guard included war correspondent Major John Langdon-Davies, and author John Brophy. Langdon-Davies engaged in an exhausting round of lecturing to '100 Battalions' of Home Guard in the winter of 1940–41.[24] His lecture was subsequently published as the manual *Home Guard Warfare*, which also included much of the content of 'Home Guard on Parade', his regular feature for the *Sunday Pictorial*. Unlike some of the other Spanish Civil War veterans, Langdon-Davies was willing and able to bridge the two worlds of the conventional military and the 'people's war'. As the publisher noted in the preface to the sixth, revised, edition of *The Home Guard Training Manual*, the successor to *Home Guard Warfare*, published in May 1942: 'Over 125,000 copies of this Home Guard Training Manual have now been sold, and it has become widely adopted since the War Office gave official sanction to its purchase out of training grant to the extent of one copy per platoon.'[25] In its scope and content Langdon-Davies' *The Home Guard Training Manual*, and its companion *The Home*

Guard Fieldcraft Manual,[26] can be said to be the definitive contemporary guides to the Home Guard.

An underage volunteer in the First World War, and subsequently a popular historian and novelist,[27] John Brophy commanded a Home Guard company in the Second World War. His manual, *Home Guard: A Handbook for the LDV*, was published in September 1940 and had been reprinted nine times by March 1942, when a revised edition, *Home Guard Handbook*, was produced, itself to be reprinted just two months later. Like Langdon-Davies, Brophy was responsible for a stream of handy pocket-sized manuals that sought to instruct and inspire. Brophy wrote in the foreword to the revised edition of the *Home Guard Handbook*:

> I believe that in general and in detail all my handbooks conform to the excellent Training and other Regulations of the Home Guard, and I should again like to emphasise that anything I write is to supplement and amplify official instructions which cannot always be made public and, if only for lack of paper, cannot be put into the hands of every member of the Home Guard. (Brophy, 1942, p. 10)

It is an odd assertion that a private individual should have the liberty to publish material 'that cannot always be made public' and that Hodder & Stoughton, Brophy's publishers, had access to supplies of paper denied to the official organs of state. Certainly, in the early months of the LDV's existence, authors such as Brophy and Langdon-Davies were filling a vacuum, but later their chief attraction must have been what Brophy himself described as 'certain informalities of outlook and phrasing' (Brophy, 1941a, p. 12). Professional writers, Brophy and Langdon-Davies kept alive the edgy feeling of novelty and threat that drove 1.5 million civilians to take up arms in the Home Guard, even as that threat ebbed away. The high-water mark of these private manuals was 1942; then the tide of the war started to turn, the public appetite for DIY combat training diminished and the Home Guard, now a properly integrated component of Home Defence – effectively a new, unpaid, Territorial Army to replace the one fighting overseas – was fully supported by the War Office.

The Home Guard generated a corpus of official documentation under the titles *Home Guard Instruction* (initially *LDV Instruction*) and *Home Guard Information Circular*. These sequentially numbered leaflets covered subjects as diverse as expenses and damages claims, the preservation of boots through the use of hobnails and the performance of anti-tank mines in the Western Desert. Contrary to Brophy's suggestion above, very great efforts were made to keep the Home Guard interested and informed, with operational lessons being passed on from as far afield as Guadalcanal. Much of this material is preserved, amongst a mass of other Home Guard material, in the National Archives, Kew, and a surprising amount is to be found for sale from specialist booksellers and online. Of particular significance to this study is a series of volumes dating from 1942–43, making up *Home Guard Instruction No. 51*. These set out the Home Guard's tactical doctrine, as well as listing the capabilities of weapons, and the organisation of platoons and squads, down to the roles of individual soldiers. They represent the final stage in the evolution of the organisation into an entirely competent, and accepted, component of Home Defence.[28]

In 1943, journalist and Home Guard Charles Graves celebrated the Home Guard (then at its apogee) in *The Home Guard of Britain*.[29] This remains the closest thing to an 'official history' the organisation ever received, although it suffers from the disadvantage of having been completed some months before the final 'stand-down'. When, in late 1944, the Home Guard did 'stand down', most members appreciated that this marked the end of a singular and formative experience (the Home Guard was officially disbanded on 31 December 1945).[30] Various commemorative publications were produced, ranging in pretension from a twelve-page leaflet produced by the Intelligence Section, 8th Wiltshire Home Guard,[31] to the 168-page *Bureaucrats in Battledress* – the history of the Ministry of Food Home Guard.[32] The intention of the authors of these and countless similar publications was lyrically expounded by Major C.E. Mansell, late Officer Commanding 'Dog Company', 20th Battalion, Kent Home Guard, in the introduction to the commemorative 'diary' of his battalion:[33]

> Sometimes on a Tuesday or a Thursday winter's evening in years to come, we shall surely be sitting at home, by the fireside, listening to the rain beating upon the window pane and the wind howling, and we shall think of those four winters when we used to turn out for Parade at the Drill Hall.
>
> Perhaps a friend will be there to share our thoughts and we shall start yarning about those Home Guard days and nights ... At such times this little book will certainly be highly appreciated by us all. It will jog our memories and help us to recall countless incidents which otherwise are bound to fade in the course of time. (Brown and Peek, 1944, p. 2)

And fade they have. Such *aides-memoir* should be historical gold dust, but the reality for the historian is usually frustration. They are, to use Beckett's phrase (1991, p. 271), 'relentlessly anecdotal'; nevertheless, they should not be dismissed. Content varies and coverage of the earlier (LDV) period can be sketchy, but careful reading is rewarded with invaluable first-hand information. The 'wartime' publications end with *Britain's Home Guard: A Character Study*,[34] written, appropriately, by John Brophy and masterfully illustrated by fellow Home Guard, artist Eric Kennington. The tone is elegiac:

> … without the Home Guard Britain itself could not exist. It guaranteed determined, skilful, organised resistance to the invader everywhere. It symbolized and made effective the will of the British people to defend their liberties, not merely while the period of acute danger persisted, but unremittingly till the continental despotism is overthrown. (Brophy, 1945, p. 9)

Several copies of an unpublished *History of the Home Guard* lie in the National Archives, the project to produce an official history having been started but abandoned.[35] After a brief revival during the 1950s, the Home Guard lapsed into obscurity until 1968, and the screening of the first episode of *Dad's Army*, which, of course, brings us full circle.

The key facet of this study is military technology and, in particular, the study of military firearms. In this context *With British Snipers to the Reich*, by Captain Clifford Shore, is of particular significance.[36] Shore, an enthusiastic, skilled and knowledgeable rifle shot, served in the Home Guard before undergoing officer selection and joining the RAF Regiment (he was 33 years old in 1940). He crossed into Europe on D-Day+1 and saw active service with the RAF Regiment, before becoming an instructor to the Army Field Sniper School in Holland. *With British Snipers to the Reich* was written immediately following Shore's demobilisation, between March and December 1946, at the suggestion of an American publisher. Although best known as a book on sniping, the references to the Home Guard, their small arms and musketry are of considerable importance. Other sources will be introduced in later chapters, but those most familiar to firearms *cognoscenti* are the works of Australia-based researcher and writer Ian Skennerton, and the 'Collector Grade' series of large-format monographs, edited by R. Blake Stevens of Ontario. Goldsmith's *The Grand Old Lady of No Man's Land* and *The Browning Machine Gun*, Laidler and Howroyd's *The Guns of Dagenham*, Easterly's *The Belgian Rattlesnake* and Ballou's *Rock in a Hard Place* are the key resources for (respectively) the Vickers machine gun, Browning machine gun, Lanchester and Sten 'machine carbines', Lewis light machine gun and Browning Automatic Rifle (BAR).[37] Other very useful and diverse technical information has emerged thanks to the efforts of the author's colleagues in the Historical Breechloading Smallarms Association. It is, of course, impossible to undertake a study such as this without recourse to one or more of the late Ian Hogg's books, and those of other noted specialists such as Terry Gander. However, wherever possible, technical specifications have been extracted from contemporary Home Guard publications, as data such as effective ranges or penetration of armour were often modified, in light of experience, by the time the equipment entered service with the Home Guard. Like Clifford Shore, the author of this book prefers to examine matters for himself, and he has examined, handled, restored and in many cases fired almost every weapon mentioned herein.

On 6 December 1944, just as the *Volkssturm*, the German equivalent of the Home Guard, was preparing for its last-ditch defence of the *Reich*, Britain's Home Guard had been stood down. A.E. Stroud, a Home Guard trained to defend a 'Tank Island' in Wiltshire, wrote, summing up the feelings of all those who had given so much time and effort to the Home Guard:

> Towards the end of 1943 and early 1944 ... it was obvious that our invasion was near with its possibility of airborne raids in this country for disruption of communications and traffic.
>
> I suppose we shall learn one day why this never happened, perhaps the answer is that we were so well prepared for it. I'm glad it didn't happen, of course, but I can't help feeling sometimes that I'd have liked to have seen our wheels go round in action just once, after all we did build a lovely machine, and never saw it work. (Stroud, 1944, p. 7)

I

THE THREAT

The Home Guard was born of a spontaneous reaction by the British public to the twin threats of invasion and subversion. In order to place the organisation, and its equipment and tactics, in context, it is necessary to explore those threats. During the First World War, large numbers of troops had been earmarked for Home Defence, and defences prepared along England's East Coast. The bombardment of coastal towns by the German Imperial Navy in December 1914 served to further heighten the possibility of invasion, or large-scale raids or landings. These never happened, but bombardment continued, using German Army or navy airships and bomber aircraft. Although the subsequent civilian casualties failed to break the will of the British civilians at home and soldiers overseas, indiscriminate 'terror bombing' became established as a strategic option. The Spanish Civil War demonstrated what could be achieved using modern bombers against the civilian population – famously at Guernica – and aerial bombardment clearly represented a significant threat to the UK mainland in the event of another European war. The danger of public morale collapsing under the torrent of bombs from bombers that would 'always get through'[1] seemed a very real one. The threat to the UK of invasion, however, diminished in the minds of both the public and military planners, who briefly examined the possibility in 1939, and discounted it. When Great Britain declared war on Nazi Germany in September 1939, the obstacles presented by the Maginot Line, the French Army, and the Royal Navy, meant that an invasion by German troops was not regarded as a serious possibility. Just eight months later that view was completely reversed, following the German advances into Scandinavia on 9 April 1940, and on the Western Front a month later. From 10 May 1940, the day Churchill became prime minister, the British watched with growing horror and alarm as the apparently unstoppable German Army sliced through Western Europe. The invasion threat had suddenly become real, and if one single factor seized the public imagination, it was the German use of parachute troops, an innovation that seemed to render the Royal Navy, England's traditional bulwark against invasion, impotent.

The possibility of airborne assault on the United Kingdom had been discussed since the first tentative ascents in hot air balloons, but in truth, air-landings had been the stuff of science fiction. That was entirely changed by the German assault on Norway; the effective use of parachute and air-landing troops there, and subsequently in the Low Countries, added instantaneous and ubiquitous invasion to the now well-established aerial threat. Importantly, the British public's response to this new threat was not to flee, or demand that the government sue for peace, but rather to insist that the population be assisted to take up arms. This happened first unofficially as vigilante groups – the so-called 'Parashots' – spontaneously formed, and then, following a radio broadcast on the evening of 14 May 1940 by Anthony Eden, the Secretary of State for War, as officially sanctioned 'Local Defence Volunteers'. In his broadcast Eden outlined the new threat posed by German parachute troops, and asked for volunteers to report to their local police stations:

> Since the war began the Government have received countless enquiries from all over the Kingdom from men of all ages who are for one reason or another not at present engaged in military service, and who wish to do something for the defence of the country.
>
> Now is your opportunity. We want large numbers of such men in Great Britain who are British subjects, between the ages of 17 and 65, to come forward and offer their services in order to make assurance doubly sure. The name of the new force which is now to be raised will be the 'Local Defence Volunteers'. This name, Local Defence Volunteers, describes its duties in three words.[2]

However, the German threat, which seemed so real and immediate with enemy troops just across the English Channel, became rather less tangible when subjected to close scrutiny. This is reflected in the first of the unofficial LDV handbooks, *Rifle Training for War*, published in July 1940. The editor struggles with the fact that, whilst in broad terms, the *raison d'être* of the LDV was obvious, its actual role was far from clear:

At the time of writing, the precise duties of the L.D.V. have not been defined. They can, however, be guessed at and whatever they have to do they will surely find a knowledge of the rifle useful. The author wishes the best of luck to all his readers. They have answered the appeal to 'repel boarders', whether they come by sea or air. (Robinson and King, 1940, p. xii)

As envisaged in *Rifle Training for War*, the operational role of the LDV appeared to consist of small numbers of concerned citizens stalking and killing equally small numbers of Nazi paratroopers, preferably before they landed:

For instance a Volunteer [*sic*] or a pair of volunteers may see two or three parachutes dropping. If the volunteer is alone and is a good shot and near enough to open fire – say within two or three hundred yards of the nearest – he may decide to attempt to get one or two, or perhaps all of them, before they land. If two volunteers are on the watch in such a situation one may go back to report whilst the better shot remains to watch and shoot if he gets the chance. (Robinson and King, 1940, p. 2)

It is not apparent what purpose it would serve the enemy to drop such small numbers of parachutists, but it is abundantly clear why downed RAF aircrew ran a serious risk of being shot by their own countrymen.

Parachutist hysteria, and a persistent willingness to credit the Germans with extraordinary military capacities, led contemporary authorities to some unfortunate overestimations of German capabilities. In dismissing these exaggerations historians can also dismiss the threat. MacKenzie, for instance, after explaining that the Under Secretary of State for War, Lord Croft, believed in the summer of 1940 that the Germans could land up to 10,000 paratroops, points out: 'the German armed forces had only 7,000 fully trained paratroopers in the spring of 1940, and had suffered quite severe losses in men and transports during operations in Holland' (MacKenzie, 1996, p. 23). Writing in *Invasion 1940* Derek Robinson puts the German parachute force still lower, 4,500 men at the start of *Fall Gelb* (Case Yellow), the invasion of France and the Low Countries, many of whom became casualties, particularly in the airborne set piece 'Battle for the Hague' (Robinson, 2006, p. 116). Although the *Fallschirmjäger* captured by the Dutch were released when Holland capitulated on 14 May, Robinson makes the point that the losses of Junkers Ju 52 transport aircraft in the campaign (213 out of 475) were crippling. Nevertheless, he estimates that in June 1940, Germany could have launched a lift of a maximum of 3,000 paratroops to England (Robinson, 2006, p. 112). Fleming, writing just sixteen years after the events he was describing, suggests that, pulling out all the stops, the parachute force might have amounted to between 6,000 and 7,000 *Fallschirmjäger*, with airlift capacity for a follow-on air-landing force of 15,000 – which as he points out, was smaller than the force that narrowly secured the rather thinly defended island of Crete in 1941 (Fleming, 1957, p. 70).[3]

Whether undertaken by 7,000 *Fallschirmjäger* or 3,000, this airborne assault could only be the overture for the main thrust, which would have to be an amphibious landing by conventional troops, bringing with them artillery and armour. Indeed, the German plan was to use parachute troops to secure the beachheads, much as the Allies would do in 1944. German plans for cross-Channel invasion have suffered from being measured against the Allied Normandy landings of June 1944 – but the Allies' Operation OVERLORD was an entirely different undertaking, if only because of the scale and preparedness of the defences. German preparations in the summer of 1940, and their chances of success, need to be measured against previous joint operations. It is instructive to consider Churchill's summation of the German assault on Norway:

> Surprise, ruthlessness, and precision were the characteristics of the onslaught … Nowhere did the initial landing forces exceed two thousand men. Seven army divisions were employed … Three divisions were used in the assault phase, and four supported them through Oslo and Trondheim. Eight hundred operational aircraft and 250 to 300 transport planes were the salient and vital feature of the design. Within forty-eight hours all the main ports of Norway were in the German grip. (Churchill, 1954a, p. 473)

Even 3,000 fully trained, equipped and combat-tested paratroops were considerably more than any other combatant nation could field in the summer of 1940, and they were backed by the world's most modern air force, undefeated in the recent campaigns in Poland and Western Europe. 'Speed, ruthlessness and determination to advance at all costs' might well have got German troops across the Channel before a shocked, demoralised and largely disarmed Britain could properly organise itself, and at that stage in the war it was impossible to believe that such a determined and capable enemy would let the opportunity slip through his fingers.

Periodical Notes on the German Army No. 28 (published by the War Office on 27 June 1940) explained: 'From the time when the German Army overthrew the restrictions imposed by the Treaty of Versailles, the offensive spirit has been stressed in all training. The result of this teaching, an offensive, violent both in speed and ruthlessness, has already been well illustrated in the campaigns in Poland and on the Western Front.'[4] The British public was never quite able to accept that such an army would fail to take any sort of direct action against the UK mainland. Writing in 1945, John Brophy put the popular view of Germany's missed opportunity:

> The probability is that it lay beyond the German imagination to conceive the state of defencelessness into which Britain had been allowed to lapse by her former rulers. Had they guessed how few tanks, guns, machine-guns, supplied with what scanty stocks of ammunition, lay between them and the greatest conquest they could hope for, they would certainly have launched their invading fleets, and reckoned any losses at sea and in the air a small price to pay. (Brophy, 1945, p. 18)

In *Invasion 1940*, Derek Robinson seeks to draw attention to a key factor in examining the practicality, or otherwise, of a German invasion of England in 1940 – the presence of the vastly superior British navy. It was this, he insists, not the Battle of Britain, and the pilots of Fighter Command, which prevented a German invasion (Robinson, 2006, p. 5): 'Historians themselves have perpetuated one mistaken belief about what happened in 1940: the myth that "The Few" alone saved Britain from invasion.' Robinson's argument about the neglected importance of the Royal Navy is well made, but it misses the point that perceptions count, and it was not the old threat of a surface invasion that really galvanised the British at the time, but the entirely new threat of airborne envelopment.[5] The counters to this apparently ubiquitous threat were Fighter Command in the air, and the Local Defence Volunteers on the ground – and that is the contemporary context in which the establishment of LDV/Home Guard must be viewed.

Periodical Notes on the German Army, No. 30, published by War Office intelligence department MI14 in August 1940, contains two sections: 'Lessons of the Battle of France' and 'Possible German Tactics in an Attack on Great Britain'. The British General Staff's viewpoint at the time is made perfectly clear:

In operations in the United Kingdom the German forces will be inferior in numbers to our own, are likely to be less well supplied with tanks and heavier supporting weapons and will also be handicapped by long and uncertain lines of communications across a sea dominated by the British Navy, and, it may be hoped, after the first 48 hours, by a shortage of food, ammunition and petrol.[6]

MI14 thus allows Robinson his point, but then (proceeding in the anticipated order of arrival in the UK) goes straight on to discuss parachute troops. After a general description of organisation and training the notes continue:

These troops might be employed against this country:-

(a)   To prepare the way for the landing of air-borne troops. For this purpose they would land near areas (in open flat ground, not necessarily aerodromes) suitable for the landing of troop-carrying aircraft. They might, for example, be landed in an open space between two woods.

(b)   To co-operate with landings from the sea. Parachute troops might be dropped in comparatively large numbers close to suitable beaches or harbours in order to cover the landing of sea-borne troops. These parachute landings might take place before or during attempts to gain a foot-hold on the beaches, etc.

(c)   To cause confusion or effect dispersion of our own forces by widespread landings in small groups. These small detachments would try to establish contact with agents and Fifth Columnists with the object of carrying out sabotage, stampeding the population and bringing the normal life of the country to a standstill. Parachutists might be used simultaneously in all three roles described above and some might be disguised in British uniforms and speak English fluently.

Point 'c', above, is of interest, because it illuminates the 'penny packet' threat of small numbers of parachutists. Next to arrive are the air-landing troops, described in the same format:

In this country the tasks of air-landing troops would probably be:-

(a)   To seize important areas in the early stages of an attack, establish [seize?] aerodromes, coastal batteries and forts.

(b)   To establish bridgeheads for troops and material landing by sea.

(c)   To create chaos, to aim at achieving dispersion of our forces and to draw off troops from areas where sea landings might be attempted.

All these tasks are likely to be undertaken simultaneously and in co-operation with parachute troops.

The air landing troops are followed in sequence by the sea-borne contingents:

- Mechanised reconnaissance units
- Armoured formations
- Motorised infantry and infantry divisions

The notes also cover:

- Engineers (some of whom will be amongst the first troops landed)
- Smoke troops
- Possible use of gas
- Irregular methods of warfare (dirty tricks)

MI14 concludes:

(a)   Once landed German forces of all kinds will use every endeavour to advance inland as far and as fast as they can. They will rely on immediate and effective support from dive-bombers to attack opposition which they are unable to overcome with their own resources. Infiltration tactics are to be expected and success will be reinforced wherever it is obtained.

(b)   Difficulties of terrain set a limit on the effectiveness of armoured forces in certain districts in this country. Their dependence on sea communications is another important limiting factor, though they may hope to obtain some fuel and food by capture.

(c)   The enemy will aim at creating civil chaos as one of the conditions for the success of his military plans. The landing of parachute and air-borne troops together with heavy air bombing, all of which will probably precede and accompany the arrival of sea-borne forces, will be employed to create this confusion.

(d)   The extensive employment of smoke (possibly in conjunction with gas) to cover the approach to and subsequent landing on beaches must be expected.

(e)   The employment of gas on a large scale is probable.[7]

This then is the British Army intelligence template for a German invasion, against which all British counter-invasion preparations were made, and it remained so for as long as full-scale invasion remained a planning contingency. It determined that the first threat for the Home Guard (as the LDV became known from 23 August 1940) would be dealing, probably unaided, with German parachutists, who may be dropped in small numbers in order to force the British Field Army to disperse, and in order to join up with Fifth Columnists. That scenario became, and remained, the principal preoccupation of the Home Guard throughout its wartime existence. In the introduction we noted that the authors of official instructions for the Home Guard made great efforts to make their publications interesting and accessible. This includes one of the more remarkable military manuals ever produced, Colonel G.A. Wade's *The Defence of Bloodford Village*. *The Defence of Bloodford Village* is a Home Guard version of the famous *The Defence of Duffer's Drift*, written by Ernest Dunlop Swinton, and still a highly regarded treatise on small unit tactics, used as a teaching aide by both the modern British and US armies. Like Duffer's Drift, the defence of Bloodford is the responsibility of a junior commander, whose nightmares of failure over a series of succeeding nights prompt him to improve various aspects of the defences, until perfection is achieved. Released in late November 1940, the booklet has a short forward by the Director General Home Guard, Major General T.R. Eastwood, DSO, MC:

> The Battle of Bloodford Village and how it came to be successfully defended as a result of the lessons learnt from the dreams of the local Home Guard Commander, makes most interesting and instructive reading.
>
> The story contains many useful hints that should help other Home Guard Commanders in planning the defence of their villages. [Shown in inverted commas on the original.] (Wade, 1940, frontispiece)

The sixteen-page booklet opens with a description of the imaginary village of Bloodford as we might encounter it after Hitler's war has been won: overlooked by a picturesque windmill on a hill, the village features an old stone bridge over the River Booze; the half-timbered Bridge Inn, with its lichened roof; Hag's Pond, still with ducking stool; the Grange; and a huddle of quaint old houses around the village green. On the green stand an old gibbet – and three destroyed German tanks, proud trophies of the village Home Guard. In the narrative, Bloodford Home Guard is under the command of Geoffrey 'Skipper' Gee (Home Guard commissions and military ranks were only introduced on 3 February 1941), resident of the Grange. After a long night spent working out a Defensive Scheme for the village, an exhausted Gee eats a large piece of cheese before heading to bed. In the nightmare that follows, Gee finds himself helplessly watching the first stages of a Nazi invasion:

> It was early morning, patches of mist still hung on the Village Green, the sun rising over OAK WOOD was reflected in the water of HAG'S POND and sundry roosters proclaimed the birth of another day. No one could be seen in the streets although the rattle of buckets and the clank of the pumps showed that early risers were astir. 'The best time of the day,' thought Gee, 'when the larks are singing and the sky is a lovely deep blue, and – My God! What's that?' for floating downwards were some tiny white specks. 'Parachutists! – Yes, eight of them, and look there's a score of them over there as well!' In agony Gee looked round. Why didn't somebody *do something*? They would come to earth only a mile away and be here in no time and yet still the buckets were rattling and the men whistling and the cocks crowing just as though DEATH was not advancing from two directions at once! (Wade, 1940, pp. 2 and 3)

Inevitably, none of the busy villagers looks up to see the descending parachutists, who 'heavily armed and dangerous' are soon 'converging on the unsuspecting village, their minds set on MURDER, PILLAGE and RAPE'. A warning from a mortally wounded child on a bicycle comes too late; the Home Guard are caught napping and massacred. Horrified, Gee watches his own dead body being hoisted onto the gibbet.

Rising, shaken, the following day, Gee immediately sets about reorganising the village's Defensive Scheme to ensure that Bloodford cannot be taken by surprise. However, poor Gee cannot get a good night's sleep. Over five nights, five more dreams follow, and awaking from each the unfortunate Home Guard Commander further refines Bloodford's defences. In the second dream, light tanks outflank the village road block and machine gun the Home Guard from behind. In the third, a Fifth Columnist dumps the Home Guard's ammunition in the river, while in the fourth, Windmill Hill, the dominating feature, is taken and held by the enemy, despite a suicidal bayonet charge by the Home Guard. In the fifth dream a German troop-carrying aircraft lands on the village green, and in the sixth, and last, the Home Guards are scuppered by the lack of a mobile reserve. Finally, the Bloodford's defences achieve perfection – just in the nick of time as the real invasion takes place. German troops and tanks attack the village and are soundly defeated by the Home Guard. Interspersing the text are twenty-eight boxed 'Points' for the reader to note, such as:

Point No. 16.

KEEP A RESERVE

This is of tremendous importance for every Defensive Scheme seems weak in parts and the temptation to employ every available man in the initial stages must be sternly resisted.

When the attack is taking place, the reserves should be used only to re-establish the defences if they are penetrated. Once this is done, they should return *at once* to reserve. (Wade, 1940, p. 11)

In its sixteen small pages, *The Defence of Bloodford* achieves many goals. Firstly, we are shown the likely component phases of a German invasion (paratroops, air-landing, armoured reconnaissance, etc.), and how, in general terms, the Home Guard can deal with each of them, thus boosting confidence (and initiative – when the ammunition is found to be missing, thanks to the treachery of the Fifth Columnist, the Home Guard are undaunted and do their best with Molotov Cocktails). Then there are specific learning points to increase military efficiency and effectiveness. Underlying all this is the juxtaposition of murderous German paratroopers with an idealised bucolic English landscape – an effective character assassination, and not entirely without foundation, as we shall see. It is interesting to note, and it is a theme we will return to, that despite the twentieth-century urbanisation, suburbanisation and industrialisation of Great Britain, the Home Guard is depicted fighting in, and for, a rural 'Dream of England'.

Robinson describes the German paratrooper, the *Fallschirmjäger*, as 'probably the most overrated soldier of the war' (Robinson, 2006, p. 108). Certainly, the threat posed to the UK by German parachute troops was overrated, both because of the shortage of men and transport aircraft, and inherent problems with their equipment and *modus operandi*. Faced with the need to confront elite German paratroopers, the Home Guard made themselves the masters of the subject, identifying the points where the *Fallschirmjäger* would be most vulnerable to attack. It was soon realised that airborne invasion would not be constituted by handfuls of Nazi paratroopers, as Hugh Slater explained, in his hugely popular book *Home Guard for Victory!* in January 1941:

> The Home Guard has developed in a rather typically English, spontaneous, way. First of all there were the Parashots. They were to patrol the countryside with shot-guns and to blaze away at enemy parachutists as they came slowly sailing down to earth. After about a fortnight it was realised that the Eschner parachute, used by the Germans, is so designed that it may take no longer than five seconds for the parachutists to be landed from the plane, and therefore the conception of potting at them as they floated through the air had to be regarded as obsolete. (Slater, 1941, pp. 11–12)

The actual time of descent was 20–30 seconds, not 'five seconds' as a moment's sensible reflection would make obvious – it would not be the only time that Slater would misinform his eager readers – but at least the danger posed to friendly aircrew was appreciated:

> Parachute troops will generally be landed from low levels, and will not come down singly or in batches of up to six men as the crews of crashed fighters or bombers will do. They will be seen, as a rule, in groups of more than six …
>
> If parachutists are seen to drop in batches of more than six from enemy aircraft, fire may be opened on them by members of the armed forces while they are in the air. In no other circumstances should parachutists be shot at while coming down.
>
> Fire should not be opened on parachutists after they have landed unless they take, or show unmistakeable signs of taking hostile action. (Slater, 1941, pp. 85–6)

Slater persists in the fiction that the Germans would deliberately crash-land transport aircraft, which, presumably, reflected a misinterpretation of the use of troop-carrying gliders, and battle-damaged Ju 52 aircraft crash-landing with troops still on board: 'A troop-carrying plane can make a pancake landing in almost any large field even if there are wooden stakes, stone piles and pits or other obstacles in the field' (Slater, 1941, p. 19).

The British gained a fuller appreciation of German airborne tactics following *Unternehmen MERKUR* (Operation MERCURY), the invasion of Crete by

22,000 airborne and mountain troops in May 1941. The second edition of John Langdon-Davies' *Home Guard Fieldcraft Manual* was published in April 1942, and the book reflects thorough understanding of the limitations of *Fallschirmjäger* equipment and tactics. The German *Ruckenpackung Zwangauslosung* (RZ) -16 and -20 parachutes were effectively unsteerable (which is why German paratroopers can be seen on contemporary newsreels furiously kicking and pedalling as they come in to land, trying to swing themselves towards a better landing place), and had risers which connected in such a way as to result in an uncontrollable face-forward landing. This limited the amount of equipment or weapons the paratrooper could safely carry during the jump, and also resulted in the need to issue knee and elbow pads to minimise injuries. Langdon-Davies explained:

(a) The Nazi parachutist on landing is seldom equipped with anything but an automatic pistol, four grenades and a long knife, which cannot be accurately used at a range of more than fifty yards. The first airborne troops to land often carry machine pistols strapped to their backs, and three or four hand grenades in their pockets.

(b) The Nazi parachutist is dazed to a certain extent on landing, and there are a high percentage of sprained ankles and other minor casualties.

(c) His clothing is arranged to assist him in his fall, and he has to re-arrange it before he is in a suitable condition to fight.

(d) The rest of his equipment comes down by a separate parachute in a container which is unrolled directly the parachutists recover from their fall. (1942, p. 36)

It may seem hopelessly optimistic, pitting the civilian militia of the Home Guard against Nazi paratroopers, but the *Fallschirmjäger* were genuinely vulnerable immediately after landing and before they had collected their weapons, as the invasion of Crete would prove. The resulting tactical pause was factored into Langdon-Davies' Home Guard exercises:

When everybody is on the alert, twelve parachutists appear at a spot which has not been indicated to the Home Guard beforehand. Their position must be about 1,000 yards from the defending position. They will indicate their landing by waving white flags. They will remain stationary for four minutes, thus representing the initial period when the parachutists are practically immobilized by the difficulty of landing.

The cylinder containing their equipment, represented by a red flag, has dropped within about fifty yards of them. At the end of the four minutes they must recover the cylinder and they will have five minutes to drag it into cover and distribute the equipment. At the end of five minutes, that is to say, at the end of nine minutes from the zero hour, they are free to move off … (Langdon-Davies, 1942, p. 35)

Nine minutes might be pushing it, judging by contemporary footage of *Fallschirmjäger* in action, but there definitely was scope for the first British troops on the scene – and that would almost certainly be the Home Guard – catching the Germans before they had time to properly organise and arm themselves.[8]

If the German Army was seen, correctly, as an essentially offensive force, it was also perceived as willing to stoop to any underhand and unscrupulous tactics in order to win. This reputation was built at the outset on supposed Nazi 'dirty tricks' during the campaign in Western Europe, and widely accepted on the British side. This imagined new form of war required special vigilance on the part of the British, as John Brophy explained in *Home Guard, a Handbook for the L.D.V.*:

Enemy parachute troops may be looked for (a) in their own uniform, (b) disguised in civilian dress to act as spies and sabotage agents. Their numbers and their behaviour should give them away if their intention is to pass themselves off as British troops. If they come in civilian disguise they will almost certainly be dropped in darkness. Genuine clergymen, nuns or farm labourers are not going to descend out of the night sky, and the pretenders should be promptly and suitably dealt with. The author of this Handbook has a 'hunch' that adolescent enemy agents may be dropped in the uniforms of Boy Scouts or Sea Scouts. (Brophy, 1941a, p. 50)

Writing seventy-five years after the event, it is difficult to comprehend the threat to national security Brophy imagined would be posed by a teenage Nazi Sea Scout, and even in the febrile atmosphere of 1940, this sort of silliness undermined the authority of the Home Guard's self-appointed guiding lights. That said, had the manuals stated that Nazi spies would appear at country railway stations and in seaside towns wet from the knees down, speaking heavily accented English and carrying Mauser pistols, torches marked 'made in Bohemia', primitive encoding equipment, and a length of German sausage, no one would have believed it – but that is exactly what did happen (Jowitt, 1954, p. 34).[9]

It is clear in retrospect that the majority of the supposed German 'dirty tricks' of April and May 1940 were imaginary, or due to incompetence and the muddle brought on by the fog of war, amplified by the speed of the German advance, which prevented headquarters from establishing themselves and threatened or broke lines of communication, compromising the Allied chain of command – 'cock-up' rather than conspiracy. Nevertheless, in August 1940 the War Office authoritatively listed a litany of 'Irregular Methods of Warfare':

The Germans do not admit that there are any 'rules' in warfare and any form of trickery or cunning which would assist them in attaining their object must be expected.

The following are some of the methods believed to have been employed by the Germans which may be described at least as unorthodox.

(a) A small party allows itself to be captured; then produces concealed weapons, kills its captors and holds an important point until reinforcements arrive.

(b) A telephone call to a demolition party in perfect English saying that the bridge should not be blown until a party of British troops have crossed. The party arrives in British uniforms, is allowed to pass and then turns on the demolition party and annihilates it.

(c) Tanks flying French flags arrive at a bridge. The defenders lead the tanks through a minefield covering the position. Once through, the tanks turn and attack the position from the rear.

(d) Spreading false rumours among the civilian population concerning the approach of German troops, thereby blocking the roads in rear of the [Allies] with hordes of refugees.

(e) Bombing and machine-gunning columns of refugees to cause blocking of roads in rear of the [Allies].

(f) Concealing A.Tk. guns in farm carts driven by civilians or troops in civilian clothes.

(g) Employment of agents to guide troops and aircraft, to increase panic among civilians and to interfere with defensive measures. They were also used for sabotage, to spread defeatism among enemy troops, and even to fire on them.

Whilst there is no doubt that the Germans would make the most of a *ruse de guerre* if they could, the suggestion that they did not admit any rules in warfare was dangerously misleading. It is appropriate at this point to juxtapose the German paratroopers' own perspective. The following is extracted from an article on German paratroops in an American military publication, *Intelligence Bulletin*, produced in September 1942,[10] with the benefit of information from the battle of Crete:

 e. The Parachutist's 'Ten Commandments'

Here is a translation of a document captured from a German parachute trooper who was taken prisoner in Greece. Its title is 'The Parachutist's Ten Commandments.'

1. You are the elite of the German Army. For you, combat shall be fulfilment. You shall seek it out and train yourself to stand any test.
2. Cultivate true comradeship, for together with your comrades you will triumph or die.
3. Be shy of speech and incorruptible. Men act, women chatter; chatter will bring you to the grave.
4. Calm and caution, vigor and determination, valor and a fanatical offensive spirit will make you superior in attack.
5. In facing the foe, ammunition is the most precious thing. He who shoots uselessly, merely to reassure himself, is a man without guts. He is a weakling and does not deserve the title of parachutist.
6. Never surrender. Your honor lies in Victory or Death.
7. Only with good weapons can you have success. So look after them on the principle – First my weapons, then myself.
8. You must grasp the full meaning of an operation so that, should your leader fall by the way, you can carry it out with coolness and caution.
9. Fight chivalrously against an honest foe; armed irregulars deserve no quarter.
10. With your eyes open, keyed up to top pitch, agile as a greyhound, tough as leather, hard as Krupp steel, you will be the embodiment of a German warrior.

Point nine of the 'Ten Commandments' is worthy of note, and, as we will discuss further in the next chapter, indicates the likely temper of operations against the Home Guard, especially in the pre-uniform LDV period.

If the British public was mesmerised by the threat of airborne invasion, it was enemy armour which fixated the General Staff. *Periodical Notes on the German Army, No. 30: A. Lessons of the Battle of France* explained:

> The armoured divisions were the decisive factor in German ground successes against Poland and in Flanders and France. There can be little doubt therefore that the Germans will make every effort to land A.F.V.s on these shores from transports (should they capture a suitable port or ports) and perhaps from smaller craft such as fishing vessels, and barges and rafts of special construction. Mention has already been made of the possible transport of light tanks by aircraft.[11]

For the public it was the ubiquity of the paratrooper menace that made it so terrifying; for the General Staff, it was the recollection of enemy armour punching through the Allied front line in France and Flanders to threaten any and everything behind:

> The main tasks of the armoured divisions were to secure control of the system of communications in the area attacked and in particular the nodal points, thus disrupting the [Allied] organization and L. of C. [lines of communication] and opening up the way for the motorized and infantry divisions. The advanced elements spread out across the road system and pushed on ruthlessly, seeking to increase the area of ground captured without in any way attempting to consolidate it. The Germans relied on speed and surprise to neutralise any [Allied] counter-measures.[12]

It is quite plain from the tone of training literature produced at the time that the overriding fear was that morale would collapse in the face of a tank threat, particularly given the fact that virtually all the British Army's anti-tank weapons had been lost, and those that survived were only marginally effective. The War Office turned to highly coloured language to rally the troops, as in *Local Defence Volunteer Instruction No. 8: Tanks and Tank Destruction*, issued in mid-July 1940:

> From the moment that enemy tanks are located they must be harried, hunted, sniped and ambushed without respite. Goliath was slain by David's sling, and the

lessons of Spain and Finland confirm that tanks can be destroyed by men who have the bravery, resource and determination to do so.[13]

Military Training Pamphlet No. 42: Tank Hunting and Destruction, of 29 August 1940, is important for the light it sheds on British Army anti-tank equipment in the period July to December 1940, and will be examined in closer detail later. In general terms it is sufficient here to note that it was produced for army use and closely matches the earlier LDV document quoted above in tone and content, albeit turning from Biblical to sporting metaphor:

> It has been proved that tanks, for all their hard skin, mobility and armament achieve their more spectacular results from their moral effect on half-hearted or ill-led troops. Consequently, troops which attempt to withstand tanks by adopting a purely passive role will fail in their task, or at the best only half complete it.
>
> Tank hunting must be regarded as a sport – big game hunting at its best. A thrilling, albeit dangerous sport, which if skilfully played is about as hazardous as shooting tiger on foot, and in which the same principles of stalk and ambush are followed.[14]

It is curious that the battle envisaged is man versus a tank, not man versus tanks intimately supported by infantry; just as the public focused on paratroopers operating in small numbers in isolation, so the General Staff seem to envisage German tanks operating on their own. This may reflect the experience of the Dunkirk campaign when the *Panzers* out-ran their support, but it probably does not reflect the reality of a post-landing all-arms operation in the English countryside.

During June 1940, as the British waited for Nazi parachutists, Hitler prevaricated, expecting Britain to come to terms. The difficulty in interpreting the events of the summer of 1940 is that the British and the Nazi high command viewed the grand strategic situation in the second half of 1940 in totally divergent ways. For the British, the second Great War had reached its climax, the seconds were out and what lay ahead was the final battle. For Hitler, the war was already over, ended, as the last had been, with the signing of an armistice in a railway carriage in the forest of Compiégne. Having been driven out of Europe and at the mercy of the most powerful air force in the world, Britain must soon come to its senses and, like France, agree to an armistice. Britain at bay characterised itself as an embattled fortress – *Joyous Gard*[15] – and Hitler concurred, instinctively preferring the traditional siege tactics of blockade and bombardment to achieve his desired outcome, rather than a costly assault. Nevertheless, *Kriegsmarine* (navy) studies for an invasion of the UK had commenced as early as November 1939, the *Heer* (army) and *Luftwaffe* (air force) following suit in December. The navy plan became *Studie England*, which included preliminary work on commandeering barges and developing a landing craft, the '*Pionierlandungsboot*', which closely resembled the mechanised landing craft or LC (Mech) used later by the Allies. Although this was a thoroughly efficient landing craft design, only two of the first 'Type 39' pattern were available in the summer of 1940, which meant that the bulk of the landing would have to be made using converted barges.[16]

   The barge expedient has proven a rich vein for speculation regarding the feasibility, or otherwise, of a German invasion. It should be born in mind that the Germans had managed to land a sizeable invasion force in Norway without any specialised landing vessels at all, while the British had withdrawn over 330,000 troops from the Dunkirk beachhead using a mixture of naval, merchant marine and civilian vessels. In both cases destroyers did the bulk of the work.[17] Furthermore, Continental river barges should not be confused with English narrowboats, and the expedient of inserting a reinforced concrete floor and replacing the bow section with a ramp resulted in something that was certainly equivalent to a tank landing craft or LC(T). To quote Dr Peter Schenk: 'the barges proved quite seaworthy and the powered ones subsequently performed well during landings on the Soviet-held islands in the Baltic in 1941.'[18] Although Hitler planned to use his victory speech to the German people at the Reichstag on 19 July 1940 to offer peace terms to the British, he also ratcheted up military preparations, and on 16 July issued *Weisung Nr 16* (Directive No. 16), the order to commence planning and preparation for a landing on the British mainland, codenamed *SEELÖWE* (Sea Lion). The directive began:

> Since England, in spite of her hopeless military situation, shows no signs of being ready to come to an understanding, I have decided to prepare a landing operation against England, and, if necessary, to carry it out.
>
>   The aim of this operation will be to eliminate the English homeland as a base for the prosecution of the war against Germany and, if necessary, occupy it completely.
>
>   I therefore order as follows:

1. The landing will be in the form of a surprise crossing on a wide front from about Ramsgate to the area west of the Isle of Wight. Units of the Air Force will act as artillery, and units of the Navy as engineers.[19]

After the war, German generals downplayed *SEELÖWE*, suggesting that it was little more than a bluff. Guderian commented: 'Even from the very beginning this operation was never taken seriously. In my opinion the lack of a sufficiently strong air force and of adequate shipping made it a completely hopeless undertaking' (Guderian, 1952, p. 138). In July 1940, the *Luftwaffe* was undefeated and had swept all before it, so Guderian's post-war comment needs to be treated with some scepticism. On reading Directive No. 16, it is immediately apparent that this is *not* a bluff. But it *is* a contingency – as is made quite clear in the first paragraph. Hitler hoped he would not need to land troops in England, but wanted to have a workable plan and forces in place if he had to: 'I have decided to prepare a landing operation against England, and, if necessary, to carry it out.' What is important in understanding the original *SEELÖWE* concept is that Hitler's 'surprise crossing' is a *coup de grâce* – the *Todesstoss* or death blow – an occupation of a beaten enemy, rather than a D-Day-style assault.

Given the scale of *SEELÖWE*, and its inevitability, the appellation 'surprise crossing' seems at first optimistic, if not naive. However, it is the crossing itself, rather than the preparations which are the 'surprise'. There is, quite sensibly, no emphasis on secret preparation – which could scarcely be achieved when large numbers of vessels and troops had to be gathered and moved to the Channel ports, and huge guns emplaced opposite the Straits of Dover. It is implicit in Directive No. 16 that these preparations will tighten the screw on *Joyous Gard*. The battered and hungry defenders would see, in the invasion barges, the besiegers' saps moving ever closer to their outworks, and know that if they did not surrender while negotiation was still possible, they would have to face the consequences of being taken by storm. Thus *SEELÖWE* should be interpreted as a *threat* rather than a *bluff*. In this respect, it was a huge miscalculation, as Peter Fleming pointed out:

Even before [Hitler] actually decided on invasion his propaganda machine was working for the British Government, instilling in even the sceptic, the slacker and the dullard a sense of drama against which it was both easy and becoming to make sacrifices and submit to restrictions, to fill sandbags and to stand in queues. (Fleming, 1957, p. 306)

German operational orders fascinated British staff officers, who thrilled at their 'brevity and simplicity'. MI14 explained in a digest of lessons from the Battle of France:

> Simplicity and absence of detail is very marked in all German orders and instructions. Only the essentials are given, subordinate commanders being left to use their own initiative to a great extent. This fact assisted greatly to keep operations highly mobile, as each situation was treated on its merits and commanders were able to use their imagination and ingenuity to overcome the particular type of resistance that was encountered.[20]

Here lies the essence of *Auftragstaktik*. 'Absence of detail' should not be confused with vagueness – *what* will be done is explained, *how* it will be done is left to the subordinate. Furthermore, detail is added where it helps illustrate the concept of operations. Directive No. 16 is as good an example as any: the commander's intent is quite clear, so is the concept of operations and allocation of responsibilities – the action required of subordinates is to *plan* for a crossing to the UK on the axis described, and *simultaneously begin preparations*.

The army dominated the operation, the navy only having primacy in matters of navigation. This reflects the concept of operations, which envisaged *SEELÖWE* as the movement of troops from one land area to another across a water obstacle: 'Units of the Air Force will act as artillery, and units of the Navy as engineers.' The English Channel is not an inland waterway, but a sea, and a particularly treacherous one at that. This is not to say that the movement of troops and war materiel across it is impossible – as the entry and exit of the British Expeditionary Force (BEF) had demonstrated, but it does require a maritime, rather than riverine, perspective. In the UK, MI14 spotted the immediate relevance in the manner in which the Germans approached major water obstacles and published the following on 27 June 1940; it forms a useful background against which the British view of German activities should be judged:

C. NOTES ON OPPOSED RIVER CROSSINGS

The following notes on opposed river crossings, taken from the German manuals, are of particular interest at the present time.

1. The attack on weakly held water obstacles should be carried out (after a quick reconnaissance) by all available infantry supported by their heavy weapons. The attack should be made simultaneously at different points, full use being made of existing bridges, fords, boats and all other means available.
2. The attack on strongly defended water obstacles requires careful preparation and above all surprise. The co-operation of engineers is also essential.

Surprise is achieved by the careful concealment of all preparations for the attack, by moving troops up at the last possible moment, and by attacking simultaneously along the whole front. Air photographs of the front should, if possible, be obtained. A reconnaissance should be made of assembly areas, approaches and possible crossing points, as well as enemy defences.[21]

This extract makes it clear that, were the Germans to regard a cross–Channel operation as a species of river crossing – which they did – then they would either launch a hasty surprise attack on a poorly defended opposite shore, or a deliberate surprise attack on a well-defended one. On that basis, the likelihood was that there would be a surprise attack.

On 19 July 1940, three days after issuing Directive No. 16, Hitler delivered his victory speech to the Reichstag, and his peace offer to Great Britain. The peace offer was treated with derision by the British; nevertheless, the *Führer* remained determined to somehow prevail directly on the British people. On the night of 1/2 August the *Luftwaffe* dropped leaflets bearing a translation of the Reichstag speech and headed 'A LAST APPEAL TO REASON BY ADOLF HITLER'. It was a headline which, viewed from the British perspective, could hardly fail to be seen as the start of the final countdown. Detailed invasion planning was indeed underway, the initial concept being for thirteen German divisions to be landed on a broad front, at Weymouth, between Portsmouth and Brighton, and between Margate and Hastings, with a follow-on force of twenty-six divisions. Given carte blanche, and following the precept that a crossing should be made by 'all available infantry supported by their heavy weapons', army planners had conceived an overwhelming over-the-beach amphibious assault that anticipated operations, techniques and equipment that would only develop later in the war. The navy was able to reject the plan, on the basis that only a crossing where the Channel was at its narrowest, near Dover, could be regarded as a realistic proposition. In late July the army agreed to a main landing between Folkestone and Eastbourne, with a diversionary landing of shock troops from motor trawlers in Brighton Bay. This latter would only be reinforced 'if the situation was favourable'. There were to be nine divisions in the first wave and seven in the follow-up. These were to hold the Kent and Sussex bridgehead for up to sixteen days while third-wave reinforcements were brought across.

Assembling the invasion fleet took time: visiting the Channel coast in August, American journalist (and influential post-war historian) William Shirer failed to find any invasion barges, and began to form the view that the invasion *was* a bluff (Shirer, 1962, p. 761). In fact the first barge, the *Rhemosa*, had been commandeered in Duisburg-Ruhrort, at 11.30 a.m. on 7 July (Schenk, 1990, p. 6). The conversion of barges into landing craft was carried out at Mannheim, Mainz, Duisburg, Amsterdam, Rotterdam and Antwerp, and eight points along the Seine between Paris and Le Havre. By the end of September the fleet consisted of 2,318 barges, 174 freighters converted to troop transports, 426 tugs, around 1,600 motor fishing vessels and yachts, and 100 coasters (Schenk, 1990, p. 8). In addition, specialised equipments were investigated and developed which anticipated those used by the Allies on D-Day. *SEELÖWE* spurred the development of some far-sighted and sensible equipment including tidal mines to help secure the Channel, amphibious and submersible tanks, the *Nebelwerfer* multi-barrelled rocket launcher and a prefabricated jetty.[22] The amphibious tanks were PzKpfw IIs fitted with floatation devices, the submersibles PzKpfw IIIs and PzKpfw IV Ausf F *Tauchpanzers*, fitted with snorkels, which enabled them to move along the seabed at depths down to 4m.[23] These were later successfully used crossing the River Bug on 22 June 1941, General Guderian subsequently recording: 'At 04.15 hrs. advance units of the 17th and 18th Panzer Divisions forded the river. For this they were equipped with the waterproofing that had been tested for *Operation Sea-lion*, which enabled them to move through 13 feet of water' (Guderian, 1952, p. 153).

The suggestion that armoured fighting vehicles (AFVs) might be landed by air, made in *Periodical Notes on the German Army No. 30*, was unrealistic in August 1940, with only Ju 52 transports and eight-seater DFS 230 assault gliders in *Luftwaffe* service, and it reflects a melding of the two greatest British fears: armoured attack and air assault. However, the Germans recognised this as a gap in their capability, and in October 1940 issued an urgent specification for a large glider capable of transporting 130 fully armed and equipped troops; an 8.8cm Flak anti-aircraft gun, its half-track tractor, ammunition and crew; or a fully armed and crewed PzKpfw II, III, IV tank, or *Sturmgeschütz* assault gun. Junkers and Messerschmitt were given just fourteen days to submit initial designs. The Junkers design was unsuccessful but the first Messerschmitt Me 321 '*Gigant*' was test flown on 25 February 1941, by which time eleven gliders had been built and sixty-two more were under construction.[24] At the time the largest aircraft in the world, the *Gigant* required air superiority and, preferably, a captured airfield to land on, if it was to be used safely, but if these were achieved, the giant transports had the potential to transform the prospects of a successful cross-Channel operation.

However, most of this special equipment would not be ready until 1941. To return to the prospects for a 'hasty' crossing in 1940, on 12 August the air war began with a strike against the British early warning system and airfields in the South East. Five radar stations were attacked, opening a gap 100 miles long in the CHAIN HOME. The station at Ventnor was damaged so severely that it remained out of service for eleven days. This was a major achievement at the very start of the air offensive; however, on 15 August, fooled by the lack of damage to the masts and by dummy transmissions, head of the *Luftwaffe*, Hermann Göring, declared that: 'it is doubtful whether there is any point in continuing the attacks on radar sites, in view of the fact that not one of those attacked has so far been put out of operation' (Fleming, 1957, pp. 224–5). The early warning given by CHAIN HOME was crucial in ensuring that RAF fighters were, if not in the right place at the right time, then on their way there. In retrospect, and with the importance of CHAIN HOME established, one is inclined to the view that, were the radar sites really too difficult to destroy from the air, a hole might have been punched through them by completely destroying several in ground attacks – anticipating the British raid on the German *Würzburg* radar site at Brunval, in February 1942. However, the Battle of Britain was not to be decided by such imaginative *coups de main*. While the Germans persisted in imagining that their air arm could achieve victory in isolation, the British, perhaps demonstrating a greater comprehension of the joint force nature of *Blitzkrieg*, continued, until June 1944, to prepare defences against ground attacks on airfields and other key parts of the air defence infrastructure – tasks with which the Home Guard became increasingly involved.

On 3 September 1940 OKW issued a directive announcing 21 September as the provisional date for the invasion. On the same day, *Luftwaffe* high command decided to mount huge daylight bombing raids on London, which would serve the double function of forcing the RAF to commit its fighters, while demonstrating the reality of 'terror bombing' to the British capital. On 5 September, Chief of Staff, *Heersgruppe A*, issued *Vorläufige Weisung für Durchführung des Unternehmens „Seelöwe"* – the preliminary instruction for implementation of operation *SEELÖWE* (Klee, 1959, p. 373), a detailed breakdown of the units involved in *SEELÖWE* and their areas of responsibility. It ended with: 'The date and approximate time of day of the first landing on the English coast has still to be announced.' The order demonstrates the difficulty inherent in planning a complex and ambitious operation for which neither the date nor time could be fixed until the *Luftwaffe* had achieved air superiority and the *Kriegsmarine*, subsequently, selected a day with appropriate weather and tides. By September 1940, given the navy's requirement for a flat calm, the army's need for eleven days to mount the operation, and the air force's inability to bring the RAF to a decisive and final battle, it was obvious to both sides that time for *SEELÖWE* was running out.

The first bombing raid on London took place on 7 September 1940 and was the most devastating aerial attack, anywhere, to that date, and sufficiently dramatic to precipitate an invasion stand-to. Alan Brooke, Commander-in-Chief (C-in-C) Home Forces, recorded in his diary:

> All reports look like invasion getting nearer. Ships collecting, dive bombers being concentrated, parachutists captured, also 4 Dutchmen on the coast. Drove in from Chequers with Dill. On arriving in office was sent for to attend COS meeting to discuss latest intercepted message concerning German plans for putting down fog. Back to St Paul's to discuss expansion of armoured forces. Finally dined with Bertie after sending out orders for 'Cromwell' – i.e. state of readiness in Eastern and Southern Commands. (Danchev and Todman, 2001, p. 105)

Danchev and Todman have inserted 'exercise' in parentheses after the word 'Cromwell' in their rendering of Brooke's diaries. Whether or not issuing CROMWELL was intended to be some form of test exercise was a subject of debate among the Home Guard themselves, as the historian of the Ministry of Food Home Guard recorded:

> About midnight on the 7th/8th September the telephones buzzed with a code word – no exercise warning preceded it – and many a Home Guard, turned out of his bed in the small hours, speculated on the chance of trying his mettle and his improvised weapons against an invader, while his officers ruminated upon the means to muster their men more rapidly in future. (Smith, 1945, p. 14)

There is absolutely no suggestion from his diary that Brooke was ordering an exercise – which was an unlikely thing to do, given the apparent imminence of a

German invasion. He was, rather, raising the level of readiness, as every indication pointed to 8 or 10 September as 'S-*Tag*', landing day.[25]

The sheer scale of the aerial bombardment of London and the ensuing devastation stunned both sides, but it failed in both of its military objectives, bringing neither the end of Fighter Command, nor civil collapse. As time ran out for the invasion, the aerial assault, which had come close to success, was steadily de-focussed, diluting the effect in a self-defeating effort to increase impact. The RAF was not only undefeated, but representing a growing threat to the invasion fleet, which was being heavily bombed. Dispersal of shipping began on 19 September, after which point *SEELÖWE* ceased to be an immediate option for 1940, a fact which was officially recognised by Hitler on 12 October:

> The Führer has decided that from now on until the Spring, preparations for the landing in England shall be continued solely for the purpose of maintaining political and military pressure on England.
>
> Should the invasion be reconsidered in the spring or early summer of 1941, orders for a renewal of operational readiness will be issued later …

Whilst the order postponing *SEELÖWE* is now generally taken as the end of the invasion threat to the UK mainland, this was by no means apparent at the time. Hugh Slater published *Home Guard for Victory!* in January 1941, and whilst he acknowledged a German invasion as a *possibility* rather than a *probability*, he went on to outline seven invasion plans of varying degrees of ambition. Plan 2 'Head on to London' almost exactly matches the actual scheme for *SEELÖWE*, with a Channel crossing on a narrow front into Kent and Sussex. Comfortingly, and very optimistically, Slater anticipated that a 'highly mechanised counter-attack force of well over 250,000' would engage the invaders within a few hours (Slater, 1941, p. 25). Therefore, in order to maintain an attacking advantage of three-to-one, the Germans would need to land around 800,000 men, with 15,000 tanks, 80,000 motor vehicles and 10,000 motor cycles 'at least'. On Slater's calculation, such a force would require 5,500,000 gallons of petrol for one week's operation. In June 1940 MI14 had assessed the front-line German tank force at twelve armoured divisions, approximately 4,800 light and medium tanks. The entire German tank stock was estimated at 7,000 – 7,500 of all types.[26] The actual figure was around 2,500 tanks (Guderian, 1952, p. 94), which had risen to around 3,000 by 1941, although a significant proportion of these were still poorly armed and armoured PzKpfw Is.[27] Unless we accept that Slater, 'late Chief of

Operations, International Brigade Staff', was completely off his head, we must assume that his aim was to accentuate the practical difficulties of the various schemes and thereby reassure the public. Anyone, army or Home Guard, patrolling the South Coast was well aware that a mere couple of hundred German tanks would present a quite sufficient challenge to defenders still awaiting effective anti-tank guns; nevertheless, Slater's book was reprinted four times before the end of the month.

Alan Brooke, as C-in-C Home Forces, started 1941 determined to use the opportunity provided by the winter weather in the Channel to strengthen invasion defences:

10 January
The PM held one of his quarterly conferences of Cs-in-C of the three services … My points were connected with the increased danger of invasion owing to Axis reverses in the Mediterranean, and danger of withdrawal of too many troops from this country. (Danchev and Todman, 2001, p. 134)

He later added to the entry:

During the discussion I raised the lamentable lack of arms that still prevailed after 1½ years of war. Shortage of rifles, .303 ammunition, tracer ammunition, Boys [anti-tank] rifles and their ammunition, anti-tank guns, tanks, armoured cars, etc etc. This did not please Winston at all …

Brooke devoted his considerable energy to improving and reorganising Home Defence throughout the first half of 1941, although it was becoming increasingly evident that Hitler's attention was fixed on the Soviet Union. Hitler's decision to turn his back on an actively hostile Britain to prosecute a new campaign against the Soviet Union was greeted with surprise by his own commanders, as Guderian recalled:

… when they spread out a map of Russia before me I could scarcely believe my eyes. Was something which I had held to be utterly impossible now to become a fact? Hitler had criticised the leaders of German policy of 1914 in the strongest possible words for their failure to avoid a war on two fronts; was he now, on his own initiative and before the war with England had been decided, to open this second-front war against the Russians? All his soldiers had warned him repeatedly and urgently against this very error, and he had himself agreed with them. (Guderian, 1952, p. 142)

The military logic behind the campaign was that the huge, but disorganised and weakened, Red Army would be quickly defeated:

> ... the supreme command was sunk in its dream of defeating the Russian Army in eight or ten weeks; this defeat would result, they thought, in the political collapse of the Soviets. So confident were they of this that in the autumn of 1941 a considerable portion of Germany's industry was switched from war production to other purposes. (Guderian, 1952, p. 151)

However, even if this outcome was achieved, the preparation, execution and recovery from the operation would lose the Germans the 1941 campaigning season against Britain, as Brooke subsequently noted against his entry for 22 June, the day *Unternehmen BARBAROSSA* (Operation BARBAROSSA) was finally launched:

> ... As long as the Germans were engaged in the invasion of Russia there was no possibility of an invasion of these islands. It would now depend on how long Russia could last and what resistance she would be able to put up. My own opinion at the time, and an opinion that was shared by most people, was that Russia would not last long, possibly 3 or 4 months, possibly slightly longer. Putting it at 4 months, and as we were then in June, it certainly looked as if Germany would be unable to launch an invasion of England until October, and by then the weather and winter would be against such an enterprise.
>
> It therefore looked as if we should now be safe from invasion during 1941. (Danchev and Todman, 2001, p. 166)

It will be noted that Brooke viewed invasion as a continuing threat, assuming that the Germans would return to deal with Britain once the Soviet Union had been dispatched. The UK's defences were in better order than one year previously, but the Germans too would be better prepared and equipped. Although dispersed, the invasion fleet remained under military control and the vessels had been modified. New specialist equipment had entered service including landing craft, the prefabricated jetties and heavy gliders – the tank-transporting Me 321 would shortly be joined by a new general purpose assault glider, the Gotha Go 242, capable of carrying twenty-one fully equipped troops, a *Kubelwagen* (jeep), or light artillery piece.

As the British Army became more involved with overseas operational commitments, the Home Defence role rested more and more heavily on the Home Guard. Thus although the actual threat was diminished, or at least deferred, the Home Guard's responsibility increased – indeed compulsory enrolment for Home Guard service, 'for the duration', was introduced with effect from February 1942, although it was evident from the middle of the year that the likelihood of a German invasion was diminishing fast. All-out invasion was not, of course, the only Home Defence threat. We have noted the galvanising effect on the British public of the actual possibility of a German invasion, and how this threat was personified in the figure of the Nazi paratrooper. Hard on the heels of this came the much older fear of betrayal. In 1940 potential enemies of the state formed a worryingly large constituency: persons of pan-German origin resident in the UK; refugees from occupied Europe, about whom little was known and who were vulnerable to pressure put on relatives at home; British Fascists, and those of the political Right who had openly admired Nazi Germany and Fascist Italy; and those of the extreme Left who, until Germany's invasion on 22 June 1941, took their orders from Germany's tacit ally, the Soviet Union. There were also unprincipled opportunists, and the lazy and careless. It would have been extremely difficult to invent an identity to embrace all these disparate groups, had it not been for Spanish General Emilio Mola, as John Langdon-Davies explained:

> **Fifth Column.** General Mola, a supporter of the Spanish General Franco, invented this phrase at a time when four of Franco's columns were closing in on Madrid. 'We will capture Madrid' he said, 'with the Fifth Column hidden inside.' That is, the secret traitors working to destroy Madrid from within. 'Fifth Column' is now used for the activities of Nazi sympathizers who secretly prepare the way for the Nazi invasion of their countries. (1942b, p. 181)

The existence of a Fifth Column in the UK was an article of faith from May 1940, indeed to deny it would be to place oneself under immediate suspicion. Belief in the existence of the Fifth Column was due not only to the fractured nature of the popular attitude to Germany and the war prior to Dunkirk – which was far from the pro-war, anti-Nazi, monolith it would be forged into, and later remembered as – but also the alleged activities of the Fifth Column in recently defeated countries such as Holland and Norway, and the Spanish prototype, as experienced by veterans of the Spanish Civil War, John Langdon-Davies, for example:

> The Nazis [have] seen long ago that in this modern world of Total War, if you desire to destroy a country by military force you must first of all see that you have paralysed their defence, weakened their will by raising up within them, allies, secret sympathisers, Fifth Column traitors, able to insinuate themselves into key positions and to weaken hopelessly the chance of their country resisting the Nazi military machine when it comes. (1941, p. 10)

In reality the closest thing to an organised Fifth Column in the UK was the 'Right Club', founded in May 1939 in an attempt to unify the various British ultra-Right organisations including the British Union of Fascists (BUF) and the Nordic League. The Earl Jowitt, who, as Solicitor-General from June 1940 to March 1942, prosecuted members of that organisation and those captured Nazi spies who were not 'turned', attributed the inability of the Nazis to establish effective supporters or rings of agents in the UK to the vigorous, indeed ruthless, way in which the UK government took action against those who constituted a possible threat:

> The suspension of our doctrine of Habeas Corpus, and the internment of suspected persons without a trial – or even without an accusation – was a harsh and hard procedure and one which is opposed alike to our traditions and our principles. But in view of our perilous situation, I, for one, do not question the necessity. (Jowitt, 1954, pp. 15–16)

This not only affected refugees and immigrants, but also stretched to Members of Parliament, as in the case of Captain Archibald Ramsay, founding member of the Nordic League and the Right Club, interned 'for the duration' without trial. As Jowitt put it: 'It is no doubt necessary that the Executive in wartime should have such extraordinary powers as would enable it to intern without accusation even a Member of Parliament; but it is only right to realise that such powers may inflict grave hardship upon individuals' (Jowitt, 1954, p. 45).

Although great pains were taken to play down the British ultra-Right during and after the Second World War, it was pervasive, and fuelled by anti-Semitism and anti-communism, which made it a comfortable bedfellow with National

Socialism – whatever those involved might claim to the contrary. BUF had numbered some 40,000 members in 1934, the Nordic League, actually founded in 1935 by Nazi agents, whilst far smaller, included such high-profile individuals as Major General J.F.C. Fuller and the Duke of Hamilton among its members. General Sir Edmund Ironside's comment on the Fifth Column, when he was still C-in-C Home Forces, was actually close to the mark: 'My experience is that the gentlemen who are the best behaved and the most sleek are those who are doing the mischief'[28] (*vide* MacKenzie, 1996, pp. 56–7). Effective as the draconian legislative measures may have been, a case can be made that the intensity with which a Fifth Column threat was sought-out within the UK silenced and subdued those with leanings toward the ultra-Right. It is wrong to characterise the Fifth Column scare as a 'grass roots' phenomenon – the threat was something impressed on the LDV and Home Guard by their superiors. Writing in late 1943, a member of 4th Battalion, Cambridgeshire Home Guard gave an intriguing summation of the whole episode:

> Did not the officers back from Dunkirk assure us that the curious cryptograms scrawled on walls and trees were precisely the same as those to be seen in France, Holland, and Belgium, before their fall? Were not the coloured flares that went up mysteriously when the Boche planes were over at night just the same as those sent up by the fifth column to give away the position of an H.Q. or battery in Flanders? We did not end this hunt of the invisible fifth column till Germany invaded Russia in 1941, and then abruptly all the signs and wonders ceased. (Smith, 1944, p. 52)

In the popular mind it was the twin terrors of Nazi paratrooper and Fifth Columnist traitor which were the Home Guard's nemesis, its natural enemy. Notwithstanding that the Home Guard actually spent most of its time preparing to defend 'nodal points' against tank attack, operating anti-aircraft artillery or locating unexploded bombs, when, by 1945, the paratroopers had failed to appear and the Fifth Column was proven to be largely illusory, the force came to be seen, unfairly, as quixotic.

Vigilance also had to be maintained, if not for invasion, then for raids and landings throughout the country. CHAIN HOME and airfields have already been identified as a useful target for a ground attack, and vital parts of Britain's manufacturing base were also extremely vulnerable. All these 'Vulnerable Points' were identified and listed for protection by the Home Guard.[29] Given the

Germans' record for unconventional operations during the Second World War, it seems remarkable that no raiding was attempted. Although they had embraced emerging technologies, including airborne warfare techniques, from before the start of the Second World War, and used them to effect to capture the Belgian fort of Eben-Emael, and elsewhere, it appears that the Germans were only stimulated into establishing special operations forces to undertake unconventional operations once the effectiveness of British commando tactics had been demonstrated – and once the outcome of the war began to inexorably slide away from them. Thus, in a curious way, the British made their own fears real. Indeed, Germany's commando mastermind, Otto Skorzeny, relied heavily on British-manufactured special weapons, including silenced Sten machine carbines, Hawkins mines and plastic explosives, captured from air drops to the Dutch resistance (Whiting, 1998, p. 20).

As the time for the Allied invasion of Europe approached, the defenders of the UK became increasingly certain that the Germans would not allow this to proceed without some form of intervention – just as they had been convinced that the Germans could not possibly miss the opportunity of neutralising the UK in July 1940. The Ministry of Food (11th Denbighshire Battalion) Home Guard were informed by their CO in a special New Year message on 31 December 1943:

> The New Year will see the launching of the combined offensive against the enemy's European fortress, and the supreme effort to secure his speedy surrender. We know enough of his military skill and resource to realise that our attack will inevitably call forth every possible effort to dislocate our offensive if, indeed, it is not anticipated.
>
> We must, therefore, regard it as certain that the opening of operations on the Western Fronts will synchronise with offensive action against this country, in which this district may be involved. This will be critical – the decisive hour when courage, determination and past technical training will be the key to success. (Smith, 1945, pp. 88–9)

Rather more realistically, 'front line' were the defenders of the aerodrome at Biggin Hill, which included 'E' Company, 20th Battalion, Kent Home Guard. A preserved operation order, dated April 1944, contains administrative instructions and an assessment of the threat. Note that the Fifth Columnist no longer figures:[30]

When Allied invasion of the continent commences, the enemy may be expected to:

(a) Bomb ports, communications, airfields and other V.P.s [Vital Points].
(b) Raid by air to disrupt communications and movement.
(c) Land enemy agents by air and sea for sabotage.

German spoiling raids to disrupt the Allied invasion were the last never-to-be-attempted threat for which the Home Guard 'stood-to'. The Home Guard had done its bit and, although the UK was still at war, and there remained a requirement for anti-aircraft defence, bomb disposal, and general local defence and security duties to be undertaken, it became increasingly difficult to maintain the commitment needed to keep this huge voluntary force operational – demonstrating, as nothing else, the extent to which maintenance of the Home Guard was a direct response to the threat of enemy troops on British soil.

2

THE CARRIAGE OF ARMS

The homely, gently quixotic, image of *Dad's Army* parading twice weekly in the church hall is more comfortable and familiar than an alternative vision of the British civilian population armed, and encouraged to fight German troops by whatever means at its disposal – in the certain knowledge that such conduct would be met with the utmost ruthlessness, indeed, in the anticipation that brutal German reprisals would serve the beneficial purpose of precipitating the entry of the United States into the war. That, however, was the reality of what came to be referred to as 'Total Defence'.[1] Historically, the German military has demonstrated a singular robustness in its handling of enemy civilians.[2] The issue is clouded by the heavy-handed Allied propaganda of 1914–18 and the racist precepts of National Socialism, but even when these are filtered out, an underlying trend remains. Christopher Dowling examined German conduct during the First World War, in the context of atrocity propaganda, in a particularly enlightening article written in 1970:

> The Germans were genuinely terrified of being shot at by unseen assailants, a form of attack they regarded as cowardly and treacherous. They imagined a civilian with a sporting rifle lay in ambush on every rooftop, behind every window and in every cellar. The novelist Walter Bloem, who was serving as a reserve officer in Kluck's *First Army* [Dowling's italics], was haunted by the 'monstrous' thought that he might be killed or wounded by a bullet fired by a civilian. When they were sniped at, the Germans dealt out ruthless reprisals. Houses and villages were burnt and suspects summarily executed. These were much the same methods as had been employed, with far less outcry, in 1871. Sometimes innocent people were shot, for the Germans believed in the

principle of collective responsibility (which had been laid down by the elder Moltke) and made little attempt to establish where the guilt lay. So obsessed were they by the spectre of the terrible *franc-tireur* that they tended to assume that any shot coming from an unexpected quarter was fired by a civilian … To protect themselves against these ubiquitous snipers the Germans, contrary to international law, seized large numbers of hostages and not infrequently executed them. (Dowling, 1970, p. 791)

Those for whom the 'model occupation' of the Channel Islands during the Second World War (in the words of Asa Briggs, 1995, p. 9) 'stimulates thoughts about what would have happened in the bigger island of Britain had the Germans invaded' should bear the Greek experience in mind. According to General Hubert Lanz, 'The Germans harboured no hatred against the Greeks. On the contrary, they admired the great past and lofty culture of Hellas' (Mazower, 1998, p. 158). But how would they react to guerrilla warfare? Mark Mazower reveals:

The Wehrmacht responded with a series of anti-guerrilla operations, based on reprisal killings and the arrest of civilian hostages. Violence, to put it simply, became the chief way of reasserting German control over the countryside. Terror became the basis for rule in the urban areas. Not solely the response of nervous soldiers in the field, the logic of violence and terror reflected the core values of the National Socialist *Weltanschauung*. (Mazower, 1998, pp. xviii–xix)

Writing shortly after the Second World War, Churchill was candid:

The massacre would have been on both sides grim and great. There would have been neither mercy nor quarter. They would have used Terror, and we were prepared to go to all lengths. I intended to use the slogan 'You can always take one with you.' I even calculated that the horrors of such a scene would in the last resort turn the scale in the United States. (1955, p. 232)

An invasion of the UK appears to represent the crossing of a boundary in the prime minister's mind that separated 'war' from the struggle for British 'national survival'. Once the latter was invoked, no holds were barred. And Churchill was not the only one prepared to 'go to all lengths'. The general preface to the Home Office publication *Air Raid Precautions Handbook No. 1: Personal Protection Against Gas*,[3] of 1937 stated that:

The use of poison gas in war is forbidden by the Geneva Gas Protocols of 1925, to which this country and all the most important countries of western Europe are parties, and the Government would use every endeavour on an outbreak of war to secure an undertaking from the enemy not to use poison gas.[4]

Yet Alan Brooke noted in his diary against the entry for 22 July 1940 (as he was succeeding Ironside as Commander in Chief Home Forces): 'I was relying on heavy air attacks on the [German] points of landing, and had every intention of using sprayed mustard gas on the beaches' (Danchev and Todman, 2001, p. 94). Brooke's willingness to make pre-emptive use of chemical weapons therefore marks a deliberate decision by the British high command to disregard international law in the interests of national survival.

In this campaign there were to be no 'innocent civilians'. If Churchill expected the British public to resist the invader by every means available to them – 'You can always take one with you' – this also appeared to be the message spread by John Langdon-Davies during his evangelising tour of Home Guard units over the winter of 1940–41:

> … the civilians can no longer stand back and say to the armed forces: 'You fight the war and we will help you, but of course we do not expect to have to take an active part in the fighting ourselves.'
>
> That has been more or less the position in wars hitherto. The civilians have helped, of course; they have made munitions or they have knitted socks, and just a few have been content to be the civilisation for which the others were fighting.
>
> But it has never occurred to people that the civilian should be asked to hit back. In this war he has to hit back, not merely because total war calls for total defence of every town, village and country field by its inhabitants, but because only by hitting back can the civilian make quite certain of keeping his own heart up, keeping a good morale, and that, as I have said, is the master key to Victory. (Langdon-Davies, 1941, pp. 49–50)

Langdon-Davies is, however, a complex case. In his weekly articles for the *Sunday Pictorial*, reprinted in *Home Guard Warfare*, his Home Guard is drawn from the civilian population, yet separate, reflecting the real difficulty of defining the status of the Home Guard. This ambiguity is compounded by Langdon-Davies' use of 'civilian' as shorthand for non-Home Guards:

All experience of war teaches us that the civilian population must be out of the town and away from any route that the enemy may take before the first shot is fired.

The reason for this is that if they see their women and children at the mercy of the enemy, the best-trained soldier or Home Guard in the world cannot be expected to fight.

Moreover, there is the grim danger that the Nazis will exact reprisals on the civilian population, as by the laws of war they are entitled to do, and once it is known that they have shot a dozen civilians in one town the morale of every other town in Britain will suffer. (Langdon-Davies, 1941, p. 123)

The quote above contains Langdon-Davies' only reference to reprisals against the civilian population. Whilst that in itself is unsurprising in a manual (Slater makes none in *Home Guard for Victory!*), what is startling is his assertion that the Nazis are 'entitled' to exact reprisals. 'Entitled' or not, it would not have required a great leap of the imagination to appreciate the sort of response that action by the Home Guard would generate. Indeed, Radio Bremen had spelt out the German attitude towards the LDV in terms which make it clear that little had changed since Walter Bloem marched through Belgium with von Kluck's First Army:

The British Government is committing the worst crime of all. Evidently it permits open preparation for the formation of murder bands. The preparations which are being made all over England to arm the civilian population for guerrilla warfare are contrary to the rules of international law. German official quarters warn the misled British public and remind them of the fate of the Polish *francs-tireurs* and gangs of murderers, whether they are priests or bank clerks. British people you will do well to heed this warning. (*Vide* Graves, 1943, p. 16; Beckett, 1991, p. 273)

Thus, for a British civilian or paramilitary to take up arms against German troops was a committed move. There is, therefore, an important element of symbolism inherent in the carriage of arms, particularly in the earliest days, which is missed by commentators concentrating on the effectiveness (or otherwise) of the volunteers' armoury. This symbolic significance was not restricted to a prospective invader. The possession of a weapon – any weapon – in a public place by a British civilian is a serious matter, and the forming of an armed group even more so. Nevertheless, the use of German parachute troops in Norway and the Low Countries prompted the formation of what were, in effect, vigilante groups, the 'Parashots'. As one countryman reminisced in the 1970s: 'The beginning of this little army was so simple as men volunteered to keep watch over our village. At this stage no drill had been practised, there were just two men with twelve-bore guns, walking as the dawn broke and waiting …' (Archer, 1975, p. 65).

Even when this energy and commitment had been channelled into the officially recognised Local Defence Volunteers, relations between the LDV and the police could be, as Norman Longmate pointed out, strained: 'It was the LDV's great delight … to pull up all policemen and ask for their identity cards, especially inspectors. One squad even tried to detain a constable, who refused to comply, while he in turn threatened to arrest them for carrying arms without a licence' (Longmate, 1974, p. 57). Amusing as such anecdotes are, it should be borne in mind that the police played a vital role in establishing the LDV as a properly constituted and armed force. Anthony Eden's plea for Local Defence Volunteers was broadcast on the evening of Tuesday, 14 May 1940. Eden instructed applicants: 'In order to volunteer, what you have to do is to give in your name at your local police station; and then, as and when we want you, we will let you know' (Cambs. and Isle of Ely TA Assoc., 1944, p. 101). The official enrolment form, Army Form W.3066, was not available until several days after the broadcast (a situation wonderfully parodied in the original 1971 feature film of *Dad's Army*). Nevertheless, at 9 p.m., and with volunteers flocking to police stations, the police managed to improvise, as a member of the Cambridgeshire and Isle of Ely Home Guard recalled:

> Invaluable assistance was given by the police in enrolling the LDV. Within a few hours they had duplicated the form setting out the questions which applicants were required to answer. These forms were checked by the police on the security side and then passed to the Home Guard commanders who selected recruits (Cambs. and Isle of Ely TA Assoc., 1944, p. 16).

Police assistance also extended to distributing firearms and uniforms, thus it was only through heroic efforts by Kent County Constabulary that 1,000 LDV, with rifles and ammunition, were patrolling the South Coast within seventy-two hours of the initial call for volunteers (Gulvin, 1980). The same was true in the vulnerable eastern counties, where – for example – 350 rifles, with ten rounds apiece, and 350 denim overalls were quickly delivered to Melbourn police station,

Cambridgeshire, for distribution to the LDV (Cambs. and Isle of Ely TA Assoc., 1944, p. 51).

In instructing volunteers to report to police stations, Eden was making use of an obvious organisational focal point, but the underlying motive was for the police to filter out 'undesirables' among the applicants. After forty years of *Dad's Army*, it is difficult to associate the word 'revolutionary' with the LDV/Home Guard. However, the whole concept of placing the population in arms was fraught with political implications. There were those, Churchill foremost among them, who saw the LDV/Home Guard as continuing a tradition of loyal defence *in extremis* that could be traced back, through the yeoman longbowmen of the Hundred Years' War, to the Saxon *Fyrd*, and there were those in the military who could accept the LDV on the basis of a second-string Territorial Army, to be administered through the TA Associations. It is quite apparent, however, that many volunteers and pundits totally rejected these views: they would not welcome any backward-looking imagery that might link them to the Volunteer Training Corps of the First World War (whose *Georgius Rex* 'GR' official armbands were variously interpreted as 'Grandpa's Regiment', 'Genuine Relics', or 'Gorgeous Wrecks'), or, for that matter, the somewhat discredited conventional military. The Home Guard was different; it was *modern*. In the words of International Brigade veteran Hugh Slater:

> The development of the Home Guard is one of the most fundamental historical significance. From the military point of view, the Home Guard, combined with the regular forces, makes a military occupation of Britain by German Fascism improbable. Politically, a fully developed Home Guard provides an absolute guarantee against both the crude Fascism of a Mosely and the more insidious Fifth Column activities of any would-be British Pétains.
>
> Because it is a Citizens' Army, the Home Guard can be fully democratic and energetically modern … (1941, pp. 119–20)

Slater was not alone in seeing the Home Guard as heralding a new era, as MacKenzie explains:

> … a small number of very active left-wingers outside of the Communist Party [saw] in the Home Guard the basis for a future people's militia. Mostly intellectuals and publicists who had at some point in the past come into conflict with

the Party line, such as George Orwell, Tom Wintringham, and John Langdon-Davies, they believed that what was needed to defeat Fascism was not just better weapons but a conviction that the war would bring about true democracy, a people's peace.

This view might have mattered as little as the small number of fellow-travellers of the Right involved in the Home Guard if it had not been very much in harmony with public sentiment in the summer of 1940 ... the old guard were running the show and calls for a democratic, egalitarian people's war were increasingly common. (MacKenzie, 1996, p. 69)

Brimming with enthusiasm for the new force, George Orwell went so far as to note that: 'a million British working men would not lightly surrender the rifles now placed in their possession.'[5] He was, as it turned out, wrong – although after the war they did hang on to their boots and greatcoats.

In any case the 'old guard' was on the alert:

As early as 15 May the police had been instructed to weed out undesirable persons from the lists of applicants compiled at police stations, and both Fascists and Communists had been barred from joining the LDV in a secret War Office order dated 27 May. The police, however, had a rather different idea of who was or was not a security risk ... in practice, as a staff officer later wrote, 'nearly all men on the police lists were accepted ...' (MacKenzie, 1996, p. 31)

This led to some strange bedfellows. In the Ministry of Food Home Guard: 'Some of them wanted the Unit to be more like His Majesty's Brigade of Guards in the days of His Majesty King Edward VII; others wanted it to be more like the Red Army in 1917' (Smith, 1945, p. 29). It is a curiosity of *Dad's Army* that the Home Guard's extremes – the exponents of guerrilla warfare with their improvised 'jam tin bombs', and the veterans in their mothballed uniforms – should be amalgamated in the single character of 'Corporal Jones'. It is possible that this has softened our perception of the Home Guard's political edge. It is clear, however, that the LDV/Home Guard was, throughout its existence, dominated by the thinking of militant (in the true sense of the word) socialists. The practical effect was that a German assault on the UK, at any time after May 1940, would have met with national resistance of a sort the Germans had not yet encountered – and would not meet until their first winter in the Soviet Union.

But what of sexual politics in this 'democratic and energetically modern' force, fighting a 'democratic, egalitarian people's war'? Women were not encouraged to participate in the Home Guard – due to conservatism both on the part of the authorities, and pundits like Langdon-Davies. When illustrating the vulnerability of tanks to determined defenders, Langdon-Davies gives the impression of Spanish women joining in with the men:

> And to make everything quite certain, the Spanish Militia co-operated with their wives.
>
> These ladies collected old rags, even the double bed blanket off the double bed, and soaked them in paraffin. They hung a rope from one side of the street to the other, through the windows above the door, and when the tank crew was hesitating as to what to do about other plans for their reception, they pulled on the rope, dropped a mass of oiled textiles on top of the tank, and set it alight with perfect confidence that the fumes would make it necessary for the tank crew to come out. (Langdon-Davies, 1941, p. 42)

This passage reveals much about Langdon-Davies – that any females involved are 'wives', the specific and rather unnecessary reference to marital beds and so on. It does, though, give the impression that the ambushing was, in this case, carried out by women. It may be that such behaviour is, like slitting the throats of bailed-out tank crew, something that could be tolerated in Spain,[6] but would be inappropriate in Britain, even in conditions of 'Total Defence' – Langdon-Davies went on to set the matter straight:

> I do not find myself always in complete agreement with that very fine woman, Dr. Edith Summerskill. She wants women to be allowed to join the Home Guard on equal terms with the men.
>
> I am against it, although probably Dr. Summerskill would consider some of our reasons mere old-fashioned prejudices.
>
> I think the average Home Guard has joined it because he wants to protect his hearth and home, and he would feel a bit annoyed if the hearth and home insisted upon coming along with him and doing some protecting.
>
> But there is a still better reason why I do not want the baker's wife to stand shoulder to shoulder with the baker at the road-block, shooting down Nazis. It is that I want the baker's wife to be doing something much more useful at home in the baker's shop.

> When the Nazis come, and if they get through the defences of the road-block, there should not be left one pound of flour, one loaf of bread, one cake in the baker's shop for them to eat. (Langdon-Davies, 1941, pp. 54–5)

One could speculate that with the additional firepower of the baker's wife the road-block might have held, but this obviously never occurred to the author. Overall, Langdon-Davies' polemic is so devoid of 'reasons' as to make discussion superfluous; against similar hostility from all sides, Labour MP and medical doctor Edith Summerskill felt obliged, in 1941, to form the 'Women's Home Defence' to lobby on behalf of women who wanted to join the Home Guard. In fact, women *were* involved with the Home Guard from the outset, and many received some informal weapons training. Vera Harrison, for example, was one of several women who enrolled in the 'Women's Home Guard' (subsequently the Women's Home Defence) in Sevenoaks, Kent. The women participated in a shooting competition at nearby Shoreham range, one winning a silver cup as second prize.[7]

It is important when considering any Home Guard issues to keep in mind the progress of the war, as Miss Bridgman, a female auxiliary from the Ministry of Food Home Guard, recalled:

> In September, 1942, when the achievements of the Russian Women were making headlines, a member of the staff of the Ministry of Food circulated a round-robin for the names of women interested in forming a Women's Home Guard. A hundred and thirty names were soon added to the list … We became affiliated to the Women's Home Defence under the chairmanship of Dr. Edith Summerskill, M.P. (Smith, 1945, p. 122).

By 1943 an estimated 50,000 women were serving alongside the Home Guard, and the government, now keen to keep Home Guard numbers up – to provide anti-aircraft crews and bomb disposal teams, and shoulder a significant portion of the Home Defence burden – agreed to the formation of a women's auxiliary. An 'urgent memorandum' from the War Office, dated 15 April 1943, set out the terms under which women could be employed 'to assist the Home Guard':[8]

1. Since the foundation of the Home Guard valuable assistance of a non-combatant character has been rendered unofficially by women.
    It has been decided to place this assistance on an official footing …

2. Duties.

(a) The employment of women will be restricted to non-combatant duties, and no duties will be undertaken by them which necessitate training in weapons. Training of women in weapons by the Home Guard is, as hitherto, forbidden.

(b) The principle duties on which they may be employed are:

(i)   Clerical and telephonist
(ii) Cooking and service of food
(iii) Driving motor vehicles

It is clear from contemporary documents that women auxiliaries were highly valued. The Salisbury Home Guard Intelligence Section, for example, depended on 'Mrs Gould, [and] Misses Townsend, Warhirst, Simmonds, Bond and Ferret', four of whom were still serving when the unit stood-down (Stroud, 1944, p. 3). The total establishment of the Intelligence Section at stand-down was two officers, seven other ranks – and four ladies. But, in the final analysis, even the politically 'modern' Home Guard had a highly traditional understanding of a woman's role.

For the modern student of the Home Guard, the female 'Auxiliary' creates a confusing clash of terminology with Home Guard stay-behind 'Auxiliary Units' – although this was not an issue at the time, as the Auxiliary Units were formed and operated in secret. In 1957, Peter Fleming – a founding member – revealed the existence of wartime stay-behind parties in *Invasion 1940* (Fleming, 1957, p. 270). In May 1968, David Lampe published *The Last Ditch*, which had the advantage of interviews with many of the key participants, if lacking the official documents revealed by research in the 1990s. In 1974 the *Sunday Telegraph* magazine added a feature article on the Auxiliary Units accompanying 'The Defence of Britain' series by Correlli Barnett.[9] The enduring fascination of special operations forces ensured that, by the end of the 1990s, the Auxiliary Units threatened to eclipse the main body of the Home Guard entirely. Even in 1974, the terms 'Home Guard' and 'Special Forces' represented opposite ends of the military spectrum, making it difficult to accept the Auxiliary Units as Home Guard formations. To appreciate that the Auxiliary Units *were* a component of the Home Guard is to appreciate the special strengths of the Home Guard, particularly in rural areas, in terms of fieldcraft, skill-at-arms and local knowledge.

Countryman Fred Archer recalled of his local LDVs:

Colonel Somerton chose his men like a dealer choosing horses. Smart young tractor drivers who spent their winter evenings in the woods, shooting the hordes of pigeons which came to roost after packing their crops … were his marksmen. These, with the ex-servicemen who had worked their small-holding between the wars, made up a company of good shots, some crack shots, potential snipers on our hill. (Archer, 1975, p. 68)

That the authorities viewed the Auxiliary Units as genuinely Home Guard is apparent from contemporary correspondence.[10] On 8 August 1940, Duncan Sandys described the mission of the Auxiliary Units in a letter to the Prime Minister:

HOME GUARD – AUXILIARY UNITS

1. I think you may care to know of the progress which is being made in the organisation of the Auxiliary Units of the Home Guard.

Object

2. These Auxiliary Units are being formed with two objects:

   (a) They are intended to provide, within the framework of the Home Guard organisation, small bodies of men especially selected and trained, whose role it will be to act offensively on the flanks and in the rear of enemy troops who may obtain a foothold in this country. Their action will particularly be directed against tanks and lorries in laager, ammunition dumps, small enemy posts and stragglers. Their activities will also include sniping.

   (b The other function of the Auxiliary Units is to provide a system of intelligence, whereby the regular forces in the field can be kept informed of what is happening behind enemy lines.[11]

No military commander would miss the opportunity to place 'humint' (human intelligence) assets behind enemy lines, but the offensive action aspect of the

Auxiliary Units' role is controversial – Sandy's list of 'offensive actions' appears tailor-made to goad the German military to take punitive measures. One could speculate that the existence of Auxiliary Units was as much political – intended to ensure that there could be no 'model occupation' – as to achieve militarily significant results.

A consequence of arming large numbers of civilian volunteers was that incidents occurred involving the discharge, negligent or otherwise, of firearms. Much has been made of this,[12] if only because, in Norman Longmate's words: 'the policy of shooting first and asking questions afterwards … was to earn for the LDV a unique position as the only army in history to have killed more of its own countrymen than its enemies' (Longmate, 1974, p. 40). Longmate's assertion regarding the LDV's 'unique position' is open to discussion, but his is a serious charge – that the LDV was more of a hazard than a help – and needs to be examined in context. Unthinkingly adopting British musketry practice with an American M1917 bolt-action rifle could have dire consequences. The M1917 lacked the magazine cut-off of the British SMLE, and some negligent discharges resulted from veterans closing the bolt and squeezing the trigger to ease the mainspring, forgetting that in the absence of a cut-off, they had just chambered a live round. Some British weapons, notably the Sten machine carbine and the ST Grenade ('Sticky Bomb'), were inherently dangerous designs and accidents were bound to occur through carelessness or complacency.

One thousand, two hundred and six Home Guards died while on duty, and, never having engaged the enemy in ground combat, statistics are not on the organisation's side.[13] Professor MacKenzie quotes an 'on-duty death rate' of 0.7 per thousand for the Home Guard, against 0.05 per thousand 'among regular troops', suggesting that a mixture of old age and lack of military competence made the Home Guard more subject to fatalities while on duty (MacKenzie, 1996, p. 124). It should be remembered, however, that the vast majority of the Home Guard were in a 'teeth arm', tasked as infantrymen, and later, gunners and bomb disposal, and their role frequently required that they be out and about during air raids. Furthermore, such statistics from the Second World War are skewed by the administrative 'tail' supporting the regular forces, as John Ellis (1990, p. 156) explains: 'In the British, American and most Commonwealth armies as many as two-thirds of the troops were involved in activities behind the front line, working in the numerous roles necessary to a mechanised army in the field.' In order to compare percentages of combat casualties to the First World War, Ellis (1990, p.

159) states that 'they must be multiplied *at least* threefold'. Logically, something similar should apply when comparing casualty statistics with the Home Guard.

Apart from accidents, there were instances when the LDV/Home Guard opened fire deliberately, occasionally at parachutists, but on several occasions when manning roadblocks. A rash of incidents occurred during June 1940, at the height of the invasion scare, and when the status of the LDV was unclear both to its members and the wider public, as one ex-LDV explained: 'we were still short of arms and uniforms. There was a certain amount of moral backing in stopping cars at night when properly armed and in uniform, but it was not so easy in a mixture of khaki and plain clothes' (Cambs. and Isle of Ely TA Assoc., 1944, p. 79). A member of the Isle of Ely Home Guard battalion recorded the period when road blocks were the LDV's chief activity:

> Invasion preparations on the other side of the Channel increased the tension. Alert periods became frequent. Road block sentries had to inspect identity cards of all passing through after dusk; lorries had to be stopped and examined to see if they were being used for conveying hostile troops or fifth columnists. About once a week some car with a particular number had to be stopped and held. If it did not stop it was to be fired upon. The general public were not too helpful and could not understand the need for these measures. Considerable trouble was experienced with junior officers of the Field Army who were most indignant at being stopped and asked to prove their identity. One motor cyclist tried to rush the sentries on the south of Wisbech. He was brought down by the first shot which struck him immediately in front of his rear mudguard. (Cambs. and Ely TA Assoc., 1944, pp. 78–9)

The foregoing, which was written in 1943, makes it quite clear that the tendency to 'shoot first and ask questions later' reflected policy, rather than – as it is often portrayed – trigger-happiness on the part of the LDV. We have already seen that shooting parachutists was featured as an LDV responsibility in the first (albeit unofficial) LDV manual. Action on roadblocks is a more difficult case, if only because the LDV was almost entirely devoid of formal administration – indeed it prided itself on a 'no bumph' culture – which has left little in the way of documentary evidence. The Cambridgeshire and Isle of Ely Home Guard history is useful in this respect, being assembled in 1943 (it was published in January 1944), when the Home Guard was at its apogee, the 'Second Front' had not yet opened, and May and June 1940 were still fresh memories:

There was a hectic background which must in many ways have resembled that at the time of the Spanish Armada or the threatened invasions of the eighteenth century. All the main points were there; the inadequate force at sea, neglected and cut to the bone; the minute and ill-found army; the suspicion of widespread treason; the wonderful volunteer spirit of the countryside. 'No bumph' was the promise from above, and bitterly have officers of the H.G. regretted ever since that it was ever given, or being given, not adhered to. Operational orders were simple. 'If anything happens, start shooting.' (Cambs. and Isle of Ely TA Assoc., 1944, p. 51)

Throughout the war strenuous efforts were made to inculcate in the British a 'watchfulness' that was close to paranoia. Apart from Fougasse's cartoons, which showed Hitler or Göring listening-in on every conversation, there were such efforts as the 1942 film *Went the Day Well?*, in which the population of sleepy 'Bramley End' overlook a series of clues and allow the village to fall into the clutches of a party of ruthless German commandos.[14] Loosely based on a short story by Graham Greene, *The Lieutenant Died Last*, which was published in the American publication *Collier's* magazine in June 1940, the film uses little of Greene's original material, and his hero, a poacher called Bill Purves, is reduced to a minor role.[15] The film does though bear a striking resemblance to some aspects of *The Defence of Bloodford Village*, discussed in the previous chapter. It too starts in an imaginary future, when the German invasion has been defeated 'and old Hitler got what was coming to him'. Although Bramley End's own Home Guard section is ambushed before they can play any part in saving the village, there is no suggestion of bumbling incompetence that we might today associate with the Home Guard. They are, rather, too trusting and gentle – 'failings' exhibited by all the villagers. For example, the disguised German commander is greatly helped in putting the village into a state of defence against counter-attack by having the Home Guard's own very competent defensive scheme explained to him by the Home Guard section NCO, as (in shades of Bloodford) they examine the terrain from a vantage point beneath the abandoned windmill on Windmill Hill.

The look of the village, including the windmill, is extraordinarily close to the description of the mythical Bloodford, and once again, the action takes place, not around some vital factory, airfield or military facility, but in a dream of rural England. The production location, Turville, Buckinghamshire, is, quite literally, the quintessential English country village, having subsequently provided the external location for *Goodnight Mister Tom*, *The Vicar of Dibley*, *Little Britain*, *Midsomer*

Murders and many more. The windmill, Cobstone Windmill, was Professor Potts' residence and workshop in *Chitty Chitty Bang Bang* and later bought and restored by Hayley Mills. In Greene's original conception, however, the invaded village has the much more prosaic name of 'Potter', and is rooted in a far more convincing 1940s British landscape. There is also some logic to the arrival of the enemy there, in this case, paratroopers:

> You would hardly expect to find Potter the scene of the first invasion of England since French troops landed near Fishguard in the Napoleonic War. It is one of those tiny isolated villages you still find dumped down in deserted corners of what we call in England Metroland – the district where commuters live in tidy villas within easy distances of the railway, on the edge of scrubby commons full of clay pits and gorse and rather withered trees. Walk for three miles in any direction from Potter and you will find cement sidewalks, nurses pushing prams, the evening paper boy, but Potter itself lies off the map – the motoring map, that is to say …
>
> That was the odd scene of the 'Invasion', though if you examined Potter carefully you may conclude it was not an accident that parachutists landed there. Potter itself could be isolated by a few snips of a wire cutter, and from that little hidden spot in Metroland half a dozen men acting quickly could do an astonishing amount of damage – a mile and a half across unfrequented common and you had the main line to Scotland and the northern coast, and one supposes that the German air chiefs had planned for such attempts which our air defences foiled. Their psychological effect might have been incalculable: they would have destroyed any sense of security Englishmen still feel …
> (Greene, 1999, pp. 46–7)

BFI Screenonline says of *Went the Day Well?*

> Turville in Oxfordshire stands in for Bramley End, the sort of village invariably described as 'sleepy'. True to form, the villagers take some time to wake up to the presence of the enemy among them. But when they are roused, they respond with determination, resourcefulness and, when necessary, a surprising ruthlessness.
>
> The film is almost cruel in the way it repeatedly frustrates its audience's hopes. After the Germans' merciless extermination of the village's small platoon of home guards, the villagers make a number of attempts to summon help …

Most extraordinary is a scene in which the postmistress (Muriel George) throws pepper in the eyes of her unwelcome lodger, then finishes him off with an axe. Shortly after, when her telephone call for help is ignored by a gossiping switchboard operator, she meets her own end, on the blade of a bayonet.[16]

Eventually a wounded small boy (further echoes of *Bloodford*) – an evacuee and poacher Bill Purvis' sidekick – gets through to the local Home Guard platoon commander, the baker in the next village, who contacts district command. The army, with Home Guard attached, retake the village and relieve the besieged villagers defending the manor house – itself an echo of the 1909 anti-German melodrama *An Englishman's Home*.

No Home Guard emerging into the sunlight after a matinee performance of *Went the Day Well?* could have the slightest doubt that 'shooting first and asking questions afterwards' was not only permissible, it was his duty. If he still harboured any doubts, *The Home Guard Training Manual* would soon allay them:

The following are the official instructions for sentries on roads:

(a) When active operations are not in progress. As reliance cannot be placed on the voice to stop motorists, the following procedure should be adopted by troops or Home Guards. By day the sentry should use ordinary police signals. By night the sentry should stop motor traffic by waving a red lamp. In either case there should be another man twenty yards behind the sentry stopping, who is ready to fire if the car refuses to halt. (Langdon-Davies, 1942b, p. 84)

Were that not enough, Hugh Slater's *Home Guard for Victory!* was reassuring on the legal consequences of a fatal shooting:

A member of the Home Guard can be charged in the civil courts for any illegal act that he may commit, but if it may reasonably be supposed that he was acting in good faith under orders he will probably not be so charged. For example, if a sentry is ordered to shoot any person ignoring the challenge, he may not be charged, even if there is a fatal result. (Slater, 1941, p. 82)

Under the circumstances, and in the context of the times, we should be cautious about characterising the LDV/Home Guard as trigger-happy.

In *The Home Guard Training Manual*, Major John Langdon-Davies explained why British civilians taking up arms against an invader were required to join the Home Guard:

> ... the laws of war, which must be obeyed by every British subject, whether or not they are obeyed by the Nazis, do not permit of civilians offering armed resistance, unless they are organised in a regular corps and wear a recognizable uniform.
>
> That is why people, who would otherwise be civilians, have to join the Home Guard and receive uniform, in order to conform to the rules of war and at the same time offer the necessary resistance to the invader. (Langdon-Davies, 1942b, p. 14)

The LDV/Home Guard was established as an officially sanctioned armed civilian association – in the belief that this would maintain a moral ascendancy – although, as we have already seen in the previous chapter, there was very little likelihood that such a device would grant any protection from reprisal or summary execution by German paratroops. The importance attached to the LDV/Home Guard must be judged by the willingness of the British government to arm huge numbers of civilians, despite widespread (and widely voiced) disenchantment with the Establishment. These legal and political issues aside, the authorities were then confronted with the challenge of making good Mr Eden's promise in his call for volunteers of 14 May 1940: 'You will not be paid, but you will receive uniform and will be armed'[17] – which was interpreted by the volunteers as a commitment to arm every member of a force that had, at a stroke, almost doubled the size of the mobilised British Army. As we shall see in the next chapter, that was very much easier said than done.

3

THE RIFLE CRISIS

On 7 October 1939, Winston Churchill, then First Lord of the Admiralty, drafted a memorandum to the Home Secretary:

> Why do we not form a Home Guard of half a million men over forty (if they like to volunteer), and put our elderly stars at the head and in the structure of these new formations? Let these five hundred thousand men come along and push the young and active out of all the home billets. If uniforms are lacking a brassard would suffice, and I am assured there are plenty of rifles at any rate. (Churchill, 1954, p. 393)

Churchill's memo anticipated the raising of the Local Defence Volunteers by seven months, and serves to illustrate the imagined prerequisites of such a force: brassards (arm bands) and rifles. We will avoid the thorny issue of Home Guard uniform, but rifles are central to this study. Modern authors have struggled to discuss the subject of the Home Guard's small arms without some significant inaccuracy. This is unfortunate, as the rifle saga is central to the story of the Home Guard, to the organisation's self-perception, and the way we perceive it today.

When, in May 1940, mainland Britain was threatened with invasion, the response from the general public was to demand that a *rifle* be made available for every male of military age. Artillery, the machine gun and chemical weapons had dominated the First World War battlefields, aerial bombardment had emerged as a viable weapon; yet the bolt-action military rifle continued to enjoy a status that is difficult for those of a post-Second World War generation to fully comprehend. The rifle was, as shooting pundit Lieutenant A.G. Banks exclaimed in his 1940 shooting manual *'A.G.'s' Book of the Rifle*: 'the cleanest and noblest of all weapons'

(Banks, 1950, p. 10). The failure of the government to provide .303in-calibre Short Magazine Lee-Enfield service rifles to all the volunteers of the LDV resulted in a legacy of resentment that obscures, and continues to obscure, the detail that weapons that did reach the LDV/Home Guard were in some respects better than those in service with the British Army. The notion that the Home Guard was ill-served lingers on, and in order to unpick reality from perception we must first establish the historical background.

In Britain, pre-eminence of the military rifle occupies a period commencing with the formation of the Rifle Volunteer Movement in 1859 and ending with the issue of the Sten machine carbine to the Home Guard in 1943. The spring of 1859 saw the 'Long Acre Indignation Meeting' and the re-establishment of the volunteer movement in response to an imagined threat of invasion from France (Cole and Fulton, 1990, p. 1). The British military rifle had ceased to be the prerequisite of the specialist sharpshooter (known as Riflemen) with the adoption of the 'Minié Rifle' in 1851, and, subsequently, the Pattern 1853 Enfield Rifle. There now existed the possibility of placing the defence of the United Kingdom in the hands of a 'nation of riflemen'. The traditional smoothbore musket was inaccurate and best used when fired *en masse* in disciplined volleys. The platoon and company drill required to do this took time and practice to master. Conversely, a rifle was accurate even in the hands of someone with the minimum of training, someone who could pick off invading enemy soldiers, as the sharpshooting American colonists had the British Redcoats in the War of Independence.

In December 1859, a National Rifle Association was established from the ranks of the Volunteer movement. When, in 1890, the NRA headquarters and ranges moved from Wimbledon to Bisley, the *Illustrated London News* explained the role of the association:

> The National Rifle Association, which is so important as an Auxiliary to the Volunteer Service, in promoting skill in the use of the Infantry weapon, holds its Annual Meeting, this year, on the newly acquired camping ground, with the ranges and offices there provided, on Bisley Common ... (Cited in Cole and Fulton, 1990, p. 16)

In the event, Britain never did achieve a nation of 'minutemen' along American or Swiss lines, but target shooting with the service rifle remained a highly respectable, if essentially middle-class, activity (Cole and Fulton, 1990, *passim*). As the British service rifle evolved, each new rifle or type of ammunition was adopted in parallel by the NRA.[1] In 1888, the .303in Lee-Metford bolt-action repeating rifle was introduced and, following the introduction of smokeless propellant, the 'Rifle Magazine Lee-Enfield Mk I', in 1895, establishing a small arms dynasty that would remain in front-line service with the British Army until 1992.[2]

The Rifle, Magazine, Lee-Enfield (MLE) had design characteristics which limited the accuracy it could achieve, even under ideal conditions.[3] After a poor showing in the Boer War, the long rifles of the infantry and the short carbines of the cavalry, artillery and engineers, were replaced by a new universal 'Short Rifle'. For many small arms aficionados this compromise concept was the last straw; as Hogg and Weeks put it:

> Universally execrated by every self-styled expert in the Western world when it was introduced, the rifle was held to be too short to be a target shooter's arm and too long to be a cavalryman's companion – and that, in fact, it was an abortionate device developed by unscrupulous government technicians by robbing wherever possible every good feature from other rifles then ruining them. (Hogg and Weeks, 1973, p. 3.17)

Nonetheless, the Rifle, Short, Magazine, Lee-Enfield or 'SMLE' entered service in 1903, reaching its definitive Mk III version in 1907. Despite inauspicious beginnings it generated a loyalty among its users which bordered on idolatry:

> The short Enfield is handy, reasonably light, reasonably accurate, foolproof, and above all, utterly reliable. You can (if you are fool enough) throw it over a wall without damaging the sights. You can rapid-fire it for scores of rounds on end until it is nearly red-hot, and it will never jam or misfire. You can drop it in sand and half fill the action with grit, or mud, but it will continue to work cheerfully. These things happen in war. (Banks, 1950, p. 177)

However, the War Office, stung by the criticism levelled at the SMLE, had commenced work at the Royal Small Arms Factory (RSAF) Enfield on a completely new rifle, designed around a powerful .276in (7mm) rimless cartridge and a Mauser action (Skennerton, 1993, p. 140). The weapon was issued for troop trials as the Pattern 1913 or 'P13', but development was halted as the First World War approached – it would have been a poor time to introduce a new calibre of ammunition, even if the .276 round had been sufficiently developed for service use, which it was not. During 1914, there was concern that production of the

"AM I AN ISLAND?"
Punch, 22 May 1940

May 1940, confronted by the German airborne threat, John Bull reaches for his SMLE. (*Punch* cartoon by Bernard Partridge)

SMLE might not meet demand, and orders for service rifles were placed with American manufacturers Winchester, Remington and Eddystone (a subsidiary of Remington) (Canfield, 1991, p. 59). Rather than tool up for the elderly SMLE, a .303in calibre version of the new P13 rifle was placed in production as the Pattern 1914 or P14. The P14 rifle was accepted into service in June 1916 (Canfield, 1991, p. 59), but substantial quantities were not available until 1917, in which year production ended (Skennerton, 1984, p. 72). Compared with the SMLE, the P14 was a rather clumsy-looking weapon, particularly with a sword bayonet fitted. At 46.25in it was 2.25in longer than the SMLE, and rather heavier, 9lb 10oz against 8lb 3oz. Unlike the SMLE, which had open sights, the P14 had aperture sights, a Mauser action, and integral five-round magazine.

Introduction of the P14 rifle was marred by problems with interchangeability of parts. In effect, each of the three American companies had been required to reverse-engineer P14s from prototypes built in the UK. The result was, that whilst each produced well-made, accurate rifles, perfectly capable of 'killing Germans' (as one of the British inspectors commented), they differed subtly in their tolerances, and, as a result, each manufacturer's weapon had to be treated as a separate sub-species: P14 W (Winchester), P14 R (Remington) and P14 E (Eddystone).[4] In the event, SMLE production was sufficient to meet the demands of front-line units, and most of the production run of P14 rifles remained in the UK for training and Home Defence, or went straight into reserve (Canfield, 1991, p. 59).[5] The only P14 rifles to reach the Western Front did so because the SMLE had failed in the technically demanding role of sniper's rifle. Winchester-made P14 rifles (held to be of superior quality and performance) were fitted with fine-adjusting aperture sights to become the Pattern 14 Winchester (Fine Adjusting), or 'P14 W (F)' sniping rifle. Ian Skennerton notes: 'In nearly all instances, the sniping schools preferred the aperture sighted Pattern 1914 W (F) to the telescope fitted S.M.L.E. rifles, and towards the end of the war it was issued in the line on a scale of 3 per battalion' (Skennerton, 1984, p. 73). The P14 (W) was also fitted with telescopic sights, and it remained the standard British sniping rifle until February 1942 (Skennerton, 1984, p. 105).

While the robust and handy SMLE was popular with the soldiery, the more modern P14 was easier to mass-produce and, as befitted its target-shooting ancestry, a deadly accurate weapon.[6] Loyalty for the SMLE notwithstanding, neither rifle had proved entirely successful during the First World War so, after the war, work commenced on a replacement. Service nomenclature changed on 31 May 1926, the SMLE became the 'Rifle No. 1', and the P14 the 'Rifle No. 3' (the 'Rifle No. 2' was a .22in calibre training rifle). To avoid confusion, in this study we will refer to the No. 1 as the SMLE and the No. 3 as the P14 throughout, as that was how the Home Guard referred to them. The new service rifle in development was initially termed the 'No. 1 Mk VI', but later evolved into a new weapon, the 'Rifle No. 4 Mk 1'. It commenced troop trials in 1931 and featured a strengthened Lee action and ten-round box magazine, whilst the aperture sights, heavy 'target' barrel and fore-end design, as well as the use of screws and fixings that were standard sizes, rather than 'gunmakers' specials' showed the influence of the P14. In total, about 3,500 No. 4 rifles were manufactured prior to the Second World War (Skennerton, 1993, p. 175). The design was considered successful, but shelved due to financial stringency. Thus, in the spring of 1940, the situation as regards British service rifles stood as follows: the Rifle No. 1 (SMLE) remained the service rifle, with substantial quantities of the Rifle No. 3 (P14) in reserve, and small numbers of the Rifle No. 4 in store, with an intention to produce more. There was, in addition, a residue of 'long' Lee-Enfields of various types, particularly the modernised Charger Loading Lee-Enfield (CLLE), which had soldiered on through the First World War.[7]

In May 1940 it was assumed that to place the nation in arms the government would simply issue a *rifle*, i.e. an SMLE, or at worst a P14, to every volunteer; as Churchill reassuringly put it, in the quote at the opening of this chapter: 'I am assured that there are plenty of rifles at any rate.' This assumption was reflected in the initial wave of publications targeted at Local Defence Volunteers; thus we have, in June 1940, the reissue of *The Elements of Rifle Shooting* by Bisley service rifle champion, Lieutenant Colonel J.A. Barlow. This was followed in July by Bisley King's Prize winner Captain E.H. Robinson's *Rifle Training for War: A Textbook for Local Defence Volunteers*. This, as we have already noted, was an update of the First World War VTC training manual. It was 'revised and brought up to date' by Gordon R. King 'Late arm.-Quartermaster-Sergeant, Royal Marine Artillery, Winner of Grand Aggregate, Bisley, 1926'. October 1940 saw Lieutenant A.G. Banks' '*A. G.'s' Book of the Rifle*, which, like Colonel Barlow's book, concentrated on the technical aspects of marksmanship, and in the same month *The Home Guard Manual*, by RSM A. Southworth, formerly Warrant Officer Instructor at the Small Arms School, Hythe.[8] In this first rush of enthusiasm we recognise the *cri de cœur* of the Rifle Volunteers, in A.G. Banks' words:

Some peoples are wiser than we. I am told, by a friend who has spent much time in Finland, that every householder there has a Service rifle, as much as a matter of course as we have an umbrella or a set of golf clubs. The Government provides the rifles. And at the week-ends the whole family sallies forth to the ranges to compete in matches. That may not be strictly true. But it is true that in February 1940 Finnish soldiers routed an enemy which outnumbered them by fifty to one. (1950, p. 20)

When updating the VTC manual, Gordon King added some information concerning the P14 rifle. He was determined to instil confidence:

You are probably armed with the 'Pattern '14' rifle. This is a better weapon than the S.M.L.E. (our present service rifle) from the point of view of marksmanship but it is not so handy in the field. It is the official 'Sniper's Rifle' and when fitted with a telescopic sight is almost ideal for this work. (Robinson, 1940, pp. 25–6)

King went on to give a brief history of the development of the P13–P14 series concluding: 'The result is the P14 and a remarkably good rifle it is.' In a memorandum dated 29 June 1940, War Office department TA2, responsible for administering the LDV, confirmed that King had been correct in his assumption that many of the LDV would be armed with the P14, stating that, 'A considerable number of 1914 pattern rifles have been issued. Ross rifles [discussed below] are now arriving up to a total of 75,000.'[9] A month later, LDV fortnightly returns showed that there were 495,294 .303 service rifles in the hands of 1,456,127 volunteers.[10]

The obvious shortfall notwithstanding, The LDVs were extremely fortunate, because, despite the assurances given to Churchill in 1939, there were *not* 'plenty of rifles'. Ian Skennerton records (1993, p. 286): 'By the end of 1940, all the 1.5 million rifles in Britain were in use and 190,000 reservists were without arms at all.' This unforeseen rifle shortage was the result of several factors. Firstly, there was the need to replace the rifles lost or abandoned on mainland Europe. Churchill (1955, p. 126) gives a figure of 90,000 rifles 'left behind at Dunkirk', but Skennerton (1993, p. 286), looking at all the campaigns up to the end of 1940, puts the loss at over 300,000. Secondly, the policy of limiting Regular Army recruitment to 60,000 men per month was abandoned by Churchill in June 1940. Between June and August 1940, 324,000 men were enlisted. As David French explains (2000, p. 185): 'they were organised into 122 new infantry battalions, not because the army needed such a large increase in its infantry, but because the only weapons it had in stock were 300,000 First World War pattern rifles.'

The reference is clearly to Pattern 1914 (P14) rifles, but, as we have seen, with the exception of 3,500 No. 4 Rifles, *any* rifles available to the British Army were 'First World War pattern'.

By August 1940, Eden's broadcast of 14 May had generated over 1.6 million Local Defence Volunteers, rather than the 500,000 anticipated, and all of these men expected to be armed.[11] Furthermore, in many districts, the LDV constituted the first line of defence against invasion or subversion and *needed* to be armed. It is quite apparent that no serious thought had been given to the possible size of the LDV, beyond an assumption that 500,000 was a reasonable figure. As a War Office report dated July 1949 laconically commented: 'in the light of experience it is at least worthy of consideration as to whether it would not have been better policy to have restricted the number of volunteers to a figure more closely approximating to the amount of equipment actually available at the time, and to have opened a waiting list for men who could not be accepted at once.'[12] That was, however, to be wise after the event, and the public relations consequences of disappointing two-thirds of the volunteers, who found themselves without rifles, were to dog the Home Guard throughout the organisation's existence.

There was another, crucial, element in the 'Rifle Crisis': although Britain had been at war with Germany since September 1939, there was almost no production of service rifles in the UK. This last circumstance was one that the government was unlikely to publicise, for excellent reasons, domestic and international, and it has failed to attract the attention of historians. The situation had arisen because production of SMLE rifles was terminated after the First World War, with the exception of commercial manufacture, for the gun trade and export, at the BSA factory at Small Heath, near Birmingham. Production at the Royal Small Arms Factory was limited to barrels and receivers, to enable old rifles to be reconditioned (Skennerton, 1993, p. 177). In 1939, in anticipation of war, sites were purchased for factories to build No. 4 rifles – Royal Ordnance factories at Fazakerley (Liverpool), Maltby (near Sheffield), and a BSA plant at Shirley (Birmingham) (Skennerton, 1993, pp. 194–5) – and contracts for No. 4 rifles were placed with Stevens-Savage in the USA and Long Branch Arsenal in Canada (Skennerton, 1993, pp. 194–5). But, as with the P14 in the previous war, it would take at least two years for the new factories to reach volume production.

Thus from September 1939 until late 1941 (or later still, as it turned out), the provision of British service rifles depended on new production at one privately owned factory, and the cannibalisation of old weapons by the Royal Small Arms Factory and the gun trade. In August 1940, an air raid destroyed the barrel mill and associated workshops at Small Heath, halting production, and further raids in November caused the machinery to be dispersed – the factory finally ceased production in late 1943. The depth of the 'rifle crisis' is illustrated by the fact that just 59,071 SMLEs were manufactured in 1940, and no No. 4 rifles at all – against 613,461 SMLEs in the second year of the First World War. In 1941 42,043 SMLEs and 33,914 No. 4s were produced – compared to 852,9826 SMLEs in 1916. Full No. 1 (SMLE) rifle figures for 1939–45 cannot easily be given, because of the methods employed to remanufacture and repair as many rifles as possible (Skennerton, 1988, p. 5), but these figures serve to illustrate the inadequacy of production. Once volume production of the No. 4 rifle in the UK, USA and Canada was under way, the crisis receded, but as Skennerton notes: 'The No. 4 does not appear in photographs with the forces until the latter part of 1942, and then this was generally with specialist units, such as the Airborne Division' (Skennerton, 1993, p. 198).

There is another .303in-calibre rifle that is relevant to this study, the Canadian Ross, which, as we have seen in the memorandum of June 1940, quoted above, was being issued to the LDV at that date. Supposedly the 'perfected' version of Sir Charles Ross' design of 1896, the Ross service rifle was a full 50.56in long and weighed 9lb 14oz. Although adopted by the Canadian Army, it was never a popular nor successful service rifle due to the tendency of its 'straight pull' bolt to jam in muddy conditions. It is worth pointing out that, whilst the Ross was unpopular with the rank-and-file, it was, like the P14, favoured by snipers, who benefited from its 30.53in barrel and straight pull action (Hogg and Weeks, 1973, p. 3.38). Ian Skennerton's study of Second World War British small arms contracts reveals an undated order for 75,000 Ross rifles from Canada, which, on the evidence of the weekly returns quoted above, we can place in, or before, June 1940 (Skennerton, 1988, p. 18).[13] The Ross rifle's inability to cope with the mud of trench warfare was unlikely to prove a serious embarrassment to the LDV/Home Guard, even in combat, but the weapon did have another undesirable feature, in that its bolt, if disassembled and then incorrectly reassembled, failed to lock in the forward position, whilst still being able to fire a round. For the firer, the consequences of such a situation were particularly unpleasant. That this was occurring (and that Ross rifles were in the hands of the Home Guard) is confirmed by an exasperated memorandum from TA2, dated 2 November 1940:[14]

Dismantling of Ross bolts

This subject is fully dealt with in the pamphlet on the Ross Rifle. Issued in July, 1940, so that there would appear to be no reason for cases of mal-assembly.

I am to add that normally there should be no necessity for dismantling the bolts of these rifles.

The plain truth about the unwieldy, but accurate, Ross rifle was that the rifle was not 'soldier proof'. Nevertheless, by early 1941 there were over 79,000 Ross rifles in use with the Home Guard. In May and June 1941, .303-calibre SMLE, P14 and Ross rifles started to be withdrawn from the Home Guard and handed over to the army.[15] By April 1942, the SMLE and P14 were almost extinct in Home Guard service, with 4,233 of the former and 2,410 of the latter in the returns (from a high of 26,249 of the two types of rifle in February 1941). The number of Ross rifles had fallen by 60,000, to around 19,500.[16] This transfer of around 80,000 .303-calibre rifles from the Home Guard to the army was achieved because very large amounts of American .300in-calibre small arms had arrived, and were being issued almost exclusively to the Home Guard.

Purchasing military equipment in America effectively bankrupted the British economy, costing the country its economic and political freedom (*vide* Ponting, 1990, pp. 196–215), and reaction to the arrival of these dearly bought weapons is crucial to the thrust of this study. To fully appreciate the issue, we must take another historical detour. As we have already established, the production of the First World War British P14 service rifle had been handled by three American factories. Entering the First World War in 1917, the Americans were themselves faced with a possible shortfall of their own service rifle – the United States Rifle, calibre .30, Model 1903, widely known as the ''03 Springfield'.[17] After considering various options, the P14 was adapted to chamber American .30-06 ammunition, and production resumed at Winchester, Remington and Eddystone. Thus the final derivative of the experimental British Pattern 1913 rifle was the US Rifle, calibre .30, Model 1917, popularly known as the 'Enfield'.

The M1917 represented a further design evolution of the original P13 concept. With lessons learned from production of the P14, the cost of a US Army M1917 was $26, compared to $42 for the original P14 design, and streamlining manufacture enabled the rifle to be produced far more quickly (Canfield, 1991, p. 63). Improvements included the deletion of unnecessary and obsolete long-range volley sights, and their attendant machining and fitting, and other minor machining processes. It should not be imagined that this streamlining of manufacture resulted in a lowering of quality; in many respects the rifle was superior to the '03 Springfield, just as the P14 was to the SMLE. The US .30-06 round is ballistically superior to the British .303 Mk.VII (having a flatter trajectory), and this further enhanced the combat performance of the 'American Enfield'. As an additional bonus, the Americans discovered that six rimless US rounds would fit into the magazine designed for five rimmed British rounds. As soon as M1917 production for the US government commenced, the problem with standardisation re-emerged, and a preliminary batch of rifles, rushed to the front line – with the best of intentions – by Winchester caused more harm to the rifle's reputation than good (Canfield, 1991, p. 62). Eventually, however, the standardised M1917 proved to be a robust and accurate military rifle.

Like the P14 in the UK, the bulk of the M1917 rifles manufactured between 1917 and 1919 were placed in reserve after the First World War (Canfield, 1991, p. 63). The M1917 was never especially popular with American troops. Partly this was due to the fact that it was a foreign design, and partly due to the same lack of 'handiness' that British P14 users complained of, when compared to the M1903 'Springfield'. Also, great emphasis was placed on technical marksmanship in US military circles, and the M1917 had a rear sight that was only adjustable for elevation, and the foresight block was punched to fix the foresight blade in place, making lateral adjustment by the firer difficult. This was because the rifles were zeroed at the factory, and each one was entirely capable of hitting a man-sized target at battle ranges, if pointed with a reasonable degree of accuracy. This is entirely different, however, to target shooting on the range, and the lack of fine adjustment was another factor that militated against the design. These are, of course, 'niggles', and are a better indicator of the loyalty engendered by the '03 Springfield, than real shortcomings of the M1917 as a battle rifle, but the M1917 was, nonetheless, reduced to war reserve status following the First World War.

US infantry adopted the M1 'Garand' self-loading rifle in 1936, thus by 1940 the US military was equipped with the M1 and the M1903 'Springfield', with further M1903 rifles and most of the production of M1917 in reserve (Canfield, 1991, p. 125). Churchill described the transfer of materiel from the US reserve stockpile:

As early as June 1 the President sent out orders to the War and Navy Departments to report what weapons they could spare for Britain and France

... In forty-eight hours the answers were given, and on June 3 [General] Marshall approved the lists. The first list comprised half a million .30 calibre rifles manufactured in 1917 and 1918 and stored in grease for more than twenty years. For these there were about 250 cartridges apiece. There were 900 '*soixante-quinze*' field guns, with a million rounds, 80,000 machine-guns, and various other items ... Since every hour counted, it was decided that the Army should sell (for thirty-seven million dollars) everything on the list to one concern, which could in turn resell immediately to the British and French.

By these extraordinary measures the United States left themselves with the equipment for only 1,800,000 men, the minimum figure stipulated by the American Army's mobilisation plan. (Churchill, 1955, p. 127)

To avoid the logistic nightmare of two calibres of service ammunition, and because supplies of .30-06 were short, every round having to be imported, the use of '.300' calibre weapons (as the British termed them) was restricted, from the outset, to 'the Home Guard or fixed defensive points'.[18]

The purchase of 500,000 American rifles represented commitment and sacrifice on both sides of the Atlantic. So how did the Home Guard react to these weapons? For the student of the Home Guard, dependent on historians, this can be a confusing matter. Longmate tells us:

The first real weapons to reach the LDV in any quantity were half a million ancient rifles, sent by the United States during June and July in response to an appeal from Winston Churchill. Their vintage was betrayed by their popular name 'Springfield 1917', or '17' for short, and they arrived caked in heavy grease, like congealed Vaseline, which had protected them during their long years of disuse. Removing the grease proved to be a dirty and wearisome job. Opinions about the Springfields varied. One experienced ex-officer considered, 'we might have been much worse served', though the weapon was 'rather cumbersome' with 'a difficult bolt action for rapid fire'. But the rifle's real disadvantage was that it fired .300 ammunition instead of .303, and to prevent the wrong calibre being used a red band was painted round the barrel. Another foreign rifle distributed at this time, the Canadian Ross, was of standard calibre, but, as one user noted, 'unsuitable for Service conditions as ... any earth or dirt may cause a jam'. Another veteran, whose platoon in Devon possessed ten Ross rifles between sixty men, regarded it as 'a grand shooting rifle, but ... a heavy ill-balanced brute to lug about'. He was delighted when their Ross's were replaced by 'light, handy and accurate' Remingtons. (Longmate, 1974, p. 70)

Longmate gives the impression that the Americans generously cleared out their attic to help the embattled Brits, although, as we have seen, the American war reserve was maintained, and the Americans *sold* that which they could be persuaded to part with. More importantly, how can M1917 rifles be 'ancient', compared to the SMLE (1907), P14 (1914), or Ross (1910) and what *is* a 'cumbersome' 'Springfield 1917', and how does it relate to a 'light, handy and accurate Remington'?

The horror of cleaning cosmoline preservative from American rifles left an enduring mark on the folk memory of the Home Guard. There was, however, nothing unique about the preservation methods applied, which ensured the weapons reached their users in as-new condition. The author can confirm that removing cosmoline is a wearisome task, but under the circumstances it seems a small price to pay, shaving days, or even weeks off the delivery time of the rifles. A conscious decision was made to avoid the additional delay of passing them through ordnance depots for degreasing – on 8 July 1940, a signal was prepared from HOFOR (HQ Home Forces) to all UK commands:[19]

To H.Q. Eastern Command – Northern Command – Western Command – Southern Command – Scottish Command – London Area.

From HOFOR   8–9 July 1940

Approx _____ rifles will arrive at your command depots during next few days (.) Imperative to have distribution ready and that no delays are caused (.) Personal message on subject has been sent to your MGA but rifles will have to be degreased LDVs themselves (.) WO is issuing instructions how to do it.

Eastern 24,000 – Northern 59,000 – Western 49,000 – Southern 49,000 – Scottish 29,000 – London Area 6,000

To return to the literature, from MacKenzie (we learn that in September 1940:

... many veterans were less than happy with what they got – especially if it involved handing in the beloved SMLE in exchange for a foreign weapon. The Canadian Ross and the US Remington and Springfield rifles, covered in the thick grease in which they had been stored for over twenty years, were longer and more unwieldy than the standard Lee-Enfield, and the Ross tended to jam when dirty (the reason it had been withdrawn from service in the First World War). (MacKenzie, 1996, p. 91)

Again, we find cosmoline and careless terminology: 'Remington' and 'Springfield' rifles – no mention of Winchester or Eddystone. K.R. Gulvin, in his history of Kent Home Guard, manages yet another version:

The first weapons to reach the Kent Home Guard in large numbers were consignments of American P14 and P17 rifles, known as Springfields, Remingtons or Eddystones, depending on which company had manufactured them ... All these rifles fired the standard American .300 rimless cartridge, which was in very short supply in Britain at this time ... Another rifle issued to the Kent Home Guard in large numbers in 1940 was the Canadian Ross rifle, which fired a different design of cartridge to either the British .303 or American .300. (Gulvin, 1980, pp. 22–3)

It should now be clear why we have laboured the history of the various different service rifles to be issued to the LDV/Home Guard. There is evidence that *some* M1903 'Springfield' rifles were supplied to Britain – Skennerton (1993, p. 198) lists 64,003 M1903 A1 and A3 rifles, 38,001 M1 'Garand' self-loading rifles, and a further 119,000 M1917 rifles as supplied by the US government to the 'British Empire', under the terms of the Lend–Lease Act, passed in March 1941. Indeed, 200 'Lend–Lease' M1903 'Springfield' rifles were purchased from the UK Ministry of Supply in 1955, by an American entrepreneur, and imported back into the United States. Now eagerly sought collectors' items, the 'Red Star' rifles (as they are known, after the museum/dealership that distributed them), include various marks of M1903, but are largely rare, first-pattern, Remington-made M1903s, manufactured in 1941–42.[20] Researchers in the United States have associated these with the distinctive order mentioned by Skennerton, and also recorded in US Army archives, for 64,003 M1903s.[21] All are marked with a red-painted band on the forward woodwork, often with '.30' or '.300' stencilled on it.[22] We can, therefore, reasonably conclude that some 1903 'Springfields' may have been included in the 500,000 rifles purchased in 1940, and that as many as 64,003 arrived in 1942 (Skennerton, 1988, p. 198) and were issued to the Home Guard. Nevertheless, as is clear from contemporary photographs and training manuals, the 'signature' weapon of the Home Guard from 1941 to 1943 was the US .30-06 M1917 rifle, manufactured by Winchester, Remington or Eddystone, but often erroneously referred to as a 'P17', 'Pattern 17', or 'Springfield'.[23]

Clifford Shore, the Home Guard-turned-sniping instructor, took every opportunity to examine and shoot any small arms that came his way. Of the M1903 he recorded: 'This Springfield rifle is seldom seen in England, and my personal knowledge of it is not extensive. But I have used it enough to know it is a first-rate rifle' (Shore, 1997, p. 197). He says of the M1917:

> The M17s which I used in England in the years 1940–43 [his Home Guard service] were really splendid weapons; I never came across a bad one. In certain quarters they were not popular, but that can be primarily and summarily dismissed with the one word 'ignorance' …
>
> Many of the Home Guard in 1940 did not like the M17; usually these fellows were veterans of the First World War and the word rifle to them meant only the S.M.L.E. …
>
> The higher velocity .300 cartridge gave slightly improved ballistics than the .303 cartridge in the P14, and I should say that the M17 was probably the most accurate rifle I have ever used … (Shore, 1997, pp. 198–9)

John Langdon-Davies' *The Home Guard Training Manual* contained a chapter on 'rifles and rifle shooting', penned by Lieutenant Colonel J.A. Barlow, author of *Elements of Rifle Shooting*. In the sixth (1942) edition Barlow summed up the situation regarding Home Guard's rifles:

> You, as one of the Home Guard, may be armed with any one of the following rifles:
>
> (a) The .303" British Service Rifle (S.M.L.E.).
> (b) The .303" pattern Dec. 14 rifle (P.14).
> (c) The .303" Canadian Ross rifle (Ross).
> (d) The .300" U.S.A. 1917 model which looks almost exactly like the British P.14, having been copied from it (Model 17).
> (e) The .300" U.S.A. Springfield rifle (Springfield).

When you first joined up you probably had a British rifle given you. If you have not already had it changed for one of the U.S.A. types, it is probable that this will happen shortly. The reason is that at first you had to be armed at once with what was immediately ready; now that large stocks of U.S.A. weapons are arriving, it is obviously better for all the Home Guard to have American weapons while the field army, which has to move about, keeps the British types.

All U.S.A. rifles, and in fact any weapons which will not take the British Service cartridges, are marked with a red band two inches wide, in order to distinguish them. (Langdon Davies, 1942b, p. 93)

The author of this study can confirm, as a regular shooter with an ex-Home Guard Eddystone M1917, that the rifle may be a little awkward to carry about, due to the point of balance being on the action (bolt and magazine), rather than just in front, as it is with the SMLE and M1903 'Springfield'. But, once one is settled in the prone firing position it comes into its own. The M1917 is, as Shore described, satisfyingly accurate, and its extra weight helps absorb the recoil of the powerful .30-06 bullet, which achieves an almost flat trajectory over normal battle ranges, obviating the necessity for accurate sight setting and distance judging. The need to import this ammunition was a problem, as Professor MacKenzie comments:

Ammunition was also scarce. Given that most of the rifles issued to the Home Guard were .300 calibre rather than the standard British .303, ammunition had to be imported along with American arms, which allowed for a maximum of 50 rounds per rifle and 750 rounds for BARs [Browning Automatic Rifles] and machine guns. (MacKenzie, 1996, p. 91)

Fifty rounds of SAA (small arms ammunition) was the normal scale of 'ready' ammunition, carried in the webbing of a British soldier. Standard issue 1937-pattern webbing included two double-pocket ammunition pouches, giving the soldier forty rounds on his belt (two chargers of five rounds in each pouch), plus ten in the SMLE rifle magazine (infantrymen normally carried rectangular 'utility pouches' instead of the pocketed ammunition pouches, each capable of holding three magazines for the section's Bren light machinegun, or grenades, as well as rifle ammunition).

In anticipation of shortages of canvas webbing equipment, a leather version of 1937-pattern webbing equipment was approved in 1939. This is often, but incorrectly, associated with the Home Guard. 1939 pattern equipment was chiefly used by training battalions and some colonial troops. Modified with belt loops, 1939-pattern utility pouches were, however, initially issued on a scale of one per gun, to accompany the Browning Automatic Rifle, an American self-loading rifle used as a light support weapon, and discussed in Chapter 5. Extended versions of '39 and '37-pattern utility pouches were later to become available to those issued with Sten machine carbines, also discussed below (Hunt, 2002, p. 18). But these were specialist exceptions; the Home Guard had its own distinctive personal load carrying equipment, comprising a leather single prong buckle belt (1903-pattern, greatcoat order), two webbing ammunition pouches and a slip-over webbing back piece with two buckles, to enable '37-pattern webbing braces to be worn. There was also a slung rubberised cotton haversack and a felt covered water bottle in a leather cradle. The bayonet (if issued) was held in a pattern 1939 leather bayonet frog. The Home Guard ammunition pouches were large enough to hold two hand grenades, or two magazines for the Browning Automatic Rifle and had two pockets on the inside of the front face, each holding two chargers of five rounds of M1906 .30in ammunition. This gave the Home Guard forty rounds on his belt, just like a Regular, plus five rounds in the rifle, with a spare charger of five rounds in hand.[24]

In 1940–41, the ammunition scale for the Home Guard would not have been considered abnormally low, were it not that very little more was held in reserve or available for training. *Operation Orders – Defence Scheme No 3* of 20th Battalion Kent Home Guard (dated 27 January 1941) noted that on the invasion alarm being given, NCOs and men would make their way to company HQs, with their mobilisation equipment, including arms and ammunition. CQMSs (Company Quartermaster Sergeants) would collect further 'available ammunition' and twelve loaded magazines for the company Lewis light machine gun: thus would Sevenoaks go to war (Brown and Peek, 1944, p. 6). Although it limited the amount of practices that could be shot with the M1917 rifle, the shortage of .300in ammunition was less of a handicap than is sometimes maintained, as the Home Guard were able to practice 'GAS' (Grouping, Application and Snap shooting), and even more elaborate exercises, with smallbore .22 versions of service rifles in local TA drill halls, and on the ranges with borrowed .303 rifles, and ammunition from the National Rifle Association, as described in *Home Guard Instruction No 38* of September 1941:[25]

Many units have shown great ingenuity in constructing miniature ranges with moving targets representing descending parachutes, dive bombers, defenders appearing at the windows of houses, round corners of models, etc., which greatly add to both interest and instructional value of this training. It is hoped to maintain a regular, though probably reduced, supply of .22-inch ammunition throughout the winter. As regards the open range, it may not be generally known that a small pool of .303-inch "small mark" ammunition is supplied weekly by the N.R.A. for issue to the Home Guard. A proportion of this ammunition is used for exercising Home Guard units who are within reach of the N.R.A. ranges at Bisley, the remainder is distributed to affiliated rifle clubs throughout the country and may be used by units.

The regulations for safety areas for ranges have been relaxed and will facilitate provision under command supervision of open ranges for Home Guard units.

Arrangements will be made locally for the loaning of .303-inch rifles by Commands to Home Guard units.

The Home Guard was but one part of the machinery of Home Defence, which included many other organisations, all of which shared the problems of supply. Indeed, the Home Guard, by cornering the American weapons, had a highly advantageous situation. On 27 May 1942, Churchill wrote to the Secretary of State for War and the Chief of the Imperial General Staff (CIGS) concerning the state of an army unit detailed to protect him at his residence at Chartwell – about 20 minutes' drive away from the M1917-armed Home Guards of 'D' Company in Sevenoaks:

A company of Young Soldiers Battalion of corps troops, Buffs, were detailed for my protection when I visited Chartwell this weekend. I naturally inspected it, and asked questions about its equipment. I was told they were short of Bren gun carriers and very short of Bren guns. The output of Bren guns and Bren gun carriers has been very good for some time. I was not aware there was any deficiency in these two items.

2. I also noticed there were in the battalion two different marks of Lee-Metford rifles. Even some platoons were half-and-half. The sighting of these rifles is different, although of course they have the same ammunition. Could you let me have a note on this, stating whether any other units are in a similar condition?

3. I request that no trouble should be caused to the company or the battalion, as I am responsible for asking the questions, which it was the duty of those concerned to answer. (Churchill, 1954b, pp. 694–5)

We can assume that Churchill, having served at Omdurman and during the Boer War, knew a Lee-Metford when he inspected one. That, as late as May 1942, British Army troops guarding the prime minister were equipped with rifles dating from 1888 and sighted for black powder ammunition, brings the rifle crisis sharply into focus, and places the imagined problems of the Home Guard and their modern, high velocity, M1917 rifles in perspective.[26]

The main criticism of the P14/M1917 series was that they were not as 'handy' as the SMLE. One important aspect of 'handiness' was the rifle's suitability for bayonet fighting. The Second World War British Army remained firmly wedded to the 'Spirit of the Bayonet' and, inevitably, this percolated down to the Home Guard (Shore, 1997, p. 308). *Home Guard Instruction No. 14* (September 1940) detailed the training syllabus, stating:

> **The Bayonet** (for units armed with the bayonet): The object is to develop the offensive spirit and give the man facility with the soldier's best method of offence and defence when he cannot shoot and he wishes to kill without noise.[27]

Given the supposed importance of the bayonet as an offensive weapon, it was perhaps inevitable that an attempt would be made to arm those who 'could not shoot' simply because they still had no rifle, by welding bayonet blades to a rifle-length piece of steel tube.[28] The result was, quite correctly, but tactlessly, termed a 'pike'. Lord Croft commended the pike to the House of Lords in a debate on 4 February 1942:

> I would rather have trained bombers for fighting in urban areas, and if a bombing attack could be swiftly followed up by cold steel, it would be most effective. If I were a bomber in such a formation – and I think I have thrown most types of bombs that have been used in the Army – I should like to have a pike in order to follow up my bombing attack, especially at night. It is a most effective and silent weapon.[29]

A very similar situation to the one which Britain found itself in during the first three years of the Second World War was faced by the American Confederate

States in 1861. Also short of firearms, and firearms manufacturing capability, Confederate authorities decided to produce pikes – 6ft wooden shafts to which a blade (sometimes spring-loaded, and sometimes with a bridle cutter) was affixed. The intention was that rather than be totally unarmed, volunteers could carry a pike until they were able to capture a musket . The concept has some theoretical merit, but volunteers armed with 'Joe Brown's toothpicks' (as they were known after the governor, who ordered 10,000) proved unwilling to close with enemy carrying firearms and the issue of pikes proved deleterious to morale, and this also proved to be the case in the UK in 1941. Pikes might (possibly) have been welcome expedients in June 1940, but by the time they were issued to the Home Guard, in late-1941,[30] they proved such a public relations disaster that, as the minister responsible, Under Secretary of State for War, Lord Croft (who had opposed them in the first place), resigned.[31] In Peter Fleming's words:

> [They] seriously annoyed the Home Guard, who by that time were armed with sub-machine guns as well as rifles, grenades and even a primitive form of anti-tank gun … The well-meant ironmongery was consigned with contumely to their unit stores. (1957, p. 202)

The infamous pikes were taken as proof that the government was not taking the Home Guard seriously, and that continues to be the way the pike saga is viewed. Professor S.P. MacKenzie, for example, devotes several pages to exposing what he portrays as Churchillian whimsy (MacKenzie, 1996, pp. 97–100). This might be a fair comment, but for the fact that the pikes were *not* an exclusively Home Guard weapon. General Sir Frederick Pile, former General Officer Commanding Anti-Aircraft Command Great Britain, explained in 1949:

> The ground defence games played by A.A. Command were very old-fashioned indeed. The shortage of rifles was such that many of our units had to give up these weapons and were given instead pikes and cudgels. The pikes consisted of bayonets mounted on heavy piping, and the cudgels were of a design so novel that the gas-pipe handles were heavier than the small iron heads. Although it was generally known that the Home Guard had been issued with these weapons, we were asked to keep quiet about having them too. It was thought that the civilian might have been depressed by the knowledge that our soldiers had no other means of defence. (Pile, 1949, p. 220)

Home Guard returns list an item 'Bayonet, standard', from March 1942, which is the infamous 'pike'. From that date, 36,884 were already held, along with 105,972 examples of the 'Truncheon, various'. The numbers would eventually climb to over 45,000 pikes and 155,000 truncheons, in September 1942, before beginning a rapid decline.[32] MacKenzie is somewhat perplexed by the apparent inability of anyone involved to halt the pike project, although, as he points outs: 'P.J. Grigg, among others, was not averse to occasionally ignoring orders from 10 Downing Street which he considered foolish if he thought he could get away with it' (MacKenzie, 1996, p. 97). He goes on to hazard that '… the explanation may be that the War Office itself was genuinely misled into thinking that pikes would be welcome by the extent to which foot drill, smartness, and bayonet fighting were encouraged in some Home Guard units.' That the pikes and cudgels were also, at the same time, issued to the anti-aircraft units of the Home Army casts the entire episode in a completely different light. The pikes were the product of a combination of an abject lack of personal weapons – without which the soldier, or Home Guard, would have no option in the face of the enemy but to flee or surrender – and the orthodoxy of the 'Spirit of the Bayonet'. It is a moot point whether the knowledge that army units were also issued pikes and cudgels would have made them more acceptable to the British public, or created alarm and despondency, but for the purposes of historical analysis, we must accept them as weapons *in extremis*, rather than Churchillian eccentricity, or an ill-conceived effort to mollify the Home Guard.

The tenth edition of former RSM, now Captain, A. Southworth's *The Home Guard Pocket Manual* was published in January 1944. The only bolt action rifle featured was the M1917, indicating the extent to which it had by that stage become the standard personal weapon of the Home Guard.[33] Ironically, almost as the *Pocket Manual* went to print, Southworth's own company, in Sevenoaks, Kent, achieved its ambition of re-equipping in line with the Regular Army. 'D' Company diary records: '19/12/43. Exchange of Rifles. The .300 Rifles were handed in and .303 No. 4 Lee-Enfield Rifles issued' (Brown and Peek, 1944, p. 31). At the next trip to the ranges, on 16 January 1944, five Home Guards achieved top-scoring 4in groups, which suggests that the new rifles were satisfactory (Brown and Peek, 1944, p. 31). A year earlier, ten 4in groups were scored with the M1917s, but these were familiar rifles (Brown and Peek, 1944, p. 23). The quality of the No. 4 rifle was, though, likely to be inferior to that of almost any other rifle the Home Guard had encountered. During three years of wartime production, manufacturing shortcuts had been introduced and quality standards eased. The keen student is directed to Ian Skennerton's *The Lee-Enfield Story* (1993), for our purposes Captain Shore's comments will suffice:

> Many of the early rifles were very poor and had many faults, and at one stage opinion was dead against the model. Bolts needed a lot of work before they functioned decently; rear sights had considerable lateral play; magazines were faulty; the bores were poorly finished due to lack of machining operations, and there was great tolerance and allowance manifest when passing the bores for gauging – anything from .301 to .305 was passed as being fit for use. Some of the rifles were terrible ... (Shore, 1997, pp. 152–4)

As we have seen, the US M1917 rifle represented an improvement on the already quite respectable P14 rifle, and was ten years, two design evolutions and one major war newer than the British service rifle, the Rifle No. 1 or SMLE. The irony that the excellent M1917 military rifle should be superseded by gimcrack wartime-manufactured No. 4 Lee-Enfields was entirely lost on the Home Guard.[34] As the war entered its final phase, the Home Guard had at last achieved parity with the army. Attitudes had also changed, and the painstaking Bisley marksmanship of Lieutenant Colonel Barlow and the traditional Rifle Volunteers now belonged to a vanished age: "'The day our platoon was issued with Sten [sub-machine] guns", remember[ed] one Edinburgh Home Guard, "I knew we were going to win the war. 'At last', I thought, 'we've ditched the fine British craftsmanship nonsense'"." (Longmate, 1974, p. 75.)

Ian Beckett sought to link the LDV/Home Guard with a 'Volunteer Tradition'. The issue is a complex one, if only because the Volunteer movement was essentially reactionary, mobilising to defend the established order, while the Home Guard was enthusiastically socialist, rejecting the 'Old Guard'. However, what the 'Parashots' of May 1940 did undoubtedly share with their Victorian forebears was the conviction that to place the nation in arms was to create a nation of skilled *riflemen*. At the outset, the civilian volunteers of the LDV were not looking for uniform, formations, rank structure – or any of the other paraphernalia of formal military organisation: their expectation was simply that the government put a service rifle – scarcely cutting-edge technology – in the hands of every volunteer. But catastrophic losses of materiel, the extraordinary response to Eden's call for volunteers, the need to re-equip an army that was expanding exponentially, and the near-total lack of new production, made even this modest expectation unreasonable. The apparent *unwillingness* (an *inability* had consequences too serious to contemplate) of an already discredited government to meet its commitment to arm *all* of the LDV was perceived as a lack of faith in the volunteers, and ensured that any subsequent issue of non-standard weapons or equipment, however suitable for their purpose, was seen as *ersatz*. It threw the volunteers back on their own resources. In the end, the arrival of mass-produced sub-machine guns, requiring the very minimum of skill to build and operate, satisfied the demand for weapons, supplanted the rifle and demonstrated the universality of Stalin's maxim that 'quantity has a quality of its own'.

4

IMPROVISATION

The type and amount of weaponry delivered to the LDV/Home Guard varied according to the level of threat, and it is therefore important to bear in mind, when considering accounts of poorly armed or unarmed LDV preparing to meet the Nazi invader, that resources were placed where they were most likely to be needed. Kent, for example, was particularly threatened. K.R. Gulvin relates that:

> On the evening of 17th May, Brigadier General Franklin [organising the LDV in Kent] was ordered to have 1,500 men on armed patrol by the next evening. On receiving the order from Eastern Command, the Zone Commander visited Chatham and obtained 1,500 rifles and 15,000 rounds of ammunition from the Chatham Command. On the following date a further 2,000 rifles were drawn …
>
> By 1030pm the following night, more than 1,000 armed men were on duty throughout Kent. (1980, pp. 9–10)

Such speed and efficiency is far from the conventional view of the early days of the LDV. However, there would eventually be over 100,000 men in Kent Home Guard alone – approximately the strength of the entire modern British Army – so 3,500 rifles would not go far (Gulvin, 1980, p. 6).

Second World War British Army tactical doctrine held that seven was the largest number of men that could be controlled in battle by voice. Accordingly, the infantry section consisted of a corporal and seven men; in order to allow for sickness, detached duties or casualties, each section had an *establishment* of ten men.[1] The LDV/Home Guard, at over 1.5 million men, was larger than anticipated and, in many respects, larger than was needed – although the necessity of maintaining efficient war work limited the amount of time each Home Guard could devote to training or operational duties. As a result, platoons and sections were administrative structures – the combat units equivalent to army platoons and sections being 'battle platoons' and 'squads'. In May 1941, each Home Guard section had an *establishment* of twenty-five men and there was, doctrinally at least, no requirement to provide arms for the squad *and* its reserves.[2] Skennerton tells us that in 1940–41 the Home Guard had one rifle between two men (1993, p. 286), while MacKenzie notes that 'even under ideal conditions at least 740,000 Home Guards would have no personal weapons' (1996, p. 91). In terms of historical perspective, it is worth noting that in the build-up to 'D–Day', in March 1944, the Maquis of the French Resistance were estimated to have one rifle for every eighteen men (Marks, 2000, p. 461); nevertheless, the shortfall of personal weapons was a source of frustration to the volunteers and, whatever doctrine or military logic might have dictated, embarrassment to the government.

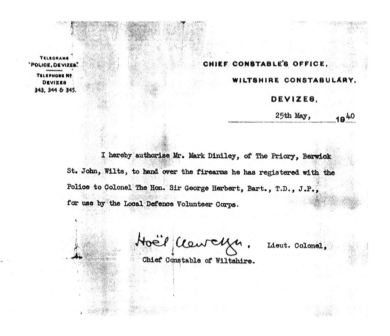

Authority to hand over privately owned weapons to the LDV. (Bapty 2000)

Since 14 May 1940, public-spirited citizens had been handing in weapons to police stations, while the National Rifle Association issued over one thousand rifles on loan to members in the LDV (Cole and Fulton, 1990, p. 41). The highest figure for (declared) privately owned rifles in the Home Guard returns is 8,019,[3] so private weapons only ever met a tiny fraction of the overall requirement. Nevertheless, they did help boost moral, particularly in areas away from the immediate threat, where official issues would be slow in coming. Mark Dineley, collector, and proprietor of theatrical armourers Bapty & Co. Ltd, placed a quantity of weapons at the disposal of the Lord Lieutenant of Wiltshire, for issue to the local LDV. Beneath his authority from the Chief Constable of Wiltshire to hand over his firearms, pasted in a scrap book, Dineley laconically noted: 'Dates from the great "Wind Up" and the organisation of the LDV and Home Guard. I armed all the neighbourhood out of my store thusly allaying a great deal of alarm.'[4] Bapty's premises in the West End of London were also striving to help the war effort, as Walter Lyall recalled in 1976:

> Until 1940 the wooden partition at the back of the landing also carried a tall, glass-fronted display case, removed by the police from a London pub, which contained a fine show of bulldog and Constabulary revolvers grouped round a .31 percussion Colt. When the war got rolling after Dunkirk Mrs Rush [the Manager] decided to break it up to satisfy the demand for handguns, just any handguns, in the Home Guard ... (Lyall, 1976, p. 309)

Like the clubs and cudgels some volunteers crafted for themselves, many of these firearms were of more symbolic than practical significance. Despite all efforts, private and public, Great Britain failed, in 1940, to become a nation of riflemen, and the emphasis shifted to improvised resistance.

Major General (Retd) Peter Pellereau recalled joining Ightham LDV (near Sevenoaks, Kent) between leaving school and going up to Trinity College, Cambridge.[5] Ightham LDV were armed with shotguns and Molotov cocktails – having received a lecture from Spanish Civil War veteran Tom Wintringham on preparing the latter.[6] The chief armament of Clifford Shore's Home Guard platoon (prior to the arrival of their M1917 rifles) was three shotguns. Shore recorded:

> Quite a number of people held the opinion that if the Hun did arrive and perforce landed in wooded areas where he would probably escape detection much more easily, and where it would certainly be better for him to hide up,

then the shotgun would be a better weapon than the rifle. There is no doubt that for very close quarter work the lethality of the 12, 16 or 20 bore cartridge cannot be dismissed lightly. (Shore, 1997, pp. 223–34)

Characteristically, Shore had some observations on shotgun ammunition:

Very tentatively we suggested to some of the more blood-thirsty volunteers that they might pour melted wax into the shot charge after loading, but warned them that with this procedure there is a very definite danger of bulging the barrel at the choke. (Shore, 1997, p. 236)

The expedient did, however, prove gratifyingly effective:

The firer took up his stance about 20 yards from the barn, put the gun to his shoulder and pulled the trigger. Most of the watchers were standing close to him and probably blinked at the noise of the explosion of the charge. They must therefore have been greatly surprised when, after the blink, they opened their eyes to find that the door had vanished! ... The door must have been in a far worse condition than was apparent from looking at it, but nevertheless it was a most spectacular demonstration, and everyone went away very impressed with the terrific power of such a projectile fired from a 12 bore gun. (Shore, 1997, p. 237)

It is relevant to note that modern hostage-rescue teams carry a shotgun loaded with lead-dust and wax 'Hatton' rounds, for the specific purpose of opening doors. Almost all the energy of the projectile is transmitted to the immediate target, with very little potential for collateral damage. This phenomenon may explain why the barn door demonstration was so spectacular. Shore continues:

... my advice was ... [to] take a 16 bore cartridge and cut it in half through the felt wad and load the half containing the shot into a 12 bore cartridge instead of the charge. The pressure developed by such a projectile would be normal, but I warned them that even with this idea there was a risk of bulging a barrel at the choke in the case of a heavily choked weapon ...

At this time quite a number of 'lethal' bullets made their appearance for use in shotguns, and I never could look at these without a grimace of distaste. Assuredly I should not have liked to be on the receiving end of such projectiles at close range. It took quite a time to persuade some men that such bullets were perfectly safe to use in shotguns ... from a full choke to a true cylinder ... (Shore, 1997, p. 237)

A 'shrapnel ball round' for shotguns was in production as early as 15 June 1940. Shrapnel balls were lead–alloy spheres 0.5in diameter, and could, according to the circular *Notes for Guidance in Examining 12 Bore Guns* (issued by TA2 on 15 June 1940) therefore pass through even a fully choked Belgian shotgun – the tightest generally available.[7] Subsequently three types of 'man-killing' shotgun ammunition were issued. 'SG' and 'LG' shot, with a spread of 3ft at 40yd – at which range SG shot could penetrate a triplex car windscreen – and Lethal Ball, which could kill at longer ranges but lacked the dispersion of shot.[8] Having already noted their sensitivity to 'dishonourable' attacks by civilians, it is germane to the discussion in Chapter 2 to see what view the Germans would have taken of volunteers using shotguns. Unlike the British, Americans have a tradition of using shotguns in war. Bruce Canfield says of the First World War US 'Trench Gun':

... The Germans accused the Americans of 'Schrecklichkeit' (barbarism) for our use of the shotgun in warfare ... On September 14, 1918, Secretary of State Lansing was presented with a formal complaint which stated:

'The German Government protests the use of shotguns by the American Army and calls attention to the fact that, according to the laws of war, every prisoner found to have in his possession such guns or ammunition belonging thereto forfeits his life.'

... The American response to the German threat was swift and firm. It stated that shotguns were not prohibited by the Hague ban.[9] It was made very clear that the United States' government would not hesitate to 'make the necessary reprisals' if the Germans followed through on even one such execution ...

The United States considered the matter closed and continued to issue trench guns ... The Germans, however ... continued to exploit the situation for propaganda purposes ... It has been said that the Germans feared the shotgun more than any other weapon they faced during World War I and their diplomatic protests certainly give this oft-repeated claim some validity. (Canfield, 1991, pp. 100–1)

British civilians were perfectly aware of the significance of taking up arms against German troops, as the historian of the 1st Cambridgeshire Home Guard Battalion recalled:

> A certain 12-bore hammerless shot gun by Evans had spent most of its forty-five years in Cambridge or in Cambridgeshire … It was a heavy weapon with Whitworth barrels, taking 2¾ in. brass 'Perfect' cases. And now in late April and early May in that year of Grace 1940, the old gun found itself a focus of unusual activity. For its owner, not unaware of what his decision implied, had made up his mind that if fighting drew near, he was turning out to join in repelling the invader, at least until turned back by troops or police on the spot. To this end then two cartridge belts were bought and joined together, forming a well-filled and well-greased bandolier, while three men, a gardener, a church verger and the owner of the gun, spent many hours in charging the powerful brass cartridges with a load more lethal than they had yet carried. (Cambs. and Isle of Eley TA Assoc., 1944, p. 31)

It should be noted that the use of shotguns as combat weapons was not limited to twelve bores:

> There was the breech-loading punt gun of 1 in. calibre, the £20 spent in cartridges and their conversion to AA. [anti-aircraft], anti-tank and anti-personal loads. The reader may smile at all this, but a steel ball (ex ball-race) 1 in. in diameter with 14 drs. of powder behind it, falls at least within the category 'S.A.P.' [semi-armour piercing]. And 26 bullets, .360 in. calibre nicely patterned at a high velocity were calculated to be a considerable danger to low-flying aircraft at least. (Cambs. and Isle of Eley TA Assoc., 1944, p. 32)

On 15 November 1940, War Office weekly returns showed that shotguns accounted for 43,697 of the personal weapons carried by members of the Home Guard – against 804,023 rifles – having fallen from a high in July of 56,033.[10] By November 1942 the figure had declined to 29,233 12-bore guns and 913 16-bores. Skennerton (1988, p. 23) notes that: 'In the general "call-up" of all firearms, considerable quantities of shotguns were also brought into service. Their main uses included guard duty and Air Force gunnery practice.' However, he lists official UK government contracts for only 1,662 assorted shotguns – dating from May 1940 to May 1943 (plus an order for 6,751 Greener Police Guns – a weapon based on a Martini action and chambering a special round – which are unlikely to have been for Home Guard use, because of their unusual ammunition).[11]

It is therefore misleading to overplay the numerical significance of the shotgun, bought or borrowed, to the Home Guard; their chief advantage appears to have been that some were on hand wherever an LDV platoon was formed. It must be said, however, that *Home Guard Instruction No. 51 Part II: Battle Drill* lists a shotgun as an alternative to a rifle or Sten machine carbine (sub-machine gun) for four of the eight members of a Home Guard 'squad', as well as the platoon serjeant [*sic*] and runner, indicating that shotguns remained as combat weapons with some units into 1943.[12] This was not to suggest, though, that half a Home Guard 'battle platoon' *would* be armed with shotguns, merely that shotguns could be used effectively by Home Guards with those duties – e.g. No. 2 on the BAR (Browning automatic rifle). Major General Pellereau recalled that all the shotguns used by the Ightham Home Guard (and, presumably, those of other units) were all safely returned to their original owners when the Home Guard was stood-down in 1944.[13]

Alongside the shotgun, the other early weapon of Ightham LDV was the Molotov cocktail. A mix of shotguns and rifles might have been adequate for potting Nazi parachutists, but they were no use against tanks, the threat that most exercised British high command immediately after Dunkirk. E. W. Ashworth notes:

> … the Home Guard still faced the problem of dealing with German tanks …
> The initial solution was the adoption of two weapons improvised during the
> Spanish Civil War (1936–39) and Finland's 'Winter War' with the Soviet Union
> (1939–40). These were the Molotov cocktail (named in 'honour' of the Soviet
> Minister for War) and the satchel charge. (Ashworth, 1998, p. 42)

The Molotov cocktail was more than a simple petrol bomb, but the distinction was unclear in 1940 and remains so today – Ashworth explains:

> The Molotov was familiar to most members of the public thanks to extensive
> press coverage during the Russian/Finnish war, in fact many Home Guard units
> managed to equip themselves with these long before the first official issue of
> small arms. This was unfortunate for some of them because the device described
> in the newspapers amounted to no more than a bottle of petrol with a petrol-
> soaked rag stuffed into or tied around its neck. Users quickly discovered that

the newspaper reports were misleading and that the weapon described in them was both dangerous and inefficient. (Ashworth, 1998, p. 42)

The 'secret ingredient' of a Molotov cocktail is the addition of a gelling agent, as the post-war US Army manual TM 31-200-1 *Unconventional Warfare Devices and Techniques* describes:[14]

GELLED FLAME FUELS – LATEX SYSTEMS   02-7

Description: Commercial rubber latex or natural latex (obtained from certain trees and plants) can be used in combination with acetic acid, sulphuric acid, hydrochloric acid or with suitable acid salts to gel gasoline for use as a flame fuel. In the commercial method, the latex is added to the gasoline mix and the mixture agitated until thickening occurs. In the natural method, the gasoline is added to the latex in a container. The container is covered and the mixture allowed to stand until it gels.

Comments: This technique was tested. It is effective.

When one appreciates the full 'recipe', the appellation 'Molotov cocktail' makes more sense. *The Home Guard Training Manual* took a slightly less scientific approach:

A mixture often made of paraffin, petrol and tar, which can be put in a bottle or tin, lit with a fuse and thrown at a tank, either to destroy part of the mechanism or to smoke out the crew. Although such methods were first used in Spain the name is a result of the great use made of it by the Finns against the Russians. (Langdon-Davies, 1942b, p. 182)

The official British Second World War recipe, as given in *Military Training Pamphlet No. 42: Tank Hunting and Destruction* (War Office, 29 August 1940), specified the inflammable substance as 'petrol and tar in approximately equal measures', but allowed that naptha, paraffin and diesel oil might also be used. Any one-pint bottle could be used, provided that it would break easily (which excluded beer and champagne bottles). The bottles were to be scored lengthwise two or three times with a diamond to aid breaking. Ignition was by 'fuzees', which could be a couple of lifeboat matches attached to the bottle with adhesive tape, rag or cotton waste soaked in paraffin and dipped in petrol 'immediately before use', or even an 18in length of cinema film.[15]

The efficacy of petrol bombs against modern armoured fighting vehicles was dramatically demonstrated in Basra, Iraq, on 21 September 2005, when rioters bombarded two British Warrior infantry fighting vehicles with petrol bombs, resulting in the crews being forced to abandon their vehicles, as Thomas Harding, Defence Correspondent for the *Daily Telegraph*, explained:[16]

> ... the driver had to open the hatches to see when the vehicle's periscope sights were damaged. A hail of petrol bombs hit the turret and burning fuel poured in, forcing the soldiers to leap out.

Private Burton, of the Staffordshire Regiment – one of the drivers – described the effect of the bombs on the crew and vehicle:

> 'Once the bomb had gone into the turret it seeped down in the back with the troops in the back.' With fire raging on the top and behind, Pte Burton had to kick open his hatch, which had jammed. 'I just jumped through the fire and got out,' he said. 'I couldn't breathe at all because of the fumes. I just needed to get out and was thinking about my life, basically.'

As early as 1940, the Germans themselves had tested Molotov cocktails, deciding that they were ineffective against current tanks, as the 'incendiary fluid did not reach the interior' (Fleischer, 1994, p. 16). The Germans subsequently revised their opinion of petrol bombs. By 1942, Germany's deteriorating military situation prompted the publication of H.Dv.469/4 *Anti-tank Defence, All Weapons* (*vide* Fleischer, 1994, p. 15). This included improvised anti-tank weapons, which the Germans divided into 'sight obscuring' and 'destroying' agents – recognising the necessity of blinding or halting a tank to enable it to be destroyed with thrown charges (or a jerry can of petrol/oil mixture with a stick grenade wired to it as an initiator). German 'incendiary bottles' were 'bottles of any size ... filled 2/3 with gasoline and 1/3 oil or burning oil [paraffin]'. Two matches were 'taped to the bottle and enclosed in wads of tow' (Fleischer, 1994, p. 15).

The need to slow, halt or blind tanks, to enable an attack, had been identified in the Spanish Civil War, and resulted in the construction of various obstacles, and the use of expedients such as blanket or tentage strung across roads or dropped from above (Slater, 1941, p. 60). There were also the famous 'soup plate mines' – ordinary china plates placed upside down in the road – which, Slater tells us, were successfully used by a British company commander during the retreat to Dunkirk to delay German armour while his troops withdrew (Slater, 1941, p. 59). This latter improvisation has the unusual distinction of featuring in *Military Training Pamphlet No. 42*, Slater's *Home Guard for Victory* and the SOE training syllabus, as an example of an effective and proven improvisation, and an early episode of *Dad's Army* and Norman Longmate's *The Real Dad's Army* for comic effect – as an illustration of the inadequacy of Home Guard anti-tank preparations.[17]

Unlike the Molotov, the Home Guard satchel charge has largely been lost to history. Ashworth notes:

> The satchel charge was widely used during the Spanish Civil War, probably originating with the coal miners of Asturia. As its name suggests it consisted of an explosive charge fitted with a detonator and short length of safety fuze in a haversack or sandbag …
>
> The Home Guard version contained about 3lbs. of explosive and the fuze was nearly always fitted with a friction igniter of the standard military type. (Ashworth, 1998, pp. 42–3)

The effectiveness of a satchel charge depends on characteristics of the propagation of an explosion, particularly with regard to the position of the detonator relative to the surface of the tank. Ashworth concludes:

> It is obvious that the chances of a thrown satchel landing in a favourable orientation are very slim … Given these facts it is easy to understand why the Home Guard much preferred the Molotov cocktail. (Ashworth, 1998, p. 43)

A certain Spanish flavour will be apparent in the improvised weaponry of the LDV.[18] Finding themselves in universal demand to expound theories of improvised warfare, Tom Wintringham and other veterans of the Spanish Civil War came up with an ambitious plan – as Professor MacKenzie relates:

> Over dinner with Edward Hulton (owner of *Picture Post*) and his friend Tom Hopkinson one evening in early July 1940, Wintringham came up with a scheme to circumvent War Office delays and procrastination in the training of the Home Guard through the setting up of a private school. The Earl of Jersey

was asked by Hulton to allow use of the grounds of his mansion at Osterley Park, just outside London. 'Could we dig weapon pits?' asked Wintringham, his imagination racing, 'loose off mines? Throw hand grenades? Set fire to old lorries in the grounds?' Lord Jersey agreed to it all, as long as the house itself was not demolished in the process. (MacKenzie, 1996, p. 71)

MacKenzie comments:

> There is no evidence to suggest that Wintringham and his staff consciously sought to inculcate political values as well as tactical roles, but in drawing comparisons with the Spanish Civil War and promoting the methods practised by the militias – heavily grounded in personal initiative and passionate commitment to the anti-fascist cause – both the school at Osterley Park and Wintringham's articles in *Picture Post* tended to invite empathy with the values that inspired the Republican war effort. (MacKenzie, 1996, p. 72)

On 26 July 1941, *Picture Post* ran a feature by Wintringham on that *sine quo non* of Home Guard improvisations – the mortar. 'We Make our Own Mortar for 38/6' ran the headline – Wintringham opened with a description of the first mortar built at the school, a year earlier:

> … Major Wilfrid Vernon made the first mortar that the Home Guard possessed. It was a clumsy piece of scrap boiler tube, set at an angle of 45 degrees in a flat lump of concrete. The concrete was its base-plate, and we aimed it by wedging up one corner or another of the concrete. The local police gave us fireworks they had confiscated from children, and from the fireworks we sorted out gunpowder to charge our comic little gun. [19]

The Bapty collection includes several Home Guard mortars and grenade throwers. Anything but 'comic little guns', all are highly finished and well thought out, and make it quite clear that such weapons should not be lightly dismissed. Where the skill existed – whether at Bapty or Osterley Park – extremely serviceable mortars could be produced. Tom Wintringham explained the process of development:

> From those days of July, 1940, we have been making many home-made mortars. We soon dropped the heavy base plate; all such a weapon needs is a spiked tail that sticks firmly in the ground. We became experts at kicking a mortar, stuck

in the ground, or wedging it with a piece of stone, in such a way as to alter the range or angle of fire, to get the second shot on the target if the first one went a little wide. And with our fifth or sixth mortar, we got the idea of making the tail in the form of a spade, so that the man handling it can dig a hole for it quickly and easily.

Powder taken from fireworks is not reliable, so we made our own gunpowder. It was not smokeless, but it worked.[20]

Apart from the mortar itself, there was also the matter of a projectile. Osterley Park mortars discharged a 'jam tin bomb', made, as its name suggests, from a standard tin can containing improvised shrapnel and a black powder charge ignited by a slow fuse, in the manner of an eighteenth-century siege mortar. The mortar featured in Wintringham's article was firing a homemade smoke bomb, but reasonably effective high-explosive/fragmentation grenades had been made out of jam tins in the Dardanelles Campaign, during the First World War.[21] The majority of the 'mortars' in the Bapty collection are bomb throwers, using single-shot rifle actions. In principle these are similar to early versions of the 4in smoke grenade dischargers fitted to British armoured fighting vehicles (AFVs) during the Second World War.[22] Without knowing what charge and projectile was used, it is difficult to assess the performance of these weapons. There is, however, no reason to imagine that they were any less effective than the contemporary AFV smoke grenade discharger, or the EY grenade-launching rifle (discussed later), and they would therefore be a useful addition to the firepower of the platoon, and provide an effective weapon for a pair of Home Guards (Nos 1 and 2 on the mortar), using only one obsolete rifle mechanism.

Like the Home Guard, Spanish Republican forces suffered from a crippling lack of artillery, which led to special emphasis being placed on comparatively simple (to build, maintain and operate) mortars, including First World War trench mortars. Each Republican 'mixed brigade' included a 'heavy weapon group', with a single heavy machine gun, mortar and anti-tank gun, which provided the organic fire-support for the brigade.[23] It is easy to see that such an organisation would have appealed to Home Guard battalions, which could not depend on indirect fire-support from artillery batteries, and there is a wry allusion to this in John Langdon-Davies's *Home Guard Warfare*:

There is another kind of war – 'Small War' or 'Guerrilla', and here everything is different. This is the kind of war which the Spaniard has fought for centuries amid his mountains – the Finn amid his lakes and forests ... In this kind of war it is no good the Infantry hoping for support from the Artillery, because nobody has the slightest idea where anyone else is. (Langdon-Davies, 1941, p. 29)

There can be no doubt that the British Army issue 2in mortar would have made an excellent weapon for the Home Guard, but demand outstripped supply of what was, small size notwithstanding, a sophisticated weapon (remaining in service into the twenty-first century[24]). In the absence of 2in mortars, the Home Guard had, initially, to fall back on their own expedients, whether they were the highly evolved mortars of the Osterley Park team, or the catapult built by employees of the Royal Mint (MacKenzie, 1996, p. 55). This later sort of device is a boon to the 'Mind my Pike!' school. In fairness to such efforts, and there seem to have been many (vide Longmate, 1974, p. 69), one should point out that a catapult – 'West's Spring Gun' – was adopted by the British Army in 1916, because it could project 'bombs' (hand grenades) in the same manner as a mortar, but without the tell-tale 'signature' of smoke or a report, and was therefore less vulnerable to location and counter-battery fire – a serious shortcoming of black powder weapons such as the Osterley mortars, and the 'sub-artillery' which would replace them (Hogg, 1992, p. 15).

Another ad hoc weapon available to the Home Guard was what we today term the victim-operated improvised explosive device (VOIED), but known at the time simply as the booby trap. IEDs accounted for the greater proportion of International Security Assistance Force (ISAF) casualties in Afghanistan, and there can be no doubting the effectiveness of this type of warfare in slowing an enemy, limiting his freedom of manoeuvre and imposing a defensive mindset. That the Home Guard were trained to prepare VOIEDs is a statement of fact, but it is harder to determine how well equipped General Service (GS) Home Guard units were to construct IEDs. Home Guard special operations Auxiliary Units were, as we shall see in Chapter 9, lavishly equipped with explosives and initiators, but the extent to which these were available to GS units awaits further research. However, they certainly were instructed in preparing electrically detonated VOIEDs, and devices using their issue grenades. *Home Guard Instruction No. 51: Battlecraft and Battle Drill for the Home Guard, Part IV, The Organization of Home Guard Defence*, published in November 1943, explained:

1. Passive obstructions can be greatly strengthened by the use of simple booby traps. They make the progress of the enemy slower and have considerable

Home Guard, who should observe the principles laid down regarding their siting :—

(a) *The 36 grenade.* This is set up in conjunction with a trip wire. The wire is permanently fixed at one end, and attached to a 36 grenade with pin removed, inserted in a cocoa tin at the other. The cocoa tin is nailed to a fixed board.

As the wire is tripped the 36 grenade is pulled out of the tin thereby releasing the lever. *See* Fig. 15.

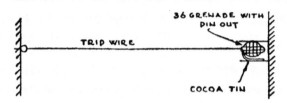

FIG. 15.

(b) *The 69 or 73 grenade.* Set up in connection with the opening of a door. The tape is partially unwound. The lead weight is fastened to the lintel of the door and the grenade supported either on the door top, or on a small ledge constructed. As the door is opened it comes in contact with a stop placed on the floor. The grenade is jarred from the door or ledge. The pin is removed by the tape. Grenade burst on hitting floor. *See* Fig. 16.

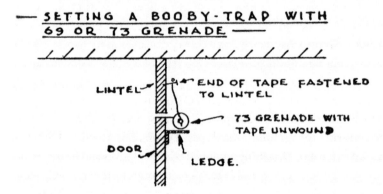

FIG. 16.

Two pages on the construction of booby traps from Home Guard Instruction No. 51, of November 1943. The No. 69 and No. 73 (bottom left) were percussion grenades. The No. 69 was a Bakelite 'offensive' grenade, which would cause limited casualties and damage as a booby trap. The No. 73 was an anti-tank blast grenade, which would be devastating in an enclosed space. (Author's collection)

(c) *Electrically exploded improvised booby trap.* This depends on the following for its effect :—

(i) A charge exploded by a low tension electric detonator.

(ii) A simple electrical circuit completed by the coming together of two contacts.

At Fig. 17 is shown a simple trip-wire trap using a clothes peg and wedge. The jaws of the clothes peg are made into electrical contacts by nailing on pieces of tin.

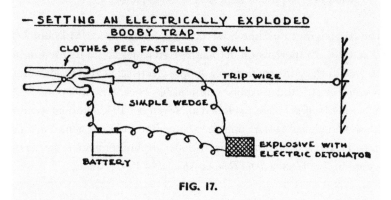

—SETTING AN ELECTRICALLY EXPLODED BOOBY TRAP——

CLOTHES PEG FASTENED TO WALL

TRIP WIRE

SIMPLE WEDGE

BATTERY

EXPLOSIVE WITH ELECTRIC DETONATOR

FIG. 17.

(d) Many other similar devices can be improvised by pieces of tin and wire, such as a trap set in a drawer with pieces of tin as contacts.

moral effect. They must be intelligently sited not to interfere with our own patrols and always be well concealed.

The methods of setting them should be ingenious and varied so that the enemy does not learn easily how to detect them.

The principles:-

(a) *Preservation of outward appearances.* If time permits, cover up all traces such as wire and spoil.

(b) *Constricted localities.* Choose a close site when setting traps [;] avoid a bottleneck when expecting them.

(c) *Double Bluff.* This is the principle of laying a well-concealed trap close to a fairly obvious one. This tends to attract the attention to the obvious one, and, in avoiding it, the well-concealed trap is set off.

(d) *Inconvenience.* The employment of obstacles and things which might be removed by troops entering the building.

(e) *Curiosity.* The principle of using booby traps in connection with souvenirs, crooked pictures, food and drink containers, etc. Never be curious. Do not touch anything unnecessarily.

(f) *Everyday operation.* Traps operated by opening or closing doors or windows, telephones, light switches, WC plugs.

The manual goes on to outline how the No. 36M grenade ('Mills bomb') and No. 69 and No. 73 (percussion detonating) grenades could be used in booby traps, as well as the construction of a simple electrical VOIED, indicating that explosive, and electrical, detonators were available. There is no mention of IEDs in *The Defence of Bloodford Village*, published in November 1940, although (somewhat ambitiously) flooded pitfalls are dug, deep enough to swallow enemy tanks (Wade, 1940, p. 6). However, Langdon-Davies includes an almost identical list of possible booby traps in *The Home Guard Training Manual* of 1942, adding:

> These can be supplemented by baiting objects [the enemy] is likely to handle. Thus the Nazi is a fanatical admirer of Hitler and is likely to waste time destroying any rude caricature of Hitler that may be prominently displayed on your mantelpiece. He is also an inveterate souvenir hunter and will take a fancy to all sorts of knickknacks. All such objects can be attached to electric cables, explosives etc., and even if they merely go off with a bang they will increase the general feeling of insecurity. (Langdon-Davies, 1942, p. 143)

Grenades started to reach the Home Guard in early 1941, and it is unlikely that there would have been the equipment or training to create IEDs before that date. However, from 1941 onwards, Home Guard defences would undoubtedly have been strengthened by the use of basic, but effective, VOIEDs.

Attempts to rationalise the rifle shortage by arguing (not unreasonably) that there were, in fact, enough rifles available for the LDV/Home Guard to meet its military commitments were doomed to failure. Frustrated, the volunteers turned to the veterans of the International Brigade, whose experience of improvised warfare suddenly assumed much greater importance than that of conventional operations. Their so-called 'Buffalo Bill' approach met with some scepticism, particularly from those cynics who pointed out that the Spanish Republican forces had actually *lost* the Spanish Civil War. Nonetheless, from the rifle crisis a distinctive ethos evolved, very early in the life of the LDV/Home Guard; suspicion of established, centralised authority, and a determination to solve problems locally with improvisation and imagination. Many of their solutions displayed a greater degree of finish and effectiveness than the improvised weapons of modern insurgents and terrorist groups.

5

PISTOLS AND AUTOMATIC WEAPONS

Could you please oblige us with a Bren gun?
We need it very badly, I'm afraid
Our local crossword solver has an excellent revolver
But during a short attack on a fort, the trigger got mislaid

In course of operations planned for Friday afternoon
Our orders are to storm the Hippodrome
So if you can't oblige us with a Bren gun
The Home Guard might as well go home

From *Could You Please Oblige Us with a Bren Gun?*,
Noël Coward, 1943

Although, in the formative days of the LDV/Home Guard, the emphasis was on the rifle, other small arms soon joined the armoury. In this chapter we will examine the Home Guard's use of handguns, light and medium machine guns, and the Thompson sub-machine gun. Some LDVs armed themselves with handguns from the outset, including, as we have seen, the contents of Bapty's display case of nineteenth-century revolvers. Bapty's owner, Mark Dineley, commanding the Berwick St John Home Guard near Salisbury, affected an American Colt 1911 government model .45 automatic,[1] and in Kent, volunteer Peter Pellereau was brandishing his grandfather's .455 Webley service revolver when he captured a downed German airman whose parachute had become entangled in a tree. In 1940, many handguns were in circulation, frequently private-purchase service weapons or military souvenirs. There were, therefore, and like shotguns, quantities of pistols of various sorts available wherever LDV units formed. However, even when handguns were ex-military small arms, they were not particularly highly valued. British doctrine and tradition places little emphasis on the pistol, which has always been regarded as a weapon of last resort and self-defence. In Home Guard service pistols were (officially at least) restricted to officers and dispatch riders.[2] The service revolver was described in training literature as being capable of 'short range rapid-fire. Only accurate in hands of an experienced shot.'[3] Nevertheless, in August 1939, 57,940 service pistols (the Enfield-designed .380in Pistol, Revolver, No. 2 Mk I or I★) were in store or on issue to the British armed forces, and a note on the War Office contract records ledger, of 2 February 1940, recorded: 'Deficiency between requirement & stock: 233,541'(Skennerton, 1988, p. 26).

Efforts were made to repair that deficiency by increasing production, purchasing commercial .380 Webley Mk IV revolvers, and placing orders in the United States with Colt, Smith and Wesson, Iver Johnson and others, for over 420,000 handguns of various types (Stamps and Skennerton, 1993, p. 88). The list of pistols ordered overseas (chiefly in the USA), during the period 1940–42, includes exotics such as 7.63mm Mauser machine pistols, and others in diverse calibres and variations of calibres (Skennerton, 1988, p. 26). Although it is tempting to see this as further evidence of desperate times leading to desperate measures, and ascribe all these weapons to the pressing needs of Home Defence, Stamps and Skennerton (1993, p. 95) speculate that the relative rarity today of some of the more exotic imports – 2,000 small-framed Iver Johnson pistols, for example – may be due to them being sent into occupied Europe for use by resistance forces. Certainly, pistols, particularly concealable ones, and those of Continental manufacture or calibre, were more likely to advance the war effort in the hands of resistance fighters than the relatively conventional troops of the Home Guard.

As we shall see later in this study, the Home Guard Auxiliary Units, which were expected to operate in a manner similar to that of the resistance movements, were issued either .380 revolvers or .32 automatics, on a scale of one per man, plus thirty-six or forty rounds of ammunition respectively.[4] The majority of imported handguns were those manufactured by Colt or Smith & Wesson, in calibres .380/.38in revolver, .455in revolver, .45in revolver or .45 Automatic Colt Pistol (ACP). Where these guns were not designed to chamber standard British service .38- or .455-calibre ammunition, they were painted with a red band and carried the calibre stencilled. Thus 'Category II .38 Special Smith and Wesson revolvers, various types' were marked with a red band painted round the rear of the barrel and the words '.38 SPECL' stencilled in black (Stamps and Skennerton,

1993, p. 95). In addition to .380-calibre pistols, 25,969 examples of the First World War service Webley Mk VI (which had been redesignated as *.455in. Pistol, Revolver, No. 1*) were ordered from Webley and Scott during the early part of the Second World War (Skennerton, 1988, p. 24).

Officially, pistols appeared with the Home Guard quite late, only featuring in monthly returns from March 1941, with an undifferentiated national total for that month of just 1,880. It is likely that there were far more, undeclared, privately owned pistols already in service. However, the number of pistols in Home Guard units climbed rapidly to 12,948 in September 1941. March 1942 saw the figure in the returns broken down by calibre for the first time, to reveal that the majority of handguns were of .445 calibre.[5] The table below shows the first and last 'by calibre' sets of entries given. There is a degree of fluctuation in the returns, and probably some inaccuracy; nevertheless trends emerge, and it is apparent that .455 and .45 were the most numerically important Home Guard pistol calibres. There also appears to be evidence of standard-issue .380-calibre weapons being withdrawn from the Home Guard in 1942. We can therefore conclude that the 'typical' Home Guard pistol was either a British .455 Webley, or an American .45 M1917 revolver – but a reasonable case can be made for almost any contemporarily available make, type or calibre.

Pistols in Home Guard Service, by calibre[6]

	.32	.32 auto	.38	.45	.45 auto	.455	Other
Mar '42	1,365	232	3,495	5,154	229	9,905	645
Nov '42	913	2,011	470	3,807	469	9,751	770

The standard pistol calibre for the British Army was .380, so the issue of .455- and .45-calibre revolvers to the Home Guard might be viewed as clear evidence that the organisation was receiving obsolete weapons. However, it is worth noting that the .455 Webley service revolver was only replaced in British Army use when it became clear that such a large and powerful handgun was too much for the soldiers of the First World War to master in the abbreviated training time that wartime conditions allowed (Skennerton, 1988, p. 24). The .380 Enfield that replaced it was, in essence, a smaller version of the earlier weapon, chambering a less-powerful round. The British .380in round was a version of the American Smith & Wesson .38in, with a heavier 200-grain bullet to increase its stopping power (Stamps and Skennerton, 1993, p. 9).[7] Combat experience has demonstrated that whilst the power of the .38/.380 round is adequate, the .45 is a guaranteed manstopper – which was why the US Army returned to that calibre for its 1909 revolver and 1911 automatic pistol.[8] Thus the .455 Webleys and .45 Colts issued to the Home Guard were reassuringly powerful combat handguns – albeit something of a handful.[9] The standard scale of issue for .380 pistol ammunition to British regular troops was just twelve rounds, and the same was allowed for the Home Guard, in a War Office memorandum on Home Guard ammunition scales of 28 July 1940.[10] However, that memorandum specifies that three rounds were to be used for practice. Thus the revolver-armed Home Guard would probably go into action with a full cylinder of six shots and half a cylinder of reloads in his ammunition pouch. Given that British doctrine assumed the revolver would only be used for self-defence in the last resort, this was not unreasonable, and in line with British Regular Army doctrine.[11]

At the opposite end of the firepower scale from revolvers were machine guns. Norman Longmate described:

> By the end of 1940 … the first automatic weapons had also begun to arrive. The first received by one West Country unit was a Lewis gun, mounted on a pivot and tripod behind which its two-man crew squatted, swinging it freely right across their front, as it poured out 600 bullets a minute. For heavier support this battalion relied on a Hotchkiss of very ancient vintage, and a veteran swore he recognised it as an old friend of the South African campaign. (1974, p. 73)

Former Home Guard Longmate was being mischievous, and inaccurate. The Lewis was a light machine gun, fitted with a small bipod,[12] and the Hotchkiss machine guns issued to Home Guard units were generally the British Gun, Machine, Hotchkiss, .303in Mks I and I★, introduced in 1916 and declared obsolete in 1946, and therefore much too young to have seen action on the veldt. Although also a light machine gun, the Hotchkiss *was* mounted on a miniature tripod. A British version of the French Hotchkiss *Mle* 09, the weapon was adopted to provide a light machine gun for the cavalry and was retained when that arm mechanised. It is conceivable that the West Country unit in question was equipped with the larger, tripod-mounted Hotchkiss *Modèle* 1914,[13] but in neither case could the weapon have served in the Boer War. What the passage does serve to illustrate, however, is the convention that any small arms issued to the Home Guard must be 'ancient' – in fact neither the Lewis, nor the Hotchkiss machine guns were even

Commercially produced manual for the .300 Lewis. The quality of the graphic design of this little manual by the Bravon Ledger Company is particularly noteworthy. The American aircraft gun illustrated has been given simple aperture sights, a British pattern wooden butt and forty-seven-round infantry magazine. These guns were initially issued without any form of mounting, to be fired rested on cover. Subsequently a rudimentary triangular bipod was developed. (Author's collection)

obsolete. The light Hotchkiss was also adopted by the US Army as the *M1909 Benét-Mercié Machine Rifle, Calibre .30*. Only 665 guns were purchased (Goldsmith, 1994, p. 200), and the gun was long out of US service by 1940, but it is possible that some were supplied to the UK (see plate 17). It should be noted, however, that there is no entry for '.300in' Hotchkiss guns in the Home Guard weapon returns.

Skennerton (1988, p. 60) records a total of 10,993 British Hotchkiss Mks I and I* reconditioned during the early part of the Second World War for service, he surmises, 'mostly with the Home Guard'. Actually the Hotchkiss LMG was a fairly rare machine gun in Home Guard service, with the first (just seven) appearing with the Home Guard in July 1941. The number slowly increased, but had only reached 100 by January 1942, and, by November 1943, just 323 were reported in service.[14] The numbers suggest an increase due to the guns being gradually released from army service, probably as more Bren guns became available.[15]

It is a curiosity of the Home Guard that improvised weapons – like the homemade mortars and Molotov cocktails, which appear rather feeble to modern eyes – could, at the time, embody values such as 'modernity' and 'a people's war', while conventional weapons of proven reliability, such as M1917 rifles, were condemned as 'old-fashioned'. This has made it difficult to give some Home Guard weapons the credit they deserve – the Lewis light machine gun being a particularly good example. Adopted by the British Army in 1914, Mk I Lewis guns started to be placed in reserve after 1938, when the Bren light machine gun entered service as the infantry's light machine gun. At the same time the Vickers 'Gas Operated'[16] supplanted the Mk II and III Lewis aircraft guns.[17] The Bren gun inspired a loyalty similar to that engendered by the SMLE rifle and, from the outset, rendered the Lewis gun completely obsolete in the minds of the army, press and public. This is unfortunate, firstly because the Lewis was one of the younger British infantry weapons (adopted two years after the Vickers Mk I machine gun and seven years after the SMLE rifle), and secondly, because the Second World War has been called – with some justification – the Lewis gun's 'finest hour' (Easterly, 1998, p. 309). Reporting to the War Cabinet on 29 August 1940, Minister of Supply, Herbert Morrison, stated that 11,000 machine guns had been lost in France, of which 8,000 were Bren guns.[18] Until this loss could be made up, Mk I Lewis guns had to be issued from reserve, but that was not the full extent of the demand. The Lewis was employed, chiefly as a light anti-aircraft weapon, in a bewildering variety of roles: on fishing boats and defensively equipped merchant ships (DEMS), on RAF rescue launches, in searchlight batteries, and on airfields. The guns even saw action on a diminutive armoured train on the Romney, Hythe and Dymchurch miniature railway on the Kent coast (claiming a *Luftwaffe* bomber that, apparently confused by the small size of the train, flew within machine-gun range). In the opening months of 1940 there was fierce competition for Lewis guns between AA Command Great Britain and the Admiralty, as described shortly after the war by General Sir Frederick Pile, formerly GOC-in-C Anti-Aircraft Command:

> The shortage of [Bofors] light anti-aircraft weapons was very great, and, in place of them, between 3000 and 4000 Lewis guns had been made available. No one pretended that these were suitable anti-aircraft weapons – indeed the R.A.F. had worked it out that, apart from a lucky accident, 850 actual hits by light machine-gun bullets were necessary to bring a plane down – but, anyhow, they were something. In February, however, the Admiralty cast envious eyes on them and demanded 800 for the protection of shipping. In March they raised this figure to 1300, and asked for a further 1600 to be made available at the rate of 250 a month. (Pile, 1949, p. 112)

General Pile's quote raises the question as to why the RAF had chosen to equip all its combat aircraft with rifle-calibre machine guns, and why the Admiralty wanted them as light anti-aircraft weapons too. The answer was that rifle-calibre guns *were* effective at close range, unless the aircraft's pilot and fuel tanks were protected with armour (Wallace, 1972, p. 36). It was in anticipation of increased aircraft armour that work was underway on the 20mm Hispano cannon for the RAF (as described in Chapter 8).[19] As it turned out, the Lewis gun was a more effective anti-aircraft weapon than was imagined, particularly against fleeting low-level targets. Indeed such was its efficacy that it was included among the guns of Anti-Aircraft Command in *Roof Over Britain*, an official booklet celebrating the command's efforts up to 1943:

> The last-war Lewis gun has been surprisingly successful, mounted singly, or in twin or quadruple for greater fire power. It has brought down many low-flying raiders who sought by diving from cloud to surprise the defences. The function of the light guns is to hold off the bomber from low-level attack, or from vulnerable points all over the country. (MOI, 1943, p. 24)

It is claimed that Lewis guns accounted for 20 per cent of the aircraft brought down by ground fire in the London area during the Battle of Britain (Easterly, 1998, p. 302). The Lewis gun was a very low-level air defence weapon, and therefore should have been used in addition to the 40mm Bofors anti-aircraft gun, rather than instead of it – which is the situation General Pile was referring to. Merchant Navy Lewis gunners were instructed that the effective anti-aircraft range of the Lewis gun was 500yd, and that, where it was available, tracer ammunition should be loaded every fifth round.[20] The DEMS manual explained:

> The Lewis gun is a light automatic gun, very simple in design and capable of a high rate of fire. It can be used with effect against men not under cover, but is of particular use at sea in repelling an aeroplane attack, when it has a most disturbing effect on the occupants of the aeroplane …[21]

On dry land, and across the countryside, some pillbox designs (the FW 3/23, for example) featured a post-mounted Lewis in the light anti-aircraft role (Wills, 1985, p. 17), while 199 Alan Williams prefabricated steel airfield defence turrets were produced with various mounting brackets for the Bren and Lewis in the ground role, Lewis in the anti-aircraft role, and Hotchkiss and Browning (q.v. below) 'for Home Guard use' (Wills, 1985, p. 22).

On 7 July 1940, Department MT7 at the War Office issued a memorandum outlining the need to provide Lewis gun training pamphlets for the LDV, indicating that at least some .303 Lewis guns were already being used by the new force.[22] The lack of training materials for the LDV was exploited by Messrs Gale & Polden of Aldershot, who swiftly republished their 75-page instruction book *The Complete Lewis Gunner*, which had been out of print since 1918.[23] As it transpired, the most significant Home Guard LMG would not be the familiar British .303 Mk I Lewis, but the .300-calibre US M1918 Savage-Lewis aircraft machine gun. Easterly (1998, p. 300) gives a figure of over 45,000 Lewis guns in .300 (US .30-06) calibre supplied to the UK during the Second World War. Of these, 4,170 were 'Mobile Army' LMGs and 41,710 aircraft guns. The latter were either mounted as light-AA for Merchant Navy use, or converted into ground-role LMGs for the Home Guard (designated the 'Mk III*'). Over 11,000 were with the Home Guard in February 1941,[24] and the Home Guard inventory of .300-calibre aircraft guns peaked at 12,756 in September 1942, with a further 3,282 .300-calibre ground-role guns and 412 .303-calibre guns in service.[25] Initially the American aircraft guns were fitted with a standard-issue wooden butt (in place of a spade grip), and crude battle sights. It was not easy to fire the guns using the tall ninety-seven-round aircraft magazine with the cheek rested on the butt in the usual manner, so only the standard infantry forty-seven-round magazines were used. As supplies of wooden butts dried up, a new fabricated butt was produced based on a modified spade grip which was much higher in the comb, making it easier to use the guns with ninety-seven-round magazines (Langdon-Davies, 1942b, p. 108).

British Mk III aircraft guns were also issued (as the Mk III★★), similarly modified (Easterly, 1998, p. 306). When these too were exhausted, guns were made up by the gun trade and light engineering firms from spare or scrap parts and deactivated drill-purpose ('DP') examples (Easterly, 1998, pp. 298–311). These reconstituted guns became the Lewis Mks IV and V (or 'SS', for 'Sea Service'). The first edition of Hogg and Weeks' classic *Military Smallarms of the Twentieth Century* records:

> **Gun, Machine, Lewis 0.303in Mark 4** (introduced on 16th August 1946). A conversion of Mark 3 guns to simplify manufacture. It is doubtful if any were ever made, as the gun was declared obsolete on the day it was approved. (1973, p. 5.58)

This is a chastening example of the dangers of jumping to conclusions. No one was seriously considering manufacturing Lewis guns, simplified or otherwise, in August 1946 – the entry is a piece of administrative housekeeping. The various wartime expedient Lewis guns could not be declared obsolete unless they had first entered the system; therefore these marks were approved and declared obsolete on the same day.[26] Indeed, wartime small arms contracts reveal that, in September 1941, Westley Richards and H. Atkin each received orders to assemble 1,000 Mk IV Lewis guns from parts. Contracts list around 44,000 Lewis guns of various marks returned to service during 1940–41, plus 15,000 ex-US .300-calibre Lewis guns reconditioned at Enfield (Skennerton, 1988, p. 59).

In 1940–45, the Lewis was still a perfectly serviceable squad automatic, and its forty-seven-round drum magazine gave a useful volume of fire in the light anti-aircraft role, while the gun's unusual air-circulation cooling system prevented it from overheating firing long bursts. Conversely, ex-aircraft Lewis guns proved quite capable of operating as terrestrial squad automatics, and in the light-AA role, had the considerable advantage of a ninety-seven-round magazine.[27] The gun did have its shortcomings, but whether in .303 or .300 calibre, the Lewis was crucial to the British war effort, and made a significant contribution to anti-aircraft defence. Yet, in the public mind, the Lewis gun remained irredeemably associated with the Great War. In the quote from *Roof Over Britain* above, for example, the official historian referred to 'the last war Lewis' – yet one does not read of 'last war' SMLE rifles, Vickers machine guns or Mills bombs. For the Home Guard to be issued with

Lewis guns was to share a scarce, valuable and effective resource – but the Lewis gun was never presented or perceived as such. Ironically, the last combat use of the Mk I Lewis would be in the hands of the German equivalent of the Home Guard, the *Volkssturm*, who were issued the '*7.7mm leMG 137(e)*' – the German designation for the Lewis guns captured at Dunkirk (Gander and Chamberlain, 1978, pp. 9 and 83).

In most Home Guard platoons the squad light support weapon was not a Lewis gun but a weapon for which there was no British equivalent, the M1918 Browning Automatic Rifle (BAR). *Home Guard Instructions* of September 1942 make clear that the BAR was the standard squad light automatic at that time:

> The organization shows that for a Browning automatic rifle. The team is known as the B.A.R. group. *Throughout this Instruction Lewis gun will be substituted for B.A.R. by those units using Lewis guns.* [Original italics][28]

It is said of the BAR that it was rather heavy for a rifle, and rather light for a light machine gun. In fact the weapon was a proto-assault rifle, styled a 'machine rifle' in contemporary documents (Ballou, 2000). Developed to provide suppressing fire from the 'marching fire' position for US troops crossing no-man's-land during the

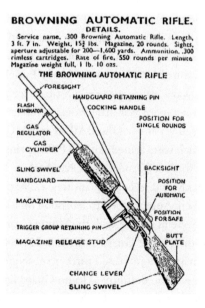

M1918 BAR from *Bernards' Manual of Modern Automatic Guns*. (Author's collection)

First World War, the BAR was originally provided with an extra-long sling and a special gunner's belt with a cup to hold the butt of the weapon, in order to facilitate accurate fire 'from the hip' (Canfield, 1991, pp. 79 and 81). The idea was to fire single shots during the approach, and a burst of full automatic to keep the defenders' heads down at the last moment to allow the 'bombers' (grenade throwers) to close with the enemy (Ballou, 2000, p. 20). In the interwar years modifications were made to the BAR, bringing it closer to a true light machine gun. These included provision of a bipod (M1918A1) and the replacement of the semi-automatic/ automatic fire selector with one offering two rates of automatic fire (M1918A2) (Ballou, 2000, pp. 128-39). These alterations were, however, peripheral, as the true character of the gun – with its light, fixed barrel and twenty-round box magazine, remained the same.

A quantity of unmodified M1918 guns remained in US reserves, and it was these that were supplied to the British. Almost 24,000 BARs reached the Home Guard between August 1940 and November 1942.[29] Although 'D' Company, 20th Kent Home Guard, had a single Lewis gun from the outset, they received their BARs rather late – the earliest reference in their *Diary* (Brown and Peek, 1944, p. 14) being: '15/2/42. Shoreham range … The B.A.R.'s were also fired by twelve members of the coy, with almost negative results.' The disappointing shooting with this unfamiliar weapon is noteworthy, but by June 1944 the BAR shooting team was able to record scores of between fifteen and eighteen, out of a possible twenty, in the Champion-at-Arms competition (Brown and Peek, 1944, p. 33). Being the squad automatic weapons, the BARs were retained when the company exchanged its M1917 rifles for No. 4 Enfields (Brown and Peek, 1944, p. 31). The BAR was a rather meagre substitute for a Bren gun as a squad automatic, but the Home Guard was little worse off than the Belgian or Polish regular forces, which used versions of the BAR as an LMG, or even US Marines and US Army units, which were armed with M1903 Springfield rifles and BARs during the early part of the war (Gander and Chamberlain, 1978, pp. 82–3). BARs arrived in the UK quickly, and in large quantities. 2,290 provisional instruction booklets were published in August 1940, to be issued on a scale of one per gun,[30] but over 20,000 BARs were in service with the Home Guard by 1 February 1941. The highest figure in the Home Guard returns is 23,684 in September 1942, although the quantity may have increased further subsequently.[31]

Although the Lewis was the definitive Home Guard light machine gun, and the BAR the most widely encountered light automatic, it was, as we have seen from Noël Coward's lyric at the head of the chapter, the Bren LMG that was the aspirational weapon in the LMG category. The Bren really did represent a genuine step forward, a truly outstanding modern LMG, which would remain in front-line service with the British Army from 1938 until the Gulf War of 1991. In terms of reliability, robustness and simplicity, the Bren gun was in a class of its own, as Gale & Polden's *The Bren Light Machine Gun: Description and Mechanism* enthused: '… it cannot be assembled incorrectly … It is practically immune from STOPPAGES provided the firer attends to the points in "PREPARE FOR ACTION" …'[32] Although not usually considered Home Guard weapons, Brens were issued to 'front-line' units, in exposed positions and those working closely alongside the army. Charles 'Chas' Medhurst who, in late 1940, joined the Polgate Home Guard platoon, about five miles inland from Eastbourne, and directly in the path of the German 9th Army in the event of invasion, recalled that throughout his eighteen months' service with the Home Guard (he subsequently served with the Royal Navy) his unit at Polgate was equipped with .303 service rifles (SMLEs) and, shortly before he left in mid-1942, was in Coward's words 'obliged with a Bren gun'.[33] In fact Bren *guns* – an extraordinary investment when 'D' Company in Sevenoaks, only 32 miles inland, had only recently received BARs. Numbers of Bren guns in Home Guard service were always small – fifty-one appear in February 1942 (probably when Polgate Home Guard received theirs), and had slowly climbed to just 112 by November 1942.[34]

Lewis gun, BAR or Bren, the light automatic was important because it was a key component of British infantry tactics. As originally formed, the Local Defence Volunteers were riflemen roaming the countryside 'rounding up' Nazi paratroopers, but very quickly the Home Guard became conventional infantry, training to operate in 'battle platoons' consisting of a platoon headquarters and three eight-man squads. By the late summer of 1942, the organisation and armament of a 'battle platoon' was as follows:[35]

Battle platoon headquarters:-

Platoon commander	Pistol, Sten or rifle
Platoon serjeant [sic]	Rifle or shotgun and No. 36 grenades (rifle)
Runner	Rifle or shotgun
Rifle-bomber	E.Y. rifle, cup discharger and No. 36 grenades (rifle)
Sniper	Rifle

Three squads each consisting of:-

Rifle group

Squad commander	Sten
No. 1 Rifleman	Rifle
No. 1 Bomber	Grenades, shotgun, rifle or Sten
No. 2 Rifleman	Sten or rifle
No. 2 Bomber	Grenades, shotgun, rifle or Sten

BAR Group

Second-in-command	Rifle or shotgun
No. 1 on the BAR	BAR
No. 2 on the BAR	Rifle or shotgun

Division of the infantry squad into rifle group and gun group served the British Army well until the introduction of the selective-fire SA80 Individual Weapon in the 1990s, and depended on the volume of fire generated by the rifle group being matched by that of the gun group, which contained an effective long-range automatic weapon. *Home Guard Instruction No. 51* explained:[36]

> Where NO light automatic is available for the B.A.R. group. This group may be composed of three men armed with rifles. The B.A.R group can be increased by the three reserve men of the squad to increase its firepower. It might be called the Fire Group. If rifles are not available for the other part of the squad the men who will make the assault should be armed with Stens, shotguns and bombs. They might then be called the assault group. They must, however, have a rifle for the sniper who will have to cover the advance of the fire group.

As noted in the previous chapter, those individuals described as carrying a shotgun were those that *could*, rather than *would* be so armed. In military terms, shotguns are close-quarter weapons – which is why, if possible, they were grouped in the 'assault group'. The other close-quarter weapon that came to the Home Guard was the sub-machine gun – the .45in Thompson and, replacing it, the 9mm Sten. Sub-machine guns appeared at the end of the First World War, but failed to generate any interest from the British military, which regarded them as – at best – police weapons. This situation changed in 1940, and the British were soon searching for a 'machine carbine or gangster gun' (Hobart, 1973, p. 9). The only one immediately available was the original 'gangster gun', the American Model 1928 Thompson.[37] This was, in manufacturing terms, a deeply conventional weapon, finely finished and blued, and fitted with walnut furniture. Typical of a high-quality peacetime product aimed at the law enforcement market. An evolution from an unsuccessful self-loading rifle concept, the gun's delayed-blowback mechanism had failed with full-power US Army .30-06 ammunition. However, it did work with the other American service small arms ammunition, the low-velocity .45 Auto Colt Pistol (ACP) round. The result was a selective-fire, pistol-calibre weapon producing a large volume of fire at relatively short range. In this respect the Thompson was in the well-established 'machine pistol' category. Nevertheless, John Taliaferro Thompson[38] chose to invent a new category of firearm to assist with his marketing efforts – giving the world the term 'sub-machine gun' (Hobart, 1973, p. 33).[39] To further complicate matters, in wartime British nomenclature, this class of gun was officially known as a 'machine carbine', although the 'Tommy gun' was widely referred to as the 'TSMG'.[40] British orders for Thompson sub-machine guns commenced on 1 February 1940, with no quantities being recorded in the contract books (Skennerton, 1988, p. 44). Hobart (1973, p. 37) lists orders for two lots of 3,000 guns from the French government, and from the British – for a paltry 450 guns – both in February 1940. By the end of 1940 British orders had increased to 107,500 guns (Hobart, 1973, p. 37) and 514,000 by April 1942 (Skennerton, 1988, p. 44). Home Guard returns show the first thousand Thompsons arriving in April 1941, and numbers climbing to a peak of 43,017 one year later, after which they rapidly declined as the weapons were transferred to the Regular Army.[41]

Auto-Ordnance Corp. in the USA produced 217,420 Thompsons during 1940–41, mostly for export to Britain; of these, Hobart (1973, p. 38) states, 'over 100,000 were lost to U-boat sinkings in the Atlantic.' Given the desperate imperative to provide sub-machine guns to the British Army, and the fact that half of the guns ended up at the bottom of the Atlantic, that *any* were issued to the Home Guard must be taken as evidence of the importance of the Home Guard as a military force – to share such a scarce resource in desperate circumstances, cannot easily be dismissed as 'tokenism'. Indeed, once sufficient supplies of the mass-produced Sten 'machine carbine' were available in 1943, all Thompsons were withdrawn from the Home Guard and issued to Regular Army units. Like the Thompson, the Sten gun was an automatic weapon chambered for a foreign pistol cartridge – but there any similarity stopped. The Sten marked a complete departure from the conventional small arms that preceded it, and will, therefore, be considered in the next chapter, alongside the Home Guard's other unconventional weapons. The sub-machine gun was new, not just to the Home Guard, but to the British Army. However, adoption of the SMG into British service did not lead to a dramatic change in British tactics – no storm troopers or tank-rider battalions. Instead, it was integrated into the standard infantry section, and standard infantry tactics. This is not to suggest, however, that the British authorities failed to appreciate the SMG's advantages and limitations. A table in Home Guard Instruction No. 51 sets out the ranges of the various section weapons:[42]

	Maximum	*Best*
Rifles and Browning Automatics	400 yards	200 yards
Stens	50 yards	10–20 yards
Revolvers	40 yards	15 yards
Shotguns	40 yards	20 yards
LMG and MMG	500 yards	200–300 yards

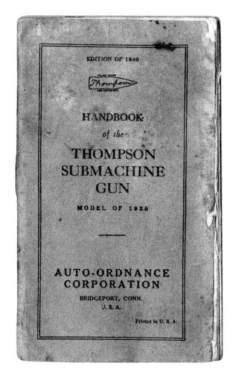

Left and opposite: The Thompson M1928 dismantled. This plate from *The Thompson Submachine Gun Mechanism Made Easy* shows the quality and relative complexity of the Thompson. (Inset) 1940 handbook as supplied with each 'Tommy Gun'. (Author's collection)

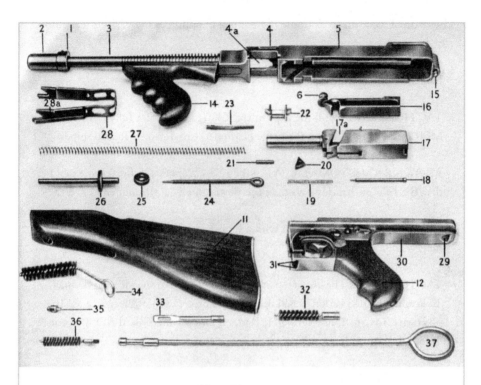

Plate III

1	*Foresight.*	
2	Cutts compensator.	
3	*Barrel.*	
4	Ejector.	
4a	Ejection port.	
5	*Body.*	
6	*Cocking handle.*	
11	*Butt.*	
12	*Pistol grip.*	
14	Fore grip.	
15	*Stud.*	
16	Actuator.	
17	*Bolt.*	
17a	Slot in bolt for H-piece.	
18	Firing pin.	
19	Firing pin spring.	
20	Hammer.	
21	Hammer pin.	
22	H-*piece.*	
23	Extractor.	
24	Recoil spring stripping tool.	
25	Buffer fibre disc.	
26	*Buffer.*	
27	Recoil spring.	
28	Breech oiler.	
28a	Breech oiler felt pads.	
29	Notch in frame for butt catch.	
30	Frame.	
31	Vertical grooves in frame for ribs of box magazine.	
*32	Barrel bristle brush, cleaning.	
*33	Cleaning rod brass loop, flannelette.	
34	Chamber cleaning bristle brush.	
*35	Cleaning rod adapter.	
*36	Barrel wire brush, cleaning.	
*37	Cleaning rod.	

* *Parts marked thus if not issued are replaced by pull-through and gauze. (See Note, p. 24.)*

The manual went on to examine the tactical handling of the various weapons:

THE RIFLE. Flat trajectory up to 400 yards. Good accuracy in hands of well-trained man.

TACTICAL USE. To fill the gaps in the killing ground not fully covered by MMGs and LMGs. To arm the battle platoon as laid down ... To arm snipers.

BROWNING AUTOMATIC. As for the rifle, except that its fire is more rapid than the rifle, so that it is a waste of fire power to give it to a sniper.

STENS. A light handy weapon with a high rate of fire and accuracy at short ranges.

TACTICAL USE. The use of the Sten may be likened to an extended bayonet. To arm the battle platoon as laid down ... To protect sub-artillery and MMG positions. To arm DRs [Dispatch Riders] and Home Guard MT [Motor Transport] companies.

SHOTGUNS. An effective man-killing short range weapon ...

TACTICAL HANDLING. ... [The] spread with SG and LG make the shotgun a peculiarly suitable and effective weapon for night patrols, and ambushes. By day it may be used to supplement the close range defence of sub-artillery positions.

REVOLVERS. Short-range rapid fire. Only accurate in hands of experienced shot.

TACTICAL HANDLING. To arm battle platoons as laid down. To arm officers and DRs (if they prefer them to Stens).

MMGs [Medium Machine Guns] and LMGs [Light Machine Guns]. These guns have the highest sustained rate of fire of any weapon with which the Home Guard is armed. The effective beaten zone of the bullets is long and narrow. MMGs are not very mobile. LMGs are more so, but both weapons are best reserved for the defences of the localities; light automatics being used for patrols.

TACTICAL HANDLING. MMGs and LMGs should be sited to fire enfilade so that the maximum number of the attackers will be within the beaten zone in any one burst. They are less easy to conceal than rifles and automatics, so should, when possible, be defiladed from the enemy.

The ranges given for medium machine guns are extremely short, considering that the tripod-mounted guns issued to the Home Guard were theoretically capable of effective fire out to 3,300yd with American M1 ball ammunition.[43] In Home Guard tactical doctrine, the medium machine gun served solely to stiffen the defence. Minor tactics, in terms of section or platoon attacks, or patrols, did not envisage the use of the MMG as fire support. Officially this was due to the weapon's lack of mobility, but there were also issues of communication – given that the Home Guard only received wireless sets from mid-1942[44] – and accuracy, as the guns issued were only fitted with iron sights, and firing on fixed lines or at registered targets were not practiced.[45]

The eclectic selection of automatic weapons provided to the Home Guard from the US reserve stockpile was a reflection of the fact that, although many of the great automatic weapon promoters and designers of the late nineteenth and early twentieth century were Americans – Maxim, Lewis, Browning, and the eponymous founder of Hotchkiss *et Cie* – the history of rifle-calibre machine guns in US service is not a happy one. The keen reader is directed to the Collector Grade series of monographs listed below in references, but it is enough to note that vested interests, nepotism, doctrinal confusion, low-quality mass production, and a very powerful service cartridge combined to ensure that the US forces never really had a truly successful infantry machine gun until the belated adoption of the Belgian FN MAG 58 as the M240 series in the late 1980s.[46] This is not to say that the guns were poor; rather that they never quite achieved the success that was anticipated, and the Americans swiftly moved on to the next latest design. They were, though, designs of weapons used successfully by other nations, and all quite suitable for the kind of intensive, but short, defensive battle envisaged for the Home Guard.

The US Army adopted Colt-built Vickers machine guns in 1915, to replace the M1909 Benét–Mercié Machine Rifle, the American version of the Hotchkiss light machine gun already described. Replacing a light machine gun with a heavy and bulky medium machine gun led to complaints from the troops, and shoddy First World War manufacturing, together with the high pressures developed by the .30-06 cartridge, resulted in the Vickers gun developing a reputation for unreliability in US service. This cleared the way for adoption of a new recoil-operated, water-cooled machine gun designed by Browning, and designated the Gun, Machine, Caliber .30, Browning M1917. Performance of the two guns is generally agreed to have been similar, but the Browning was American-designed, and cheaper and easier to manufacture (Goldsmith, 1994, p. 212). The Americans were keen to replace the Vickers with the Browning, and as soon as production was established, the US government's Vickers guns were either converted into aircraft machine guns or placed in reserve. The British, on the other hand, who had adopted the Vickers in 1912, found the combination of gun and .303in cordite-propelled bullet a perfect match. The British Mk I Vickers MMG remained in service until 1968, enjoying a reputation for reliability that was second-to-none. Thus, while the Americans were relieved to get rid of their stock of Vickers guns, the British were delighted to receive them. 7,071 US M1915 Vickers machine guns were supplied to the UK in 1940–41 (Goldsmith, 1994, p. 229). In February 1941, 124 aircraft guns and 832 ground-role versions were with the Home Guard. By January 1942, American ground role Vickers machine guns in Home Guard use had peaked at 1,405, but aircraft guns had fallen to fifty-one.[47] Vickers aircraft guns would have overheated very quickly in the ground role, as ventilating slots were cut in the barrel casing to enable the aircraft's slipstream to cool the gun. This meant they could not hold water, as required on the ground, and it is most likely that they were converted back to ground role specification by replacing or patching their casings. It is also a comparatively straightforward matter to convert Vickers guns from one calibre to another.[48] Of the M1915 Vickers supplied to the UK, 1,000 were converted to .303-calibre at RSAF Enfield Lock between July 1942 and January 1944 (Skennerton, 1988, p. 47).[49] By the end of 1942 there were just seventy-six US Vickers aircraft guns and 130 ground-role guns showing on Home Guard returns, but the number of .303 Vickers had rapidly increased from just two in May 1941 to 655. What is interesting is that during the 'darkest days' of 1940–41 *all* these easily converted Vickers machine guns were kept in the 'Home Guard calibre' of .300 (.30-06) – once again reinforcing the importance attached to providing good automatic weapons for the Home Guard.

The Browning water-cooled machine gun, which supplanted the American Vickers, served as the US infantry support machine gun from 1918 until the end of the Korean War. Its air-cooled derivative, the M1919, remained in action worldwide into the 1990s. The Second World War US Army M1917A1 Browning differed from the original M1917, as supplied to the Home Guard, in a few small modifications – chiefly a strengthening bracket riveted across the bottom of the receiver. This was a response to a problem with the receiver side plates parting under the pressure of sustained fire with powerful .30-06 rounds for prolonged periods of sustained fire – not an issue likely to affect Home Guard facing German invaders, who would probably be fighting a short, sharp and bloody battle. To all intents and purposes the 'BMG' was a weapon the Home Guard shared with the US armed forces. M1917 Brownings in British service are generally seen mounted on the M1918 tripod, a rather sophisticated device, which incorporated fine traverse and elevation adjustments, flexible leg joints – to ensure the gun was perfectly level on uneven or sloping ground – and the use of light alloys to keep the weight manageable. All this sophistication was a luxury, and although there is nothing inherently wrong with the M1918 tripod, it was another example of America's muddled and wasteful machine gun procurement policy.[50] The opportunity to clear such embarrassments out the stores, and benefit financially, was seized in 1940 (Goldsmith, 2008, p. 58). *Home Guard Instruction No. 26-1941, Miscellaneous Notes* makes it clear that M1917 and M1917A1 tripods were also in Home Guard service, the former having its own instructions, the latter being covered in *Instruction No. 26*. The M1917A1 tripod was the version in current use with US forces.

The 1940 British instruction manual for the M1917 Browning sought to accentuate the similarity between the Browning and Vickers medium guns, because of the familiarity old soldiers would have with the British Vickers.[51] However, the Browning won the respect of the Home Guard in its own right; Graves (1943) states that the Browning was preferred to the Vickers:

> Home Guard in Cornwall: On September 18th [1940] machine guns were issued at last. The general opinion is that the Browning MG is a much better weapon than the Vickers …

Polgate Home Guard, on the Sussex Coast, had a 'BMG' in late 1940, while 'D' Company, in Sevenoaks, 32 miles inland, only received theirs in July 1943 (Brown and Peek, 1944, p. 25).[52] There were already 4,331 Browning machine guns in Home Guard service in February 1941, a figure that reached 6,330 in November 1942.[53] The gun weighed 30lb and the tripod approximately 45lb. Each 250-round belt of ammunition weighed 14½lb, and seven pints of cooling water added another 6¾lb of weight to be carried by the team – a load that frequently led Home Guard units to improvise trailers for their BMG.[54] Interestingly, in view of the dire situation usually depicted, former Home Guard Browning gunner

Charles Medhurst could not recall there being any shortage of .300 ammunition for the BMG – indeed, he remembered regular firings with the gun on the Downs at Willingdon.[55]

The other American 'heavy' machine gun[56] supplied to the Home Guard, and displayed in the September 1940 'march past' photograph (see plate 17), is the M1918 Marlin-Rockwell tank machine gun. A derivative of J.M. Browning's first automatic weapon design, the Colt–Browning Model 1895 'Gas Hammer' machine gun, the Marlin-Rockwell, and various related guns, saw service with the Home Guard, although chiefly in anti-aircraft roles. The original M1895 design tapped off gas near the muzzle which impinged on an arm that swung down and to the rear, reloading the gun. It was the action of this arm which earned the M1895 its soubriquet of 'Potato-digger'. Eccentric as the M1895 mechanism appears, it actually worked rather well, to quote Hogg and Weeks:

> However odd this action may appear there is no doubt that, owing to the mechanical linkage it produced a very progressive and gentle movement of the bolt which gave particularly effective and clean extraction and kept the rate of fire down to a practical value. (1973, p. 5.69)

Production of the Colt-Browning machine gun was passed to Marlin-Rockwell in 1916, and under their auspices Colt's improved M1914 design received a series of further modifications and improvements, including replacing the distinctive 'gas-hammer' with a conventional piston and cylinder. When the United States went to war in 1917, the gun was already in use by the Italians and Russians, US, Canadians and British, in various versions (Ballou, 200, pp. 44–5).[57] As a result of the urgent need for machine guns, several models were introduced into US service, including the M1917 improved ground machine gun, the M1916, M1917 and M1918 aircraft machine guns, and the M1918 tank machine gun.

The original Colt 'Potato-digger' is one of those quirky designs, like the Madsen LMG,[58] that turns up in odd places – one being London District, where thirteen 'Colt machine guns' appeared in the Home Guard returns in June 1941. This is undoubtedly what Charles Graves is describing in *Home Guard of Britain* (1943):[59]

> 34th County of London Battalion, Home Guard: About this time [1941] a parcel of forty heavy Colt guns were received as a gift from an American

friend, and having these and a good number of personnel of a disbanded unit they were organised as an MG Company to man river defence block-houses commanding the Thames river. Soon after they grew into battalion size, and were absorbed into 'R' Zone. Their training had been given to them by Grenadier Guards sergeants who, considering that the Colt guns were new to them, did a remarkably efficient job. It is not generally known that a machine gun battalion equipped with 1914 Colt machine guns served in World War Two, even though they never saw combat.

Inevitably our attention is drawn to the age of the guns – ignoring the fact that this vintage is two years younger than the service Vickers machine gun. As described, the number of 'Colts' with the Home Guard shot up to ninety-eight in March 1942, fifty-four of which were in London District.[60] Analysis of the statistics is not helped by the returns simply listing 'Colt machine guns' (Marlin guns were listed separately), which, in theory, could cover anything that the Colts ever manufactured, from the somewhat antediluvian M1895 to the modern MG38B (a successful commercial derivative of the water-cooled M1917).[61] If this is a problem for the modern researcher, it was too for those trying to keep track of American weapons in British service at the time. On 25 July 1942, the Assistant Director of Small Arms and Ammunition, Inspection Board of United Kingdom and Canada, in Washington, DC, submitted a report, listing the various Browning derivatives (including BAR types, aircraft and .50in calibre weapons), the user guide or manual appropriate to the weapon, and the mount. The report's author explained:

1. A large number of different types of Browning Machine Guns have been shipped from North America to the UK during the period 1939–1942. In the first place, old war-stock batches, received from US government sources, and in the second place, odd lots from other sources were shipped. These included a number of early types of both commercial and US service weapons. In the third place, British contracts placed with firms in the USA led to the production of a number of commercial type weapons. Subsequently, as these contracts were converted to, or superseded by, Lend–Lease contracts, deliveries of commercial weapons were succeeded by deliveries of standard US service weapons.

2. Not infrequently difficulty is experienced in identifying these various Browning Machine Guns on account of the facts that:

    a.   Some of them are called Colt guns and some Brownings.

    b.   Some of them are gas operated and some recoil operated.

    c.   Some of them are automatic rifles, with or without bipod mountings, and some machine guns, medium or heavy.

    d.   Some of them are air-cooled and some water-cooled.

    e.   Some of them are fixed type [aircraft] guns and some flexible type.

    f.   Some of them are commercial type guns and some standard US service weapons.

3.   To clarify the situation, the attached tables of the various Colt-Browning Machine Guns of 0.30 inch and 0.50 inch calibres and their mountings have been drawn up so as to indicate the correct nomenclature of, and relationship between, each.

4.   As a general rule, though a number of these weapons have been made by firms other than Colt's Patent Fire Arms Manufacturing Company, the majority of them were in the first place manufactured by that firm, and all of them were made chiefly to Browning Patents. Consequently these guns have become known under both names, Colt and Browning. Strictly speaking, however, the term 'Colt' should be reserved for the commercial models and the name 'Browning' applied only to the service models, except in the case of the 1914 Colt gas operated machine gun, and the later models derived from it, the service models of which are termed Colt M1914, Colt M1917 and Marlin M1917.

5.   Many of the later models of commercial weapons are of similar design to the latest types of US service weapons, but the commercial guns are generally made to commercial drawings and inspected to commercial standards, while the US service weapons are made to US Ordnance drawings and inspected to US Ordnance standards. Consequently the components of the former, though often of the same design as those of the latter, cannot be regarded as fully interchangeable with them, except in the case of the Colt MG40-2, MG52-2 and MG53-2 Machine Guns, which are in fact the same as the Cal. .30 Aircraft M2, the Cal. .50 Watercooled M2, and the Cal. .50 Aircraft M2 Browning Machine Guns, respectively, with which they should have full interchangeability of parts. (Cited in Goldsmith, 2006, p. 74)

The US Army purchased 1,470 Marlin-Rockwell ground-role guns during the First World War, all of which were used only in training. More widely successful were the tank gun, and the aircraft variant of which 38,000 were built, some seeing operational use in 1918 (Easterly, 1998, p. 247). Although a serviceable machine gun, the Marlin was eclipsed by Browning's later recoil-operated machine guns, and was relegated to the reserve. In a memorandum to the War Cabinet of 29 August 1940, UK Minister of Supply, Herbert Morrison, stated that the Americans had supplied 2,600 'tank machine guns', by which he probably meant Marlin-Rockwell M1918 guns. The minister went on to point out that owing to all the American small arms being in a different calibre, they would have to be 'issued to the Home Guard or fixed defensive posts'.[62] The M1917/18 Marlin is not, though, widely seen in Home Guard service, and, like the Hotchkiss LMG, most of the guns were used by the Merchant Navy in the light anti-aircraft role (Hogg and Weeks, 1973, p. 5.69). Marlins only appear in Home Guard returns in February 1942, with 594 guns recorded, a quantity that had only climbed to 1,451 by November 1942.[63] It is likely that the majority of these guns were in the anti-aircraft role, for factory defence (see Chapter 9).

We have already established that it was neither possible, nor necessarily desirable in terms of the overall war effort, to provide a rifle for all 1,600,000-plus Home Guards; furthermore, the issue of rifles favoured those areas most directly threatened. Nevertheless, it is quite clear that the Home Guard *was* under-armed, and gaps in the armament of the battle platoons existed which needed to be plugged by issuing grenades, sub-machine guns and shotguns – as well as taking advantage of the American medium machine gun windfall. It is difficult to take serious issue with the way in which these weapons were deployed. What emerges is the thoughtful use of limited resources. It is useful to bear in mind Peter Fleming's comments on the deployment of the Home Guard:

> ... it was a largely static force and it would therefore be misleading to assess its operational influence on the invasion – had it been launched – in terms of its total strength; for the attack on south-east England would initially have had to overcome opposition only from those Home Guard units whose homes lay in its path. The battalions in Belfast, Glasgow, Cardiff, Bristol, Liverpool, Manchester and other places remote from the decisive battlefield about the capital might have seen action; but by the time German troops came within range of their rifles the issue would have been decided ... (1957, p. 205)

This factor clearly influenced planning, and the distribution of resources. It is quite apparent that the type and quantity of weapons and ammunition supplied to Home Guard units varied between those directly 'in harm's way', such as the Polgate Home Guard in Sussex, and those in less immediately threatened areas. Furthermore, those with the unenviable task of distributing weapons took the Home Guard sufficiently seriously to issue a significant quantity of automatic weapons which, far from being 'cast-offs', could all have found vital work with the army, Royal Navy, Merchant Navy, or defending aerodromes.

MACHINE GUNS IN HOME GUARD SERVICE[64]

	February 1941	March 1942	November 1942
Hotchkiss LMG		124	323
Lewis LMG (.303)		121	195
Lewis LMG (.30)	2,277	2,642	3,282
Lewis LMG (.30) (air)	11,598	12,397	12,393
Bren LMG		61	112
Vickers MMG (.30)	737	1,007	130
Vickers MMG (.30) (air)	236	326	76
Vickers MMG (.303)		250	655
Browning MMG	4,331	5,283	6,330
Marlin MMG		918	1,451
Colt MMG		98	80
Hispano 20mm HMG		71	81
Other MGs	1,250	26	67

1. Two serving members of 32 (Surrey) Battalion, Home Guard, pose for photographer J.A. Porter to illustrate the transformation of Britain's Second World War civilian militia over the four and a half years of its existence from the Local Defence Volunteers of May 1940, armed with little more than a brassard and a sense of purpose, to the well-equipped and well-trained (and, in many cases, conscripted) Home Guard at 'stand-down' in November 1944. (IWM HU 18501)

2. The author fires an ex-Home Guard M1917 rifle in a military-style competition course of fire at the National Shooting Centre, Bisley. The next firer on the point is using a Canadian Ross, another rifle used in extremis by the British in 1940. (Dr J. Butler)

3. *Fallschirmjäger*, as shown in the British manual *The German Army in Pictures*, published by department MI14 at the War Office, in January 1941. (Author's collection)

4. Two images of German paratroopers from *Home Guard Instruction No. 3* published in October 1940. The illustration on the right shows the *Fallschirmjäger* recovering their weapons container, the point in the landing when they were considered to be most vulnerable to counter-attack by the Home Guard. The Home Guard were expected to know how to operate German weapons, in case they were able to capture a container. (Author's collection)

5. The Rifle, Short, Magazine Lee–Enfield (SMLE) was the Home Guard weapon of choice. This example is a Mk III manufactured in 1911, but the wooden furniture is typical of a Second World War rebuild. Also shown are examples of LDV/Home Guard literature from the early period, ball ammunition in chargers, brass oil bottle and flannelette and a 'War Grade' beer bottle used for Molotov cocktails. (Author's photograph)

6. In the absence of sufficient rifles, dummies, antiques or broom handles could at least be used to learn or revise the principles of rifle drill. This rare survivor is stamped with the address of the retailer, Gamages department store in the City of London. It is displayed with a late-pattern (khaki) LDV brassard. (Author's photograph)

7. The Canadian .303in Ross rifle on the ranges at Bisley. This Mk 3 may well be one of the 75,000 purchased by the UK in 1940, as the only Ross adopted by the British Army was the Mk 3B, which was fitted with a magazine cut-off. (Author's photograph)

8. The M1917 rifle, the definitive Home Guard personal weapon from late 1940 to late 1943. US-supplied accessories included the 'NobuckL' sling, bayonet, and cleaning kit-cum-oil bottle with pull-through and bristle brush. Also .300 drill round, with a .303 drill round for comparison, and one of the distinctive Home Guard ammunition pouches. Each rifleman was issued with fifty rounds of .300 (.30"-'06) ammunition, here displayed using inert rounds and empty cases. (Author's photograph)

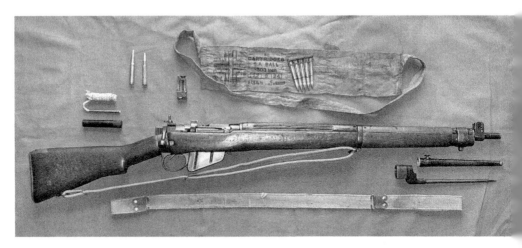

9. A US-manufactured No. 4 Mk I* Lee–Enfield. The Mk I sight was slow to manufacture, resulting in the introduction of the L-shaped Mk II battle sight. Other items are Bakelite oil bottle, pull-through, a .300 round for comparison, Mk VI .303 round, fifty-round bandolier, and a charger of five Mk VII .303 rounds. Beneath the 37-pattern webbing sling is a cotton and plastic 'austerity' sling, and spike bayonet. (Author's photograph)

10. A 12-bore brass cased 'Lethal Ball' round by Kynoch (left) and ½in shrapnel ball. (Author's photograph)

11. A Home Guard grenade thrower in the Bapty collection. This highly evolved design consists of an obsolete Martini rifle action (mounted with its trigger guard towards the camera), to which has been attached a standard issue grenade launching cup for the No. 36M grenade (Mills Bomb), the whole being adjustable for elevation and traverse, and mounted on a spiked base plate. (Bapty 2000 Ltd; author's photograph)

12. Hertfordshire Home Guards firing a homemade 3in mortar, from *Training Course for Home Guard Instructors*. The shoulder tabs and lack of area markings suggest this picture was taken early- to mid-1941, when homemade ordnance was, supposedly, being suppressed in favour of official 'sub-artillery'. The officer on the right of the picture is probably Lieutenant (later Captain) C.A. Marques MBE, designer of the 3in mortar and bombs illustrated. (Author's collection)

13. A Lewis Mk IV light machine gun. Built during the First World War as a Mk I infantry LMG, this gun was converted into a Mk III aircraft machine gun, then rebuilt during the Second World War as a ground-role gun. Mk IV guns had a Bren gun-type coil return spring exiting through a hole in the rear of the receiver. (Infantry and SASC Collection; author's photograph)

14. The BAR (Browning Automatic Rifle) was a signature Home Guard arm, serving as the squad light-support weapon. Automatic fire was at first discouraged, later forbidden, due to the lack of a quick-change barrel or bipod. For accuracy, the gun was rested on cover, as shown, with Ross rifle-armed Home Guards, on a 'rifle range in the North', 24 September 1940. (IWM HU 86079)

15. BAR ancillaries including a cotton 'bandoleer' for sixty rounds of .30 ammunition and the provisional BAR manual, issued on a scale of one per gun from 28 August 1940, as well as an unofficial Gale and Polden guide. The distinctive Home Guard ammunition pouches (left) each held two BAR magazines (left and centre), as well as twenty rounds of rifle ammunition. (Author's photograph)

16. Home Guards on the green, Dorking, Surrey, 1 December 1940. It is interesting to note that Dorking Home Guard, on a direct line between the planned German landing beaches and the capital, are (apparently) armed with a Mk I Bren light machine gun and a Thompson sub-machine gun, when many other Home Guard units were still waiting for .300 calibre rifles. (IWM 5844)

17. Home Guard march past with new American weapons, 11 September 1940. (L–R) M1918 Marlin tank machine gun; M1915 Vickers; M1917 Lewis gun; Browning M1917 machine gun; M1918 BAR. Behind the BAR a Home Guard is carrying a tripod; behind him is what appears to be a Hotchkiss LMG, or possibly the US version, the model 1909 Benét-Mercié. (IWM H 4058)

18. The M1917 Browning machine gun in British service, taken from the Gale and Polden booklet *The Browning Heavy Machine Gun .300 calibre model 1919 (water cooled) Mechanism Made Easy*, published in 1942. The firer is a Regular Army instructor, and the gun is mounted on the M1918 tripod. Note that the pistol grip is held with the left hand, while the right is used to adjust elevation and traverse. (Author's collection)

19. A Colt Model 1895 'Potato Digger' in the Infantry and Small Arms School Corps Collection. Odd and old-fashioned, these guns actually functioned very well and several were used in blockhouses to defend the River Thames. (Infantry and SASC Collection; author's photograph)

20, 21. An incomplete early Marlin-Rockwell 'Colt M1917' machine gun in the Bapty collection. Note the gas cylinder below the barrel (top), which replaced the swinging arm of the original Potato Digger. The style of sight (below) indicates this particular gun was intended for ground-role use. The metal loop is the cocking handle; the pistol grip and trigger are missing from the rear of this example. (Courtesy of Bapty 2000; author's photograph)

22. Sten Mk I*. Over 100,000 were produced, and the gun saw service with some Home Guard units.

23. Sten Mk II. The definitive wartime Sten. Unlike the Mk I, which was only produced in relatively small numbers (by Sten standards), over 2 million Mk IIs were produced, and this was the version most widely featured in the various unofficial manuals.

25. An EY rifle prepared by Mark Dinely's 'Berwick St. John Arsenal' for his Home Guard platoon (stamped on butt). Note the lack of magazine, strengthening bolt below the breech and cord binding to the fore end. Conversion of what had been a Drill Purpose (DP) rifle to an EY grenade launcher was making excellent use of an unserviceable weapon. (Reproduced by kind permission of Bapty & Co. Ltd; author's photograph)

26. No. 247 'Bakelite' or 'All-ways' fuse dismantled. The safety cap (top) has been unscrewed from the fuse body (bottom), and the closing cap (second from top) removed. The concave underside of the closing cap is visible, which ensured that the fuse still operated if the grenade struck side-on. Below the closing cap is the ball, and below that the pronged striker (missing its creep spring); below the striker is the cap pellet. (Author's photograph)

27. Released in July 1943, this official photograph is one of series showing the manufacture of ST grenades, 'just off the secret list', at Kay Brothers' Kayborough Works. Mrs Colman (nearest camera), Miss Brearley and their colleague are fitting 'woollen jackets' (which held the sticky glue) to each of the 2½ million grenades manufactured by the works. (Official photograph; author's collection)

28. A War Office training team demonstrates a Mk I Northover Projector to members of Saxmundham Home Guard, 30 July 1941. The mount could be set much lower in operational use. The photograph illustrates the white smoke 'signature' generated by the Northover's gunpowder propelling charge. (IWM H12293)

29. 'Men of the 2nd Gordon Highlanders demonstrate the Northover Projector to Major General F. Keith Simmons, GOC Singapore Fortress, and other senior officers, 17 October 1941.' Evidence of Regular Army use of the Northover Projector from a most unexpected direction. (IWM FE15)

30. At first sight quintessentially Home Guard, but actually a naval weapon, the Mk I (compressed air) Holman Projector being demonstrated to a group of Royal Marines in July 1942. Note the anti-aircraft sight. A similar projector was emplaced to protect coastal defence guns at Tynemouth Castle. This example is mounted on a naval 12-pounder gun limber. Mk II projectors were steam powered; the Mk III was self-loading, but not placed in production. (Official photograph; author's collection)

31. 'Members of the Post Office Home Guard receiving lessons on how to load the Spigot Mortar, 21st June 1943.' (Official photograph; author's collection)

32. Regular Army troops man a 29mm Spigot Mortar on its mobile mounting in a weapon pit – an illustration from the 1942 manual. It is clear from this picture why the Spigot Mortar's legs needed to be both strong and long. In action great efforts were made to camouflage the position and thus preserve the element of surprise. (Author's collection)

33. A Spigot Mortar detachment in position using a concrete pedestal mounting. The ammunition number (right) is removing a drill round from the concrete roofed ammunition store, another of which is situated to the bottom centre of the picture. From the manual of 1942. (Author's collection)

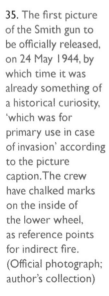

34. Spigot Mortar pedestals are the most enduring memorial to the Home Guard, with hundreds, possibly thousands, still existing throughout the UK. Typically the pit has long since been backfilled, as in this example excavated by the author in woods near Churchill's residence at Chartwell, but the concrete holdfast and stainless steel pivot remain in surprisingly sound condition. (Author's photograph)

35. The first picture of the Smith gun to be officially released, on 24 May 1944, by which time it was already something of a historical curiosity, 'which was for primary use in case of invasion' according to the picture caption. The crew have chalked marks on the inside of the lower wheel, as reference points for indirect fire. (Official photograph; author's collection)

36. Bognor Regis sea front, defended by a 6-pounder 6cwt tank gun on an extemporised field carriage with wire spoke motor-car wheels. The photograph appears to show live firing in progress, with an ammunition number standing by with the next round (centre) and an officer spotting the fall of shot (centre right). (Via Peter Hamblin, Military Vehicle Trust)

37. 29 March 1942: 'Members of 1st Battalion (Exeter) Home Guard training with an 18 pounder field gun at Okehampton Range.' The pole trail limited the extent to which the gun could be elevated, thus curbing the range of the 18-pounder Mks I, I* and II. (IWM H18273)

38. 'Gun crews of the Southern Railway Home Guard anti-tank unit running to their guns for action during firing practice at Army ranges in Kent. August 6th 1943.' The Home Guard gunners are running to 'take post' on QF 75mm 'S' Mk 2* guns (American split-trail M1916s fitted with pneumatic tyres). The range is the coastal artillery training depot at Lydd. (Official photograph; author's collection)

39. **Above:** Home Guards march past a twin No. 2 Mk I 'Z' mounting, March 1944. The original caption states: 'The intense barrage put up by the "projectors" is ... used to combat enemy air attacks and it has proved very effective, a number of enemy aircraft having been destroyed ... Home Guards, under Anti-Aircraft Command ... enable regular soldiers to be released for active service on other fronts.' (Official photograph; author's collection)

40. **Below:** Newly manufactured Beaverette Mk II. (Author's Collection)

41. **Above:** Detail from a group photograph of an unnamed Home Counties factory Home Guard unit flanked by their Hispano-Suiza 20mm light anti-aircraft guns. The rather agricultural but undeniably effective nature of the mounting, which converts this aircraft cannon into a ground-based gun, is noteworthy – as is the fact that these Home Guards in reserve occupations are of a reasonable military age: dads, but not granddads. (Author's collection)

6

STEN GUNS, PETROLEUM WARFARE AND GRENADES

The contention that the Home Guard was equipped with 'weapons which in reality were of dubious fighting value, but which in all probability would never have to be fired in anger and could be presented as worthwhile' bears heaviest on the unconventional and emergency weapons developed during the desperate days of 1940 and placed in production via unorthodox routes, frequently, it is claimed, at the insistence of the prime minister (MacKenzie, 1996, passim). The extent to which these extemporised weapons were used by forces other than the Home Guard is an important test of that hypothesis. So too is an understanding of the real capability these weapons offered, in order to determine if they were indeed of 'dubious fighting value'.

Of all the unconventional weapons developed for Home Defence, those most closely associated with the Home Guard are the 'sub-artillery'. Where this term originated is now unclear, but it was used, from 1941, in official publications, to describe a small group of unconventional support/anti-armour weapons eventually comprising the Northover Projector, the Blacker Bombard and the Smith Gun. These weapons, and a selection of grenades graced with soubriquets such as the 'Woolworths Bomb', the 'Sticky Bomb' and the 'Talcum Powder Grenade', will forever be associated with the Home Guard, and – at first sight – appear to support the contention that the organisation's armoury was, at best, whimsical and optimistic, and at worst (to borrow a phrase from the American Civil War), 'liable to do as much execution to the shooter as the shootee'. In this and the following chapter we will examine these equipments and challenge this view. However, first, we must continue where we left off at the end of the last chapter, by examining the most successful of all the unconventional weapons developed by the British in the early stages of the Second World War – the Sten gun.

K.R. Gulvin (1980, p. 24) comments: 'Although intended as a Home Guard weapon, the Sten was later in general issued to the Field Army …' Heart-warming as it is to read an association of the Home Guard with a successful development in weaponry, Gulvin falls into the trap of confusing 'Home Defence' with 'Home Guard'. Home Defence forces included the 'Field Force' (army) and airfield defence forces, as well as the Home Guard, all with a desperate need for weapons. Stens first entered service with the Regular Army in the latter part of 1941 (Laidler and Howroyd, 1995), and were issued to the Home Guard from March 1942, at which point Thompson sub-machine guns were withdrawn and issued to the army. Curiously, Longmate suggests that this occurred as early as 1941:

> In 1941 Tommy guns were no sooner issued than they were withdrawn again for use by the Commandoes; but soon afterwards the Home Guard received a new automatic weapon, the Sten … (1974, p. 75)

Thompsons were certainly still in service with Kent Home Guard in August 1942, as they are specified on the HQ Company, 20th Bn, training programme of 26 August (Brown and Peek, 1944, p. 22). Their first reference to the Sten is in January 1943 (Brown and Peek, 1944, p. 23). The changeover is reflected in the Home Guard returns, which show that in November 1942, 12,895 Thompsons were in use by the Home Guard, but that figure was just half the previous month's total, indicating that the guns were being rapidly withdrawn.[1]

Stens had arrived eight months earlier, with 7,914 appearing suddenly in the Home Guard returns for March 1942. The first areas to receive them were Northern, Scottish, Southern and Western Commands. The following month there were 72,929 Stens with the Home Guard, distributed nationwide – an astonishing rate of production and introduction. By November the figure had almost reached a quarter of a million – 248,234.[2] Sten guns eventually made up 40 per cent of the Home Guard armoury, and were greeted, as we have seen, with enthusiasm by those who appreciated that the gun represented a healthy new utilitarian approach (Longmate, 1974, p. 75). They were brutally simple, poorly finished with dangerous characteristics, but undeniably effective, cheap and simple to manufacture – the BSA factory at Tysley was able to assemble 47,000 Sten guns in a single week in 1943 (Laidler and Howroyd, 1995, p. 7).

Sten gun aide memoir 'strictly reserved for use in the Home Guard', published by the Bravon Ledger Company in September 1942, when there were already 225,656 of the new guns in Home Guard service. (Author's collection)

The first request from the BEF for a 'machine carbine or gangster gun' had been back in December 1939, to which the Board of Ordnance responded by supplying seven sub-machine guns for trials.[3] In January 1940 the Board had tested a 'Schmeisser'. The gun was of 7.65mm calibre, and must have been an example of the Hugo Schmeisser-designed MP28. The MP28/II design was, as its nomenclature suggests, already 12 years old when tested by the Board, and was a modification of the MP18/I that had entered service with German storm troops in the final months of the First World War. Production had been undertaken in Belgium since 1934, and the weapon had been adopted by Belgian forces, as well as enjoying sales to Portugal, China, Japan and various South and Central American countries, including Bolivia. The British, testing the gun in January 1940, were, therefore, considerably 'behind the curve'.

MP28s saw little Second World War German service, generally with garrison troops, security police or *Volkssturm*. It was replaced in production by the pressed steel, folding stock MP38, a captured example of which was tested by the British in July 1940. Initially referred to as the 'German parachutists' machine carbine', the Erma-built MP38 was subsequently referred to by the Board (and the rest of the world) as the 'Schmeisser', despite having no connection with the designer, and giving rise to considerable potential for confusion.[4] Seven months had elapsed since the British Army had urgently requested machine carbines, without any tangible result, so although the American Thompson sub-machine gun did not use standard UK ammunition, and although they cost a hefty £50 each, the Thompson was adopted for army and Home Guard use. In August 1940, with the army apparently satisfied with Thompsons en route, the Admiralty requested 10,000 copies of the 'Schmeisser' (MP28), and the Air Ministry, having been impressed by the 'folding stock Schmeisser' (MP38), requested 10,000 copies of the more modern gun.

Eventually it was agreed to produce 50,000 British versions of the MP28/II (Hobart, 1973, pp. 71 and 73). At first sight it seems perverse to have opted for this over the modern and popular MP38, however, the shaping of a wooden stock was straightforward, and the receiver was a simple piece of seamless tube, extending the full length of the gun to hold the barrel securely and provide a forward hand grip. The barrel and trigger mechanism presented no particular challenges, and the gun was therefore quicker and easier to get into production than the MP38, which would require more complex tooling. Adopting standard UK .380in (9x17mm) pistol calibre was abandoned due to poor penetration, and it was agreed that the weapon would fire the 'enemy' 9x19mm Parabellum round (there was a precedent, as the BESA tank machine gun fired the Continental 7.92mm '8mm Mauser' round) (Laidler and Howroyd, 1995, p. 4). Production was given to the Sterling Engineering Co. Ltd of Dagenham.

Seconded to Sterling was automotive engineer George Lanchester, one of the owners of the eponymous motorcar company, and successful designer of armoured cars. Lanchester and Sterling were tasked by the Ministry of Supply to get the '9mm Schmeisser Carbine' in production as quickly as possible. Test firing was carried out in November 1940, with the production order for 50,000 guns at £14 each being issued in June 1941. One might expect that Britain's first domestically produced, and rather old-fashioned, sub-machine gun would be issued to the Home Guard, but almost the entire production went to the Royal Navy, with whom the gun remained in service until the 1960s. A few were used by British troops in India, but the urgent requirements of Home Defence notwithstanding, Lanchesters went to sea (Laidler and Howroyd, 1995, p. 7). The army, as we have seen, put its faith in the Thompson, and shared their precious weapons with the Home Guard. This, perhaps more than anything else, demonstrates the seriousness with which the arming of the Home Guard was viewed.

The gun on which the MP28 and its derivatives, including the Lanchester, was based, the German MP18/I, had been developed in the final months of the First World War and was an *ersatz* design, intended to be manufactured cheaply and easily. The improved peacetime MP28/II was rather more luxurious and carefully constructed, but its heritage remained – hence the use of a tube for the receiver, rather than one machined from a solid steel billet. This commended itself to wartime manufacture, but Enfield designer H.J. Turpin believed the original concept could be taken further. In January 1941, with development of the Lanchester still underway, Turpin deconstructed the light automatic to produce the most basic automatic firearm built up to that time, using narrow, thin-walled steel tube for the body of the gun, a simple cylindrical bolt with a fixed firing pin, a welded steel butt and simple battle sights. The only wood on the gun was an insert in the small of the butt and the fore grip. This was a true 'second generation' sub-machine gun, the Sten Mk I.

Given prevailing prejudices, it is little short of miraculous that the Sten entered service, as it contradicted every accepted tenet of British military small arms: that self-loading or automatic weapons would only encourage the soldier to waste ammunition; that pistol ammunition lacked range and penetration; and the design itself had dangerous characteristics making it prone to runaways and inadvertent discharges. When BSA established a production line at Tynsley, in September 1942, 200 Stens were built. The following month that figure rose to 1,000, 2,000 in November, and by July 1942 – when 100,000 had been built – production was running at 20,000 Sten guns per month. The Royal Ordnance Factory at Fazakerley reached the same rate during 1943–44 (Hobart, 1973). The guns cost between £3 and £5 each (Skennerton, 1988, p. 32). In comparison, the highest production of Lanchesters was 3,410 per month (Laidler and Howroyd, 1995, p. 7).

Apart from being easy to manufacture, the Sten did the job it was required to do, without wasting manufacturing effort on refinements that would mean little under less-than-optimal real-life combat conditions. If imitation is the sincerest form of flattery, then the copying of Stens worldwide – including in wartime Germany – indicates that the design was fit for purpose (Hobart, 1973, p. 84). Adoption of the Sten marked a sea change in the British attitude to military firearms. Of the various marks of Sten, it is the Mks I*, II and III that are relevant to the Home Guard.[5] The Mk I* was a Mk I with the vestigial woodwork and flash hider deleted, the

Mk II was the definitive Sten, with a removable barrel and magazine housing that swivelled to close the feed and ejection ports, while the Mk III was a redesign of the gun to facilitate manufacture by the toy company Lines Bros, makers of Tri-ang products. Lines built toys using thin steel sheet, so the receiver of the gun was rolled from a sheet of steel and the various fittings welded in place. Although not the most numerically important Sten, this was truly a glimpse into the future of military small arms. It is interesting how easily the £5 Sten was able to replace the £50 Thompson sub-machine gun in Home Guard service. Writing in January 1944, the chronicler of 6th (34th GPO) Cambridgeshire Battalion, Home Guard (Cambs. and Isle of Ely TAA, 1944, p. 64), recorded: 'In 1941, Tommy guns began to arrive and although they were later withdrawn, issues of Sten guns in 1942 and 1943 have provided ample replacement.'

Innovative solutions to the shortage of small arms were one thing, but if German tanks had come ashore on Britain's South Coast in the summer or autumn of 1940, there would have been very little to stop them. The Home Guard's best hope was to halt the *Panzers* with barricades and then pelt them with Molotov cocktails or satchel charges. Even if the army had still possessed its full complement of 2pr anti-tank guns and .55in Boys anti-tank rifles – which it did not – it is probable that the Home Guard approach would have been at least as effective. Ian Hogg notes:

> … there were only 167 anti-tank guns left in Britain, and it was imperative to get more manufactured in order to re-equip formations and also meet the demands of a rapidly expanding army. The question was whether to put the 6-pounder or the 2-pounder into production. The latter was chosen, since production was running and the troops were familiar with the gun; putting the 6-pounder into production would have meant a delay of six or eight months before the first guns appeared, after which would come the problem of re-training …
>
> Nevertheless, the Director of Artillery [also] placed an order for 6-pounders in June 1940, on the understanding that the production would commence only when the immediate demand for 2-pounders had been satisfied. The result was that the first [6-pounder] guns appeared from production in November 1941. (Hogg, 1998, p. 138)

The defeat of German armour remained the key challenge up to the end of 1941. Like the volunteers, the authorities turned to petrol-based weapons

– under the auspices of the Petroleum Warfare Department. E.W. Ashworth (1998, p. 47) states that while large flame traps, designed to flood defiles with burning petrol/oil mixture 'were not, strictly speaking, Home Guard weapons since they formed part of the regular force's defensive layout. The smaller versions, known colloquially as 'fougasses', 'demi-gasses' and 'hedge-hoppers' could be improvised in the field and were used extensively by the Home Guard.' Fougasses (also referred to as flame fougasses and barrel fougasses) and demi-gasses were barrels filled with incendiary liquid which would be ignited and blown forward by an explosive charge, while hedge-hoppers threw the barrel into the air. These weapons were prepared by Royal Engineers Chemical Warfare companies, as part of district defence plans, because the blocking, or otherwise, of routes was too important to be handled with unit-level improvisations. *Military Training Pamphlet No. 42, Tank Hunting and Destruction*, of 29 August 1940, stresses: 'This form of ambush should be prepared only where approved by general officers commanding-in-chief or such officers to whom they may delegate the authority.'[6]

The idea of a remotely fired buried charge, propelling a mass of stones and rubble towards an attacking enemy, was familiar to Vauban, but the Second World War British version of the fougasse was significantly more dangerous. Each installation consisted of four 50-gallon oil drums, as described by Adrian Armishaw:[7]

> Early fougasse barrels were filled with an incendiary liquid comprising 25% petrol and 75% gas oil. They had a 5lb propelling charge of gunpowder against the rear face, and an 8oz ammonal opening charge on the front, which also helped ignite the mixture … Two replacement incendiary mixtures were developed; either a 40% petrol 60% gas oil mixture (40/60 or standard mixture), or a tar, lime and petrol gel known as 5B …
>
> After further research and testing by the PETROLEUM WARFARE DEPARTMENT the charge on the front of the barrel was found to be unnecessary and [that an] ammonal charge alone at the rear was sufficient. Electron turnings (90% magnesium 10% aluminium) [were] placed between the charge and barrel to ensure effective ignition.

Reproduced below is a secret instruction from Salisbury Plain District Headquarters concerning the handing over to the local Home Guard battalions of barrel fougasses installed by 64 Chemical Warfare Company. What Home Guards made of the note that OPs (observation posts) should be provided with a getaway

Subject:- <u>Barrel Fougasses</u>.   S E C R E T.

From:- S.P. District.   4. 2. 42.   S.P.D. SG/13/80/G.
----

1.   Barrels have been installed by 64 C.W. Coy. as notified in
their letter 64/832/15 of the 5th January, 1942.

2.   H.G. Bns. will please take charge of these barrel sites, inspect
them regularly, see that they are not tampered with, and carry out
any necessary maintenance of the camouflage.   Any repairs requiring
R.E. assistance should be reported to this H.Q.

2.   (In the event of any Bn. being unable to locate barrels installed
in their area from the map reference given, Bns. should ask 64 C.W.
Coy (Tel. BROMHAM 94) to send out an N.C.O. to show them the position.
As 64 C.W. Coy. may not be available for long, very early action
should be taken.)

3.   Bns. should forthwith detail two men per site to be responsible
for inspecting and maintaining fougasses, and for firing them when
the occasion arises.   Early arrangements are being made to train
these personnel.

4.   Charges, cable and firing boxes are in process of being made up
and will be issued as soon as possible.   It is hoped that training
puffs will also be provided shortly.

5.   Where this has not already been done, H.G. Bns. should select
and construct O.P's from which fougasses will be fired.

6.   <u>O.P's.</u>

    (a) Should command a good view of the road in both
        directions and of the area of flame.

    (b) Should be well dug in, not too close to the road
        well concealed and should provide a get-away if
        possible.

    (c) May be sited on either side of the road.

    (d) If desired, two O.P's can be constructed to cover
        one site and wired up so that the fougasses can be
        fired from either O.P., i.e., so that if one O.P.
        is spotted and knocked out, the other can fire the
        fougasse and vice versa.

Instruction from HQ Salisbury Plain District to Home Guard Units regarding Barrel
Fougasses, February 1942. (Reproduced by kind permission of Bapty & Co. Ltd)

'if possible' (paragraph 6.b) is anyone's guess, but in February 1942, the enemy
threat was still serious enough for what was effectively a suicide mission to be
officially considered worthwhile.

The scenario of determined volunteers command detonating a powerful IED
under a military vehicle has been seen often enough in Northern Ireland, and
latterly Iraq and Afghanistan, for there to be no doubt that these devices would
have seriously inconvenienced an attacking force. Although an extemporised and
essentially simple weapon, the fougasses' destructive power impressed the Home
Guards who saw them demonstrated:

This can be described as a flame-thrower, electrically detonated and very vicious in its effects. It was designed to be dug in to re-inforce [*sic*] a road block; only a few members of the Unit saw demonstrations arranged in secrecy in remote places, but we all had lectures on them and most of us would have liked to see one go off. (Smith, 1945, p. 46)

That these spectacular weapons – the placing of which required the approval of General Officers Commanding – were placed under the responsibility of the Home Guard, is a clear reflection of the organisation's relevance in the overall scheme of Home Defence.

Fougasses were constructed by the Royal Engineers, but the Home Guard themselves did produce extemporised flamethrowers, such as the 'Nuttall flamethrower', produced by Staffordshire Home Guards. Mounted on an engineless Austin Seven chassis, the fuel contained in the Nuttall's 50-gallon drum was sufficient to generate a 75ft jet of flame for 3 minutes.[8] The official equivalent was the Harvey flamethrower, which used nitrogen to propel 22 gallons of creosote over a burning pad of cotton waste soaked in paraffin. Although the resulting flame jet lasted just ten seconds,[9] the authorities were sufficiently impressed with the Harvey flamethrower to order 2,000 in July 1940, at an estimated cost of £60,000 (Skennerton, 1988, p. 75). The Harvey lacked both mobility and duration of flame; nevertheless it remained in service long enough

THE HARVEY FLAME-THROWER

The Harvey flamethrower in action; an illustration from *Tank Hunting and Destruction* of August 1940. The vertical cylinder was mounted on a pair of 18in wheels, enabling it to be transported 'very much in the manner of a porter's barrow'. It was officially categorised as 'static'. (Author's collection)

to arrive in the Home Guard arsenal in March 1942, with 458 reported in Home Guard returns. By November 1942 the total had risen to 804.[10] That, in 1940, '41 and '42, the British Regular Army was anticipating fighting German tanks with what was, in effect, a large fire extinguisher full of creosote, once again serves to put the supposed deficiencies of Home Guard weapons of the time into context.

In a report on the British Home Guard for the United States War Department, and based on a visit that took place between 17 October and 8 November 1941, H. Wendell Endicott analysed the flame weapons, and, quoting a War Office survey, reported that the British had concluded that simplicity was the key to success:[11]

> The Hedgehopper requires such a scientific placement that it is not sure of reaching the right spot, and is being discouraged as a weapon of the Home Guard … The emphasis is being placed on the 'Fougasse', as it is considered much more efficient. It can be placed in any length along the road, and can be more effective. It can be operated by remote control, and can be kept in complete control. With the greater importance given to the 'Fougasse', both the Harvey Flame-thrower and the Home Guard Flame-thrower are expected to be withdrawn as Home Guard weapons, but no final official decision has yet been reached.

Wendell Endicott's comments are interesting, not least because he has the Harvey flamethrower in Home Guard service, and possibly being withdrawn, some four months before it appears on the monthly returns. The 'Home Guard flamethrower' he mentions was a kit produced by the Petroleum Warfare department, consisting of a 50-gallon drum, 100ft hose, connections, a hand pump and instructions. The Home Guard were required to construct a simple two-wheeled carriage for the device, and assemble a nozzle and ground spike from gas pipe. Crewed by five or six men, the flamethrower could produce a 60ft flame jet of blazing 40–60 'standard mixture' for around 2 minutes. The 'HG' flamethrower first appears in Home Guard returns in May 1942, with 310 listed, the total then fluctuates over the succeeding months, between 257 and 275, until the returns cease showing weapons in November 1942.[12] The significance of this fluctuation (if not a typographic error) is unclear, but it is apparent that the 'HG' was not a particularly important Home Guard weapon, despite its name.

Another approach to the problem of defeating enemy armour was to find better alternatives to the Molotov cocktail and satchel charge – which would have the added bonus of regaining the initiative from Tom Wintringham and Osterley Park. The result was a series of anti-tank and anti-personnel grenades which quickly entered service with the Regular Army, and with which the Home Guard were also expected to become proficient. In March 1941 *Home Guard Instruction No. 26* announced: 'Home-made grenades – The grenades to be issued to the Home Guard will be restricted in due course to recognized Army types. Meanwhile the production of unauthorized home-made grenades must cease.'[13] In the British Army of 1939–40 the term 'grenade' was synonymous with the No. 36M grenade or 'Mills bomb'. The most successful of a plethora of British 'bombs' developed during the First World War, Mills' design first entered service as the No. 5 in 1915. During the First World War the bomb was fitted with a rodded base to be used as a rifle grenade (the No. 23), and modified and improved to become the No. 36 (subsequently No. 36M), which could be used either as a hand grenade or fitted with a base plate or 'gas check' to become a rifle grenade, fired from a discharger cup clamped to the muzzle of the SMLE rifle.

When, on 5 August 1940, Lord Woolton was persuaded to write to the Secretary of State for War to request uniforms and equipment for 450 members of the Ministry of Food LDV, amongst other items listed were 200 'Mills Bombs', twenty-four rifle grenade dischargers and 'rifle grenade accessories for 50 grenades' (Smith, 1945, p. 30). Anthony Eden was obliged to reply that 'resources did not permit of immediate issues to all members of the Home Guard on the scale suggested'. Mills bombs eventually arrived, at approximately the same time as the M1917 rifles, marking the end of the shotgun-and-Ross-rifle phase of the MOF Home Guard's history. No. 36M grenades are not featured in the first (August 1940) Edition of Southworth's *Home Guard Handbook*, but are to be found in the March 1941 reprint of Brophy's *Home Guard – A Handbook for the L.D.V* (Brophy, 1941a, p. 95). They were certainly in Home Guard service by May 1941, when 2nd Lieutenant S.J. White, of the 1st Essex Battalion, Home Guard, was one of the first of several Home Guards to win bravery awards for picking up a smoking grenade, accidentally dropped during practice, and throwing it over the safety parapet.[14]

It is interesting that, although the Mills bomb entered service in 1915, a year after the Lewis light machine gun, and two years earlier than the M1917 rifle, this was never viewed as a shortcoming. Various new designs were introduced during the Second World War, but the Mills bomb remained *the* 'hand grenade' then, and for some time after the war. The key factor here is the continued use of the grenade (like the 1907 SMLE rifle and 1905 Vickers machine gun) by the army, which conferred a perception of continued relevance and effectiveness, vintage notwithstanding. To quote *Grenades for the Home Guard*:

> The No. 36 grenade was designed during the Great War 1914–1918 for trench warfare. So efficient did it prove that it still continues to be part of the Army equipment, and in the process it has undergone only slight modifications. Its mechanism is simple and safe, and troops can be rapidly trained to its use. It is small in size and can be fairly easily carried as compared with the enemy stick grenade. (Manders, undated, p. 8)

No. 36M grenades could be thrown 25–35yd by hand, but the rifle grenade discharger extended this to an impressive 80–200yd (Manders, undated, p. 10). The grenades were issued in boxes of a dozen, with a metal canister containing twelve fuses (4 seconds for hand grenades, or 7 seconds for those to be used with the discharger cup). Grenades for use with the discharger also came with twelve gas checks (base plates) and .303 blanks, each containing thirty grains of Ballistite. The shock of discharging a rifle grenade resulted in the rifle becoming 'somewhat spoilt as a precision weapon', to quote the author of *Grenades for the Home Guard* (Manders, undated, p. 27). A special rifle was designated for grenade launching and marked 'EY', indicating that it should only be used to fire ball ammunition in

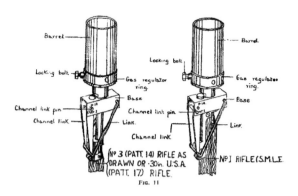

The No. 2 Mk I discharger cup could be fitted to the SMLE, P'14 and M1917 rifles without modification. Officially accepted in August 1942, it featured in the July 1942 edition of *Small Arms Training*, Vol. I, No. 13, *Grenade*. (Author's collection)

an Emergency.[15] Service rifles were already in short supply, making this a wasteful arrangement, and it is curious that more use was not made of old 'long' Lee-Enfield, Lee-Metford and .303 Martini carbines, the obsolete actions which were used for the 4in smoke grenade dischargers used on armoured fighting vehicles.

As we have seen, the Bapty collection contains a very impressive grenade launcher built by Home Guards, using a No. 1 Mk I discharger cup, fitted to a .303 Martini action and mounted on a base plate. Although in the absence of .303 Ballistite cartridges it has not been possible to test this weapon, there is no doubt that it would work very effectively. Provision of EY rifles for the Home Guard was greatly simplified by the development of an adaptor 'Adaptors, Discharger, 2½in. Grenade. No. 1', officially adopted for service on 7 August 1942 (Skennerton, 1993, p. 356). This enabled the No. 1 discharger to be fitted to the P14 and M1917 rifles, and on the same date a simplified discharger cup, the No. 2 Mk I, was introduced, which could be fitted to the SMLE (Rifle No. 1), P14 (Rifle No. 3) or M1917 without modification. The army gradually lost interest in the rifle grenade, preferring to use the 2in mortar and Projector, Infantry, Anti-Tank (PIAT), but the rifle discharger remained a key Home Guard weapon until 'stand-down', both in anti-personnel and, as we shall see, anti-tank roles.

Although useful for killing AFV crews if it could be dropped into the vehicle,[16] the No. 36M was no use in defeating armour. In the British infantry platoon of 1940, that duty fell to the .55in Boys anti-tank rifle, a weapon which, although amongst the best of its type, had proven unable to halt the heavier German tanks. As we have seen, while the popular imagination, including that of the LDV/Home Guard, was gripped by the spectre of the Nazi parachutist, it was the threat of *Panzers* running unchecked that most alarmed the General Staff. In the aftermath of the Battle of France, three new grenades swiftly entered service to give British infantry some means of tackling German armour – the No. 73 Anti-Tank Percussion grenade, the No. 74 Sticky Type grenade, the No. 76 Self-Igniting Phosphorous grenade – all of which featured in *Tank Hunting and Destruction*, published by the War Office on 29 August 1940.

They were followed (as far as the Home Guard was concerned) by the No. 68 Anti-Tank Rifle grenade, the No. 69 Bakelite grenade and the No. 75 Hawkins grenade (or mine). *Tank Hunting and Destruction* makes it clear that it was all-hands-to-the-pumps when it came to stopping German armour: 'Although this task is primarily one for the specially equipped tank-hunting platoons, the responsibility is not theirs alone. Every soldier and every member of the Home Guard should be trained in the methods of tank hunting and in the use of special anti-tank weapons.'[17] Thus the Home Guard, who at this stage were mostly still hopefully awaiting service rifles, found themselves expected to master a selection of challenging and dangerous anti-tank grenades.

Ubiquitous in the Home Guard, the AW bomb (named for its manufacturer – Allbright and Wilson of Oldbury, leading purveyors of white phosphorous), also known as the Self-Igniting Phosphorous (SIP) grenade and the Grenade, Hand or Projector, No. 76, was a successful effort to provide an improved Molotov cocktail. It consisted of a 'short-necked half-pint clear glass bottle'[18] containing benzene, gelled with rubber, some water and phosphorous. The bottles were sealed, removing the hazards of spilt fuel and fumes, and ignited instantly on breaking. It was said that a significant disadvantage of the AW/SIP/No. 76 grenade was that if dropped it would go off – but the same was true of the Sten gun. Of all the variations on the Molotov cocktail theme developed during the 1930s and '40s, the British No. 76 SIP grenade was the only one to feature in the US Army training manual *Unconventional Warfare Devices and Techniques*, prepared for the US Special Forces in 1966 (see above).[19] Ian Hogg (1979, p. 163) states that the grenade was also issued to army units in the UK during 1940–41 'but it was

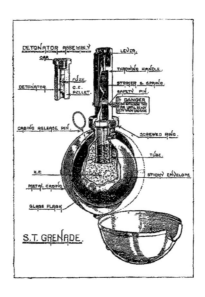

Cut-away illustration of the No. 74 ST grenade from *Small Arms Training pamphlet No. 13 Supplement No. 2* of August 1941. (Author's collection)

largely issued to the Home Guard. It was officially declared obsolete in February 1944 …' *Military Training Pamphlet No. 42, Tank Hunting and Destruction* makes it clear that the grenades listed were intended for Home Defence Army units, and that the Home Guard should also be trained in their use (the author's copy was originally issued to a 2nd Lieutenant A.N.Young, Royal Horse Artillery). During the course of the war, as the burden of Home Defence rested increasingly heavily on the Home Guard, it was forgotten that the unconventional weapons rushed into service in 1940–41 were issued to the army first, which significantly alters the way in which this equipment should be viewed.

No. 76 SIP grenades were issued in 53lb wire-bound wooden partitioned cases of two dozen. This fragile and highly flammable glass grenade did not commend itself to mobile warfare, as the author of Grenades for the Home Guard was forced to admit:

Method of carrying. The box seems the best means of transportation. This means a two-man load. (Manders, undated, p. 61)

In the context of a largely immobilised British force awaiting a German invasion, the glass No. 76 SIP grenade made very good sense. The heavy crates could be cached near choke points where the defenders might expect to ambush German AFVs. In other contexts the grenade had rather more disadvantages than advantages, and it soon was in service only with the Home Guard, who continued to train for defensive operations on their own ground in the UK.

Part of the popularity of the No. 36M Mills grenade was its inherent safety. The grenades were shipped without their fuses, which were fitted only when the grenades were about to be issued. The striker was held clear of the firing cap by the tip of the hand lever, and the lever was held safely in place by a pin. When the grenade was about to be thrown the pin was removed, the thrower's hand keeping the lever depressed. If the thrower changed his mind, he could replace the pin and return the grenade to his pouch. If he threw the grenade, then as he did so the lever flew off, the striker hit the firing cap and ignited a short length of fuse. The fuse burnt for four seconds (or seven in the case of discharger grenades), before igniting the detonator which exploded the grenade. In the case of discharger grenades, the cup of the discharger held the lever in place in the same manner as the thrower's hand. The time delay system had much to commend it, particularly if the grenade was being thrown into a room, bunker or trench. But it was very unsuitable for use against moving vehicles, as the grenade would roll

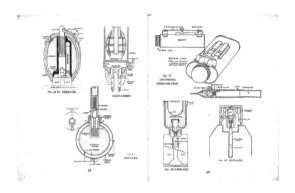

A selection of grenades in use with the Home Guard. (Author's collection)

off and explode once the vehicle had passed. What was needed was a percussion fuse, but one that would ensure the grenade remained unarmed until well clear of the thrower, and then detonated as soon as the grenade struck – regardless of whether it struck right way up, sideways or upside down.

This tall order was met by the No. 247 'All-ways' fuse. This featured a Bakelite screw cap which, once removed, revealed a length of cloth tape and a lead weight. On throwing, the tape unwound until, at its full length, it pulled the safety pin from the fuse body. At that point the fuse was armed. Inside the fuse body, a firing cap sat at the base of a heavy cup, the 'cap pellet', beneath a sharply pronged striker which sat under a lead ball. If the fuse struck a hard surface 'right way up' the lead ball drove the striker down to fire the cap. If inverted, then the weight of the cap pellet drove the cap onto the striker. If sideways, the ball was driven against a slope in the closing cap of the fuse, forcing it to bear down on the striker.

The No. 247 fuse was brilliantly simple, and was mated to a cylindrical tinned plate container, holding almost 4lb of explosive, to produce the Anti-Tank Percussion grenade, later designated the No. 73 Anti-Tank grenade (Hand). The resulting grenade bore a strong resemblance to a contemporary Thermos vacuum flask, and was popularly known as the 'Thermos bomb'. It was also known as the 'Woolworths bomb', probably because of a comment in one of John Langdon-Davies' lectures, subsequently published as *Home Guard Warfare*: 'The Finns could not afford sufficient expensive full-sized [anti-tank] mines, but they used to construct little ones out of material, all of which could probably be bought by you or me at a Woolworths store …' (Langdon-Davies, 1941, p. 44).

The No. 73 was a powerful grenade capable of blowing the tracks off any tank, but it could not be thrown far – about 10yd – and this meant that the grenade presented a real threat to the thrower, as the War Office training pamphlet of August 1941 explained:

> The object of this grenade is to damage armoured fighting vehicles, the best effect being obtained when used against the track or suspension of a tank. Owing to its weight and shape it can only be thrown quite short distances, 10–15 yards; and, owing to the powerful nature of the grenade, it is absolutely essential that the thrower is behind cover. The use of it, therefore, is limited to ambushes or road blocks.[20]

The No. 73 had the hallmarks of a 'Victoria Cross weapon', and it is probably not surprising that troops preferred the Sticky bomb – which allowed the tank to trundle away from the thrower before exploding, or could be placed on a parked vehicle, allowing the tank-hunter time to slip away. The Sticky bomb, or No. 74 ST grenade, used a Mills-type firing mechanism, and solved the problem of attacking moving tanks by remaining glued to the vehicle while the fuse burnt. Introduced for Home Defence in 1940, and forever associated with the Home Guard, the Grenade Hand, No. 74 ST ('Sticky Type') was privately developed and entered service via MD1, the department responsible for the provision of weapons to clandestine organisations including SOE (Cornish, 2003). MacKenzie records that, following a demonstration on 28 July 1940, Churchill:

> Personally ordered that the weapon go into production … When the Ordnance Board opposition seemed to be causing delays, he sent a sharp note to his scientific adviser, Professor Linderman: 'Sticky Bomb. Make one million. WSC'.[21] (1996, p. 93)

The bomb consisted of a glass (later Bakelite) sphere filled with nitro–glycerine, to which a wooden handle, containing a firing mechanism, was screwed. The sphere was covered with stockinette material soaked in a birdlime-like glue, protected until the moment of throwing by a sprung, two-part metal cover. The bombs were fragile and tended to leak nitro–glycerine, which, quite apart from being an explosive sensitive to impact, caused severe headaches and 'nitro–glycerine poisoning'.[22] In the opinion of the Board of Ordnance, as recorded by Ian Hogg (1979, p. 162), 'the whole article is most objectionable'. MacKenzie (1996, p. 177) interprets Churchill's determination to overrule the experts as further evidence of what he terms 'a manifest desire on the part of the Prime Minister and War Office to maintain public confidence in the usefulness of the Home Guard through public gestures'. There is, of course, the alternative view that, while the Board of Ordnance might have, given time, come up with a better alternative, time was the one thing Britain did not have. The No. 74 ST grenade was a 'bird in the hand' during the eighteen months when Britain's anti-tank defences consisted of Molotovs, and a few 2pr guns and .55in rifles.

Curiously, the ST grenade was popular with the Home Guard – probably because it was, in Ashworth's (1998, p. 44) words: 'effective against the side or roof plates of all contemporary German tanks.' Ashworth states that 'the army remained reluctant to have anything to do with it, leaving its use almost exclusively to the Home Guard'. The army manual *Tank Hunting and Destruction* of August 1940, whilst setting the extensive safety precautions to be observed when handling ST grenades, was enthusiastic about the grenade's potential, but realistic about its performance:

> The S.T. grenade is most effective against baby tanks and armoured cars having plating under 1 inch thickness. It is not effective against plating exceeding this thickness.
>
> Medium or heavy tanks encountered will probably be vulnerable only on the roofs, engine casing and under parts.
>
> The S.T. grenade should be considered as a portable demolition charge which can be quickly and easily applied. One of the safest and easiest methods of application is to drop the grenade from the upstairs window of a building overlooking a road along which a tank is proceeding ... [23]

Similar sentiments are to be found in the grenade training manual issued a year later:

> For night raids on tank parks, the grenade is an ideal weapon. It can be regarded as a portable demolition charge and planted by hand instead of thrown, so long as the operator retreats in such a direction that he is protected from the explosion. With practice and training, the grenade can be thrown about 20 yards. [24]

The grenade was the product of manufacturing chemists Kay Brothers, makers of a well-known adhesive, 'Coaguline Cement'. Kays were tasked to develop a way of making a 2lb bomb stick to an armoured fighting vehicle long enough to detonate, ensure that the bombs did not stick to each other, or the thrower, and develop an adhesive that would remain effective across the range of climates experienced by British troops. The No. 74 ST grenade met all these criteria, and Kay Bros were responsible for fitting the adhesive-soaked knitted sleeves to the glass spheres of the grenades, and attaching the handle. Kays' own records put production of No. 74 ST grenades by their Kayborough Works at Reddish at 2½ million bombs, and state that the grenade saw service in North Africa, Italy and in France during the latter part of the Second World War.[25]

Most sources agree that, apart from the Home Guard, No. 74 ST grenades saw service in occupied Europe, via SOE, as demolition charges (see Hogg, 1979, p. 163). Army use of the No. 74 ST grenades has been virtually forgotten, although they were extensively used in action by the British Eighth Army during 1942 – as in this example, one of many recorded in the New Zealand official war history:

A 23 Battalion man who had strayed from his company was armed with a sticky bomb with which he set a tank alight. By the illumination thus provided Sergeant Lord (B Company) climbed onto another tank, shot the commander and dropped a grenade inside, while others fired tommy guns through the slits, killing the crew and setting it on fire also. Lord killed the commander of another tank in the same manner, but the crew climbed out and surrendered before they could be dealt with. The rest of the tanks scattered into the darkness.[26]

The action took place at Ruweisat Ridge, during the early stages of the Battle of El Alamein, when many weapons then or later issued to the Home Guard saw operational service, including another innovative anti-armour weapon, the No. 68 Anti-Tank grenade (rifle). The shaped charge or high-explosive anti-tank (HEAT) round is usually associated with Second World War German developments, particularly demolition charges and the *Panzerfaust*. However, the first HEAT anti-armour projectile to enter service with any army was the British No. 68 rifle grenade, issued from February 1941. Fired from the 'EY' rifle fitted with a 2½in discharger cup, No. 68 grenades saw some service with the BEF in 1940, with the Eighth Army in the Western Desert, and from 1941 to 1944 with the Home Guard (Hogg, 1979, p. 160). Unlike the No. 36M, the No. 68 was designed only to be used as a rifle grenade. It was fired from the prone position, with the rifle the correct way up, almost horizontal, and butt braced against a sandbag or similar, the grenade following a relatively flat trajectory to the target.

The No. 68 had an effective range of 75–100yd, and was aimed through a simple sheet metal sight clamped to the rifle. The bomb could penetrate 2in (50mm) of armour, making it rather more than twice as effective as the Boys anti-tank rifle (20mm penetration, ideal range 300yd), and even the 2pr anti-tank gun (42mm penetration), although it lacked the range of either weapon (up to 1,000yd, but 300–500 being ideal, in the case of the 2pr).[27] Undoubtedly difficult to use effectively, the No. 68 was the infantry's best hope against armour until the arrival of the 6pr anti-tank gun and PIAT in 1942, and it was another weapon which the army and the Home Guard shared.

However, this takes us somewhat ahead of the narrative. To return to the darkest days of July–August 1940, and the familiar Mills bomb; the No. 36M 'Mills' grenade is sometimes referred to as a 'defensive' grenade, a term based on the fact that that the 20–100yd lethal radius of its fragments (Manders, undated, p. 10) exceeded the distance it could be thrown, and therefore it was best thrown from the safety of a trench or similar cover at an exposed (i.e. attacking) enemy. The term is not, and never has been recognised in British military circles, if only because the Mills bomb was universally used in offensive action.[28] Nevertheless, early in the Second World War there was recognition that some type of 'offensive' grenade, i.e. one that would stun an enemy, but not inflict casualties on one's own side, would be useful. The result, introduced in February 1941, was the No. 69, a plastic hand grenade, consisting of a No. 247 'all-ways' fuse attached to a simple Bakelite body. The No. 69 was widely used by the Home Guard, and sometimes employed as a training 'thunderflash'. In May 1942, Captain Southworth (formerly RSM Southworth, and author of the *Home Guard Pocket Book*) demonstrated No. 36M grenades and No. 69 grenades to Sevenoaks Home Guard. CSM Brown and Sgt Peek recorded (Brown and Peek, 1944, p15): 'Capt. Southworth's stroll along the "road" apparently carelessly throwing 69s all around him produced a fitting finale.' Officially, the grenade was described thus: 'a light hand percussion grenade for offensive action. The area of burst is very limited and it can, therefore, be thrown standing in the open. The material effect is small but the moral effect is considerable, particularly at night since each man, thinking an H.E. grenade has been thrown believes himself (in the darkness) to be the only one left alive.' The pamphlet added: 'the grenade can also be used for adding realism to exercises with troops … they will be regarded as having a danger area of 30 yards.' By November 1943, *Home Guard Instruction No. 51* was already describing the No. 69 grenade as: '*not a general issue, but is found in operational stocks in some localities*' [original italics].

If the soubriquet 'Woolworth bomb' did originate in Langdon-Davies' lecture, then it was perhaps more appropriate for what Norman Longmate calls the 'Talcum Powder grenade', as this really was a 'small mine made from common materials'. Introduced in 1942, the Hawkins grenade, or No. 75 grenade, to give it its correct name, consisted of a screw-topped rectangular tinned plate container, of the sort commonly used to hold talcum powder. Soldered to one face were two fuse pockets, protected by a plate. The 'grenade' nomenclature was applied because it was theoretically possible to throw the 'grenade-mine' into the path of an oncoming tank. The rectangular 'talcum tin' shape ensured that it would land with the fuse uppermost or underneath, in a good position to be crushed as the vehicle rolled over it. Generally, the grenades were placed or buried, like normal mines, or strung together in such a way that they could be dragged into the path of an oncoming vehicle. *Home Guard Circular No. 43* (15 December 1943) reported on experiments undertaken by the Eighth Army to assess the effectiveness of the No. 75 Hawkins grenade:

3. *New Experiments with the 75 grenade*
The Eighth Army recently made experiments with the 75 grenade, using a captured German Mark IV tank, which was towed at about 6 m.p.h. This is what happened:-

A single grenade was placed so that one of the tank's tracks went right over it. This shattered two links of the track, causing a clean break.[29]

The No. 75 and No. 75A (with diagonal fuse pockets) were widely used by British and American troops (it was known as the 'Mine, Light, Anti-tank, M7A2' in US service). It remained in service until 1955 and was used against British troops in Aden. Apart from anti-tank use, the Home Guard were taught to use two No. 75s taped together as a demolition charge for 'mouseholing' when fighting in a built-up area.[30]

The anti-tank grenades developed in 1940–41 were best suited to the defence, and as the tide of war turned, the No. 73 Anti-Tank Percussion grenade and No. 74 'Sticky bomb' in particular became less suitable for an army now on the offensive on every front. The new airborne troops and Commandos, in particular, were unwilling to struggle with bulky and fragile grenades. A solution was found in the No. 82 or Gammon grenade (named after its inventor, Captain 'Dick' Gammon MC, 1 PARA). This was remarkable, in that it consisted of nothing more than a No. 247 all-ways fuse to which a small cloth skirt was attached, closed with elastic to form a bag. Regular troops were issued plastic explosive, and a quantity of this was placed inside the bag to form the charge of the grenade. Although the size of the bag was supposed to limit the size of the charge, quite alarming amounts of PE could be squeezed into a Gammon grenade, particularly when it was being used as a demolition charge. By adding a handful of gravel or pebbles, a useful anti-personnel effect could also be achieved. The combination of the No. 36M and the No. 82 Gammon grenade was quite suitable for most purposes during the latter part of the war, and the other grenades were increasingly left to the Home Guard, who were not generally issued PE, and in any case, had a static, defensive role. This is why they have become so strongly associated with the Home Guard. It is entirely typical of the people and time that British grenades were given homely nicknames. This should not detract from the fact that these grenades were at least as effective as any others fielded by the combatant nations at that time – or that tank hunting was dangerous and the odds of success would be slim. Good or bad, these grenades were all standard issue throughout the army, Royal Air Force airfield defence units, and the Home Guard too.

7

SUB-ARTILLERY

The arrival of new small arms and grenades at the end of 1940 provided the opportunity to ban homemade weapons, and replace Osterley Park with an official school and training teams.[1] Osterley had championed the Home Guard mortar, and there remained the problem of indirect fire support, as the homemade mortar had become a Home Guard byword, and quickly reached a reasonable level of sophistication. Their immediate replacement was an officially produced, but unconventional, weapon, which was developed as the 'Northover (Bottle) Mortar',[2] entered service as the 'Projector 2½ in Mks I and II',[3] but was universally known as the 'Northover Projector'. Major Northover was a Home Guard officer whose 'projector', described, somewhat harshly, by Ian Hogg (1979, p. 160) as 'a primitive smoothbore gun', replaced the homemade mortar as principle Home Guard support weapon. The 'NO' (**N**orth**O**ver) suffered from the same drawback as the Osterley Park mortars, in that its gunpowder propelling charge generated a distinctive cloud of white smoke, and the added disadvantage that, at 134lb it was decidedly heavy.[4] On the other hand, it could discharge the No. 76 SIP grenade, the No. 36M grenade, and the No. 68 grenade – all a great improvement on jam tin bombs – to a range of 300yd (150–200 effective).[5] Furthermore, the professionally produced, pre-packaged black powder charges were safer and more effective than the homemade version or recycled fireworks.

The Northover Projector was officially described as: 'primarily an ambush anti-tank weapon to be sited as part of the defences to fire enfilade on likely tank approaches'.[6] The first 277 examples were issued to London District in June 1941, and by the following month 6,630 were in the hands of Home Guard units, illustrating the speed with which the weapon could be manufactured and distributed. The highest figure in the Home Guard returns is 18,992, in

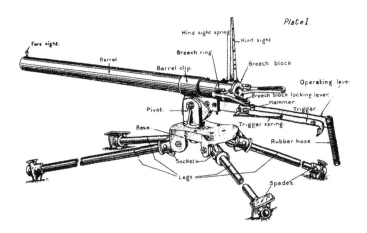

The 2½in Projector Mk I. Thirteen thousand of these guns were produced by the Bisley Clay Target Company between August 1940 and July 1941. The four-legged mount enabled the gun to be carried 'stretcher-wise'. (Author's collection)

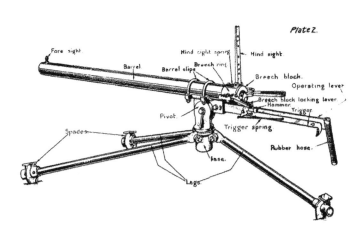

The 2½in Projector Mk II. Eight thousand were built by the Selection Manufacturing Company in 1940. The most obvious modification is the tripod mount, but more important was the welded boss holding the foresight, which prevented the sight being screwed too far in, thus obstructing the barrel and causing the round to explode in the bore. (Author's collection)

September 1942, falling off by a dozen the following month (the last for which figures are given). Skennerton lists contracts for a total production of 21,000 Northover Projectors between August 1940 and December 1941.[7]

A special version of the No. 76 SIP grenade was produced for the Northover Projector, with a diameter of 2½in, rather than the 2¾in of the hand-thrown version (Manders, undated, p. 60). It had thicker glass, and a green, rather than scarlet, crown cap as a distinguishing mark. These grenades did still sometimes break up in the bore of the projector, with a flamethrower-like effect (although usually with no lasting ill-effects on the crew). Conversely, they could be difficult to ignite unless they struck a hard object squarely and with force (Smith, 1945, p. 46). During the latter stages of the Northover's career, a paper sleeve and fibreboard base ring were used in an effort to protect the grenade from the shock of firing (Smith, 1945, p. 46),[8] and the projector was sometimes used without its mount, rested on cover, rather like a light mortar or rocket launcher.[9] Certainly simple and robust, the Northover does not deserve to be described as 'primitive', particularly when compared to its Soviet equivalent, the *Ampulomet 1941 System Kartukov*. Essentially similar to the Northover Projector, the *Ampulomet* saw action at Stalingrad in 1942, and used a gunpowder cartridge to propel a spherical 127mm diameter glass incendiary bottle containing diesel oil and phosphorous up to a range of 250m.[10]

The Northover Projector should not be dismissed as a joke – it was, for example, fired by a percussion cap 'of the standard military type',[11] not a 'toy pistol cap' as MacKenzie states (1996, p. 94). The Northover was carried by platoons engaged in 'offensive defence' (i.e. counter-attacking) as indirect fire support – analogous with the 2in mortar of the army – as well as in ambush or defensive positions.[12] It was envisaged that, in action, the Northover could disable a light tank by hitting the running gear with a No. 68 grenade, then destroy the vehicle or smoke out the crew with the No. 76 SIP. Using the No. 36M grenade, the projector could be used 'in any suitable anti-personnel role',[13] which made it extremely versatile, and it remained in service long after more potent and more conventional weapons were introduced. Confirmation of its demise is to be found in the *Home Guard Information Circular No. 53* of 9 August 1944: 'Consequent on equipments having been declared obsolete, the undermentioned handbook relating thereto is hereby *cancelled*. Handbook for the Projectors, 2½ inch, Marks I and II on Mountings 2½ inch Projector, Marks I and II, 1941. Copies of this handbook will be disposed of in confidential waste.'[14]

Whilst the Northover was not universally popular, particularly because of its smoke cloud signature, it did make a positive impression on those who appreciated the urgency of quickly providing some kind of support weapon to regular troops and Home Guard preparing to take on invading German tanks. In his report of February 1942, US War Department special observer H. Wendell Endicott says of the Northover Projector:[15]

> I consider this an amazing weapon – effective – accurate – simple in construction – easy to operate, requiring no expert technique – no maintenance problem – produced at low cost.

He goes on to describe a demonstration given in March 1941 at ranges of 75–200yd, twenty shots were fired with one 'blow' (a No. 76 SIP grenade breaking in the bore) and the accuracy was 'surprising'. Reporting on another, in October 1941, with the projector fired at targets 150–250yd away, Endicott observed two 'blows' out of thirty shots fired, noting that 'if the target had been a tank [the Northover Projector] would have scored one hundred percent hits'.

The Northover Projector was to become absolutely associated with the Home Guard, yet it is evident from *Military Training Pamphlet No. 42, Tank Hunting and Destruction*, of 29 August 1940, that the weapon was developed for army use, and was one of the 'special weapons' the Home Guard were *also* expected to master. At the time *Tank Hunting and Destruction* was published, the 'Northover (Bottle) Mortar' was not yet in production, and the pages devoted to the weapon were marked 'to be issued later'.[16] In December 1940, it was a Regular Army officer, 2nd Lt Young of the Royal Horse Artillery, the owner of the pamphlet presently in the author's possession, who duly pasted the amendment in, now marked 'Northover Projector'. As late as October 1941, the Northover was being demonstrated by Regular Army troops in Singapore (see plate 29), although no record has yet come to light of combat use.

It is sometimes said that the Northover Projector also saw naval service, and even downed a German bomber, but this is not quite true (Ashworth, 1998, p. 46). The maritime equivalent of the Northover was the Holman Grenade Projector. The product of a Cornish engineering company,[17] the Holman Projector also fired the No. 36M grenade from an unrifled barrel, but did so using compressed air or steam from a vessel's boiler as the propellant. The Holman was supposed to protect vessels such as armed trawlers from air attack, by launching No. 36M grenades into the path of oncoming aircraft. Large numbers were produced, but they were never particularly popular, except as a means of light-heartedly bombarding friendly forces with potatoes or empty tins.[18] The issue of around

4,500 Holman Grenade Projectors to the Royal Navy and merchant marine does, though, serve to place the Northover Projector in context, as it illustrates the extent to which this sort of unconventional weapon was taken seriously in 1940–41.

Typically the Holman scared off attackers, but they could actually down an enemy aircraft, as the following RAF report for 2 August 1940 describes:

> A report has been received from *SS Highlander* that she was attacked by two enemy aircraft at about 2345 hours on 1st August, 6 miles south of Stonehaven. She claims that one He115 [*a large seaplane torpedo bomber*] was brought down by a Holman projector and crashed on the poop deck, and that the other aircraft crashed into the sea in flames due to Lewis gun fire. Both aircraft are stated to have made aerial torpedo and low machine gunning attacks.[19]

The He 115 was a substantial aircraft, with a crew of three and a 73ft wingspan, and downing two, with a Holman Projector and a Lewis gun, demonstrates what could be achieved with emergency weaponry – given luck and the right combination of circumstances. Holman Projectors were also used in coastal defences, and may have been encountered by Home Guard coast artillery units.

The hypothesis that emergency unconventional weapons such as the Sticky bomb and Northover Projector were produced merely as 'public gestures' to quieten the Home Guard is further undermined by the fact that both were officially 'secret', and could not be discussed, which is why they do not feature in the numerous unofficial manuals produced in 1941–42.[20] To quote John Brophy, writing in June 1941:

> *Anti-Tank Weapons.* – In order to preserve secrecy and add to the effect of the unpleasant surprises awaiting the invader, only those weapons which were in general use before the outbreak of war may be described or even named in public print. No one will question the wisdom of this ruling. Since the L.D.V. days when Molotov cocktails were first made and tested in this country, a sizeable range of anti-tank weapons has become available to the Home Guard. Those units which are stationed in areas regarded as most vulnerable are supplied first, but it can safely be said that very soon after this book is published (if not before) every Home Guard formation will have several of these new and secret weapons among its armaments. (1941b, p. 64)

Brophy was obviously trying to make his audience feel special, laying great stress on the imminent arrival of 'secret' equipment. He went on:

> Nor will it be long before the whole range – some items of which are exclusive to the Home Guard, so that supplies will not be held up while deliveries are made to the full-time Army – is available for every unit.

In pressing the point, Brophy may have gone too far, and laid the foundations for the subsequent conviction that the sub-artillery and the anti-tank grenades which arrived at this time were 'Home Guard only'. This, as we have already established, was dangerous, when the Home Guards themselves were determined that they should be, as closely as possible, equipped as per the standard British line infantryman of the time.

Hollow charge anti-tank warheads, such as the No. 68 grenade, are least effective if they arrive on target at high velocity or spinning – in other words, they commend themselves to means of delivery other than conventional high-velocity rifled ordnance. Thus the combination of the low-velocity, unrifled Northover Projector and the hollow charge No. 68 grenade was, in theory at least, an ideal anti-tank weapon. The No. 68 was never the major ammunition for the Northover, the phosphorous incendiary No. 76 SIP grenade being the preferred projectile throughout the projector's service, and this was doubtless due to the No. 68's rather lacklustre performance. To significantly increase the penetration of a hollow charge warhead it is necessary to increase its diameter, which was impossible with cup or tube-type dischargers, such as the EY rifle or the Northover Projector.[21] Efforts were made to increase the potency of the No. 68 grenade,[22] but it was clear that if the British infantry was to take on the *Panzers* on anything approaching equal terms, a more powerful weapon was required, and one that could be put into production quickly.

Colonel L.V.S. Blacker, a Territorial Army officer, had offered a spigot-type smoke grenade launcher, the 'Arbalest', to the British Army in 1939, which was rejected in favour of the 2in mortar (Hogg, 1979, p. 148). Blacker now designed a Spigot Mortar he named the 'Bombard', which fired a large high-explosive anti-tank round, and which was developed into a serviceable weapon with the support of MD1 (Cornish, 2009, p. 35). Blacker had a Churchillian taste for antiquarian nomenclature, and we have seen how irritating this could be to the modern-minded volunteers. The official terminology for his weapon – '29mm Spigot Mortar' (a reference to the diameter of the spigot) – made it one of a minority of British weapons to be given a 'modern' metric designation. Nevertheless, David Carroll comments beneath an illustration of Sevenoaks Spigot Mortar crew:

> Officially known as the Blacker Bombard ... the Spigot Mortar possessed a short barrel ... It was an ungainly piece of equipment – a highly whimsical contraption, in fact, whose name and appearance suggest that it might have been more comfortably employed in the rough-and-tumble of the English Civil War rather than Britain's mighty struggle with Hitler's Germany. Although the Spigot Mortar came widely into use with the Home Guard ... more than one ex-member of the force has complained of its unpredictability when firing, coupled with a daunting lack of accuracy in the field. (1999, p. 72)

Setting aside confusion regarding the correct historical context for a bombard,[23] this description is unhelpful – particularly in view of the recorded reaction of Sevenoaks Home Guard to the Spigot Mortar:

> 17/5/42. Demonstration at Sandpit, Shoreham Lane.
> A spigot mortar team ... also gave a demonstration with practice bombs. The shooting was remarkably accurate and created a good impression, especially as this was the first occasion on which many of us had seen the mortar in action. (Brown and Peek, 1944, p. 15)

The roof armour of a tank is its weakest point – just 26mm in the case of a Tiger I – and that is where the Spigot Mortar round would strike.[24] Henry Wills (1985, p. 68) records the reaction of one ex-tank crewman to a Spigot Mortar demonstration against a concrete pillbox:

> I would think that 5–10 rounds were fired by the spigot mortar. Looking back on my tank experience, I doubt if anything would have survived after the first hit. I do not recollect any misses. An effective tool ...

Whether Brophy's ruling that 'only those weapons which were in general use before the outbreak of war may be described or even named in public print' applied to official manuals is a moot point. Certainly, the tactical field manuals prepared for the Regular Army between August 1940 and September 1941, such as the series making up *Operations, Military Training Pamphlet No. 23* (The War

Office, various dates from 1940–42), avoid any reference to sub-artillery, although, as we shall see, Colonel Blacker's Bombard certainly was in service with British Empire troops towards the end of that period. In truth, the volumes of *Pamphlet No. 23* published in late 1940 and 1941 describe a model British Army equipped with 18pr and 25pr field artillery, Bren light machine guns and 'Army tanks' that totally fails to reflect the threadbare reality of the time. It is therefore not surprising that until very recently most sources gave the impression that sub-artillery was developed and produced specifically for the Home Guard, and that the 'real' army would have nothing to do with it. Increased interest in the Home Guard has resulted in more research and, whilst an element of 'Mind My Pike' lingers on, there is now no escaping the fact that these devices were developed as weapons for the perilously under-armed British armed forces in general, not as political gestures to quieten a supposed restive and influential Home Guard lobby.

In fairness to modern authors, however, Home Guards themselves are unhelpful when it comes to sub-artillery, as the following posting regarding the Blacker Bombard on the Portsdown Tunnels research website demonstrates:

> Going through the web site of Portsdown Tunnels under 'invasion' I came across the Spigot Mortar; the Blacker Bombard. During part of my time spent as a private in the Chesterfield Home Guard I was in the Blacker Bombard Squad. However during my 5 years in the Army (infantry) nobody I spoke to had ever heard of the Blacker Bombard. Old soldiers I have spoken to since had never heard of it and I feel sure they thought that I was making it up. Thank you very much for providing the proof that there was such a weapon.
>
> The base of the Mortar had four legs made out of 2 inch red band tube which slotted into the base of the Mortar itself. We were suppose [*sic*] to be mobile. When firing it we had to lay down and there was a padded roller at the end of the firing butt and you had to rest your head on this to look through the site [*sic*]. When you fired the thing the front end jumped up and the roller hit your forehead and nearly broke your neck. I only fired this contraption once thank goodness. The Blacker Bombard squad consisted of six men and a Sergeant. It was really the days of *Dad's Army*. At 18 I joined the real Army.
>
> HARRY BRADBURY, Derbyshire – January 2007[25]

Mr Bradbury's recollections illustrate the difficulties and dangers of relying too heavily on the testimony of surviving former Home Guards, whose two teenage years in the organisation have been overlaid by service in the army and sixty or so subsequent years, and many showings of *Dad's Army*. His colleagues in the 'real Army' were not quite so well-informed as he might have been led to believe, and the 29mm Spigot Mortar/Blacker Bombard was a more proven piece of equipment than he, and most modern commentators, imagine. And just as a point of order, it is worth quoting from the safety precautions in the 29mm Spigot Mortar (Blacker Bombard) training manual: 'The number 1 will not rest his head on the rubber pad when sighting. This pad is fitted as a safeguard should the bombard recoil excessively.'[26]

Spigot Mortars are a well established family of weapons, with the German *Granatenwerfer* of 1916 being an early successful example. Replacing the conventional gun barrel with a steel rod, fitting into a tubular tail on the projectile, which also contained the propellant, enabled a relatively small, light and unsophisticated launcher to fire a very large projectile. British forces made extensive use of Spigot Mortar technology during the Second World War, including the Blacker Bombard (29mm Spigot Mortar), the PIAT (Projector, Infantry, Anti-Tank), Petard (290mm Spigot Mortar), Hedgehog (multiple launcher for 7in anti-submarine depth charges) and Hedgerow (a version of Hedgehog fired from landing craft to clear mines). These were all systems developed by MD1 (Cornish, 2009, p. 35).

According to the Blacker family, the prototype Blacker Bombard was mounted on a 2pr gun anti-tank carriage.[27] In service, however, the 29mm Spigot Mortar was provided with a robust cruciform 'portable mounting' of steel tube, secured with angle-iron pickets, and four pedestal mountings, designed to be cast into substantial concrete posts.[28] Each 20mm Spigot Mortar was supplied with twelve anti-personnel rounds and twenty 20lb high-explosive anti-tank rounds, which were propelled by a small black powder charge, and more than a match for any contemporary tank.[29] The 29mm Spigot Mortar was officially described as 'the most destructive of all the Home Guard anti-tank weapons' at a time (in 1943) when these included conventional 2pr anti-tank guns and .55in anti-tank rifles.

Documents in The National Archives reveal that army high command reacted with considerable enthusiasm when the Blacker Bombard was demonstrated and tested at Bisley in April 1941.[30] According to GHQ Home Forces, the weapon's performance 'fully justified its adoption as an anti-tank weapon both by regular formations and the Home Guard'. There had been teething troubles and initial scepticism, as is clear from a minute dated 30 April 1941, from one R.J. Sinclair to Engineer Vice Admiral Sir Harold Brown CBE, KCB, Director General Munitions Production at the Ministry of Supply:[31]

I am told that the result of the demonstration yesterday of special Anti-Tank weapons were extremely favourable to the Blacker Bombard and the S.T. [Sticky] Bomb.

Neither of these weapons, of course, are new, but initial defects which made them very much less effective appear to have been overcome and, in particular, the new fuze which D. of A. [Director of Artillery] has designed for the Bombard ammunition has altered the whole complexion of the weapon so far as its effectiveness and desirability from the point of view of the General Staff is concerned.

Sinclair goes on to confirm a General Staff requirement for 14,000 Blacker Bombards/29mm Spigot Mortars, and 3½ million rounds of ammunition. GHQ Home Forces intended to issue Spigot Mortars on a scale of twenty-four per anti-tank regiment, eight per infantry brigade anti-tank company, two to every Home Guard company, and twelve each to detachments of regular troops defending aerodromes. The training of Home Guard instructors would take place at the new official training school, No. 1 Home Guard Training School, at Dorking.[32]

However, and despite the enthusiasm for the Spigot Mortar at senior levels, something of a rural revolt broke out in Wiltshire, when a demonstration failed to convince the local Home Guard that the Spigot Mortar was the support weapon of their dreams. Devices such as the Sten gun, Northover Projector and Blacker Bombard pushed the limits of what could be accepted as a viable and reliable weapon system, and already being at the limit, any further degradation or lowering of standards was likely to have unfortunate results. A rush to issue 29mm Spigot Mortars resulted in early examples leaving the factory without complete sights (the range calibration was printed on a piece of paper), and this, together with an initial batch of poor quality ammunition (referred to in the minute quoted above), undermined confidence in the weapon.[33] The situation was inflamed because the local Home Guard commander was unable to attend, and sent as his representative a lowly HG Lieutenant – one Mark Dineley, proprietor of Bapty & Co.

Dineley was frustrated because he had previously failed to interest the government in a reasonably priced and viable sub-machine gun design, the Hungarian Király, back in May 1939, long before the purchase of the expensive Thompson SMG, and the development of the Lanchester and Sten – which he regarded as 'poor weapons'.[34] Now his 'Berwick St. John Arsenal' was to cease production of highly finished mortars and bomb-throwers and adopt the Blacker Bombard/29mm Spigot Mortar. The demonstration was clearly mishandled, and there is undoubtedly an element of 'not-invented-here syndrome' in Dineley's report, but he makes some valid and intelligent comments about the arming of the Home Guard:[35]

> The Priory
> Berwick St. John
> 3 November 1941
>
> Dear Major Collett,
>
> Under your instructions, 3 NCOs and myself went and attended the Blacker Bombard demonstration at Bulford Camp this morning.
>
> ### The Weapon
> This is an adaption of the old German Stick 'Grenaten Werfer', Types 1915 and 1916.
>
> In these mortars the bomb contains the charge and barrel, which is slipped on to a spigot on the mortar, which has the striker running through it.
>
> This has never been a particularly satisfactory type of mortar and has long been abandoned as unsuitable, i.e. since 1916.
>
> The mortar is a box of tricks, heavy, clumsy and the sighting fragile. The firing mechanism, activated by Bowden cable, will, as Bowden cable always does, go wrong, especially if someone picks it up by it.
>
> It has the normal mortar disadvantages, the most noticeable of which is muzzle loading, meaning exposure [of the] crew when used for flat firing, its normal use against tanks.
>
> It requires a crew of 5, has no very great range and the bombs [are] fragile – the tails get bent and, also owing to their type dirt in the tail tube produces misfires.
>
> ### Tactically
> The weapon is purely static as now made. The bed, made of vast tubes, has to be nailed into the ground by a sledgehammer. The mortar body is clumsy and, as before stated, the bombs long and fragile. Any attempt to move it means the use of a lorry and the attendant hiring troubles, and it takes 5 men about 5–10 minutes to get it into action. When in action its range is short, 100–300 yards, lacks accuracy or reliability (20% misfires and lost fins at demonstration).

It is a weapon which can only be used in open country given a sufficiency of men and time and then is not very good.

It can be used in static defence positions covering road-blocks with better success.

Fitted with wheels or on a car it might be used with some success against crash-landing planes.

Outside this and at road blocks, it is, as far as I can see of very little use to the H.G. Normal Stokes 3" mortars would have been better.

It is a weapon and better than nothing but that is all and Country Platoons, in a large number of cases, would be far better without it, as too many of their few men will tend to be occupied with it instead of harassing the enemy with their L.M.G.s.

There are not enough Infantry to protect it and it is not a mobile or useful enough arm to be worth protecting.

From some personal experience one can have too many kinds of weapons. The Home Guard, in Country Districts, would be better off with Rifle, Sub-machine Guns, L.M.G., Heavy M.G., Grenades – Some Platoons Stokes, some Mobile A.T. Guns, or A.T. Rifles, plus some Land Mines.

The Blacker Bombard is the last weapon I would issue, heavy, complicated, fragile and not super-excellent.

The men I took agree, as did most of the spectators.

(Signed) Mark Dineley
Lieut.

Dineley's report opens a window into the minds of Home Guards, eighteen months into the organisation's existence, and with the war going badly on all fronts. It is clear that the Berwick St John platoon commander is still thinking primarily about enemy airborne troops 'crash-landing planes' and his men harassing enemy infantry with Lewis guns. He is at a loss to understand how the situation will be helped by a weapon only suited to static defence, covering road blocks. That, of course, was precisely how the General Staff wanted to see the Home Guard employed – dug in, in static positions, acting as an endless series of road blocks to slow the enemy and allow the Field Army manoeuvre force to attack at the time and place of its choosing. To say that the Home Guard would be better off with anti-tank guns and anti-tank rifles was stating the obvious, and suggests that even someone as well acquainted with the military and the

British arms industry as Mark Dineley, was unaware of just how severe the losses of conventional equipment were, and (more importantly) how difficult it was proving to make them up. As we shall see in Chapter 8, the Home Guard was in the queue for 2pr anti-tank guns, and anti-tank rifles, but would not (for the most part) receive them until they had been replaced in army service in 1943. Until then, the 29mm Spigot Mortar/Blacker Bombard, even if it was 'not super-excellent', was the best alternative solution for destroying enemy tanks – and that was the British General Staff's most pressing concern.

It is entirely typical of the Home Guard that no one was afraid to air their views, and that the forthright opinions of a Home Guard lieutenant from a Wiltshire hamlet should finish up preserved in the Blacker Bombard files at the National Archives. It was eventually necessary for Brigadier Collingwood MC to reassert military authority and bring the matter to a close, in a minute to Colonel F.G. Drew, GSO1 Home Guard, Salisbury Plain District. The brigadier also makes it crystal clear that the 29mm Spigot Mortar/Blacker Bombard is a weapon the Home Guard shares with the Regular Army:

> I am sorry to hear that members of the Wiltshire Home Guard are inclined to be pessimistic about the Blacker Bombard. I think this is a pity as it has many good points. People who have recently returned from the Home Guard School at DENBIES are most enthusiastic about it.
>
> It undoubtedly had teething troubles to start with but these have now been largely overcome and the number of duds [*misfires*] are now very few.
>
> The issue to the Home Guard and Regular Troops has been on a fifty-fifty basis and I notice that Static Headquarters in 5 Corps District are making good use of their bombards for defending approaches to their Headquarters.

The Spigot Mortar appeared in Home Guard returns in August 1941, but with a nil return, indicating that the weapon was anticipated, but introduction was delayed. The first 130 only appeared in October, curiously, 123 of these were in Northern Command. The following month, when Dineley attended the demonstration in Bulford, 2,150 Spigot Mortars were with the Home Guard, a figure that rose rapidly to 7,643 by February the following year. The highest entry in the Home Guard returns is for 17,954 in September 1942, although that is undoubtedly less than the eventual total, as they were still reaching Home Guard units in 1943. One of these was the Ministry of Food Home Guard, who, being based on the Welsh coast, were a low priority. The author of their unit history said of the

Northover Projector: 'Those of us who had much experience of the Northover Projector prayed fervently that we might never have to employ it to betray our position when attacking a tank' (Smith, 1945, p. 78). He was, though, much more impressed by the 29mm Spigot Mortar: 'Unlike the Northover Projector, the Spigot Mortar, although unorthodox in design was extremely accurate and effective, and had indeed been put to very good use by the defenders of Stalingrad, delivery to whom had for a time precluded its supply to the Home Guard.'

It is clear from the Ministry of Supply files that, once the initial resistance was overcome, demand for the 29mm Spigot Mortar skyrocketed, before the strategic situation began to shift from defensive to offensive and orders were cut back, in August 1942. The initial requirement of 14,000 weapons was increased to a 'finite requirement' for 24,500. Eventually orders were placed for 32,500 mortars, the same number of mobile mountings, and 18,000 static mountings. Fretful minutes in the Ministry of Supply files from 1942 show civil servants trying to determine just how many Spigot Mortars were ordered, delivered and actually needed. It was eventually agreed that 32,195 29mm Spigot Mortars (or Blacker Bombards, as the Ministry insisted on calling them) had been accepted for service, plus 30,275 mobile mountings and 18,162 static mountings.[36]

Not all of these went to the Home Guard or even British troops. As Henry Smith describes in the history of the Ministry of Food Home Guard quoted above, 29mm Spigot Mortars/Blacker Bombards were supplied to the Soviet Union. As at 30 June 1942, military items supplied to the USSR included 250 Blacker Bombards.[37] A Ministry of Supply minute from February 1942 shows this to be part of a total requirement of 5,000 Spigot Mortars for the Soviet Union.[38] It would be interesting to know if the Spigot Mortars saw any action on the Eastern Front. Chamberlain and Gander (1975a, p. 51) state that Blacker Bombards saw operational service 'in North Africa during the siege of Tobruk and were used by some Indian Army units with varying degrees of success'. This is corroborated to some extent by *Home Guard Instruction No. 40*, of November 1941: 'The mortar is effective against heavy tanks at short ranges and has been taken into use in the Middle East.'[39]

There is, though, a ringing endorsement of the combat performance of the 29mm Spigot Mortar, dating from May 1943, when the following entry was published by the War Office in *Home Guard Information Circular No. 27*:

4. The Spigot Mortar
The following extracted from a letter received from a theatre of operations is published for information.

'… Spigot mortars were used extensively to thicken up A.Tk. [anti-tank] defences in our area of … RIDGE – i.e., a defensive and static role during Oct., '42 … They were used with good effect in fwd coy's FDL's [forward company's forward defensive locations] on … RIDGE where the enemy had observation at some 500 yards range. His fire, both mortar and SAA [small arms], was accurate and heavy and our mortar fire did not have much effect. A spigot mortar was put in position during the night and succeeded in subduing the enemy's fire using AP [anti-personnel] bombs …

'… Even if we had more inf. A.Tk. guns we would still use spigots in defence as they were so very inconspicuous, have a tremendous hitting power and are very simple to teach and learn …'[40]

The entry was sponsored by War Office department HG1(T), i.e. Home Guard training, and raises the question of where this action, in which the 29mm Spigot Mortar proved so effective, took place, and who the satisfied user was. The date of October 1942 suggests the place was *Ruweisat* Ridge, and the troops involved were from the Eighth Army. A somewhat bemused exchange on an internet forum thread reveals that records in the Australian War Memorial archives show the 9th Australian Division was equipped with 29mm Spigot Mortars at El Alamein.[41] The New Zealand official war history, which is replete with references to weaponry discussed in this thesis – Sticky bombs, Hawkins mines, and the Spigot Mortar – and amply demonstrates the degree to which British Dominion forces of 1942 were users of weapons that we now associate solely with the Home Guard, indicates that the 29mm Spigot Mortar reached New Zealand troops in North Africa in June 1942:

> The ground at Minqar Qaim was extremely hard and, although the urgency of the task kept many of the troops digging till well after midnight on 26–27 June, some slit trenches were still very shallow and sangars had, in some cases, been built up from the excavated rocks. The digging-in of the spigot mortars, the new but rather big and clumsy infantry anti-tank weapons which were supposed to be most effective if a hit was scored at 100 yards range, proved virtually impossible in the time available. The news that the enemy had 'broken through' at Charing Cross stimulated the diggers to make fresh efforts.[42]

The Kiwis' difficulties become apparent when one considers the recommended design of a Spigot Mortar position (see plates 32–34), which was a deep circular trench, surrounding a central core or pillar on which the mortar stood. This was necessary to afford 360 degrees of traverse and cover to load and fire the weapon, in actions that were expected to take place suddenly and at very short ranges.

There is a longstanding association of the operational use of the 29mm Spigot Mortar with Indian troops, and, given the location and the date, we can be reasonably certain that the satisfied user quoted in *Home Guard Information Circular No. 27* was an officer of the 4th Indian Division. The Indian dimension was elaborated to the author in correspondence with a retired Indian Army officer, J.G. Rawlinson, who in 2002 wrote to the author describing his period as an instructor at the Indian Company Group (ICG) at the Small Arms School at Saugor (now Sagar), between May 1942 and April 1943. Expecting to take over the sniper course, Captain (acting unpaid) Rawlinson found himself responsible for the 29mm Spigot Mortar:

> In June [1942] the first Spigot Mortar, also known as the Blacker Bombard after the inventor, arrived in India. This was an ungainly weapon with a large tripod, on which sat the 'gun', a spigot which fired the bomb. This had a head the size of a football filled with explosive, and a tubular tail which fitted over the spigot. It was an anti-tank weapon with a range of about 500 yards. The mortar had been brought out from England to India by a Captain Faber and sent to Saugor. I recall the delays and frustrations in getting the ammunition from the depot in Bombay, where it had been stored on arrival. Indian red tape held up despatch by about two months. I worked with Captain Faber on the running of courses, which included the drills. (Rawlinson, 2002)

Thus 29mm Spigot Mortars arrived at the Indian Army training centre, and with New Zealand troops in action against the *Afrika Korps*, one month after one was first demonstrated to the Home Guard in Sevenoaks, Kent. This suggests that, at the very least, 'front-line' Home Guard units were being accorded the same priority as Empire and Dominion fighting troops. That Spigot Mortars were in use in the Indian small arms training school prompts the question of whether they were also used operationally in the Far East. Mr Rawlinson was fairly certain this was not the case:

> I have no knowledge of the use of the Mortar outside Saugor, and I cannot say whether it was ever used 'in anger' in Burma. I rather doubt whether it would fit in with the Burmese jungles. It was ungainly, difficult to transport,

and with [*sic*] its limited range allowed it to be easily located and destroyed by the Japs. I did know it had been used in the Western Desert, but I do not know to what effect.[43]

The National Archives do, in fact, hold records of experiments in mounting a 'Blacker Bombard' on a Sherman tank, which took place in 1944, under the auspices of Allied Forces South East Asia.[44] Beyond that, operational use of the Blacker Bombard/Spigot Mortar on operations in the Far East awaits further research.

Mr Rawlinson's reply echoes Mark Dineley's observations on the Spigot Mortar's shortcomings, which turned initial enthusiasm into disillusionment. The Spigot Mortar was extremely heavy: the gun itself weighed 112lb, the pivot 56lb and each leg 44lb, and it was moved in five man-loads, exclusive of ammunition (increased to seven in an amendment of 1944).[45] Had it been deployed on a 2pr gun carriage, or even a simple trolley, like the Soviet *Sokolov* Maxim machine-gun carriage, as Dineley suggested, its use might have been easier. As it was, its short range and immobility were tactical limitations that could render it a one-shot gun.[46] In the defensive context of the UK, this problem was countered by preparing a series of up to four weapon pits for every Spigot Mortar. Each pit contained a concrete pedestal onto which the firing post could be quickly mounted. Well camouflaged and defiladed, these positions made the most of the mortar as an ambush weapon.

The Northover Projector, although easy to produce, had a performance that was, at best, marginal; the 29mm Spigot Mortar, although undeniably effective, lacked mobility. Both these faults were addressed by what E.W. Ashworth calls 'the last and best of the privately developed weapons, the Ordnance Smoothbore (OSB) gun 3in Mk. I, or "Smith Gun"' (Ashworth, 1998, p. 46). The gun was developed by Major (Retired) William H. Smith, the managing director of Trianco Ltd, a firm of structural engineers. Writing in the *Journal of the Ordnance Society*, in 2005, Terry Gander says of the Smith Gun:

> Mr Smith must have been a very capable engineer. Appreciating that priority had to be given to speed of production at a time when every source of raw materials was already hard pressed, he placed emphasis on simplicity and incorporation of as many non-critical materials as could be managed. Taking heed of these basic requirements he approached his project with a completely open and original mind. (Gander, 2005, p. 60)

It is clear from the correspondence in the Ministry of Aircraft Production files that initially, in the spring of 1941, the Smith Gun was viewed with considerable enthusiasm. It was anticipated that the army would order 20,000 guns, with further orders for the Royal Navy 'for all ships', the RAF wanted the gun for airfield defence, and there would undoubtedly be orders from the Empire and Dominions and probably the Soviet Union too.[47] Under the circumstances, it made sense to pay-off Smith as quickly as possible and, in effect, buy the rights to his gun. In April 1941, very substantial payment of £30,000 was agreed, with some graciousness on Smith's side, payable monthly as war loans. Although there was great enthusiasm for Smith's gun, it was its ammunition that created the biggest stir. The Smith Gun fired a 3in shell which benefited from an 'obturator case', which expanded on firing to seal the shell in the bore. Both bore and shell could be a slack fit, allowing the barrel to be manufactured from ordinary drawn steel tube and hugely easing manufacturing tolerances for both gun and projectile. It was even anticipated that Smith's obturating system might be applied to 'Stokes guns', i.e. conventional muzzle-loading mortars, to extend their range.[48]

At first sight the Smith Gun resembles a conventional artillery piece and limber, but, although not as radical a solution to the tank threat as the German *Panzerfaust*, it displayed highly original features. Its low weight enabled the gun and limber to be towed by a 10hp car, a single horse, or as separate loads behind motorcycles, and its large wheels enabled the crew to manhandle it into position over rubble or broken ground.[49] Coming into action, gun and limber (correctly termed 'trailer, artillery, No. 39') were tipped on to their left-hand wheel. This allowed the gun to be traversed through 360 degrees with the minimum of effort. The 54in, low-velocity, smoothbore barrel fired a 6lb 3in calibre, finned HEAT round, with an effective range of 200yd (100yd 'best'), and an 8lb fragmented cast iron anti-personnel round, fitted with a No. 245 fuse, or the ubiquitous No. 247 'Bakelite' fuse. This was effective at 650yd, 'best' being 150yd. The gun could also fire high-explosive or smoke 3in mortar bombs.[50] By way of comparison, the maximum range of the conventional 2pr anti-tank gun was (by 1943) 500yd, 200yd 'best', and it had no anti-personnel capability.[51] The Smith Gun could penetrate 3.15in (78.75mm) of armour, or put a 2ft diameter hole in a 9in reinforced concrete wall.[52] Ten 8lb shells, or five 10lb bombs, were carried on the gun, and another forty 8lb shells or twenty 10lb bombs on the limber.[53]

In late spring 1941, orders were placed for 6,000 guns and limbers, and 2,600,000 rounds of ammunition. The provisional manual for the gun, now designated 'The 3in OSB Gun' (OSB standing for 'Ordnance Smooth Bore'), was

3-INCH OSB GUN—COMING OUT OF ACTION IN THE OPEN USING TOGGLE ROPES.

COMING OUT OF ACTION IN THE OPEN — BY USING TOGGLE ROPES

A Smith gun coming out of action, illustrated in Home Guard Instruction No. 52, *Battlecraft and Battle Drill for the Home Guard, Part IV, The Organization of Home Guard Defence*, published by GHQ Home Forces in November 1943. Contrary to the traditional bucolic image of the Home Guard, the Smith gun is portrayed in action in a blitzed urban landscape. The gun presented a tall target in open ground. (Author's collection)

issued in July 1941 and the gun was carried as a nil return on Home Guard returns from August. However, the first examples – just six issued to Northern District – did not appear until February 1942. This appears to have been a two-month troop trial, with the guns withdrawn in April. In May 1942, ten guns appeared in London District, the following month there were 145 on Home Guard strength. A year after the gun first appeared on the returns there were just 1,328 in service with the Home Guard. The highest figure in the returns (November 1942) is 2,187.

All members of Sevenoaks Home Guard were expected to show a 'working knowledge' of the Smith Gun, Northover Projector and Spigot Mortar in the training schedule of December 1942, the Smith Gun, like the Spigot Mortar, having arrived earlier in that year.[54] Similarly, the fetchingly blue-painted Smith Gun in the historical collection of the RAF Regiment is stated to have entered service with that organisation in 1942.[55] The slow roll-out to the Home Guard is almost certainly due to this Ministry of Aircraft Production project going to meet MAP requirements (such as airfield defence) first, which is interesting, as, once again, it calls into question the 'Home Guard only' view of sub-artillery. To give an impression of the way Home Guard support weapons were organised, September 1943 saw 6 (Ministry of Food) Platoon of E Company, 2nd City of London (Civil Service Battalion), Home Guard, become that company's designated Sub-Artillery [*sic*] Platoon. The platoon was equipped with one Smith Gun, two Spigot Mortars, one Boys anti-tank rifle and a Lewis gun. Subsequently two Vickers machine guns were added to the platoon's considerable firepower.

Tactical deployment of the Smith Gun is extensively covered in *Home Guard Instruction No. 51, Battlecraft and Battle Drill for the Home Guard, Part IV, The Organization of Home Guard Defence*, of November 1943, which stresses the need for covering fire, to the extent that a three-man Browning Automatic Rifle (BAR) group is assigned to the Smith Gun detachment. Whether this is a result of operational experience with conventional (i.e. 2pr) anti-tank guns is unclear (War Office manuals dealing with anti-tank guns in defence, stress concealment, flash, mutual defence against encirclement, and siting within defended localities[56]), but it was already a recognised factor when the manual for the Smith Gun was issued in July 1942: 'The gun should never be called upon to operate unsupported by infantry and the detachment should be provided with small arms and grenades for self defence.'[57] This requirement to provide personal weapons for the gun crew is important, because it totally undermines the oft-heard assertion that crew-served weapons were issued to ameliorate the shortage of Home Guard weaponry.

The 1943 battle drills manual drives home the point about covering fire, with a series of parade ground drills in which the BAR group participates alongside the gun and crew:[58]

Each man comes to attention in turn, calls out his number and duty, and stands at ease. The duties are:-

Detachment Commander. – I command the detachment, am responsible for all orders, select the gun site, and control the fire.

No. 1. – I fire the gun. I also load and set the range when in the open.

No. 2. – I assist No. 1 and pass ammunition. I load, and set the range when the gun is firing from behind cover.

No. 3. – I carry ammunition from the trailer to the gun site. I also drive the towing vehicle.

BAR Group. – We are attached for covering fire and all-round protection.

The image of the BAR group chanting their *devoir* in unison is delightful. The 3in OSB Gun (Smith Gun) was listed as one of the three heavy weapons available to Home Guard mobile battalions and companies, alongside the anti-tank rifle and 2pr anti-tank gun, which started to reach the Home Guard during 1943, as 6pr guns and PIATs became increasingly available for the regular forces.[59] It is worthwhile pausing to compare the capabilities of all the Home Guard weapons as they were given in November 1943, the apogee of the force in terms of training and equipment:[60]

Northover Projector using:-	*Maximum*	*Best*
68 grenade	60 yards	50 yards
76 SIP grenade	120 ,,	70 ,,
36 grenade–		
4 sec. fuze	150 ,,	—
7 sec. fuze	200 ,,	—
29-mm Spigot Mortar:–		
20 lb. HE anti-tank	200 ,,	100 yards
14 lb. HE anti-personnel	750 ,,	400 ,,
3-inch OSB Gun:–		
8 lb. HE anti-personnel	650 ,,	150 ,,
6 lb. HE anti-tank	200 ,,	100 ,,
2-pr., armour piercing shot	500 ,,	200 ,,

The original design of the 3in OSB Gun was geared to anti-tank operations, with open sights and a 360° free traverse. Nevertheless, through its service life there were efforts to develop it as a gun-howitzer in the indirect fire role. The 29mm Spigot Mortar's long range and hard-hitting anti-personnel shell made it a useful infantry mortar, as had been demonstrated at Ruweisat Ridge. But opening fire compromised the position, weapon and crew, necessitating an immediate move, which was easier said than done, given the weapon's lack of mobility. As a result, priority was given to anti-tank action, holding fire until the last possible moment. To quote the manual: 'it will be realised that the element of surprise essential to success will be lost if the mortar is first used on anti-personnel targets at long ranges.'[61] The 3in OSB Gun, although lacking 100yd on the Spigot Mortar, still had a respectable range, particularly in close country or an urban area, and the bonus of mobility. It is interesting to note that by November 1943 the 3in OSB Gun's anti-personnel capability was being listed above its anti-tank performance. This is also reflected in the notes on tactical handling:

> *In defence* the anti-personnel shell should be used to cover dead ground by either direct or indirect fire, the gun can be fired off any sort of ground provided the wheel base is roughly level. Owing to difficulties of concealment, alternative positions should be selected and prepared …
>
> *In reserve* the gun can be retained by the Force commander with the reserve to reinforce any threatened locality with the minimum of delay …
>
> *In counter attack* the gun can support infantry with fire from a flank. It can be used to dislodge enemy established in a building. Having wheels, it is more suitable than the Northover for use with standing patrols … [62]

For indirect fire the entire gun, by virtue of the fact that it rotated on its lower wheel, and with a little DIY from the crew, became a dial sight, a system that was both simple and workable:

3. *Indirect Laying*

    i. When gun and target are not intervisible, the method of 'indirect laying' is adopted. This method requires that a scale of leads should be painted or chalked on the base cone … A stick or post is planted about 50 yards in front of the gun on the estimated line to the target. For the first round the gun is laid on the post over the open sight and clamped. An arrow is chalked on the base wheel opposite the '0' graduation. The range is set on the quadrant sight, thus depressing the line of sight and displacing the bubble. The bubble is brought back to the centre of its run by means of the control levers and the elevation locking lever clamped. The observer, who is away from the gun but in a position to see the fall of shot, orders fresh ranges as required, and these are applied to the sights, and the gun relaid from round to round as already described. The correction to direction is estimated and ordered as lead. The layer traverses the gun until the lead ordered is opposite the arrow [on the base cone of the gun mounting], and reclamps. The following table shows the amount of lead which should be ordered … [63]

The Smith Gun, or 3in OSB Gun, was an imaginative and workmanlike weapon, and there is no reason to doubt that given the chance it would have given a decent account of itself. Certainly, the nearest equivalent, the German 8.8cm *Racketenwerfer 43 'Püppchen'*, a simple artillery piece that fired a rocket-propelled HEAT round from a smooth-bore closed barrel, proved effective in the limited service it saw (although the *Panzerschrek* shoulder-fired rocket launcher used a similar round more economically and saw more extensive service). There remains the question of to what extent 3in OSB Guns produced served beyond the Home Guard. In 1975 Chamberlain and Gander stated that 'the Smith Gun was issued to Home Guard units and at one time it was intended to issue it to regular Home Defence units, but that does not appear to have happened'.[64] Ashworth, writing more recently, states: 'A total of 4,000 Smith Guns were built with a small proportion being used by the Regular Army and RAF regiment for the static defence of airfields.'[65] Air Ministry records in The National Archives make it quite clear that 3in OSB Guns were widely used for 'aerodrome defence' during the period 1941–43, with RAF personnel being trained as gun crews,[66] and, as we have seen, one RAF example actually survives in the historical collection of the RAF Regiment.

However, the Smith Gun/3in OSB Gun does not figure in any of the Western Desert accounts that show extensive use of other contemporary unconventional weapons – the Hawkins mine, Sticky bomb and 29mm Spigot Mortar – by Commonwealth troops. Records survive of experiments carried out in 1943, to determine if a Smith Gun could be dropped by parachute from a Wellington bomber aircraft, in order to provide a support weapon for airborne troops (an airborne derivative of the 6pr anti-tank gun was subsequently adopted), but the 3in OSB Gun only saw service in the UK. Given that the 29mm Spigot Mortar saw quite extensive service in the Western Desert, it may seem strange that the powerful and versatile 3in OSB Gun did not. Indeed, it will be apparent that the anticipated Smith Gun 'gold rush' failed to materialise. The most serious shortcoming of Major Smith's gun was its most innovative feature, the fact that it went into action using its 4ft-diameter wheel as a turntable. The gun needed to be levelled with sandbags or similar if it was to be used on any sloping or uneven ground, and in its firing configuration was also very tall, overall width (i.e. height 'in action') being 5'6". In open ground this presented far too large a target for an anti-tank weapon with a 'best' range of 100yd. For these reasons the 3in OSB Gun would not have commended itself to use in the undulating and barren desert. In the hedgerows of Kent and Sussex, or in blitzed towns, the gun had rather more potential, and much training seems to have centred on using the gun in urban warfare.

Understanding the issues surrounding the development and use of the British Second World War 'sub-artillery' is absolutely pivotal to a comprehension of the wider arguments concerning the arming of the Home Guard. Although issuing unconventional crew-served weapons might have helped ease the embarrassment caused by the shortfall of conventional arms for the Home Guard (a contention which is disputed, in any case), there were also recipients, such as the army county battalions, Dominion and Empire forces and the RAF Regiment, whom the government would not have felt politically obliged to placate. The clue to understanding the sub-artillery is in the nature of the equipment itself. The LDV formed as a result of popular anxiety about German paratroops, with whom the Home Guard remained fixated until well into 1941. It is abundantly clear that the sub-artillery and anti-tank grenades of 1940–41 were developed as anti-*Panzer*, not anti-*Falschirmjaeger* weapons, and were a reaction to high command, not grassroots, concerns. They were issued to Home Defence units – army, RAF *and* Home Guard – not to keep the Home Guard feeling important, but in response to the army command's own nightmare scenario that German armour would get ashore and there would be nothing to stop it, resulting in panic and *Panzers* pushing inland unchecked.

Of the various weapons devised in 1940–41, the Blacker Bombard/29mm Spigot Mortar and the Sticky bomb were the most practical, but in the case of the unwieldy Spigot Mortar, only in operations based on prepared defence. Accordingly, both saw widespread service in the Western Desert, until the military balance shifted, and operations switched to the offence, at which point, like the trench mortars of the First World War, the Spigot Mortar was left behind.[67] In the UK, where the military task remained defensive, the sub-artillery remained relevant. As regular troops were drawn away to other theatres of war, the operation of these equipments increasingly fell to the Home Guard, which is one reason why they are so strongly associated with that organisation. Short memories in the army, and Brophy's suggestion that some of the new anti-tank weapons were 'exclusive to the Home Guard', together with the fact that most operational use was in the hands of Dominion and Empire troops, led to the belief that these were 'Home Guard only' weapons, which continues to this day.

There is a real need to challenge a narrative convention, which, when discussing sub-artillery, appears unshakeable. To take an example concerning the

3in OSB Gun on the internet, a most important research resource for modern schoolchildren, the National Army Museum website states:

> The Smith Gun was designed by the Trianco toy company at the beginning of the Second World War (1939–1945). It was one of several homemade pieces of artillery produced in Britain during the desperate days of 1940 when the threat of German invasion was at its greatest …

After explaining that the gun entered service in 1941 with the Home Guard and for airfield defence, it concludes:

> The Smith Gun was one of the many weird and wonderful devices used by Captain Mainwaring and the Walmington-on-Sea Home Guard of TV's 'Dad's Army'. This is one of the few remaining examples in existence anywhere in the world.

The 3in OSB Gun/Smith Gun is, of course, exactly as 'homemade' as the Mk III Sten gun (as manufactured by toy manufacturer Tri-ang), and the sub-artillery deserves a better reputation. The Home Guard's automatic distrust of anything not on issue to Regular infantry has been noted, and the weapons were not without their shortcomings, resulting in an understandable, and unfortunate, conflation. Seen objectively, and in context, the sub-artillery must be viewed as a genuine attempt to provide defensive anti-tank weapons quickly, at a period, between the summer of 1940 and the winter of 1942, when the outcome of the war was by no means a forgone conclusion. The three weapons, the Northover Projector, the Blacker Bombard and the Smith Gun, were less successful than they might have been, not because they were poorly constructed – they were not – or because they didn't work – they did. Their shortcoming was their lack of mobility, in artillery parlance, not the ordnance but the carriage. It would have taken very little work to mount each weapon on the sort of simple two-wheeled carriage used for the German *Püppchen*. That they were not so mounted is a reflection of the military mindset when they were first accepted for service, which saw assaulting *Panzers* being checked by desperately held fixed lines of defence, whose defenders had nowhere to run, no prospect of reinforcement or withdrawal, and would seek to degrade the attackers by attrition.

8

ARTILLERY

Thus far in this study we have followed the arming of the Home Guard from the initial distribution of service rifles to the LDV in the most threatened coastal areas of England, through various stages of unofficial and official improvisation; the arrival of military reserve stock and commercial small arms from the United States, and the issue of current British-issue Sten sub-machine guns, No. 4 service rifles and Bren light machine guns, finally bringing (at least in some areas) the Home Guard armoury in line with that of the British Regular Army. In this chapter we will look at parallel developments, which saw the Home Guard armed with the really big guns – coastal artillery, field artillery, anti-aircraft and anti-tank artillery (in which latter category we will, for convenience, also consider the Boys anti-tank rifle). In doing so we will illustrate the manner in which the Home Guard evolved rapidly from a civilian militia to a valued military resource completely integrated into the structures of Home Defence. We will also continue to rehabilitate serviceable weaponry that has gained an undeservedly poor reputation.

Writing after stand-down, on 29 December 1944, Director General Home Guard described the roles of the Home Guard as follows: Infantry and General Service including anti-tank; anti-aircraft; bomb disposal; coastal defence; MT columns; water and mounted patrols.[1] The first of these refers to infantry skills, which still made up the bulk of Home Guard activity, and bomb disposal, MT columns, and water and mounted patrols fall outside the scope of this study. In this chapter we will start our examination of the 'big guns' by looking at the Home Guard's involvement in coastal defence. The Home Guard began to be recruited to augment Royal Artillery coast artillery personnel in the latter part of 1941. At that time coastal batteries were very much 'front-line' positions, expected to engage enemy raids and landings, marauding enemy warships, surfaced submarines and attack craft. They also provided covering fire for naval inspection parties sent to examine passing shipping, and for friendly ships as they lay in harbour. The possibility of involving the Home Guard in coast artillery started to be examined in July 1941,[2] and reflected the move away from the static defence of the UK favoured by General Ironside, to the mobile forces championed by his successor Alan Brooke (Danchev and Todman, 2001, p. 94). Brooke needed to extract troops from the coast batteries in order to build up the armoured divisions that would be the effective counter to a German invasion, but do so without compromising the effectiveness of his first line of defence.[3] The idea was to replace each of the higher gun numbers (i.e. those men whose duties were mostly handling ammunition[4]), with two Home Guards (to allow for part-time working), and also raise a Home Guard platoon for local defence of each battery. The chief difficulty lay with maintaining full readiness whilst depending, in part, on part-timers, and it took until September 1941 before HQ Home Forces and Director General Home Guard had thrashed out the detail and recruiting could begin.

The importance of coast artillery had been established in the reign of Henry VIII, when a chain of purpose-built coastal artillery forts were constructed, many of which were so well placed they were still being manned during the Second World War. It was also painfully emphasised in June 1667, when a Dutch fleet captured the fort at Sheerness in Kent and entered the Medway, to wreak havoc amongst the anchored British fleet. The threat did not pass with the end of the age of sail as, during the First World War, the Kaiser's High Seas Fleet bombarded English coastal towns, including Scarborough, Hartlepool and Whitby. The bombardment of Hartlepool by the German battlecruisers, *Seydlitz* and *Moltke*, and heavy cruiser *Blücher*, commenced at 8.10 a.m. on 16 December 1914, and in 40 minutes 1,150 shells were fired at the shore gun emplacements and harbour, killing nine and wounding twelve of the coast artillery crews, as well as killing eighty-six civilians and wounding 424. Hartlepool's Heugh and Lighthouse batteries fought back, firing 143 6in shells, damaging three of the German ships, including the *Blücher*.[5]

Britain's shore batteries were abandoned in the 1950s,[6] and there is, therefore, a temptation to look on Second World War coast artillery as being old-fashioned and in decline. This is certainly not how it was viewed during the Second World War, indeed 153 new 'Emergency Coast Batteries' were built in 1940. We can (and admitting considerable latitude and blurring of boundaries) usefully categorise the coastal gun positions into the following groups:

- ▸ Coast Artillery Batteries: Established and formal positions, many of which were sited in artillery forts that had been in occupation (and an almost continuous state of development) for four hundred years
- ▸ Emergency Coast Batteries: Properly configured gun positions built hastily in 1940 to defend vulnerable coastal points that had previously been overlooked
- ▸ Beach Batteries: Improvised positions in which a gun of almost any type or vintage might be bolted to some form of firing platform from which it could be used to engage an enemy landing force over open sights

One Emergency Coast Battery, at Workington docks, on the Cumberland coast, has been examined as part of a wider study of the Workington Home Guard, by Russell W. Barnes, to whom I am indebted for kindly allowing me to share his research.[7] Workington serves as a useful example of the completeness and sophistication of some Emergency Coast Batteries, and the importance of the role played by the Home Guard in the coast defences. Construction of the Emergency Coast Batteries at Workington and Bransty (Whitehaven) began in July 1940, while nearby Maryport received a Beach Battery at the same time. The three installations together formed 406 Coast Battery, manned by 561 (later 562) Regiment, Royal Artillery. Two 4in BL (Breech Loading) Mk VII guns were emplaced at Workington, two more at Whitehaven, and one at Maryport. The 4in guns at Workington dated from 1912 and 1914 (the design having been first introduced in 1908), and they would have originally been mounted in the secondary armament positions of major warships, such as a Dreadnought battleship, or as primary armament on a cruiser.[8] The Admiralty Gunnery Branch handbook describes the guns as follows:

> There are three designs of 4-inch BL guns. The Mark VII is a high velocity gun, having a M.V. of 2,852 f.s. It is mounted as an anti-torpedo craft gun in large ships, and in the main armament of smaller ships. The Mark VIII and VIII★ are medium velocity guns, having a MV of 2,287 f.s. They are mounted in light craft where heavy deck strains cannot be allowed.[9]

Apart from their use on warships and in shore emplacements, these versatile guns were widely used to arm merchant ships during both World Wars. At Workington, the guns were emplaced in separate concrete casemates 30yd apart. Each could traverse through 80 degrees and had a range of 2,000 to 10,000yd, with 6,000yd as the limit of effective fire.[10]

At Workington gunfire was directed from the Battery Observation Post (BOP), which was equipped with a 4ft 6in Barr and Stroud prismatic coincidence rangefinder (replaced in April 1942 with an 80cm rangefinder[11]) and a Dumaresq, a device which calculated the speed of a target relative to the line of fire, to enable the correct deflection (aim off) and range to be given to the gun-layers. The equipment was the same as that was carried by a well-armed Defensively Equipped Merchant Ship (DEMS).[12] In addition, the guns were flanked on either side by two 'Defence Electric Lights' or 'DELs'. These were searchlights, positioned 323yd apart, controlled from the BOP, which could be used to illuminate and range a target at night. These arrangements were quite sufficient for the intended role of the battery, which Russell Barnes describes as follows:

> Enemy attacks by fleet action on the West Cumberland coastline were considered unlikely. It was thought that the greatest threat would be an audacious invasion attempt with violent assaults on coastal defences by the use of gas, dive-bombers and machine-gunnery. Enemy troops would use light craft and parachute landings in an attempt to secure a beach-head. Port and harbour installations were considered to be under threat from close-range warship gunfire and blockships. Enemy submarines were thought to be a likely form of attack.[13]

Construction of the batteries was undertaken by civilian contractors under Royal Engineer Works supervision, and the technical aspects were the responsibility of experts from the Coast Artillery School and a specialist gun mounting party. In operation, apart from Royal Artillery personnel, there were also Royal Marines, who were responsible for signalling to shipping in the Solway Firth, and naval personnel – who made up the Royal Naval Examination Party, which boarded ships halted under the battery's guns in the designated area known as 'Workington Roads'.

The reader will have noticed that there is no mention of Home Guard – and this is an important point. The early history of the Workington Emergency Coast Battery serves to illustrate the extent to which ad hoc, extemporised defences were constructed for army use. It also illustrates the commonality between emergency armament for Home Defence and emergency maritime armament, which we have noted in previous chapters. At the time of the battery's construction, in the summer of 1940, there was no prospect of the Local Defence Volunteers (as they still were at that stage) participating in its operation. This changed, however, in December 1941, when recruiting advertisements for a new Home Guard unit were placed in local newspapers.[14] In the case of Workington, many of the men who responded were Special Constables, who had not been encouraged to join the Home Guard up to that point, as they had other emergency and volunteer duties. The Home Guard coast artillery volunteer unit formed in January 1942, and began training alongside Regular personnel, reaching a sufficient standard of competence to be awarded Royal Artillery shoulder flashes and be entitled to wear the white lanyard of the trained gunner.[15]

The Royal Artillery battery was divided into three eight-hour watches, with eight (or, ideally nine) men crewing each of the 4in guns. The Home Guard contingent joined with the Regulars at night, parading at 7.25 p.m. and being dismissed at 8 a.m. The coast artillery task was 'for real', and required high levels of competence and vigilance. There were a number of occasions when the batteries at Workington and Whitehaven actually fired across the bows of vessels not flying the correct signal, or not responding to signals from the shore. This fire could either be a burst of machine-gun fire from a Lewis gun, or a 'Bring-to' round – a sand-filled projectile from one of the 4in guns. It is recorded in the War Diary of 561 Regiment (of which only two months' entries survive[16]), that on 20 September 1941, Workington fired two bursts of Lewis gun fire across the bows of one fishing boat trying to enter the harbour with the incorrect signals and a week later fired a 'Bring-to' round across the bows of another. The other surviving month, April 1942, also saw Workington firing a 'Bring-to' round, this time at a merchant ship, and stopped another merchantman with warning bursts from the Lewis gun. The same month Whitehaven fired two 'Bring-to' rounds. This suggests that either these were two particularly active months, or the batteries were required to fire warning shots quite frequently.

By 'stand-down', in November 1944, 7,000 Home Guard were employed in coast artillery, freeing around half that number of Regular gunners for duties elsewhere (Brophy, 1945, p. 41). The professionalism of the Home Guard in this demanding role, and the extent to which they integrated with the Regular Army was praised by Major Winter, Commanding Officer 562 Regiment (as it had become), when all the Home Guard, including the coast artillery units, was stood-down in November 1944:

It has been given to me, as Regimental Commander in Coast Artillery for more than four years, to be in at the birth of several fine bodies of Home Guard Coast Artillery Personnel, and to watch them and try to help in their steady advancement towards becoming Gunners of high proficiency and outstanding zeal. Of these colleagues of mine, men whom it has been a delight and honour for me to number as operational members of my Regiment, there is no section, sub-unit or battery which stands out more prominently as an example of the qualities and attainments required for this great service, than the Workington Coastal Artillery Home-Guard.[17]

Ian Hogg (2002, p. 194) lists the following naval guns as having been made available by the Admiralty and subsequently emplaced in Second World War Emergency Coast Batteries:

6in Gun Mks 7, 11, 11★, 12, 12A, 13, 16
5.5in Gun Mk 1 (naval gun of 1915 unrelated to the Land Service 5.5in gun)
4.7in Gun Mk 5
4in BL Gun Mk 7
4in BL Gun Mk 9
4in QF Gun Mk 4
12pdr
3in
3pdr

He goes on to say:

[A]nother offer was of twenty-seven French 138mm guns removed from the French warships *Courbet* and *Paris*. These were said to be the 1910 model, but it turned out that they were a mixture of 1910, 1918, 1923, 1924, 1925, 1927 and 1929 models, none of which was exactly the same. They were provisionally allocated the nomenclature 'Ordnance QF 138mm Mk 6 or Mk 7' depending on the original model, an odd selection since there never was a Mk 1 to 5. In February 1942, the director of Artillery reported that he had had the guns carefully examined at Hilsea Ordnance Depot; all were so worn as to be at the end of their useful life, one so badly that no trace of rifling remained in the bore. The offer, therefore, was declined.

Contrary to the assertion that the French 138mm guns were declined, 561 Regiment's War Diary has the following entry for 12 April 1942: 'Whitehaven – 138mm Gun proofed and pronounced ready for action.'[18] *Courbet* and *Paris* were Dreadnoughts, launched in 1911 and 1912 respectively, and rebuilt in the 1920s (Moore, 2001, p. 184). *Courbet* was seized in Portsmouth, after the Franco–German armistice, and disarmed and 'hulked' in April 1941, subsequently being sunk as a breakwater during the Normandy landings,[19] *Paris* was seized in Plymouth and spent the remainder of the war as a depot ship. In addition to their main armament of twelve 305mm (12in) guns, each ship carried twenty-two 138mm (5.4in) guns for anti-torpedo boat defence – the same role for which British Dreadnoughts carried 4in Mk VII guns.

The 'Mk 6 or 7' designation can best be explained by the fact that seven different year marks of 138mm gun were salvaged from the two ships, and presumably only the most recent, i.e. those dating from 1927 and 1929, were deemed still useable. This might also explain why only twenty-seven out of a possible forty-four 138mm guns were offered for coastal service. As we have already seen, the Ordnance authorities tended to display a cautious attitude that was at odds with the seriousness of the situation in 1940–14. However, common sense clearly prevailed, and the sketch by former wartime army cadet Frank Lewthwaite clearly shows two 138mm guns from what he identifies as 'the cruiser' *Paris* emplaced at Whitehaven.[20] Removing standard-issue 4in (*c.* 105mm) guns, for use elsewhere, and replacing them with non-standard, but powerful, 138mm (*c.* 5.4in) guns, and whatever ammunition was seized with them, makes good sense, as the change over took place in the spring of 1942, when the prospect of enemy action against the Cumberland coast was greatly diminished.[21]

Having started with the emplacement of 4in BL guns at Whitehaven, Workington and Maryport, we have now added Lewis light machine guns and a pair of French 138mm guns to the armament used by the gunners of 561/562 Regiments and their Home Guard colleagues. In fact the War Diary, although only a fragment survives, allows us to add still more weaponry. We know, for example, that the beach battery at Maryport was equipped with a French 75mm gun on a static mount, and that this gun was removed on 28 April 1942, following the arrival of a '75mm Fr Mobile Gun' on 6 April. Whitehaven lost the second of its 4in guns and gained a '6pdr 6 cwt Mobile Gun' on 29 April.[22]

The 6pr 6cwt was a shortened version of the 6pr 8cwt Hotchkiss naval gun of the 1880s, and was used as the main armament of First World War British 'Male' tanks ('Females' being armed with Lewis or Hotchkiss machine guns). These 6pr guns were quite widely used in the Second World War for emergency defences, both on the coast and inland, on mounts varying from field carriages to armoured trains. It is tempting to imagine that they were salvaged from the 265 war-surplus 'Presentation Tanks', donated by the Army Council to various civic authorities in 1919, as thanks for the efforts made to generate War Savings – almost all of which were, unfortunately, scrapped in 1940. Sadly, this swords-into-ploughshares-into-swords theory founders on the fact that the presentation tanks were all machine-gun-armed 'Females'.[23] This in itself is interesting, as it suggests that the 'Males', or at least their armament, were preserved for possible future use. The 57mm/2.24in 6pr 8cwt of the Mk I tank, and the shortened 6pr 6cwt of its successor, as fitted to the Mk IV tank of 1917 (the first specialist tank gun ever manufactured), were the largest calibre guns mounted as main armament on British tanks until the arrival of the 6pr 7cwt in 1941. Although supplanted by the 3pr, and later the 2pr, during the inter-war years, it is apparent that numbers were retained in store after the First World War, still mounted in the curved vertical mantlets needed to fit the side sponsons of First World War tanks.

In 1940 these guns were returned to service in a variety of mountings. In 'front-line' Sussex, for example, the beachfront at Bognor Regis was defended by a 6pr 6cwt on a field carriage (below), and at Bodiam Castle, one appears to have been mounted in a Type 25 pillbox instead of a 2pr anti-tank gun.[24] The 6pr was designed to fire a high-explosive (HE) shell, but for anti-tank use during the Second World War solid steel armour piercing shot was provided. The Home Guard took over its first 6prs from the army in October 1941. Forty-nine 6pr 'light coast defence guns' were in Home Guard service in March 1942, and 124 by November 1942[25] (the last month for which figures are available). Clearly, these improvisations were developed for Home Defence use by the army and subsequently passed on to the Home Guard, and it would be unfair to characterise the 6pr 6cwt field gun, delightfully Heath-Robinson as it undoubtedly appears as a 'Home Guard' weapon.

Apart from the emplaced 4in guns, Workington Emergency Coast Battery was, like Maryport, also equipped with a mobile French 75mm gun, and it might seem odd issuing these field pieces to coastal artillery. In fact there was nothing new in this, as coast batteries and coaling stations throughout the Empire were always equipped with field or mountain guns as 'movable armament', chiefly to defend against landward attack.[26] This was the case at Workington, where the 75mm field gun was used to defend the battery from landward, for training, and to supplement the 4in guns in the coastal role. The Emergency Coast Battery's responsibilities were given, in declining order of priority, as follows:[27]

▸ Anti-shipping
▸ Support of the Royal Naval Examination Service

▶ Defence of the Beach and Shoreline
▶ Landward Defences

The landward defences at Workington consisted of three 'dug-outs', two behind the north searchlight position, and one north of the BOP (Battery Observation Post). Around a third of the small garrison could be spared for local defence, and in addition to the 75mm gun, the battery was armed with SMLE rifles and (later in the war) with Sten guns and Bren guns. The final defensive element of the batteries at Workington and Whitehaven consisted of 'Z' twin anti-aircraft rocket launchers. We will be looking at 'Z' AA in more detail later, but first we will look in broader terms at the Home Guard's use of field guns and anti-tank guns.

In Chapter 3 we noted Churchill's description of the transfer of war material from the USA to the UK in the summer of 1940:

> As early as June 1 the President sent out orders to the War and Navy Departments to report what weapons they could spare for Britain and France … In forty-eight hours the answers were given, and on June 3 [General] Marshall approved the lists. The first list comprised half a million .30 calibre rifles manufactured in 1917 and 1918 and stored in grease for more than twenty years. For these there were about 250 cartridges apiece. There were 900 *"soixante-quinze"* field guns, with a million rounds, 80,000 machine-guns, and various other items … Since every hour counted, it was decided that the Army should sell (for thirty-seven million dollars) everything on the list to one concern, which could in turn resell immediately to the British and French.
>
> By these extraordinary measures the United States left themselves with the equipment for only 1,800,000 men, the minimum figure stipulated by the American Army's mobilisation plan. (Churchill, 1955, p. 127)

The '*Soixante-Quinze*' (*Matériel de 75mm Mle 1897*) was a French field gun that transformed field artillery at the end of the nineteenth century. The first true Quick Firing or 'QF' field gun, the '75' used a fixed round of ammunition – shell and cartridge, with a primer in the base – much like an oversized rifle round. At the time most artillery was loaded with a separate shell, bagged propelling charge, and a tube primer inserted into the breech block – the system used in the naval 4in guns at Workington, and known as Breech Loading, or 'BL'. The combination of fixed ammunition, a quick-acting rotary breech mechanism and carriage recoil, which permitted the barrel to recoil almost its full length in a cradle (so the gun did not need to be laboriously re-laid between shots), gave the French '75' a world-beating rate of fire, up to twenty rounds in a minute, compared to the four rounds per minute of a typical BL field gun.

Britain responded with two new QF field guns, a 13pr for the Royal Horse Artillery and a functionally identical, but slightly larger, 18pr for the Field Artillery, which entered service from 1904. They were joined in 1908 by an excellent 4.5in field howitzer. The '75' was the main French field gun during the First World War, and the 18pr gun and 4.5in howitzer the main British ones – the lighter 13pr gun proving less useful once trench warfare made its mobility less of an advantage. Design limitations emerged during the 18pr's first ten years in service – the gun's pole trail, recuperator and breech mechanism all needed to be improved in the light of experience, and specifications for a new equipment were drawn up in 1913–14, but not acted on, due to the outbreak of the First World War. Design shortcomings notwithstanding, during the First World War 99,397,670 rounds of 18pr ammunition were fired on the Western Front alone, making up the greater part of the total British artillery expenditure of 170,305,595 rounds (in comparison, 13prs fired 1,520,155 rounds) (RAI, 1919, p. 66). A new version of the 18pr, the Mk IV,[28] entered service in the final two months of the First World War, featuring a variable-recoil hydro-pneumatic recuperator, box trail carriage and single action 'Asbury' breech, which were features found on the 4.5in howitzer. In this respect, the design of the 18pr Mk IV presaged the idea of combining field gun and field howitzer in a single 'gun-howitzer' equipment. The gun's increased elevation (achieved because of the box trail) extended its range from the 6,525yd of the Mk I/II to a maximum 10,400yd.[29]

Following the First World War another version of the QF 18pr Mk IV was adopted, with a split trail carriage, and all variants of the gun continued to serve during the inter-war period, with the older types passing to Territorial Army and training regiments.[30] The drive to achieve longer range led to the development of a new 25lb, 3.45in-diameter shell, and, as a temporary measure, from August 1936, 1,000 QF 18prs Mk IV were re-barrelled to produce the 'Ordnance QF 25pr Mk I', often termed the '18/25-pounder'.[31] Work was also undertaken to design a purpose-built 25pr gun-howitzer, and this was approved for service in December 1937, although the first batteries were not operational until May 1940. The first use of the new 'QF 25pr Mk II on Carriage 25pr Mk I', universally called simply 'the 25-pounder', was during the campaign in Norway. The new gun achieved a maximum range of 13,400yd (Henry, 2002, p. 24).

As we have seen, during the First World War Britain turned to American industry to augment domestic artillery production, and 851 18prs and 100 13prs were manufactured in the United States (RAI, 1919, pp. 12 and 18). When America entered the First World War, the principle field gun of the US Army was the 3in M1902, an elderly design that was meant to have been replaced by a modern, quick-firing split trail 3in (*c*. 76mm) gun, the M1916. However, there had been considerable difficulty manufacturing the recuperator system for the M1916 in the United States, and the programme was further delayed by a last-minute decision to chamber the gun for French 75mm ammunition (Breer, 2007, pp. 2 and 3). In the absence of their own gun, the Americans adopted the French *Soixante-Quinze*, as the 75mm Gun M1897. Initially French-manufactured guns were bought (Breer, 2007, p. 10), and while tooling up for domestic manufacture of the M1897, the United States also produced a stopgap 75mm version of the British 18pr – in much the same manner as the M1917 rifle had been produced using P14 tooling. The resulting field gun was designated the 75mm Gun M1917 (British).[32] The M1897 75mm gun was still the standard US field gun in 1940, particularly in its modernised M2 form with a split trail and pneumatic tyres, although work was well advanced on its replacement, the 105mm howitzer M2A1, which entered production in 1940.

The 900 guns purchased by the British from the American reserve stocks in 1940, as described by Churchill, did all chamber the French 75mm round, but only a proportion were actually *Mle 1897 'Soixante-Quinzes'* – the eventual inventory of '75s' included M1897, M1916 and M1917. The British gave the guns the following designations:

M1897 – Ordnance QF 75mm Mk 1 or Mk 1★ (The star indicated modernised, 'Martin-Parry conversion' carriages with pneumatic tyres)

M1916 – Ordnance QF 75mm 'S' Mk 2 or Mk 2★ (The 'S' standing for split trail, the star for pneumatic tyres)

M1917 – Ordnance QF 75mm Converted Mk 1 or Mk 1★ (The gun was 'converted' in the sense that the design was converted from that of an 18pr. The star designated pneumatic tyres)

In 1940, 395 M1917s arrived in the UK, the guns having been purchased by France, but diverted to Britain following the fall of France. Britain also purchased 500 M1897s – making up the bulk of Churchill's 900 guns. A further 170 M1916s were released to the UK under lend lease in 1941.[33] Apart from using the M1897s on field carriages, a pedestal mount was developed, the 'Mounting 75mm Mk 1', which would have been the type used for the static 75mm gun in the beach battery at Maryport.[34]

After Dunkirk, 100 18pr, 210 18/25pr, 30 25pr Mk II, 200 4.5in howitzer and 135 heavier guns were all the field artillery remaining in the UK.[35] By the end of July 1940, manufacture, reconditioning, and utilising obsolete equipments had raised the UK field artillery park to 3,100 guns, or 52 per cent of requirement.[36] The 820 American 75mm guns added another 29 per cent of the requirement.[37] The American '75s' were immediately used to re-equip British field artillery batteries, as well as Allied units forming in the UK, such as the Free Polish and Free Czech armies.[38] Hence, in his study of wartime defences at Walberswick, on the Sussex coast, D. Sims says:

> The provision of field artillery was also increased during June and July [1940]. Taking the area from Sandymount covert to Southwold, on 1st June 1940 some five field guns were able to fire on this part of the coast. By mid July, this number had increased to thirteen and would remain at this figure until October. The quality of ordnance had improved too; 136 Field Regiment, for example, who had one troop at Sallow Wood Covert were re-equipped with a full compliment of 75mm field guns in late August. (Sims, UEA, 2008)

As the Royal Artillery re-equipped with 25pr Mk IIs, older British equipments and '75s' were 'pooled' and then released for anti-tank defences. The process was described in a secret memorandum from Headquarters Home Forces to regional commands, issued on 23 September 1941, which is reproduced in full below, as it gives useful context as to what was occurring in other areas of Home Forces:[39]

> SUBJECT: Manning of surplus Field Artillery Equipments by units other than Field Regiments R.A. SECRET

> Reference this Headquarters letter, number as above, dated 9 Aug, the Commander-in-Chief directs that surplus artillery equipments, allotted to Commands on a pool basis, shall be given to units in the following order of priority:-

> (i)   Defence Regiments.
> (ii)   Coast Artillery Batteries.

(iii) Super Heavy and Heavy Batteries.

(iv) Home Guard.

2. Defence Regiments

75mm. or 60-prs should be allocated to Defence Regiments to replace the 4" Naval guns, the withdrawal of which is to start shortly. It should be possible for the personnel of the existing detachments to man a number of these equipments in excess of the existing number of 4" guns. Moreover, in some places the same detachment may usefully be able to man two guns; one sited to enfilade the beach, and one sited to shoot landwards against localities where air descent may be expected. There is no objection, where necessary, to siting the two guns up to, say, 200 yards apart: but in these circumstances each gun should be complete with its own dump of ammunition.

3. Coast Batteries

75mm. guns should be allotted as supplementary weapons for protection landward and to cover areas where enemy air descent is possible.

4. Super Heavy and Heavy Batteries

75mm. guns should be allotted as supplementary weapons to engage targets with direct fire from within the battery's protective wire. These batteries will thus give added depth to the system of anti-tank defence.

5. Home Guard

The policy should be to allot initially to Home Guard surplus 18-pr, 13-pr and 4.5" Hows, since ex-gunners of the last war will be familiar with these weapons. Later, if any 75mm. equipments remain surplus after the requirements of priorities (i), (ii) and (iii) have been met, these may be offered also to the Home Guard.

It should be emphasised that the first priority in the use of Home Guard with guns is in Coast Artillery Batteries, where these are sited in the vicinity of Home Guard units (H.F. 4022/9/G(s.D.) dated 19 Sep 41 refers).

G.H.Q., Home Forces   (Signed) H.C. Loyd

23 September, 1941   Lieut. General

                                             Chief of the General Staff

It is an interesting reversal that, in the case of field artillery, the American equipment would go to the Regulars and the British equipment to the Home Guard. Points to note are the withdrawal of 4in naval guns, which were used both as fixed coast artillery (as at Bransty, where, as we have seen, the guns were removed a few months later, in the spring of 1942) and on self-propelled (lorried) mobile mounts. The memorandum reflects the situation at Workington, as described by Russell Barnes, and it is important to note the emphasis placed on getting Home Guard gunners into coast batteries.

A solid steel 18-pound armour-piercing shot Mk IIIT could defeat 62mm of armour plate,[40] and it, or its 75mm equivalent, would be likely to disable or destroy anything struck at the sorts of operational ranges to be encountered in southern and eastern England. Home Guard returns show the first two 18prs with the Home Guard in Southern Command in June 1942. By November, Home Guard units were operating two 3prs, 124 6prs, four 13prs, nine 18prs, two 60prs, six 75mms and eleven 6in mortars.[41] Field guns were distributed individually to boost the tank-killing potential of Home Guard units, as recorded in the following reminiscence from the small village of Bunwell, Norfolk:

Later in the war Bunwell was supplied with a field gun which was kept at Home Farm. My father had been a gun layer in the navy so he was put in charge of the gun. He went on a course, at Dorking, with the Regular Army and on his return was promoted to Lieutenant. He selected a crew of mainly younger men to handle it; Frank and Jack Brown used their Ford tractors to pull it. Training was done in the farmyard on Sunday mornings.[42]

MacKenzie is dismissive of the conventional artillery supplied to the Home Guard:

[I]t remained War Office policy to keep introducing 'new' weapons to the Home Guard (while keeping as much existing equipment in service as long as possible) for the sake of appearances. Hence the allocation of 100,000 obsolete Boys anti-tank rifles in July 1943, and then a relatively small number of 'special' Home Guard 75mm anti-tank guns. The 75mm anti-tank gun was a hybrid, consisting of the shortened barrel of the now-obsolete 3" anti-aircraft gun mounted on the modified carriage of a First-World-War-vintage 4.5" Howitzer. It had a maximum range of 10,450 yards, a muzzle velocity of 2,500 ft/sec., and was mostly used for coastal defence. Only when very obsolete weapons (such as the Northover Projector and the dreaded pikes) could be replaced at once with marginally less ineffective cast-offs from the Army (such as the 18-pounder field gun or 2-pounder anti-tank gun) was anything taken out of service. (1996, p. 135)

The passage takes us into the same murky waters that we previously encountered when unpicking the reality behind the Home Guard's supposedly 'ancient' grease-encrusted M1917 American rifles. The reader will be alive to the dangers of pejoratives such as 'First-World-War-vintage' and 'obsolete', which are meaningless in a context where many First World War (and earlier) weapons continued to serve with distinction. We have also established that the 'marginally less ineffective' 18prs were quite fit-for-purpose as Home Defence anti-tank guns,[43] and cannot, in all seriousness, be lumped together with the Northover Projector and 'Croft's Pikes'. The 'special' 3in/75mm anti-tank gun MacKenzie refers to is something of a mystery. The US Army combined a 3in AA gun with the carriage of the 105mm (4.1in) howitzer to produce an interim heavy anti-tank weapon, the 3in M5, which saw extensive service with the US Army from 1942 onwards (Hogg, 2002, p. 88), and the Americans also used some 75mm M2 field guns as anti-tank. A self-propelled version of this gun, mounted on the M3 halftrack, was extensively used by US and British forces in North Africa and Italy.[44]

As we have already discussed, the M2 was the ultimate evolution of the French '75', the gun being mounted on an M1916-type split trail carriage, and there is clearly scope for confusion here. In the passage quoted above MacKenzie references K.R. Gulvin's *Kent Home Guard: A History*. Gulvin, as we have already seen, can be a little uncertain on matters of military technology, and his description of the Home Guard's supposed special 75mm/3in anti-tank guns on 4.5in howitzer carriages is illustrated with a photograph of the Southern Railway Home Guard from the same series as the shoot at Lydd, illustrated. The guns in question most certainly are not mounted on the 4.5in howitzer carriage, as that had a box trail, as opposed to the split trail depicted, nor do they have the barrels of anti-aircraft guns; they are in fact American 75mm M1916M1A1s.

As far as the British 3in anti-aircraft/anti-tank gun is concerned, in 1941 an attempt was made to counter the increasing armour thicknesses of German tanks by producing a powerful self-propelled anti-tank gun. This consisted of a Churchill tank hull with the turret and 2pr gun replaced by a large, fixed armoured box or casemate. Through the box's vertical front armour projected a shortened 3in anti-aircraft gun. The result was a tank destroyer, roughly similar to those later built by the Soviets and Germans.[45] The service history of the vehicle is rather obscure, and at least one website ascribes them to the Home Guard, which would have given the Home Guard a very impressive weapon system indeed.[46] Known as the Carrier, 3in Gun, Churchill Mk I (armoured fighting vehicle designation A22D), the 3in tank destroyer was developed following a General Staff requirement issued in September 1941. The vehicle was ready for testing by February 1942, by which time it had already been decided that the requirement should be reduced from 100 to twenty-five, in order to concentrate on production of conventional turreted Churchill Mk IV tanks armed with the 6pr anti-tank gun. However, as the modified hulls had been built by the manufacturers, Beyer, Peacock and Co., the order was reinstated, although only fifty were completed.[47]

It is not widely known, but Churchill 3in Gun Carriers briefly saw service with UK-based British and Canadian armoured brigades. In June 1942, Heavy Support Squadrons of nine 3in Gun Carriers were formed, attached to brigade headquarters.[48] They were disbanded in March 1943, when sufficient 17pr anti-tank guns became available.[49] Subsequently Churchill Gun Carriers were used in training and (without guns) to test the Snake minefield breaching system.[50] It is unlikely that a system as large and complicated to operate and maintain as the Churchill Gun Carrier was passed on to the Home Guard – but not impossible, and research continues.[51] However, the remaining fifty 3in 16cwt guns (as the shortened anti-tank gun version of the 3in 20cwt anti-aircraft gun was designated) were fitted to 17pr gun carriages. Of these, twenty-five were kept in the UK for Home Defence, and would certainly have been encountered by the Home Guard. The remainder were sent to the Middle East. Virtually no documentation exists concerning this hybrid, but it does fit with Gulvin's reference to anti-tank guns made up of 3in anti-aircraft guns on 4.5in howitzer carriages (the 17pr carriage would have been a better choice for a direct fire, high-velocity anti-tank gun, but surplus 4.5in howitzer carriages were available). The resulting weapon would have been both potent, firing a 12½lb armour-piercing shot capable of penetrating 100mm of armour at 200yd,[52] and practical. However, it had already been overtaken by the 6pr 7cwt and 17pr anti-tank guns.

Hybrid artillery certainly was produced, such as the 6pr 6cwt tank guns on field carriages already described, as stop-gap anti-tank weapons for army use, and later inherited by the Home Guard, but the idea that a 75mm gun was built specially for the Home Guard can be dismissed as a conflation of the use of American 75mm guns, and various stop-gap hybrids placed in Home Defence service in 1940–41. Compared to the other weapons associated with the Home Guard, conventional artillery arrived late and initially in fairly insignificant numbers. The Home Guard operated an increasing quantity and range of field artillery from the winter of 1942, as they took over responsibility for beach batteries from the army. The distribution of Home Guard conventional artillery was national, with the largest proportion being in Southern Command (but not South Eastern Command), followed by Scottish and Northern Commands.[53]

Having established that the field guns and artillery hybrids which found their way into service with the Home Guard were quite suitable for the direct-fire anti-tank role required of them, we need to examine whether the same can be said of the specialist anti-armour weapons, the 2pr anti-tank gun and the Boys anti-tank rifle. The first Boys anti-tank rifles appear on Home Guard returns in March 1942, with seventeen rifles listed, spread over Northern, Southern and Eastern Commands, and the Home Guard holding remained in the teens, climbing to twenty-nine by the end of the year.[54] At this period the rifle was still very much standard infantry equipment, giving the lie to the suggestion that the Boys was obsolete when issued to the Home Guard. However, both the Boys and the 2pr anti-tank gun only became wide-scale standard-issue Home Guard weapons from mid-1943, when Regular infantry regiments began to re-equip with the 6pr 7cwt anti-tank gun and PIAT infantry anti-tank Spigot Mortar. The reader may recall from previous chapters that Number 6 Platoon, E Company, 2nd City of London (Civil Service) Battalion – civil servants who had been left in London following the departure of the rest of the Ministry of Food to Colwyn Bay – became, in September 1943, their battalion's specialist sub-artillery platoon. The platoon was equipped with one Smith gun, two Spigot Mortars, a Lewis gun and a Boys anti-tank rifle, a grouping that produced a support weapons or heavy weapons platoon, echoing the arrangements of the republicans in the Spanish Civil War. In the North East, Workington's Home Guard battalion had four 2prs and no less than nineteen Boys anti-tank rifles.[55] Workington's 2prs were distributed piecemeal to the rifle companies, one each to B and D companies, based in the town itself, and two to E company, defending the Heavy Duty Alloys aircraft parts 'shadow factory' at Distington.[56]

It is widely stated that both the Boys anti-tank rifle and 2pr anti-tank gun were already obsolete at the outbreak of the Second World War, but, like most common places we have encountered in this study, it is not really true.[57] The typical anti-tank equipment for all combatants during the early stages of the Second World War was a high-powered armour-piercing rifle, and a small high-velocity artillery piece. Comparative performance figures are unreliable, due to the number of variables involved, but the British 40mm 2pr anti-tank round was at the upper end of performance. The 2pr could penetrate 42mm of armour, at an angle of 30 degress, at 1,000yd, 53mm at 500yd,[58] which meant that it could disable or destroy all German armoured vehicles in service in 1940, including early PzKpfw IIIs and IVs. To illustrate, the 10mm armour of the pre-war Panzer III was increased to 30mm on the front, sides and rear in the *Ausführung* (batch) D,E,F (1939–40) and G (1940–41) models, which was still within the 2pr's capabilities. The H (1940–41) model had an additional 30mm plate bolted to the front, making it impervious from that angle at more than 500yd, and the J (1941–42) model had 50mm of solid armour at the front and rear. Likewise, the Panzer IV started with 14.5mm of frontal armour, increased to 30mm on the *Ausf* B model. The turret armour was increased to 30mm on the *Ausf* C; the D model (1939) had its side armour increased to 20mm, and *Ausf* E had 50mm on the bow and an additional 30mm *appliqué* on the glacis, at which point it became invulnerable to the 2pr from the front, except at very close range. Hull armour only reached 50mm in April 1941, with the F variant (Perret, 1999a, 1999b).

Thus the 2pr could defeat any armoured fighting vehicle the German Army could field in 1940, and it remained effective, in theory at least, into 1942/3, when Panther and Tiger tanks entered service.[59] Even then, the Panther had 40mm side armour, which was, theoretically, within the reach of the 2pr (the Tiger had 60mm hull armour). This places the gun in context, and shows that the War Office decision to continue 2pr production in 1940, even if it delayed the introduction of the 6pr anti-tank gun, was absolutely correct. At the outbreak of war, the 2pr gun was operated by anti-tank regiments of the Royal Artillery. Once the 6pr 7cwt became available in quantity (from November 1941), the Royal Artillery began re-equipping with new guns and the following year 2prs were passed to infantry battalions (Hogg, 2002, pp. 73 and 75). When the 17pr anti-tank gun entered Royal Artillery service in 1943, the 6pr was passed to the infantry and the 2pr passed to the Home Guard. It is hard to fault the logic of this, as the 2pr was still capable of dealing with any light armour that might be air-landed in some sort of raid, and even the heavier German tanks at close ranges. In Home Guard service the operating range of the 2pr was given as a very realistic (even pessimistic) 500yd maximum, 200yd 'best'.[60]

The 2pr gun remained in British Army service in the Far East until 1945, and in Europe it was the main British tank armament until 1942. It was also fitted to British armoured cars throughout the Second World War and beyond.[61] It is therefore incorrect to describe the gun as obsolete; it clearly had limitations, but, in one guise or another, it remained an important anti-armour weapon throughout the Second World War. The manner in which the Home Guard would deploy the 2pr anti-tank gun was set out in *Home Guard Instruction No. 51, Part IV, The Organization of Home Guard Defence*:

(f)   *The 2-pr.* The 2-pr is an accurate and quick-firing A-tk weapon with a flat trajectory. It is small and easily concealed. It can be manhandled and towed on the road behind any vehicle capable of carrying the crew of four and a supply of ammunition. The maximum range at which fire will be opened is 500 yards, but the best range is 200 yards.

Tactical handling. In view of its longer range, the primary use of the 2-pr is to cover likely tank and soft vehicle approaches to the defensive locality which are beyond the range of the Home Guard sub-artillery weapons. It may also be used as a reserve A-tk weapon in the hands of a commander to destroy any tanks which may penetrate his locality, and to replace any anti-tank weapons which may have been overrun.[62]

The chief shortcoming of both the 2pr and the Boys anti-tank rifle was their size. Both weapons were bulky and heavy, limiting their mobility. Neither offered a commensurate return in terms of hitting power, for the burden they imposed. Neither weapon was likely to achieve an outright 'kill' – with the enemy tank 'brewing up' – and the Boys was unlikely even to achieve a 'mobility kill', halting the enemy tank in its tracks. That is not to say that the rifle did not have any effect on enemy armour, as a .55in bullet penetrating the interior of the tank could do considerable damage to the crew, but it was unlikely to have any *visible* effect, and this undoubtedly contributed to the rifle's unpopularity.

Although rated amongst the best anti-tank rifles, the Boys quickly fell out of favour with the infantry due to its weight, lack of hitting power, muzzle blast and recoil.[63] *Small Arms Training, Volume I, Pamphlet No. 5, Anti-Tank Rifle*, of April 1942 describes the factors affecting the performance of the rifle:

Although the bullet will penetrate the armour of light A.F.V.s up to 500 yards, and inflict casualties on the crew, fire should be withheld until the range is well within 300 yards. The angle of impact of the anti-tank rifle bullet on the armour has a greater influence than the range at which it is fired. For example, while the penetrative power is only 10 per cent. less at 300 yards than at 100 yards, it is 25 per cent. less when the angle of impact is over 20 degrees, and 50 per cent. less at over 40 degrees at the latter range … The exact moment of fire must therefore be decided by the firer's determination to hit the selected part of the tank fair and square, rather than by range only. As a general rule the .55-in. anti-tank rifle bullet will penetrate all parts of the Pz. Kw. Mk. II light tank, at 250 yards range at an angle of impact of 20 degrees or less. It does not penetrate the armour of heavier tanks except in certain points such as the rear of the turret and cupola of the Pz. Kw. Mk. IV at very short range. When shooting at German tanks of the [sic] Pz. Kw. Mk. III and larger tanks fire should be aimed, if it is possible, at vulnerable points, especially on the junction point of turret and hull and gun mantle, to cause burring over of working surfaces and thus produce jamming.[64]

Pamphlet No. 5 also gives the following penetration figures, it will be noted that the rifle was effective against early and lighter tanks, as well as armoured cars and half tracks:[65]

Effective attack

Range	Normal		20 degrees		40 degrees	
yd	in	m/m	in	m/m	in	m/m
100	.91	23.2	.67	17.0	.43	11.0
300	.82	20.9	.63	16.0	.38	9.6
500	.74	18.8	.60	15.3	.35	8.8

TABLE II

Performance against brick walls and shingle

	Brick walls	Shingle in sandbags
Greatest penetration …	14in	10in

The Boys rifle was superseded in regular army service with a portable one-man derivative of the Blacker Bombard, a miniaturisation made possible by the use of a hollow charge warhead. The weapon started life as the 'Baby Bombard', but was subsequently adopted, in August 1942, as the 'projector, infantry anti-tank' or PIAT. The 'PIAT' was a handful – heavy, difficult to cock, and with recoil nearly as spectacular as that of the Boys rifle, but it could, and did, knock out Tiger tanks, which made it worth the effort.[66] The PIAT was not issued to the Home Guard, who were not required to be as mobile as Regular infantry, and therefore could continue to make use of the Blacker Bombard/29mm Spigot Mortar, with its big anti-tank bomb and useful anti-personnel round. However, as the Boys rifle passed from regular service it was added to the Home Guard arsenal. In November 1943, in Home Guard service, assessment of the performance of the Boys anti-tank rifle was realistic:

> *Tactical handling.* The A-tk rifle is *not* effective against heavy armour, and heavier A-tk weapons should be used for this purpose. It can, however, break the tracks of heavy tanks. The bullet can pierce light armour and put soft vehicles out of action. It can be allotted to those parts of the defences where suitable targets are most likely to approach.[67]

By the time it reached the majority of the Home Guard, the anti-tank rifle was discredited with its users, and this is how posterity continues to remember it. Indeed, when Hogg and Weeks published their authoritative *Military Smallarms of the Twentieth Century* in 1973, very heavy rifles were regarded as totally extinct, an evolutionary cul-de-sac:

> The career of the anti-tank rifle lasted a mere three decades from the first tanks of World War 1 to the close of World War 2 … The thickness of tank armour rapidly outstripped the efforts of the designers to produce a tank-killer light enough to be operated by one man yet still fire conventional fixed-case ammunition, and so the military turned to handheld rocket projectors, recoilless guns and similar devices: the anti-tank rifles, cumbersome and ineffective, were discarded. (Hogg and Weeks, 1973, p. 6.01)

Actually, very heavy rifles never entirely went away and they have enjoyed a huge renaissance since the Balkan conflicts of the 1990s. The Barrett M82 'Light 50', firing the M2 Browning heavy machine gun .50in round, is a favoured long-range sniping weapon at ranges out to 2,000yd, and long-range sniping and 'anti-materiel' rifles exist in calibres up to 20mm. The Boys rifle played a role in the development of large calibre sniping, as examples converted from .55in to .50in Browning and fitted with tank telescope gunsights were used in the long-range sniping/harassing role by US-supported Nationalist Chinese forces in Taiwan during the Korean War.[68] Fired from a Home Guard defended locality, the Boys could have easily halted any vehicle that German parachutists might commandeer, and shoot through most forms of cover to hit the soldier behind. In terms of a modern sniping application, though, wartime deployment of the Boys rifle was limited by the lack of a telescope sight and, more importantly, the rifle's broader uses were obscured doctrinally by the fact that it had been introduced specifically as, and was always thought of as, the 'anti-tank rifle'. It would be naïve to suggest that the 2pr and the Boys anti-tank rifle were ideal anti-armour weapons – they were not. Their performance had been outstripped by tank development by late 1942 and the PIAT and 6pr 7cwt were better, more effective, anti-armour weapons for the infantry. But the 2pr and Boys were neither useless nor obsolete. The 2pr could knock out any armoured (or un-armoured) vehicle the Home Guard were ever likely to encounter, and the Boys anti-tank rifle, although restricted to lightly armoured and un-armoured targets by the time it entered Home Guard service, was a useful weapon at a road block, and with imagination, could have been used in ways that anticipated the modern anti-materiel rifle (AMR) role.

To conclude our examination of the Home Guard and artillery we must look at air defence – an arena in which the Home Guard played a particularly important role. The late-1930s had seen the adoption of the sophisticated Swedish-designed 40mm Bofors automatic canon, to replace the Lewis gun in the light anti-aircraft role, and the elderly, but popular, 3in 20cwt anti-aircraft guns of the Royal Artillery Heavy AA Regiments began to be superseded by a powerful new 3.7in gun.[69] Both new equipments represented a significant increase in capability, and were allied to a 'Kerrison predictor', a mechanical analogue computer that fed settings directly to the gun layers, in order to ensure that the target aircraft and shell arrived at the same point in the sky at the same time. However, they were both 'a lot more gun' than the weapons they supposedly replaced. As we have seen, the Lewis continued to be extensively used throughout the Second World War in the light AA role – and with some success – chiefly due to demand for the Bofors gun consistently exceeding output.[70] The very big, very heavy and complicated '3.7' was at first regarded with suspicion, and it was the familiar, relatively light and simple, First World War 3in 20cwt that served with the British field armies in the early part of the Second World War.[71] Eventually it was recognised that the considerable advantages of the 3.7in gun outweighed its disadvantages and the 3in 20cwt anti-aircraft gun was slowly phased out, 100 being earmarked for conversion to the 20pr 16cwt anti-tank guns, described above.[72]

The best defence against massed air attack (particularly at night) quickly proved to be massed anti-aircraft artillery, firing barrage patterns through which the enemy was forced to fly in order to reach the target. Guns were marshalled into 'Gun Defended Areas', such as 'Thames and Medway (South)', which stretched from Dartford to Sheppy and defended the south-eastern approaches to London. The area contained seventy-two HAA (Heavy Anti-Aircraft) guns grouped in four-gun batteries or 'sites'. In 1940 these consisted of eight 3in guns, eight 3.7in mobile guns, twenty-four 3.7in static guns and thirty-two 4.5in guns. By 1944, although the number of guns remained the same, the 3in and 4.5in guns had been replaced, the total number of 3.7s being increased to sixty-four, and the balance made up of four twin 5.25in mountings.[73] The gun crews (eleven men for each 3.7in), plus accompanying height finders, predictor operators, battery command post staff and so on, absorbed an immense amount of manpower (and there were also barrage balloon and searchlight crews to take into consideration). This soon led to the employment of women in the batteries. The charter for the formation of mixed anti-aircraft batteries was issued in May 1941, and the first confirmed aircraft to fall a mixed battery was brought down on 8 December 1941 (MOI, 1943, p. 59). Although women shared the gun pits with men, they were not permitted to serve the guns – their duties included radiolocation, height and range finding, and operating the predictor and the aircraft identification telescope.[74]

The Home Guard participated in air defence as part of their infantry duties, one Home Counties platoon, for example, shot down a low-flying Dornier Do 17 in August 1940, with 180 rounds of rapid fire from P14 rifles.[75] However, the topic of aircraft recognition was demoted in the Home Guard training syllabus in March 1942, on the basis that the Home Guard was not issued tracer ammunition, making it impossible to engage aircraft accurately at heights above 2,000ft. Below that altitude, it was determined, aircraft would be immediately recognisable by their national markings or 'their hostile action'. Therefore, it was unnecessary to waste time on more aircraft recognition than was necessary for 'self-defence'.[76]

However, at the same time training was underway of the first specialist Home Guard anti-aircraft artillery units. Like the coast artillery, Home Guard air defence artillery began with recruiting in late-1941, as described by Sir Frederick Pile, GOC-in-C, AA Command, writing shortly after the war:

The same pressure, the same claims of pure mathematics that had forced the hands of those opposed to the acceptance of A.T.S. [female auxiliaries], now forced their hands into the acceptance of the Home Guard being used in A.A. Command. The greatest snag was that Home Guards were not allowed to perform more than 48 hours' training and duty in 28 days. Even in the event of air raids, they were unable to volunteer for extra duty without permission from their civil employers. This meant that we couldn't immediately hand over the most important defences to them. But they could be used both on some of the light anti-aircraft defences of factories and railways and on the new rocket deployment designed to reinforce existing anti-aircraft defences. (Pile, 1949, p. 224)

Although the Home Guards were part-timers, they could, unlike the ATS, serve the guns. The first Home Guard units were ready in early summer 1942,[77] and in September, General Pile was able to rebalance AA manpower. At its peak his command absorbed half a million men and women, and by further increasing the use of Home Guards, it was eventually possible to free 71,000 male soldiers for other duties.[78] By the time Home Guard 'Ack-Ack' units were stood-down in 1944 there were 141,198 Home Guards in Anti-Aircraft Command.[79]

The first weapon system selected for Home Guard Ack-Ack gunners was one we previously encountered earlier in this chapter, as part of the defences at Workington and Whitehaven – the 'Z' anti-aircraft projector. The 'Z' projector reflected practical experience which showed that hundreds, even thousands, of anti-aircraft shells were fired for each plane shot down.[80] Under the circumstances, a shotgun approach was the best way to intercept a bird on the wing, and the 'Z' projector was designed to put as much explosive in the air as possible, in the shortest possible time. The system comprised of the usual battery command post arrangements, but the guns were replaced with considerably less expensive and sophisticated rocket launchers or 'projectors', each capable of firing, first a single, and later, two, 3in 'unrotated projectiles' or UPs. British development of anti-aircraft rockets had begun in 1934 and resulted in a 2in rocket which eventually saw wartime service on merchant ships, and some limited use in coastal batteries, utilising the 2in Rocket Mounting Mk II or 'Pillar Box' – a twenty-rocket volley mounting (Chamberlain and Gander, 1975c, pp. 49–52). However, in 1937 the Committee on Air Defence Research directed that work should concentrate on a 3in projectile with a similar lethality to the 3.7in anti-aircraft gun round. Trials were undertaken in 1939, and by September 1940 1,000 3in projectors had been built. The initial 'Projector, 3in, Mk I' fired a single rocket, and was rather less sophisticated than its successor, the Number 2

Mk I, which was a twin rocket launcher. Both types saw operational service in the UK and North Africa, and the Mk I was adopted by the Royal Navy for DEMS (merchant shipping) use. A mobile launcher, the Projector, 3in No. 4, which could fire nine rockets, was mounted on the carriages of the 100 3in anti-aircraft guns retired and converted into anti-tank guns, discussed previously. The final version, the Number 6 projector, which fired twenty rockets, entered service in 1944 (Chamberlain and Gander, 1975c, pp. 49–52). Initially the Mk I projector (see below) was deemed suitable for Home Guard use, as described by the former GOC-in-C AA Command:

> The single-barrelled U.P. projector was selected for their use, chiefly because of the simplicity with which the equipment could be handled.
>
> The first of these units was formed in Liverpool and went into training in October 1941. (Pile, 1949, p. 225)

For the defence of major targets each 'Z' battery consisted of sixty-four twin projectors. Each projector was operated by a crew of two, so the whole arrangement was considerably more economical than a conventional HAA battery. Nevertheless, sixty-four projector batteries still required considerable manpower. Home Guard batteries were formed, around a core of Regular Army personnel. Summing up the Home Guard's contribution to the war effort, Director General Home Guard said of the 'Z' AA batteries:[81]

> Home Guard have taken over all duties in connection with rocket batteries and apart from a very small regular component for maintenance of the equipment and for training, these equipments are manned entirely by the Home Guard.

The 'Z' projector is, quite rightly, associated with the Home Guard, and the weapon was, it is true, a Sten gun, to the 3.7in gun's rifle, but like the Sten it was cheap, easy to mass produce and deadly – and, although unguided, it represented the future of air defence.[82] Like the Sten, the 'Z' projector was a weapon that the Home Guard shared with the army, although in this case it was in the form of mixed Home Guard, regular and ATS batteries, with the three organisations working alongside and completely dependent on each other.

Air defence also formed a major part of the duties of the Home Guard factory units, which were formed from the workforce to guard key industrial installations. The official summation was as follows:[83]

L.A.A. [Light Anti-Aircraft] All important factories and undertakings are defended against low flying and dive bombing attacks by factory workers who are enrolled in the Home Guard and are prepared to man the guns on receipt of the alarm

At Workington, for example, 'E' Company of the local Home Guard battalion, which was responsible for security at the High-Duty Alloys 'shadow factory', reorganised in January 1944 to include a light anti-aircraft troop, designated 'C' LAA troop, and equipped with eight Marlin machine guns and nine 20mm Hispano-Suiza cannon. The nearby Workington Iron and Steel Works also formed a Home Guard LAA detachment, equipped with an impressive eighteen 20mm Hispano-Suiza guns. Both detachments were disbanded in September 1944.[84] We encountered the .30-06-calibre Marlin machine gun in Chapter 5, noting that many went to the merchant navy for anti-aircraft use. The Hispano-Suiza was a French-designed 20mm aircraft canon, originating in a license-built Oerlikon design, but evolved into a more sophisticated weapon that would be mounted between the 'V' cylinders of a Hispano-Suiza aircraft engine, firing through the propeller boss (Wallace, 1972, p. 78).[85]

At the outbreak of war the 'Hispano' cannon was regarded as the pre-eminent weapon of its type, undergoing service trials and development with various European air forces, the French Air Force, the US Navy and the RAF. Described as 'one of the most important guns used by the RAF' (Wallace, 1972, p. 77),[86] it was eventually fitted to numerous fighter and attack aircraft, including the Whirlwind, Spitfire, Hurricane, Tempest and Beaufighter, as well as the post-war Shackleton maritime patrol aircraft and Vampire jet fighter, amongst others. At the outset its only significant limitation as an aircraft weapon was that it was fed from a drum magazine, which meant it had to either be mounted in such a way that the magazine could be replaced by the crew of the aircraft, or settle for a rather limited supply of ammunition (sixty rounds).[87] The problem was resolved by development in early 1941 of a belt-feed mechanism, interchangeable with the magazine.[88] In the ground role, however, the drum magazine was no problem, and the Hispano-Suiza was used in single and multiple light anti-aircraft mountings by British Commonwealth and US forces during the Second World War. It saw further action with various armies after the Second World War.

Hispano-Suiza 20mm cannons were manufactured in the UK and, from January 1942, in the USA, where they were standardised as the M1. Large quantities of M1 guns were supplied to the UK, but failed to perform as well as the British guns. In the early stages of the Hispano gun's development, difficulties had been experienced with 'soft strikes' (stoppages due to a failure to ignite the round – relatively easy to clear on the ground, by re-cocking the gun, but enough to put a gun out of action if wing-mounted in an aircraft). The cause had been identified as poor-quality cartridges which 'crushed up' when fed into the chamber. This was resolved by shortening the chamber by 2mm. The Americans resolutely refused to make a 2mm adjustment to the chamber of their guns, as it was an ammunition rather than gun design fault, and refused to standardise with the improved British Mk II gun, as they were redrawing the plans from millimetres (as used by the British and French) to inches to suit their production methods (Wallace, 1972, pp. 176–8). According to British aerial ordnance specialist G.F. Wallace, as a result, 'it was decided by the Director of Equipment that no American-built Hispano 20mm guns would be issued for installation in RAF aircraft'. Nevertheless, 'some thousands' were delivered. Some of these were re-chambered to British dimensions and fitted with triple-wire recoil springs (more resistant to breaking than the single wire springs used by the Americans), and fitted to ground mounts but (according to Wallace) 'never used in action', and they are undoubtedly the ones issued to the Home Guard for factory defence (Wallace, 1972, p. 178). Hispano 20mm anti-aircraft guns were in use for airfield defence as early as August 1940 (where they most certainly did see action) and subsequently saw service in all theatres with RAF 'ground gunners' and their successors the RAF Regiment.[89]

Anti-Aircraft Command GB made considerable use of Hispanos, because they were ideal for engaging fleeting targets and only needed a single operator, compared to the crew required for a 40mm Bofors. For example, sixty Bofors guns were withdrawn and replaced by 200 Hispanos to combat 'tip-and-run' air raids on the South Coast in 1942 (Pile, 1949, p. 242).[90] The Hispano first appears in Home Guard records in March 1942, seventy-one guns distributed around the country in threes and fours, with the exception of Western Command, which had twenty. By September of that year eighty-seven were reported – although it is clear that very many more were eventually issued, particularly in the approach to D-Day.[91] References to the Hispano-Suiza are rare; *Home Guard Instruction No. 60* of December 1943 lists the '20mm Hispano gun' among other Home Guard weapons, noting that care had to be taken to keep the gun serviceable:

> In order to get best results with the 20mm Hispano gun, a high standard of care of arms must be maintained. Dust covers should be kept on the gun whenever the situation permits.[92]

Dust covers notwithstanding, the use of surplus Hispano aircraft cannon on simple AA mountings, manned by factory workers who were in the Home Guard, was an intelligent and effective way to boost low-level anti-aircraft defences of vital installations.

The use of Home Guard on Ack-Ack duties was not without its difficulties, both because of the numbers of Home Guard required to man the numerous shifts for each site – around 1,400 per rocket site (Pile, 1949, p. 225) – and the quality of manpower, which was declining, with the Ministry of Labour 'directing' men into Home Guard AA units.[93] As AA Command's manpower was further eroded, the Home Guard assumed an ever larger and more important role, and, during 1942, the Home Guard started to be used on 3.7in guns. Once again, to quote the Director General Home Guard:[94]

> H.A.A. Home Guard assist existing regular batteries by taking over certain guns and by manning extra guns on existing sites.

The Home Guard performed sufficiently well that units were rotated, those from the Midlands and North, quieter areas later in the war, coming south to relieve gunners in the South East, which was still an active area. This gave the opportunity for men used to the basic 3.7in mobile HAA gun to experience the latest state-of-the-art remotely controlled, power-operated static mountings, and gain operational experience against a live enemy.

Home Guard anti-aircraft and coastal defence units stopped parading for duty in September 1944, and the Home Guard was officially stood-down the following month. The organisation's contribution to the manning of anti-aircraft and coastal artillery batteries illustrates the extent to which the part-time soldiers were trusted to take on front-line roles, and the way most rose to the challenge. It is important to remember that they were unpaid, and, typically, working long hours in work that was already important to the war effort. Home Guard duties were undertaken at night; they slept if they could, and went to work the following day. Much of the artillery of Home Defence was an eclectic mixture of the improvised, elderly and superseded. This is *not* a reflection of the way the Home Guard was regarded or treated by the authorities, but the way in which the last drops of usefulness were squeezed out of whatever equipment was available. Most of these stopgaps and improvisations were originally manned by army personnel before they were handed over to the Home Guard, and all of them worked sufficiently for the limited duties they were expected to perform.

9

AUXILIARY UNITS

The history of the Auxiliary Units is intimately related to the topic of arming the Home Guard, as the lack of arms for the original LDV was one reason why an 'asymmetric' (in modern parlance) resistance to a German invasion was prepared and organised. Auxiliary Unit organiser Major Nigel Oxenden MC★ commented in his post-operation report for the War Office, *Auxiliary Units History and Achievement 1940–44*:

> The organisation of a guerrilla force had the double advantage of building up a body of men to work behind the enemy's lines with much more success than would probably attend the road block efforts of the Home Guard proper, and doing it moreover, without drawing upon the country's scanty supply of small arms. Their mission was to 'create havoc and destruction among the enemy's supplies and communications'. (Oxenden, October 1944, published 1998, p. 1)

Oxenden placed the 'birthday' of the Auxiliary Units as 2 July 1940, the date Colonel Colin McVean Gubbins began assembling a staff of junior officers, known as 'IOs', who were to form guerrilla cells in coastal districts from 'Caithness to Wales':

> Their mission was to find reliable men, about thirty each, to leave them a 'dump' of assorted explosives and incendiaries, to help these 'dump-owners' to form their cells of five desperate men, to train them in the use of weapons that were as new to them as to the trainees, and to provide the cells with some form of 'hideout'.

When researching his 1968 study *The Last Ditch*, David Lampe became (wrongly) convinced that there was no official documentation recording the existence of the Auxiliary Units. He was therefore delighted to find, in the 1943 Auxiliary Units textbook *'The Countryman's Diary 1939'*, a reference stating 'Auxunit packing is O.K.',[1] which he took to be a unique surviving reference naming the organisation.[2] We now know it refers (with unhelpful ambiguity) not to the men, but their sabotage equipment packs. As Oxenden went on to explain:

> The first dumps, afterwards called 'packs', and finally Aux Units, were contained in cardboard boxes that disintegrated if buried or left out in the rain, and included, besides 10lbs of Plastic Explosive and a mass of feeble and uncertain incendiaries, a hollow bronze casting of a lump of coal that could hold two ounces of H.E. and a detonator. This museum piece was a clue to our proposed activities in July 1940 – the crippling of our railway system, assumed to be in use by the enemy. (1998, p. 4)

Why Oxenden calls the dummy coal in the pack a 'museum piece' is unclear, as these items must have been comparatively recent, albeit belonging to the pre-history of special operations. Mark Seaman, in discussing the origins of SOE, specifically MI(R) and Section D, makes reference to a 'brown book of devices' published at the end of 1939, and now lost: 'mention of its contents offers confirmation that, even at an early stage, [Commander] Langley's team [the experimental component of Section D] had already ... developed explosive devices camouflaged as pieces of coal or logs of wood' (Seaman, 2000, p. 4). It is likely that this booklet has thus far eluded rediscovery because it was produced as an 'anti-sabotage' handbook for Royal Navy boarding officers inspecting merchant shipping, rather than a saboteur's catalogue, as was done later, once war had started. Research into sabotage equipment was, at that stage, 'purely experimental' and supposedly defensive in nature.[3]

Oxenden's cynicism regarding dummy coal was shared by Major Leslie Wood, Commander Langley's second-in-command, and subsequent Officer Commanding, of Station XII, the SOE research centre at Aston House, near Stevenage. As remembered by Wood, the coal was required for use by the French Resistance:

> The idea was we should produce camouflaged pieces of coal which, in fact, contained high explosives. Our gallant boys were to risk their lives planting

some of these in the bunkers used by locomotives ... Well, of course it was absolutely ridiculous – made me so angry, the thought of risking our chaps' lives for such a futile thing. Luckily, in those days I was still quite a good mathematician, and I'd got with me a very good volume on the Law of Averages. I worked out properly, so that it could be checked, the chances of one piece of coal ever getting into the fire-box of a French locomotive that happened to be in the right place and happened to be taking troops. It worked out at one in ten million, or something like that. I wish I had kept that file – I didn't like to. It came back – and this is absolutely true, this is a proper official War Office file, red tape and everything else, and across it was written 'Bless you.' But that was crossed out and underneath was 'God Bless you.' And that was crossed out and underneath was 'May the good Lord shine the light of His countenance upon you for ever and ever, Amen. Signed.' That finished the whole thing because nobody could ever refute those figures. (Turner, 2006, p. 95)

Whatever majors Oxenden and Wood's opinion, far from finished, 'Explosive Coal' continued in production throughout the Second World War, and still featured in the *Descriptive Catalogue of Special Devices and Supplies* issued by 'MO1 (SP)', i.e. Aston House, in 1945 (Seaman, 2000, p. 193).[4] It was never again issued to the Auxiliary Units though.

One of the original IOs, Lieutenant Stuart Edmundsen, took delivery of a lorry load of fifty 'packs'. Edmundsen recalled that each pack contained (Warwicker, 2004, p. 5):

5lbs gelignite
3 Mills bombs
2 Magnesium incendiary bombs
Box detonators
Instantaneous fuse
Fast burning fuse
Slow burning fuse
Selection of 'Time Pencils', delay switches ranging from 10 minutes to 2 weeks, colour coded
Pressure switches
Trip switches
Coils of trip wire
A crimping tool
Sticky tape

It will be immediately apparent that there is some difference between Edmundsen's description of the pack contents and Oxenden's. Whether this reflects regional differences (Oxenden being on the East Coast, Edmundsen in the South West), or recollection of equipment schedules that differed over time is unclear. At least two 'marks' of Aux Unit pack are recorded, and the presence of gelignite rather than plastic explosive suggests that Edmundsen's were the later type of 'Mk. I', Oxenden's being the earlier pattern.[5] What is clear is that this equipment was all intended for acts of sabotage, with nothing, with the possible exception of the Mills bombs, being provided for self-protection. This led to a famous intervention by the prime minister, as recorded by Oxenden:

> In August Col Gubbins, in his weekly report to the C.I.C., which was always read with interest by the Prime Minister, recommended the issue of revolvers. Mr Churchill added a note, 'these men are to have revolvers.' Accordingly four hundred .32 Colt automatics were distributed at once, and the next month a 100% issue of .38 revolvers was made, followed much later by ammunition that fitted them. (1998, p. 4)

Oxenden noted the psychological significance of the Auxiliers' weapons:

> These, and hunting knives, were a great source of pride to the auxiliers, and a valuable recruiting draw. They enhanced a reputation for toughness that the unit was building up, as opposed to the 'church parade' activities of the ill-equipped Home Guard proper. The limit was reached when an individual was apprehended by police at a London terminus wearing a balaclava, a battledress without any sort of flash or title, and conspicuously armed with a revolver and a knife.

We have already examined the provision of handguns in Chapter 5. Further to that we can add that ex-Auxilier and researcher Robert (Bob) Millard has identified the following types as issued to Auxiliary Unit patrols – .32 Colt Special Police, .32 Colt Police Positive, .32 Colt Semi-automatic, and Smith & Wesson .38/200 British Service Revolver.[6] It is apparent, therefore, that the immediate issue of 400 .32 handguns was made up of something of a potpourri of assorted Colts, from civilian stocks available in the UK, while the '100% issue of .38 revolvers' in September will have come from the order of 65,000 revolvers placed with Smith & Wesson at the end of May 1940 (Skennerton, 1988, p. 27). In common with the remainder of the Home Guard, Auxiliary Units personnel made the most of whatever privately owned and First World War trophy handguns were available to them. Makes confirmed as in use with patrols included .455 Webley, and Beretta and Mauser pistols.[7] The Auxiliary Units also appear to have been beneficiaries of the 'Committee for American Aid for the Defense of British Homes'.[8] These privately donated American weapons, or some of them, were channelled through Section XII at Aston House,[9] which is how Auxiliary Unit patrols in Bath came to be issued ex-New York Police Department Colt revolvers and black leather police holsters.[10]

Although a weapon not particularly valued in British military doctrine, the handgun was at least familiar and an existing service weapon. Fighting knives were an entirely different matter. Various private purchase and improvised 'trench knives' had been used during the First World War, but in 1940 the British soldier's sidearm was still a 21¾in 'sword bayonet', which was particularly unsuited to close combat, except as an attachment to the Lee-Enfield rifle. Silent killing of sentries at close quarters required a completely different arrangement and weapon – a situation which became increasingly apparent in June 1940, with the formation of the 'Independent Companies' and 'Special Service' units, later to become the Commandos. The immediate response was the issue of a hunting knife, the 'RBD', as what today might be termed a 'survival knife', suitable for combat or utility duties. The RBD was a large, 'clip point' Bowie, originally produced with a 9½in or 10½in blade. The knives issued during the Second World War appear to have had 7in blades, and current research suggests that all of the Wilkinson stock went to the Commando Basic Training Centre at Achnacarry.[11] Very similar knives were produced by Sheffield cutlers including William Rodgers, and there are three recorded Auxiliary Unit 'hunting knives'; all three being Bowie knives by another Sheffield knife maker, Joseph Rodgers. The knives are described by researcher Richard Ashley at the British Resistance Organisation museum as having a '5½ in blade of very thin construction'.[12] 'Special service' personnel of all sorts would have received an RBD or similar Bowie knife, if they were lucky – at least one Auxilier was issued with a Stanley kitchen knife.[13]

In November 1940, the doyens of close-quarter fighting, W.E. Fairbairn and E.A. Sykes, met with 'Jack' Wilkinson Latham at the Wilkinson premises in Pall Mall to discuss the production of a purpose-built fighting knife, a meeting apparently enlivened by a vigorous simulated knife fight between the two ex-Shanghai policemen.[14] Fairbairn and Sykes left one of their Shanghai fighting knives with Wilkinson. This was a rather short, double-edged dagger, with a simple flat aluminium guard and a turned, knurled, brass hilt of 'Coke bottle' shape, held together with a pommel nut. The double-edged blade was ground from a Pattern 1903 Lee-Metford bayonet, and the dagger was dated 1937.[15] A prototype 'Fairbairn-Sykes fighting knife' was swiftly produced by Wilkinson and, after some modifications, approved by the two experts. This knife had a rather longer blade than the original Shanghai knife as it was designed to kill after penetrating the thickest clothing of any enemy soldier, which at that point in the war, was considered to be a Russian in full winter clothing.[16] Robert Wilkinson Latham shows on his website an extract from the Wilkinson order book, with an order dated November 1940 for '500 RBD and commercial knives', which he states was a cover for a preliminary order of the new F-S fighting knives. He is certainly well placed to know, and the quoted price (13 shillings and sixpence each) is the same as would later be charged for the F-S knife.[17] But there is also a listing for '1,000 F-S knife first pattern' in the same entry, and it may well be that Wilkinson had already provided 500 RBDs and similar knives, and was balancing the books before embarking on production of the new fighting knife.

F-S knives (and the RBDs) did not fall under the Chief Inspector of Small Arms, but were special operations stores, alongside time pencils, limpet mines and so forth. Contracts to supply F-S knives were issued to Wilkinson by 'Room 55a, the War Office'.[18] This was the War Office 'front' address for Station XII procurement, which maintained secrecy, by making it unnecessary for suppliers to visit Aston House, as FANY[19] typist Ishbel Mackenzie recalled:

> Aston House needed lots of technical supplies from companies like ICI who thought they were dealing with a War Office department E.S.6 (WD) in London. We couldn't reveal the Aston House address, so when someone at ICI telephoned and said, 'look I'm going to be in London this morning can I pop in and see you at E.S.6 (WD)?' we had to say, 'Well I'm sorry but major so and so is terribly busy this morning, perhaps in a day or two, may I ring you back?' Then you waited until our representative hurtled up to our room [55a] at the War Office in London to meet them and act out the pretence of working there permanently. No outside business people were allowed to visit Aston House. (Turner, 2006, p. 179)

Wilkinson's contract book records deliveries to Knebworth (the railhead for Aston House) and Weedon (location of the Army Small Arms Depot), and 'Station 6

(WD)', which was another cover title for Aston House.[20] In a monograph on the F-S fighting knife, William L. Cassidy notes:

> The first government order of the Fairbairn-Sykes [fighting knife] came 14 January 1941, from one of Fairbairn's colleagues at SOE. In the absence of a formal contract (security demanded that such matters be dispensed with), Wilkinson's own order number 960 was written for 98 Fairbairn-Sykes knives: 50 to be sent to Knebworth, whence they were removed to SOE's Station XII; 48 sent to Weedon, bound for SOE's Depot School near there. From these two centres the first specially purchased Fairbairn-Sykes knives were disbursed to other SOE schools and centres.
>
> Wilkinson Sword Company awakened to demand for the weapon. According to Robert Wilkinson-Latham, 'Deliveries were made to certain specified depots but the bulk of the production as it became available was held at the London showrooms, where they were given out against signed chits.' For not only SOE, but the whole of Britain's special forces clamoured for the Fairbairn-Sykes. 'The day they arrived,' Fairbairn remembered, 'there was a near riot in the rush to buy them.'[21]

Contracts were issued, but from Station XII (in the guise of 'Room 55a, War Office'), and are not therefore recorded under the Chief Inspector of Small Arms contract lists examined by Skennerton (which include other items, such as bayonets, ordered from Wilkinson, and inspected by the CISA 'viewer' and stamped at the factory). SOE had its own quality control and inspection operation at Aston House, from where stores were shipped to whichever part of the special operations structure required them.[22]

Weapons and sabotage equipment for the Auxiliary Units were collected and packed at Aston House, from where they were moved to the Auxiliary Units HQ at Coleshill House, near Swindon,[23] then to the area IOs, and from the IOs to the patrol leaders (Oxenden, 1998, p. 13). Therefore F-S knives for the Auxiliers came from the stock modern researchers have identified as 'SOE'. Cassidy puts the number of knives supplied to SOE by Wilkinson at 3,019,[24] which is some 500 fewer than the total number of Auxiliers on strength in 1941,[25] so many more knives must have been supplied to the special forces establishment to meet the requirements of the Auxiliary Units and the other components of SOE. It is worth noting that some 100 companies are believed to have been manufacturing or retailing F-S knives by 1942 and collectors' interest and research has tended to concentrate on Wilkinson.[26] Although Wilkinson's part in the development of the original knife is beyond dispute, it is quite possible that William Rodgers is the more important manufacturer, in terms of quantities of knives on operational service. Estimates of wartime British F–S knife manufacture put the total at some 2,000,000 knives, of which 231,769 were produced by Wilkinson.[27] What is certain is that no Auxilier could have received an F–S fighting knife before December 1940, any issue prior to this date being a hunting knife or similar. The majority of surviving F–S knives with confirmed Auxiliary Unit provenance are of the second pattern, however, Robert Millard notes:

> We had an early 1941 issue of the second pattern [unlikely to have been before August 1941, Wilkinson's introduction date of the second pattern F–S knife], straight crossguard, not stamped ... Geoff Bradford (now deceased) from a Devon patrol had a third pattern knife which he gave to Parham [BRO Museum]. Captain Ford, I/O in the Ramsey area also had a third pattern knife.[28]

Researchers recognise some fourteen variations of the F–S knife in use during the Second World War, including wood-handled versions which were available for aircrew, and variations on the second pattern F–S with so-called 'beaded' and 'roped' brass grips. These are regarded by some as the best balanced and finest F–S knives built, and are believed to have been produced by William Rodgers.[29] There is also a variant with a rather narrow steel hilt, variously referred to as the 'arctic' version (on the basis that it has turned up in Norway, and the shape of the grip and pommel might have suited gloved hands), or the 'French Resistance' or *ersatz* version (on the basis that it may have been produced cheaply and in bulk prior to D-Day). An *ersatz* F–S knife was issued to an Essex Auxilier, and a reference to the Arundel patrol in Angell's *Secret Sussex Resistance*, suggests they too had this pattern: 'When the men of Arundel Patrol were issued with these knives, they found the handles too narrow, so wound them round with plastic tape to build up the grip to the desired thickness' (Angell, 1996, p. 45). Issue to the Auxiliary Units would seem to run counter to the argument that this particular type of knife was a 1944 bulk order for D-Day, as, by that time, the Auxiliary Units were in decline. Further research is continuing on these weapons.[30]

Other close-combat weapons used by Auxiliers included home-made fighting knives, including punch daggers made up from broken fencing foils, and at least one example of the 'smatchet' (a heavy-bladed machete-like fighting knife,

215

which was another of Fairbairn's inventions), as well as wire garrottes, and various clubs, knuckledusters and coshes.[31] If the F–S knife was a rapier, then the smatchet was a broadsword, a big knife or short machete with a heavy blade to deliver a cutting blow. Fairbairn, single-mindedly, and rather optimistically, promoted the smatchet as the ideal weapon for any man not carrying a rifle, in his 1943 book *Get Tough*:[32]

> The psychological reaction of any man, when he first takes the smatchet in his hand, is full justification for its recommendation as a fighting weapon. He will immediately register all the essential qualities of a good soldier – confidence, determination, and aggressiveness.
>
> Its balance, weight, and killing power, with the point, edge or pommel, combined with the extremely simple training necessary to become efficient in its use, make it the ideal personal weapon for all those not armed with a rifle and bayonet.
>
> Note. – The smatchet is now in wide use throughout the British armed forces. It is hoped that it will soon be adopted by the United States Army.[33]

Fairbairn's quote captures the character of the man, and his absolute determination to close with the enemy and fight hand-to-hand. Although the smatchet did have some users, troops, on both sides of the Atlantic, 'not armed with a rifle and bayonet', seem to have preferred the option of a sub-machine gun.

While there can be no doubt that being issued a fighting knife greatly boosted the owner's moral and self-esteem – whether he be an Auxilier or Commando – there was, and remains, some question over the practicality of a knife that was designed (if brilliantly) for the single purpose of killing another human being. Silently and deliberately killing an enemy soldier with a knife requires the very highest standards of skill, fieldcraft, fitness and nerve. It is likely that the Auxiliary Units achieved these standards, but, in reality, the only real advantage of killing with a knife over, for example, the silenced firearm, is that the victim can be lowered and dragged away, rather than toppling over with a clatter of arms and equipment. Given the relatively few instances of fighting knives actually being used in this way, they were in danger of becoming weapons of symbolic significance, no more practical than an officer's sword. This was apparent by 1944, when Oxenden was recording his 'lessons learned' from the Auxiliary Units experience (Oxenden, 1998, p. 27):

The knife is perhaps the hardest and noisiest way of killing a conscious man, but is light to carry. The rubber club might be useful on occasions; but both these are rendered superfluous by the Welrod [silenced pistol], and call, in addition, for a very high degree of luck and skill in stalking.

Oxenden's mention of the Welrod is interesting, as he was obviously very impressed by this SOE silenced pistol, although there is no evidence it ever was issued to the Auxiliary Units. It does, however, lead us to consider the patrols' other weapons. All Sussex patrol leaders were given the following list of stores to be held at the patrol leader's house (Angell, 1996, p. 67):

Rifles .300	2
Thompson sub-machine gun	1
Thompson SMG sling	1
Sten guns	4
Sten gun [magazine] fillers	4
Pull throughs	6
Gauzes	10
.22 Rifle with rod	1
Cells for telephone	4
Rifle slings	2
Thompson SMG magazines	10
Box w/cleaning brushes Thompson SMG	1
Sten gun magazines	up to 32 per patrol
Sten gun slings	4
Oil bottles	6
Rum	1 gallon
Telephones	2
Goggles NP [night patrol simulating?]	3pr

It is obvious that, while the remainder of the Home Guard never had quite enough weapons for all its members, the five-man (after spring 1941, seven-man – Oxenden, 1998, p. 6) Auxiliary Units patrols had something of an embarrassment of riches. This arsenal was, however, accumulated over time, and with variations – the list shown being for Sussex patrols, directly in the path of a German invasion or raid. As we have established, the first weapons – apart from grenades and explosives – were knives and pistols, received in August and September 1940, along with rubber truncheons, which appear to have been withdrawn, at least from some patrols. These were followed by rifles, on a scale of two per patrol. As usual, memories of the rifles' manufacturer are hazy and confused, but we can be confident that they were standard Home Guard-issue M1917s, which arrived in the UK in July 1940.[34] Oxenden (1998, p. 5) regarded the rifles as something of a mystery: 'American rifles, on a scale of two per patrol, were an early issue, nobody quite knew why, and this item was never afterwards changed.' Giving the patrols a couple of rifles does not seem unreasonable at a time when the only other personal weapons available were pistols. In Oxenden's words, the rifles 'came into their own' from the summer of 1942, when the Auxiliary Units started to concentrate less on resisting an all-out invasion (which was now vanishingly unlikely), and more on disrupting a temporary landing or raid (Oxenden, 1998, p. 17).

What was really required was a light automatic weapon, and initially Browning Automatic Rifles were issued, one per patrol. A full-length self-loading rifle is awkward in a role that involves infiltration and clambering in and out of an underground hide. Oxenden (1998, p. 5) states that the BAR was: 'extremely popular, though quite alien to our role, and was later exchanged in England for the more portable Tommy Gun.' The Thompson SMG would appear to be very well suited to the Auxiliary Units role (it even had an easily removable stock), and it is interesting that a scale of just one per patrol seems to reflect a stringency with these guns, despite the very high priority the Auxiliary Units enjoyed. Although Thompsons were popular with the army, SOE preferred the Sten, regarding it as lighter, simpler, easier to conceal and more natural to aim for reflex shooting than the Thompson.[35] This may be why the scale of issue was not higher – the 'Tommy Gun' perhaps also being regarded as too clumsy for the Auxiliary Units. Andrew Taylor, Director of the British Resistance Organisation Museum, noted that by 1943 two types of patrol existed – Type A, equipped with the .45in Thompson SMG, and Type B equipped with (presumably a single) 9mm Sten machine carbine (Warwicker, 2004, p. 168). The 'Raid Role' from the summer of 1942 saw a special issue of Stens to coastal patrols (Oxenden, 1998, p. 17) – which explains the rather lavish armoury of the Sussex patrols, shown in the list above.

One item on the patrol list that has excited a great deal of interest is the '.22 Rifle with rod'. These were described by Oxenden:

.22 rifles of various patterns, fitted with silencers and telescopic sights, the first of 500, began to arrive, but long before delivery was complete, the telescope was found to be a mistake, adding little to accuracy even when carefully zeroed, and being so easily shifted by handling that ranging shots were always necessary. However it was too late to stop the issue, and many rifles had no backsights, the telescopes having been fitted in their place. (1998, p. 12)

The interest is due to the fact that these rifles would appear to be a tangible link with the Auxiliary Units' supposed assassination role. In John Warwicker's phrase: 'many Auxunit patrols regarded themselves as Judge, Jury and Executioner when collaborators were identified' (Warwicker, 2004, p. 168). There is no doubt that the idea of Auxiliers ruthlessly sniping Quislings and Fifth Columnists seems to hold a certain fascination, even if it is peripheral (at best) to their operational role. Skennerton (1988, pp. 21–2) lists contracts for 12,500 'miscellaneous .22 rifles' placed between April 1940 and January 1943; many of these are quite obviously trainers for use on indoor ranges, but others, specified as being supplied with telescopic sights, are probably the rifles Oxenden refers to, and give some indication of the types and make. The following extracts show the date the contracts were placed, description of the weapons purchased, supplier, quantity and (sometimes) unit price:

19.8.41	Win. s/s w/5X scope	Salter & Varge	10
	Win. s/s w/scope and peep sight	Salter & Varge	10
	Win. rep. w/5 shot mag & 5X scope	Salter & Varge	10

(The first two entries above, from August 1941, were Winchester single-shot rifles, ten fitted with 5x magnification telescopic sights and ten with telescopic sights and peep sights, supplied by Messrs Salter & Varge. The third entry was for five-shot repeaters.)

2.10.41	Win. Mod 69 BA w/5X scope	Geo. Greene	10	£6ea
	Win. Mod 72 BA w/5X scope	Geo. Greene	10	£8ea

(Winchester Model 69 and 72 bolt-action rifles with 5x magnification telescopic sights.)

31.1.42	Remington b/a s/s & Weaver scope	Remington Arms	10
	Remington rep & Weaver scope	Remington Arms	10

(Remington bolt-action single shot and repeating rifles with Weaver telescopic sights.)

Amongst all these batches of ten rifles, an undated contract from 1942 shows two bulk orders from Salter & Varge:

–.–.42	repeating rifle	Salter & Varge	250
	s/s rifle with scope	Salter & Varge	230

Salter & Varge Ltd, of Empire House, St Martins Le Grand, London, were noted for their game rifles and shotguns.[36] These two orders are intriguing, as they may account for the bulk of Oxenden's 500 rifles, the other orders only adding up to seventy weapons (although many more .22 rifles were ordered without a telescopic sight being specified). There is no more detail of date than '1942' on the contracts list, and it is difficult to reconcile the entry with a crucial contract with Parker Hale discussed below, as it is placed below it in the list. However, it is entirely conceivable that this was the order for the bulk of the Auxiliary Unit rifles.

Most relevant to any discussion of Oxenden's 500 .22 rifles is an entry for March 1942:

13.3.42	.22 rifle silencers, fitted for	Parker Hale	660	19/3ea
	For use by Home Guard		

The very existence of this contract is interesting, as it shows that, unlike the F-S knives, conventional contracts were placed for the silenced rifles, through the CISA system. A total of 660 silencers fitted to .22 rifles gives enough for one for each Auxiliary Units patrol – 576 patrols, as at 1941 (Lampe, 2007, p. 160), but described as 'rather more than 640' by early 1944 (Warwicker, 2004, 235) – plus a residue for the Regular Army Scout Sections, which were part of the Auxiliary Units structure (Warwicker, 2004, p. 68), and for training, or spares. The contract could have been drafted once the work was completed ('on termination' – although that is not specified). So, judging by the contract list, the earliest issues of .22 rifles with telescopic sights could have been in August 1941, but a delivery date of the final weapons is unlikely to be much earlier than March 1942.[37] This timing fits well with a diary entry by Firle (Sussex) patrol leader Bill Webber, recording the first issue of silenced .22 rifles in his area occurring at a patrol leaders' meeting at Allington Farm on 30 April 1942 (Angell, 1996, p. 35).

It has been said – by no lesser authority than the UK National Rifle Association online historical resource – that, apart from silencers, Parker Hale also fitted these

660 rifles with the No. 42 straight sighting telescope.[38] The No. 42 is similar to the army's No. 32 sniper's sight, which was developed in 1939 for use on the Bren light machine gun, but saw all of its military service on the sniper version of the No. 4 Lee-Enfield, the No. 4(T).[39] Once the idea of mating the Bren to a telescopic sight had been abandoned, all efforts concentrated on the No. 4(T) rifle/No. 32 'scope combination. Development took until March 1941, with the first snipers' rifles delivered in December 1941 (Laidler, 1993, p. 6). The No. 42 scope (and subsequent Nos 53 and 55), are identical to the No. 32, with some minor differences in optical arrangements between the marks. However, a major difference is that none of the three has any facility for adjusting range or deflection, in other words, the cross hairs are fixed. The development and use of these sights remains subject to discussion, but they were chiefly built for use with BESA machine guns mounted in tanks. There is, however, evidence that some of these sights were fitted to Winchester Model 75 self-loading .22 rifles, fitted with Parker Hale silencers, for use by the Auxiliary Units. The timing (delivery to the Aux Unit patrols in April 1942) is reasonable, and the combination is workable – and rather more robust than contemporary civilian 'scopes of the day. In what quantities these combinations were produced is difficult to determine, but they may well be the 250 repeating rifles in the Salter & Varge order that do not have telescopic sights specified.

Lampe (2007, p. 78) states that the .22 rifles were fitted with a 'powerful telescopic sight and a silencer, [and] fired high-velocity bullets capable of killing a man a mile away'. This is to seriously overestimate the power of a .22 bullet – and there is no evidence that the ammunition used was anything than standard .22 'long rifle' rim-fire.[41] This ammunition is marked 'dangerous to one mile',[40] but that is not to suggest that one could deliberately hit a target at that range, as velocity falls off and the bullet drops dramatically after a few hundred yards. In any case, high-velocity ammunition is the last thing one wishes to fire from a silenced weapon. There are three areas to consider when silencing a firearm: Firstly, there is the mechanical noise of the mechanism operating, which, in a single-shot bolt-action .22 is minimal – and becomes even less of an issue if the weapon is carried to the firing point loaded and cocked, and does not need to be operated again once the shot is fired. It is slightly more on a repeater, but still negligible. Secondly there is the 'report', the sound caused by high-pressure gases leaving the muzzle as the bullet exits. This can be defeated by trapping the gases and allowing them to dissipate their energy using a tube containing a series of baffles, attached to the muzzle of the weapon – the 'silencer', more correctly termed a 'suppressor', a device successfully demonstrated by Hiram Maxim on a series of rifles, including a .22 Winchester, in 1909. The sound of Maxim's Winchester firing was described by the *New York Times* as: '… a "click" about as loud as one would make by snapping the trigger of an old-fashioned musket.'[42] The final element is the 'ballistic crack', a small sonic boom, caused by the bullet, or air surrounding the bullet, travelling faster than the speed of sound (*c*. 1,100ft/s depending on conditions). This can be obviated by using ammunition which is already sub-sonic, such as the .45ACP round used in the Thompson SMG, or bleeding gases from behind the bullet to reduce muzzle velocity to a sub-sonic rate.

A .22 rifle can be virtually silent if subsonic ammunition (around 950ft/s) is used, but this low-velocity ammunition further diminishes the hitting power of what is already a low-powered round. With a muzzle velocity of 1,085ft/s, standard .22LR ammunition, such as that used by the British Army on miniature ranges, is subsonic to transonic under most temperatures experienced in the UK.[43] On firing, the Auxiliary Unit sniper would have made some sound, but one that would be almost impossible to pinpoint, or even identify as a shot. But, there remains the problem of the round's hitting power. Oxenden (1998, p. 12) was quite specific about the purpose of the silenced .22 rifles: 'These weapons were intended at first for the sniping of enemy sentries, and to fill the larder.' .22 rifles are typically used to shoot small game or vermin such as squirrels, rats or rabbits at ranges out to 150yd. Foxes can be shot at up to 80yd, and American figures give 65yd for animals as large as coyotes – and these must be head or chest shots. In 1970 a Home Office committee, convened to examine police use of sniping rifles, examined various options and calibres. On the subject of .22 ammunition the committee reported:[44]

> The .22" Long Rifle rim-fire cartridge which is made in the United Kingdom lacks hitting power even in the sporting, high velocity versions and is accurate only within 100 yards. Even, up to this range, and some way beyond it, it is much inferior in hitting power to the recommended pistol cartridge.

We can conclude that, as originally conceived, the Auxiliary Unit sniper might have expected to drop an enemy with a well-aimed shot (avoiding his steel helmet, if worn) at around 50–75yd range. Robert Millard, whose patrol was armed with a Winchester repeater, elaborated:

> Re: .22 sniping. I have tried to think pragmatically about this. In my two visits to Coleshill [training centre, in early and late 1941] nothing was said about

sniping sentries, they were to be dealt with by the F–S knife, the garrotte (a problem with a coal scuttle helmet, tunic collar and chin strap) and a blow to the temple or carotid artery with the rubber truncheon. Two of us were rifle club members so 100 yds with target sights was standard. Rabbits at 75 yds with a scope was also a familiar shot. However, these were shots taken at leisure and under no stress. We practised in a quarry at about 100 yards and with a scope I could make a head shot in twilight conditions BUT no stress, a still target and a comfortable firing position. A sentry is not going to be standing in the open with the moon behind him … we had a Winchester 74 which is a semi automatic so two or three quick chest shots was a possibility.

Given the relatively short range, the lack of adjustment on the No. 42 sight would not represent too much of a problem, as long as the sight was squarely mounted on the rifle. A telescopic sight would certainly help ensure absolute accuracy, and 'gather light' in poor light conditions, but the .22s were definitely not going to assassinate anyone at ranges out to 1 mile. As Oxenden commented (1998, p. 12): 'In the end they proved their value for competitive training.'[45]

During the Second World War, much more effective silenced weapons were available to the special operations community – the De Lisle carbine, silenced Sten guns, and Oxenden's favourite, the Welrod pistol. Post-war Territorial Army four-man stay-behind patrols were issued a single L34A1 silenced Sterling sub-machine gun, a weapon consanguineous with the Lanchester machine carbine and the De Lisle carbine.[46] The L34A1, it was assumed, would deal with any silent killing that needed to be done, no thought being given to the use of fighting knives, garrottes or coshes. We might, therefore, reasonably expect to see a silenced Sten or De Lisle carbine in service with the wartime Auxiliary Units, but the key here is timing. Work on the De Lisle and silenced Mk II Sten did not begin until mid-to-late 1942 (rather later for the Welrod[47]), by which time the Auxiliary Units had already identified the requirement, and met it by issuing silenced .22 rifles in the winter of 1941–42. This undoubtedly reflected the benefit of having an organisation containing numbers of poachers and gamekeepers, who would have been familiar with silenced smallbore rifles. By 1943, when specially built silenced military small arms started to become available, the contingency for which the Auxiliary Units had needed them was impossibly remote, and organisation itself was deliberately keeping a low profile to avoid being stood-down.[48]

Thus far we have made every effort to stress the effectiveness of Home Guard weapons that have traditionally been characterised as ineffective. It might therefore seem strange that we have rather diminished the Auxiliary Units' two 'signature' weapons, their F–S fighting knives and silenced rifles. However, the aim has been to achieve a balanced assessment of the Home Guard's military effectiveness, and to concentrate on the Auxiliary Units' daggers and sniping is to totally miss the point. The Auxilier's personal weapons and small arms were never more than a means to end, a way of ensuring the success of their real task, which was demolition and destruction using explosives and incendiaries. Oxenden makes this quite plain in his recommendations, should a similar force ever again be called into being:

> PERSONAL WEAPONS. There are strong arguments against the carrying of firearms on night operations [the only sort of operation seriously considered for Aux Unit patrols]. One shot could betray the presence of the patrol and turn the attack into a headlong rout.
>
> The only weapon of this sort that could be used without wrecking the chances of the attackers is one that is silent and fitted with luminous sights. Such a pistol has been produced under the name of 'Welrod'.

To illustrate the sort of use to which Oxenden would have seen Aux Unit firearms put, it is worthwhile reproducing the 'general instructions for use' from the Welrod manual,[49] although it must be stressed that there is no evidence of Auxiliary Units ever having used this weapon:

Function:
The 9mm. Welrod is a silent single shot pistol, intended for use by specially trained operators for specific tasks.

General Description:
The Weapon is a specially constructed single shot pistol with a detachable silencer. It is silent, reliable in action and easy to conceal. It is accurate up to 30 yards in daylight or 20 yards on a fairly light night, but is most effective when fired in contact with the target.

Notes on use:
The gun has three distinct and separate uses:

a) For aimed and deliberate shots in daylight or darkness. The effective range of the gun with normal handling is 15/30 yards. For deliberate shots, extreme accuracy is required and can only be obtained by correct trigger squeeze, i.e. a gradual squeeze by the whole hand. With training and practice it is possible to obtain very accurate groups at the distances mentioned. The gun should be held with the thumb and forefinger of the left hand as close up to the muzzle as possible, the pistol grip being held by the right hand. For standing shots, the left elbow should be as close to the body as possible and the rear of the gun approximately 6"/7" from the operator's eye.

b) Without its silencer and used as a single-shot weapon.

c) By use of the weapon at the closest quarters, i.e. with the muzzle against the target. For this purpose no special training is required.

We have seen that each Auxilier was issued a quantity of equipment and weapons to keep at home, while more was stored by the patrol commander. The third and final component of the patrol's equipment was stored at their underground hide or OB (operating base) (Angell, 1996, p. 69):[50]

Grenades 36M	48
Aux units Mk. II	1
Compass magnetic	1
Tyre cutter	1
Spare detonators	50
First aid set	1
Monocular and case	1
Primus stove	1
Lamps hurricane	2
Pick and helve	1
Pouches basic	2
Shovels	2
Det. Carriers	8
M.E.B. [?]	48
Elsan and Elsanol	1 [*Chemical toilet and fluid*]
Tripwire rolls	24
Trapwire rolls	24
Ammunition .450	1200
,, 9mm	1250
,, .22	200
Bottles AW	48
Release switches	50

Pull switches	50
Pressure switches	50
Paraffin	up to 10 gals. per patrol
Thermometer	1
Shell dressings	up to 4 per patrol
Telephone cable	already laid
Plastic H.E.	up to 30lbs per patrol
L. delays 1hr	15) unless L. delays for aux unit
L. delays 3hr	15)　Mk II have been issued
Cotton waste	½lb
Crimping tools	4
C.T.I. (where issued)	60 [copper tube igniters]
Striker boards	24
Magnets	24
Time pencils (where issued)	240
Camouflage cream	3 black
,,	3 green
,,	3 brown

The OB stores list brings us full circle, as it includes fifteen 'packs', in this case the 'Aux units Mk. II', as well as significant additional quantities of explosives and initiators of various sorts. The inclusion of Mk II Aux Units and L-delay timers puts this list late in the Auxiliary Units brief history, probably 1943. It is interesting to note that the patrol has two cases of 'AW Bottles' (No. 76 SIP grenades), but the Sticky bomb (No. 74 grenade) is not mentioned, although it featured in the first two editions of the Aux Unit textbook, the 'Calendar 1937' and '1938'.[51]

The Auxiliary Unit mission started out, as Oxenden put it, as: 'the indiscriminate and malicious damage of anything that worked' (Oxenden, 1998, p. 5). Incendiarism and wrecking the transport infrastructure was a role recognisable to *francs-tireurs* of the Franco-Prussian War and Lawrence's Arab irregulars of the First World War. However, as we have seen in previous chapters, in 1940–41, British high command was rather more vexed by the threat of *Panzers* running unchecked across the Home Counties than the *Deutsche Reichsbahn Gesellschaft* taking over the Southern Railway. In short order, the Auxiliary Units patrols became some of the specialist 'tank hunters' referred to in *Tank Hunting and Destruction* of August 1940.[52] Working on Lawrence's dictum that materiel is harder to replace than men, in those vital hours and days after a landing, the fifty snorkelling PzKpfw III and IV '*Tauchpanzers*' would have been a worthwhile target for patrols, whose operational life expectancy was only ever going to be measured in days. In Oxenden's words (1998, p. 5): 'Briefly, sabotage gave place to attack by night, mainly upon A.F.V.' Tank and steamroller hulks were arranged in the grounds of the Auxiliary Units headquarters at Coleshill House to represent AFVs parked-up in a tactical laager, for the Auxiliers to practise placing Sticky bombs and other charges on the vehicles at night (Lampe, 2007, p. 77).

Apart from ST and SIP grenades, the Auxiliers were also issued, as we have seen, with No. 36M (Mills) grenades, and, later, the No. 77, a phosphorous smoke grenade, using the ubiquitous No. 247 'All-ways' fuse. This grenade never reached the remainder of the Home Guard (nor indeed did any smoke grenade or generator, the No. 76 SIP being used instead). The No. 77, which was in service by July 1942, was described as a 'hand percussion smoke grenade'.[53] It was not, strictly speaking, a weapon, as it was designed to burst producing an instantaneous, but short-duration, smoke screen. Being phosphorous, it did however have a useful anti-personnel effect. For the Auxiliary Units patrols, this combination of instant and noxious smoke was an excellent way to discourage pursuit, and the Auxiliary Units took to the No. 77. In November 1943 Auxiliary Units placed an order for 50,000 No. 77 grenades (exceeding their issue recommendation by 2,500 per cent), which was optimistic and, at that stage in the war, asking for trouble. The issue was eventually approved in January 1944, subject to being phased over three months (Warwicker, 2004, p. 48). Oxenden placed the No. 77 grenade alongside the Welrod as an item required for any Auxilier of the future:

> The No 77 is the grenade that would prove most useful on patrol. There is no indication of the point from which it is thrown, and there is no chance of taking cover from it. It would always baffle pursuit.
>
> In short no arms are needed but the Welrod for attack and the 77 for defence.
> (1998, p. 27)

To return to explosives, the period 1940–41 saw increasing use of a diversity of initiators, including time pencils, and pressure and pull switches. The time pencil was one of the earliest and most important products of MI(R). Commander Langley began work to produce a simple, silent, reliable timer which could fire an HE charge or incendiary, in early 1939. Work on the rate at which corrosive solutions ate through wire were carried out in laboratories at the University of London. In the UK 12,800,000 'pencil time fuses' were produced, more in the

USA, and it was copied by other nations including the USSR.[54] Throughout British special operations the 1940–41 period was one of exuberant enthusiasm and experimentation, characterised by a boyish attitude to explosive devices. Booby trapping was elevated to something of a team sport, and Commandos, Station XII, and the rest, competed to see who could most surprise visitors from the other sections with exploding lavatory seats and mattresses rigged with coils of instantaneous fuse – calculated to levitate the occupant of an army cot just short of the ceiling.[55] This gaiety doubtless owes much to the irrepressible character of Major Leslie John Cardew Wood, who succeeded Langley as Officer Commanding Station XII at Aston House. The war news was shaky, but within the special operations community, anything and everything was possible.

This culture encouraged offensive spirit, inventive solutions and an easiness with explosives, but for the part-timers of the Auxiliary Units there were disadvantages as use of explosive devices became more complex. Mid-1941 saw targets begin to shift towards airfields, threatening any German air bridge and efforts to maintain

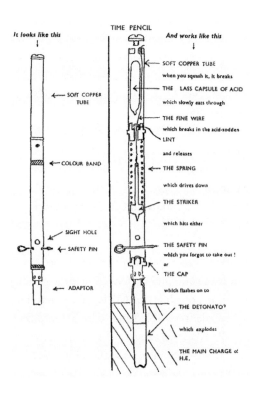

The Time Pencil, as illustrated and explained in *The Countryman's Diary 1939*. (Author's collection via John Warwicker and Robert Millard)

local air superiority. The patrols were also reorganised to be able to mount large-scale 'group' attacks, which, as MBRO Director Andrew Taylor has pointed out, seriously compromised the original, relatively secure, cellular structure of the force (Warwicker, 2004, p. 34). Oxenden comments:

> Operational complexity at this time was accompanied by a boom in 'practical jokes'. New mechanisms and new ideas for booby traps were constantly cropping up, and although they may have increased the 'explosive-mindedness' of some of the auxiliers, they unquestionably produced a state of mental fog in the remainder. This was realised later, and teaching amended accordingly. (1998, p. 11)

As we have noted with relation to the Auxiliers' small arms, the final recommendation in Oxenden's report was simplicity. Just as the possession of an armoury of firearms was more likely to result in the patrols being compromised, so the construction of elaborate booby traps was more likely to defeat the object of the mission:

> Once the matter was seriously questioned it became increasingly obvious that the auxilier had been in some respects over-rated, and that such a policy would inevitably mean confusion and inefficiency in action.
>
> Tests of cross-sections of the unit here and there showed that, after two years training, less was known about the use of explosives than in 1940, that many of the 'toys' since issued would never, and could never successfully be used, and that liaison between patrols was little more than wishful thinking, and questionable at that. At one stroke our policy had been cleared of much hampering undergrowth. From now on the patrol was self-contained and would fight alone; from now on the rank and file would not be asked to think. (Oxenden, 1998, p. 15)

A practical outcome of the rethink was the development of a one-size-fits-all 'unit charge' that could be pre-prepared and used for almost any sabotage task. Oxenden explained:

> 1lb was fixed as a weight of explosive that was light enough to carry in reasonable numbers, and powerful enough for all practical purposes. A simple make-up was adopted as official, universally taught, and illustrated in our revised textbook, the 'Calendar 1938'. Briefly, the charge had one ounce of primer and a twelve inch tail of detonating fuse, to which were taped two time pencils with

detonators. The fuse itself ended in a double loop, for threading when necessary onto a 'ring main'.

The auxilier would not now be asked to play with bits and pieces in the target area, or to devise 'booby traps' under the noses of enemy sentries, where his powers of thought might not be at their clearest; his work would simply be to get in and place a unit charge, a form of fieldcraft that had reached a very high standard. (1998, p. 16)

By the time the final Auxiliary Unit manual, 'The Countryman's Diary 1939', was issued, the unit charge had further diminished to ½lb.[56] Where larger amounts of explosive were required, multiple charges were used on a 'ring main'. Each man was to carry nine or ten of these down the front of his battledress blouse, in waterproof paper bags (to prevent the explosives giving a severe headache). It is evident from the OB stores list that the patrols had considerable stores of

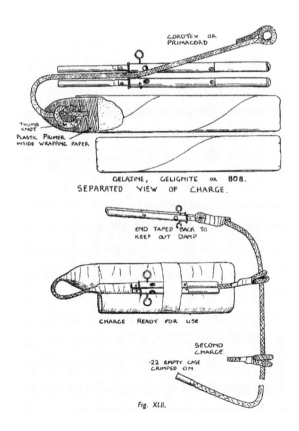

CORDTEX OR PRIMACORD

THUMB KNOT
PLASTIC PRIMER INSIDE WRAPPING PAPER

GELATINE, GELIGNITE OR 808.
SEPARATED VIEW OF CHARGE.

END TAPED BACK TO KEEP OUT DAMP

CHARGE READY FOR USE

SECOND CHARGE
·22 EMPTY CASE CRIMPED ON

Fig. XLII.

The 1lb unit charge, as illustrated in the Calendar 1938. (Via Robert Millard) explosive, and the potential to do a great deal of damage for as long as they could remain operational. To reinforce the point, it is worthwhile listing the explosive stores recorded by a Royal Army Ordnance Corps NCO when the explosive stores of the five Auxiliary Unit patrols in Dengie Marshes in Essex were finally handed over to the authorities on 7 April 1964 (Lampe, 2007, pp. 146–7):

14,738 rounds of ammunition for pistols, rifles and sub-machine-guns, including a quantity of incendiary rounds

1,205lbs of gelignite, of Nobel 808 and of plastic explosive, most of it in a safe enough condition to take away

3,742ft delayed action fuse

930ft instantaneous safety fuse

250ft detonating cord

1,447 time pencils

1,207 L-delay switches [a later form of time pencil which, instead of relying on acid, is triggered by induced metal fatigue]

1,271 detonators of various types

719 push, pull and pressure-release booby-trap switches

314 paraffin bombs and

340 igniters for these bombs and for the safety fuses

131 fog signals

121 smoke bombs

212 thunderflashes

571 primers

36 1lb slabs of gun cotton

4 hand-grenades

10 phosphorous grenades

33 time-pencils and booby trap switches attached to made-up charges

The Home Guard Auxiliary Units patrols demonstrated that outstandingly high standards of professionalism could be achieved by unpaid part-timers. They also demonstrated the need to concentrate on doing a small number of things very well, and avoid the temptation to increase interest and variety at the expense of quality. These conclusions were equally applicable to the Home Guard as a whole. In the end, commitment and determination, a few phosphorous grenades and a unit charge, were as much as the Auxiliary Units really needed, everything else was simply impedimenta.

10

THE MATTER OF PERSPECTIVE

In his diary entry for 10 August 1940, Alan Brooke, then General Officer Commanding Home Forces, recorded his dismay at having to lose three tank regiments – one cruiser, one light, and one army tank – for service in North Africa, just when a German invasion of the UK seemed most likely. In his notes added later to the entry, he elaborated:[1]

> This does not seem much when considered from the point of view of later years in the war, but in the early days even this small contribution constituted a large proportion of the total of my armoured forces. To make matters worse at this time, Beaverbrook, who was minister of Aircraft Production, began to form an army of his own to protect aircraft factories in the event of invasion. He acquired large proportions of armour plating for the production of small armoured cars called 'Beaverettes', with which he equipped Home Guard personnel of factories for their protection. This was at a time when I was shouting for every armoured vehicle I could lay my hands on with which to equip regular forces. The whole thing was fantastic. How could individual factories have held out, and what part could they have played once the main battle for this country was lost?

It is sobering to consider that the Standard Beaverette, the armoured fighting vehicle that was the source of such friction between Brooke and Beaverbrook, was an ad hoc construction, consisting of a Standard 12hp saloon car chassis, on which was mounted an open-topped armoured body of 9mm steel, reinforced behind with 3in of oak planking. The vehicle carried a crew of three, and was armed with a single Bren gun. The first two patterns of the car had an attractive sports car styling, although the 2½-ton body, and narrow vision slit, positioned well forward of the driver, made it difficult and arduous to drive. The Mk III Beaverette dispensed with civilian-style mudguards in favour of a boxy bonnet and shortened hull of 12mm armour, topped by a 'dustbin' turret, the overall effect being of a child's drawing of an armoured car (these vehicles were also known as 'Beaverbugs'). The final, Mk IV version had a stepped glacis, in order to move the vision slit closer to the driver.

Having argued the merits of the 2pr anti-tank gun, which could penetrate 53mm of armour plate, and the Boys anti-tank rifle, which could penetrate 21mm at 300yd, it will be apparent that, as an armoured fighting vehicle, the Beaverette offered very meagre protection. It also had limited cross-country performance, due to its two-wheel drive and the additional weight of the armour. Nevertheless, the 'Beaverette Light Reconnaissance Car' was the only armour available to re-equip various Regular Army armoured units in 1940. The Regular Army used their Beaverette en masse, or at least they were massed for the benefit of publicity photographs. In Home Guard service they tended to be individual vehicles, or ones and twos, chiefly for the defence of factories, a task that was also undertaken by older AFVs, such as Rolls-Royce armoured cars, and homemade armoured vehicles, which were probably at least as effective as the Beaverette. Beaverettes also played a key role in the defence of airfields; the later Mks III and IV were rather more 'mobile pillboxes' or machine-gun posts than armoured cars, the tall hull and turret giving a good field of fire. The last hurrah of the Beaverette came in April 1943, when 168, mounting Lewis guns, formed part of the coastal defensive anti-aircraft 'fringe' against German 'tip-and-run' air raids.[2] As the threat of airborne invasion or raids diminished, some Beaverettes in factories became tractors, at Cowley, for example, hauling aircraft scrap to the furnaces,[3] or runabouts, while others lingered on airfields, towing air cadet gliders.[4] Some Mk IVs served with the Irish Army until the 1960s.

General Brooke's frustration makes sense from the perspective of a military commander with insufficient resources tasked with defending the British mainland from invasion. But it also betrays a failure to comprehend the fragility of the country's manufacturing base, and the impact that damage to it might have on the UK's capacity to wage war in the technological age. We have already seen the dramatic effect on small arms production of the destruction of the BSA Small Heath rifle barrel plant. Another vital, specialist Birmingham factory was that of SU Carburettors. The vulnerability of the country's carburettor manufacturing was vividly described in the post-war publication *Calling All Arms*, which celebrated the wartime achievements of the Nuffield Organisation:[5]

… by comparison with other Birmingham works, the factory was quite small, employing about 700 people up to the outbreak of war. Yet within its narrow confines, right up to the Battle of Britain, *all* the aero-carburettors for the R.A.F.'s Spitfires and Hurricanes were made. And if this single factory had been destroyed, Britain would have been unable to put into the air any new fighters for a period of at least twelve months. The RAF would have suffered a mortal blow.

If petrol is the life-blood of a warplane, then the carburettor which supplies the engine with this petrol is its very heart. The danger was apprehended in 1939, when Riley's began to lay down a plant to duplicate the S.U.'s work. But it was technically and humanly impossible to get this highly intricate and delicate mechanism into production in anything under a year.

So, if the Germans had but known, and had sent over 500 bombers – even at the cost of losing every one of them – or had sacrificed as many parachutists and gliders as they did at Crete, for the sole purpose of blowing the little S.U. works sky-high, history would have taken a calamitous turn indeed in those dark days of 1940.

When the threat of a German invasion hung over this country, the British authorities began to get a little anxious.

However, one Saturday afternoon that summer, the S.U. factory received an unexpected personal visit – it was, of course, kept very hush-hush – from Admiral Sir Edward Evans – 'Evans of the *Broke*'.[6] He went over the premises and said: 'Now, you're very important. We have to arm you.' He sanctioned the construction of strongposts, which were specially designed by one of the firm's technical staff. These had two storeys with bunks in the lower one. A 40-ft. iron observation tower was built on the roof, so that spotters might keep a constant look-out for enemy parachutists.

The promised arms duly arrived – one armoured car, machine-guns, and rifles. The workers banded themselves into a smart Home Guard unit, under the direction of the managing director, who had been a member of the Honourable Artillery Company for many years.

General Brooke was a highly intelligent and capable officer – was he correct in thinking that the battle for Britain could only be won or lost on the beaches, by the British Army, or was Lord Beaverbrook correct in retaining scarce military resources to secure unique and irreplaceable manufacturing capability? On balance they were both correct – and neither case is helped by the fact that German tactics were based on a third course, that of bludgeoning the UK population into compliance by terror bombing. What appeared 'fantastic' to a military strategist might seem prudent to an economist. Brooke was looking at the matter at the operational level, while Beaverbrook was being strategic, and from that perspective, his factory Home Guard units were, in some respects, a higher priority than the Regular Army.

The relevance and effectiveness of the Home Guard has been judged in terms of a Nazi invasion that never happened, Nazi parachutists who never arrived, and Fifth Columnists who probably never existed. This is unfair, because what the Home Guard did do was provide a trained, uniformed and armed military presence throughout the entire UK. It freed army personnel from anti-aircraft command and the coastal artillery, and enabled vital points – 'VPs' – to be defended on their own resources by providing guards, patrols, sentries and anti-aircraft gun crews from within the workforce. It is perfectly clear, from General Brooke's response to it, that the invasion threat was real and credible, and lasted from May 1940 to the 'Turn of the Tide' in 1942. During that time every effort was made to strengthen the UK's defences, of which the Home Guard was a key part. The extent to which the Home Guard was able to shoulder the responsibility for Home Defence as the Regular Army became more committed overseas reflects extremely well on these unpaid part-timers, who, for the most part, were already engaged in war work of national importance.

This study grew from the observation that Home Guard weapons in the Bapty collection were of a significantly better quality than popularly imagined, which suggested that the combat power of the wartime Home Guard was being seriously underestimated. Subsequent examination of the few modern books on the subject revealed that (with the possible exception of Ian Beckett) the authors had accepted the poor quality of the Home Guard arsenal without question; indeed Professor S.P. MacKenzie, the most important academic source on the subject, based his hypothesis on the premise that Home Guard was armed with 'weapons which in reality were of dubious fighting value, but which in all probability would never have to be fired in anger and could be presented as worthwhile'. In contrast, it should now be clear that monopolising imported American weapons placed the Home Guard at a significant advantage over other components of Home Defence.

The accurate, high-velocity, M1917 rifle was ideally suited to the Home Guard who, even the authors of training manuals finally admitted, were better off relying on marksmanship than 'cold steel'. Of the Home Guard's automatic weapons, the Browning Automatic Rifle (BAR), whilst not as good a section automatic as the Bren gun, was sufficiently highly regarded by US forces to have remained in service until the Vietnam War. The Browning medium machine gun was another highly effective weapon that the Home Guard shared with American troops, while the Vickers machine gun – although unpopular with the Americans – continued to serve with British infantry battalions until 1968. The Home Guard's main light machine gun, the Lewis, had only retired from front-line service with the British Army in 1938 and still equipped some of the TA units of the BEF. Far from being a 'cast-off', the Lewis was in universal demand – particularly in a light anti-aircraft role – throughout the Second World War.

Professor MacKenzie dismissed the Home Guard's unconventional weapons: 'mass production of cheap, ineffective weapons such as the Northover Projector allowed the War Office to have its cake and eat it too. Maintaining the Home Guard from 1941 onward cost about £1,000,000 a month ... a tiny fraction of what was being spent on the Regular Army' (MacKenzie, 1996, p. 177). But this is just too cynical: the Sten gun, for all its shortcomings, was one of the most successful British small arms designs of all time. The ST grenade ('Sticky bomb') saw service in the Western Desert and occupied Europe, and was not obsolete until 1955; the 29mm Spigot Mortar ('Blacker Bombard') too saw action with the Eighth Army in the Middle East. The Northover Projector differed little in effectiveness from the Holman Projector, which equipped fishing boats, merchant vessels, and minor naval vessels, and the Smith Gun was issued to RAF Regiment airfield defence units. These were not, on the balance of evidence, tokens to appease a noisy Home Guard 'lobby', but genuine attempts to provide weapons at a time when demand entirely exceeded Britain's capacity to produce. They were also optimised for static defence, which is why they continued to meet the requirements of the Home Guard, whilst becoming obsolete for the Regular Army, as it turned to the offensive.

As the demand for manpower to meet Britain's military commitments became unsustainable, the burden of Home Defence increasingly fell to the Home Guard. MacKenzie states that:

[When] there were no more sub-artillery curiosities dating from 1940 to draw upon ... it remained War Office policy to keep introducing 'new' weapons to the Home Guard ... for the sake of appearances ... Only when very obsolete weapons (such as the Northover Projector and the dreaded pikes) could be replaced at once with marginally less ineffective cast-offs from the Army (such as the 18-pounder field gun or 2-pounder anti-tank gun) was anything taken out of service. (MacKenzie, 1996, p. 135)

To suggest that service weapons such as the 18pr or 2pr were only marginally more effective than the Northover Projector is either to significantly overrate the performance of the Northover or underrate the performance of two mainstays of the regular artillery during the early part of the Second World War, and such statements cannot help form a coherent idea of the Home Guard's military potential. Over time the Home Guard acquired a suite of weapons – improvised, obsolescent, current and experimental – which constituted the Home Defence arsenal. Effective ranges were shortened and tactics altered to continue to make the most of each weapon (the Northover Projector being a prime example) and weapons moved back from 'front-line' Home Guard units to less immediately threatened ones. It is difficult, when all things are considered, to find fault with such a strategy.

In the final analysis, the Home Guard arsenal had two significant shortcomings: firstly, there were not 'plenty of rifles' – an already discredited government failed to meet the immediate public expectation of a service rifle for every volunteer, leading to the perception that the authorities were not taking the volunteers seriously. Indeed, there were always more volunteers than weapons – although, from the arrival of the first US shipments in late summer 1940, the Home Guard, as a domestic Resistance Army, was luxuriously equipped, compared to the French Forces of the Interior, for example. Secondly, there was the perception that any equipment issued that differed from that of a British line infantryman was *ersatz*. The weapons that were issued were different to those the Home Guard, particularly those with previous military experience, expected to receive but were, within the limitations in which the Home Guard was expected to operate, fit for purpose. There was, though, automatic hostility against anything that was different from the standard Regular Army issue – such as the M1917 rifles – even when sober examination makes it clear that they were at least as good as any other rifles in British hands at the time. The ease with which the Home Guard accepted shoddy wartime-manufactured No. 4 rifles and Sten guns indicates the extent to which they would settle for anything, as long as they shared it with the Regular Army.

This attitude owes much to a feeling among Home Guards that neither the authorities nor the public, nor the other armed services was taking them seriously. Any examination of the contemporary documents held in The National Archives immediately indicates how much official thought and effort was expended on the Home Guard – although the failure and delays in arming and equipping the LDV/Home Guard was taken by the volunteers as proof to the contrary. We noted in Chapter 2 that LDV security roadblocks were likely to be ignored by some civilians and military, despite the fact that they were officially sanctioned, and playing an important role in anti-invasion security measures. Certainly there was, and remains, a difficulty in accepting that the bank manager and clerks, the butcher and the undertaker – as depicted in *Dad's Army* – or Langdon-Davies' baker, could play any meaningful role in military operations, both at the time and since.

When the author was researching, at an early stage in this project, requests for information through local newspapers resulted in a flurry of letters, only two of which were from individuals with first-hand experience of the Home Guard, Chas Medhurst and Peter Pellereau. Both these men took a dim view of the portrayal of the Home Guard in *Dad's Army* – they had both been young Home Guards, and therefore represented by Ian Lavender's character 'Private Pike' in the series. Pellereau, it will be recalled, rounded up a downed *Luftwaffe* airman, whilst brandishing his grandfather's Webley revolver, and went on to have a distinguished military career, while Medhurst at 16 was a stalwart of the Browning machine-gun team, in a Home Guard unit that lay almost exactly in the path of the planned German invasion, and subsequently served in the Merchant Navy. However, most of the correspondence received was along the lines of 'my great uncle was in the Home Guards in the War and it was *exactly* like *Dad's Army*!!!' That is the 'cherished narrative', and that is how we *want* to see the Home Guard.

Peter Fleming examined the British reaction to the threat of Nazi invasion in some detail, and concluded that, in the absence of invasion, or any significant conflict, on British soil for many generations, the prospect was never entirely real in the minds of the British public:

Would tanks, one day, come nosing through the allotments? Would tracer bullets flick across the recreation ground? Would field-grey figures carrying stick-grenades and flame throwers work their way along the hedges towards the flimsy pill-box opposite the Nag's Head?

Reason, and their leaders, told the British that these things were very likely to occur; but the mental pictures which they formed of them, though highly coloured, were somehow not really alarming. They retained an affinity with patriotic melodrama; they were illustrations to a stirring tale of adventure rather than images of a dreadful reality. The British contemplated them with a morbid relish, but without complete conviction. (Fleming, 1957, pp. 80–1)

When none of the supposed threats the Home Guard was preparing to meet materialised there remained a feeling of self-consciousness – that 2 million men and women and their families and co-workers had in some way been the victims of an elaborate practical joke, and left looking slightly silly. The prosaic, but vital, work the Home Guard did as a key component of the defence of the UK was overlooked. The cherished image of old men and boys preparing to meet the Nazis with pikes is a synthesis. It combines a folk memory of the period, in June and July 1940, when the LDV (largely made of volunteers in their prime, but not yet liable for call-up) impatiently awaited the arrival of its weapons – and the latter part of the Home Guard's existence, 1943–44, when the rapacious demands of conscription increasingly confined the Home Guard to the middle-aged and under-aged. As we have seen, the pikes were, in any case, shared with the regular troops of Anti-Aircraft Command. One cannot help but notice the devastating effect of those adjectives 'old' and 'First World War' – and conclude that there is one rule for describing Home Guard equipment, and another for everyone else's. Describing the Home Guard's rifles as 'First World War' is to suggest that there was another kind. There wasn't. The cherished SMLE of the Regular Army dated from 1907, and the only truly modern rifle was the No. 4 Lee-Enfield, which was not generally available until 1943 – at which point it began to be issued to the Home Guard.

In order to make the argument that the weapons of the Home Guard were fit for purpose, it has been necessary to examine them all, to avoid the charge of being selective with the evidence. There is a great deal of ground to cover, and having made the point in general terms, there is now scope for much more detailed examination of the various areas. The reasons for the shortage of service rifles in 1940, and the development, sponsorship and service history of the sub-artillery are two subjects that merit further serious examination. More broadly, the Home Guard returns, held at The National Archives, have only been used in the most basic manner in this book, to illustrate when a certain item entered service, and how many were in use at a given time. The returns have considerably more potential for statistical analysis. It would, for example, be most interesting to model the roll-out of new weapon types across the country. One would expect to see a 'wave' spreading inland from the south and east coasts, but the indications are that this is not the case, and new items like Sten guns plugged gaps in less front-line areas first. In many ways, Home Defence, 1939–45, offers an ideal opportunity for research that is both accessible and innovative, and prime examples used in this study are the University of East Anglia 'Defence of Walberswick' project[7] and Russell W. Barnes' 'Defence of Workington'.[8]

To usefully examine Home Defence we have to get past what Calder characterised as the 'Myth of the Blitz'. Ian Beckett has noted the extent to which even contemporary images of the Home Guard differ from reality: 'many contemporary accounts were redolent with a rustic imagery of oak, elm, cow-byres and village cricket grounds that paid only lip service to the realities of a force largely urban and industrial in composition' (Beckett, 1991, p. 278). We have seen how, from the very outset, the emotional levers of the Home Guard were pulled not by vicious street fighting in the London suburbs or tank-killing in 'metroland', let alone standing watch over the SU carburettor factory, but defence of a rural 'Dream of England'. By the same token, Omdurman veterans back in uniform, 'Three Generations Serving Together', and antiquated or eccentric arms made the best press for the contemporary media.[9] Such is the power of these myths that, bolstered by *Dad's Army*, they filter and constrain our understanding of the reality of 'Total Defence'. In more mundane reality the Home Guard, drilling twice a week and exercising with the 'Field Force', while world war raged around and above them, must have been – at the very least – the equal of the pre-war Territorial Army. Historians need to set mythology aside and – with an affectionate nod to *Dad's Army* – recognise the Home Guard as the United Kingdom's most fundamental response to 'Total War', and a real and potent component of Home Defence during that period when the eventual course and outcome of the Second World War was entirely uncertain.

NOTES

Introduction

1 For example, the SMLE rifle was adopted in 1907, the Vickers machine gun in 1912, the 4.5in howitzer in 1908 and the 60-pounder gun in 1905.

2 Held, since April 2000, by a new company, Bapty (2000) Ltd.

3 *'Allo, 'Allo!*, a BBC sitcom written by Jeremy Lloyd and *Dad's Army* co-writer David Croft, first aired between 1982 and 1992.

4 Of the eighty episodes of *Dad's Army*, only one referenced women joining the Home Guard, and that was seen through the perspective of a romantic entanglement for Captain Mainwaring. See: Summerfield and Peniston-Bird, 2007, p. 257.

5 Longmate, N., *The Real Dad's Army* (London, 1974).

6 MacKenzie, S.P., *The Home Guard* (Oxford, 1995).

7 Summerfield, P. and C. Penniston-Bird, *Contesting Home Defence* (Manchester, 2007).

8 Beckett, I.F.W., *The Amateur Military Tradition 1558–1945* (Manchester, 1991).

9 Steppler, G., *Britons, To Arms!* (Stroud, 1992).

10 Fleming, P., *Invasion 1940* (London, 1957). Currently in print as *Operation Sea Lion*.

11 See: www.britarch.ac.uk/projects/dob.

12 Ward, A., *Resisting the Nazi Invader* (London, 1997).

13 Carroll, D., *The Home Guard* (Stroud, 1999).

14 Gulvin, K.R., *Kent Home Guard: A History* (Rainham, Kent, 1980).

15 See: www.wartimememories.co.uk/secret/auxiliaryunits.html, for example, for a useful source of Auxiliary Unit memoirs.

16 Mace, M., *Vehicles of the Home Guard* (Storrington, 2001), and Hunt, R., *Uniforms of the Home Guard* (Storrington, 2002).

17 Barlow, J.A., *The Elements of Rifle Shooting* (Aldershot, 1932, 1942).

18 Robinson, E., *Rifle Training for War: A Textbook for Local Defence Volunteers* (London, 1940).

19 Southworth, A., *The Home Guard Pocket Manual* (Stonehouse, 1940).

20 Bernards 'Key to Victory' series (London, undated, *c.* 1941).

21 Elliot, A., et al., *The Home Guard Encyclopedia* (London, undated, *c.* 1941).

22 *Bernard's Manual of Commando and Guerrilla Warfare: Unarmed Combat* (London, undated, *c.* 1941).

23 Slater, H., *Home Guard for Victory!* (London, 1941).

24 Langdon-Davies, J., *Home Guard Warfare* (London, 1941), frontispiece.

25 Langdon-Davies, J., *The Home Guard Training Manual* (London, 1940, sixth [revised] edition 1942, facsimile reprint, Aylesford, 1998).

26 Langdon-Davies, J., *The Home Guard Fieldcraft Manual* (London, 1942).

27 As described in the frontispiece of *A Home Guard Handbook*, Brophy was also the author of *A Home Guard Drill Book and Field Service Manual*; *Advanced Training for the Home Guard*; *The Five Years: A History of 1914–1918* etc.; and co-editor of 'Songs and Slang of the British Soldier' (Brophy, *A Home Guard Handbook*, frontispiece). He also wrote the Great War novel *The World Went Mad* (London, 1935).

28 *Home Guard Instruction No. 51: Battlecraft and Battle Drill for the Home Guard, Parts I–IV* (GHQ Home Forces, 1942, 1943).

29 Graves, C., *Home Guard of Britain* (London, 1943).

30 Home Guard parades became voluntary on 6 September 1944. The organisation was officially disbanded with effect from 31 December 1945.

31 Stroud, A., et al., *Intelligence Section Home Guard* (Salisbury, 1944 [Bapty archive]).

32 Smith, H., *Bureaucrats in Battledress* (Conway, 1945).

33 Brown, G. and A. Peek, *1940–44: Being a Diary of 'D' Company 20th Bn. Kent HG* (Sevenoaks, 1944).

34 Brophy, J. and E. Kennington, *Britain's Home Guard: A Character Study* (London, 1945).

35 TNA WO 199/3243.

36 Shore, C., *With British Sniper to the Reich* (Georgetown, 1948).

37 Goldsmith, D., *The Grand Old Lady of No Man's Land* (Coburg, Ontario, 1994), Goldsmith, D., *The Browning Machine Gun: Vol. II, Rifle Calibre Brownings Abroad* (Coburg, Ontario, 2006). Laidler P. and D. Howroyd, *The Guns of Dagenham* (Coburg, Ontario, 1995). Easterly, W., *The Belgian Rattlesnake* (Coburg, Ontario, 1998). Ballou, J.L., *Rock in a Hard Place* (Coburg, Ontario, 2000).

Chapter 1

1 Stanley Baldwin's speech in Parliament, 10 November 1932, set out a terrifying view of modern aerial warfare, describing a civilian population helplessly at the mercy of random and unpreventable air attacks: 'I think it is well also for the man in the street to realise that there is no power on earth that can protect him from being bombed. Whatever people may tell him, the bomber will always get through, and it is very easy to understand that, if you realise the area of space. I said that any town within reach of an aerodrome could be bombed. Take any large town you like in this island or on the Continent within such reach. For the defence of that town and its suburbs, you have to split up the air into sectors for defence. Calculate that the bombing aeroplanes will be at least 20,000ft high in the air, and perhaps higher, and it is a matter of simple mathematical calculation – or I will omit the word "simple" – that you will have sectors of from 10 to hundreds of millions of cubic miles to defend. I beg pardon. I am not a mathematician, as the House will see. I mean tens or hundreds of cubic miles. Now imagine 100 cubic miles covered with cloud and fog, and you can calculate how many aeroplanes you would have to throw into that to have much chance of catching odd aeroplanes as they fly through it. It cannot be done, and there is no expert in Europe who will say that it can. The only defence is in offence, which

means that you have to kill more women and children more quickly than the enemy if you want to save yourselves.' See Hansard, 10 November 1932, for the speech and debate in full http://hansard.millbanksystems.com/commons/1932/nov/10/international-affairs (accessed 29/5/2016).

2 'Mr Eden's Appeal', as appended in Cambs. and Isle of Ely TA Assoc., 1944, p. 100.

3 Fleming gives German Army High Command (OKH, Oberkommando des Heeres) reported strengths on 11 July 1940 as 400 Ju 52 aircraft, each capable of carrying twenty men, and 110 gliders, increasing to 1,000 aircraft and 150 gliders on 16 July (Fleming, 1957, p. 70).

4 *Periodical Notes on the German Army, No. 28* (War Office, 1940) p. 8.

5 In making his point, Robinson underplays the immediate impact that effective attack and reconnaissance aviation had on maritime operations. In an American Air Command and Staff College paper on the lessons of the Norwegian Campaign, Major Brian T. Baxley concluded (Baxley, 1997, p. 29): 'Airpower alone did not seize and control Norway in 1940, but its decisive use during Operation Weseruebung denied the dominant British forces the use of the land and sea.'

6 *Periodical Notes on the German Army*, No. 30 (War Office, 1940) p. 16.

7 *Periodical Notes on the German Army*, No. 30 (War Office, 1940) p. 24.

8 *Home Guard Instruction No. 51, Battlecraft and Battle Drill for the Home Guard, Part III,* Patrolling (War Office, January 1943, p. 15), in describing the characteristics of German parachute troops, states that: 'they can free themselves from their harness and collect arms and ammunition in under five minutes'. There is a good scene-setter for this chapter in the *fallschirmjäger* video posted by 'WorldwarIIhistorian' on YouTube at www.youtube.com/watch?v=DBc41_f8eZI . The fighting in a built-up area sequence in particular gives a very good impression of what similar combat in the UK would have been like (accessed 4/12/2010).

9 For that matter, no one would have believed that in May 1941 a few rural Scottish Home Guards would find themselves guarding a parachutist calling himself *Hauptman* Horn, who turned out to be none other than Hitler's deputy, Rudolf Hess.

10 Reproduced at www.lonesentry.com/articles/parachutists/index.html (accessed 13/3/2010).

11 *Periodical Notes on the German Army No. 30* (War Office, 1940) p. 19.

12 *Periodical Notes on the German Army No. 30* (War Office, 1940) p. 1.

13 TNA WO 199/3237, *Local Defence Volunteers Instruction No. 8: Tanks and Tank Destruction,* July 1940.

14 *Military Training Pamphlet No. 42, Tank Hunting and Destruction* (War Office, 1940).

15 *Punch,* 24 July 1940. Joyous Gard was the castle of Lancelot. It reverted to its original name of 'Dolorous Gard' in the strife that followed the condemning of Guinevere.

16 The *Pionierlandungsboot* was almost identical to later Allied landing craft, but could be split longitudinally to facilitate transport by rail. Subsequently 450 were built and used operationally in the Greek islands, Mediterranean and Eastern Front. L534, a later Type 41, is preserved in Germany (Schenk, 1990).

17 Fleming, 1957, p. 151. However, half the German destroyer force was sunk during the Norwegian operation.

18 One formerly commandeered German river barge is preserved at Henrichenburg. Built in 1929, the *Franz Christian* has a 200hp diesel engine and capacity of 289 tonnes. After conversion into landing craft *B 8 Pmot* she stood-by in Boulogne for

the invasion of England, before seeing active service in the Baltic from 1942 to 1945 (Schenk, 1990). An interesting sidelight is cast on how seriously contemporary British military authorities took the barge concept by the fact that 1,000 'dumb' (i.e. unpowered) Thames barges or lighters, roughly similar to the Continental river barges, were requisitioned in April 1942 to make up for a shortage of specialist landing craft for use in the 'Second Front' landing contingencies SLEDGEHAMMER and ROUND-UP. The British barges were to be fitted with stern ramps, and, like the German barges, towed and beached by tugs or launches. Some were reinforced internally with concrete. Subsequently 400 of these vessels took part in OVERLORD, largely as specialist craft and fitted with engines, wheelhouses and rudders. Landing Barge Vehicle (LBV).37, formerly the barge *Zulu*, even crossed to Normandy using sweeps (oars) and an improvised sail, following an engine failure. Barges were particularly valued because of their shallow draft, tough construction, and ability to rest on the bottom in tidal waters while still loaded. See: www.naval-history.net/ WW2MiscRNLandingBarges.htm (accessed 11/12/2010). Barge variants included: Landing Barge Flak (LBF), Landing Barge Gun (LBG), Landing Barge Vehicle (LBV), Landing Barge Engineering (or 'Emergency Repair', LBE), Landing Barge Oil (LBO), Landing Barge Water (LBW), Landing Barge Kitchen (LBK) and Landing Barge Cable (LBC).

19 Trans. Schenk, 1990.
20 *Periodical Notes on the German Army No. 30* (War Office, 1940) pp. 12–13.
21 *Periodical Notes on the German Army No. 28* (War Office, 1940) p. 7.
22 Schenk, 1990, passim. The *Kriegsmarine* was concerned by the time it would take to seize and open a port, bearing in mind the inefficiency of unloading the converted barges over the beach. This resulted in the issuing of specifications for a prefabricated jetty which could be carried or towed across the Channel and assembled on the invasion beachhead. Dortmunder Union and Krupp Rheinhausen both tendered designs, the Dortmunder design was relatively conventional and took about twenty-eight days to work up to full operation. The Krupp design was much more radical and could be working in 24 hours. Development continued through the winter of 1940–41 and the units were tested at Zeebrugge and inspected by the army and navy on 30 July 1941, the Krupp design being declared the more effective. However, by then the military situation had changed and further development was halted and orders for eight jetties were cancelled. In the summer of 1942 both structures were moved to Alderney and assembled in Braye Harbour, as an extension of the quay, for the landing of defence stores. The 'German Jetty' was scrapped in 1978 – its long civilian career testimony to the quality of its design and construction.
23 Schenk, 1990, p. 14. 'Tank Detachment B', port of embarkation Ostend, comprised thirteen PzKpfw II amphibious tanks, thirty-nine PzKpfw III submersible tanks and twelve PzKpfw IV submersible tanks, which were to land east of Dymchurch.
24 www.waffenhq.de/index1024.html (accessed 11/12/2010).
25 Fleming (1957, p. 281) was quite clear on the matter, stating that the problem was that 'hardly anybody knew what *Cromwell* really meant'. The former Auxiliary Unit organiser explained that on receipt of the code word, troops were to take up their battle stations, certain civilian telephone and telegraph lines were to be taken over by the military, and liaison officers were to take up their duties with the civilian administration.

26 *Periodical Notes on the German Army No. 30*, War Office, 1940, p. 1.
27 Delaney (1996, p. 125) gives German tank strengths for BARBAROSSA as 3,332 vehicles, comprising 410 PzKpfw Is, 746 PzKpfw IIs, 149 PzKpfw 35(t)s, 623 PzKpfw 38(t)s, 965 PzKpfw IIIs and 439 PzKpfw IVs.
28 See: MacKenzie, 1996, pp. 56–7.
29 TNA 199/3237, *List of VPs*, 1941.
30 *Operation Order No. 1, E Coy, 20th Bn. K.H.G.*, Badgers Mount, April 1944 (Collection of Mr Harvey Vallis).

Chapter 2

1 See: Langton-Davies, 1942, p. 11.
2 See: Crankshaw, E., *Bismarck*, London, 1981, 1982, for reference to *francs-tireurs* and Prussian repression. Also: Lord Russell of Liverpool, *The Scourge of the Swastika* (London, 1954, 1956) p. 225, for the conclusions of the Bryce Report of 1915.
3 *Air Raid Precautions Handbook No. 1 (1st Edition): Personal Protection against Gas*, HMSO, 1937.
4 *Air Raid Precautions Handbook No. 1 (1st Edition): Personal Protection against Gas*, HMSO, 1937, p. 3.
5 Beckett, 1991, p. 271, quoting from Orwell and Angus (Eds.), *Collected Essays, Journalism and Letters of George Orwell*, London, 1968.
6 '... a tank deprived of motion is no longer a Goliath of modern warfare, it is a mass of junk. The people inside have very soon to come out to get fresh air, and then the Spanish Militia knew exactly what to do, because, after all, it was an old Spanish custom.' Langdon-Davies, 1941, p. 38.
7 See: 'Mum's Army were at home on the range', *Sevenoaks Chronicle*, 26 June 2003, p. 18.
8 TNA WO 199/3243.
9 Pryce-Jones, D., 'Colonel Gubbins's Secret Army', *The Sunday Telegraph* magazine, No. 496, 10 May 1974, p. 20.
10 See: Churchill, 1955, p. 519: 'I have been following with much interest the growth and development of the new guerrilla formations of the Home Guard known as "Auxiliary Units".' (Prime Minister to Secretary of State for Defence, 25 August 1940).
11 This letter is copied in full in Angell, 1996, pp. 9–10.
12 See: *Secret History*, 'The Real Dad's Army', passim.
13 Mellor, *Casualties*, 138, 836, *Statistical Digest of the War*, 13, quoted in MacKenzie, 1996, p. 123.
14 Cavalcanti (Dir.), *Went the Day Well?*, Ealing Studios, London, 1942. Based on a story by Graham Greene published in *Collier's Weekly*, June 1940. See Calder, 1991, p. 260 for a discussion of this film.
15 See BFI Screenonline: http://www.screenonline.org.uk/film/id/454179/index.html (accessed 14/2/2010).
16 BFI Screenonline: http://www.screenonline.org.uk/film/id/454179/index.html (accessed 14/2/2010).
17 From the full text of Eden's appeal, Appendix A, Cambs. and Isle of Ely TA Assoc., 1944, p. 100.

Chapter 3

1 A process which continued until the adoption of the L1A1 Self-Loading Rifle in 1960 (Cole and Fulton, 1990, p. 91).

2 The L42 7.62 NATO sniper rifle, the last Lee-Enfield in front-line service with British troops was declared obsolescent in April 1992.

3 The design of the bolt causes it to be placed under compression on firing, while the nature of the receiver causes the resulting forces to be distributed asymmetrically. The barrel is considered too light for really accurate shooting and can be displaced by warping of the full-length stock.

4 Information regarding the introduction of the P14, Edwards, A., unpublished MA dissertation, and lecture presentation to the Historic Breechloading Smallarms Association, 'The P14 Rifle', 18/1/2010.

5 As Edwards explained on the Great War Forum: 'The actual total of Pattern 14s received in the UK was 1,117,850. The difference between this figure and the approximate 1.2 million manufactured is accounted by 100,000 rifles sent direct to India and about 25,000 that were lost at sea to U-boats. Also, considerable quantities were sent to Russia in WW2 as part of the allied aid effort.' http://1914-1918. invisionzone.com/forums/lofiversion/index.php/t64636.html (accessed 19/2/2010). Many P14 rifles were sold to the Baltic States during the inter-war period.

6 The accuracy of the P14 with indifferent ammunition deteriorates over longer ranges due to the 'flip' characteristics of the barrel. However, it outclasses the SMLE over battle ranges of 300–600yd. See Banks, 1950, p. 179.

7 The Royal Navy, including Naval Battalions, made extensive use of 'long' Charger Loading Lee-Enfields, during the First World War.

8 Later Captain Southworth MBE.

9 TNA WO 199/3237 HOFORS memo, 29 June 1940.

10 TNA WO 199/3247 LDV/Home Guard returns.

11 TNA WO 199/3247 LDV/Home Guard returns.

12 TNA WO 199/3243, *Home Guard History and Organisation*, July 1949.

13 See also: HOFORS memo (TNA WO 199/3237, above). Note: Chamberlain and Gander (1976, p. 9) state that, in 1940, 70,000 Ross rifles were sold to the UK from US stocks purchased for training during the First World War. However, Skennerton, in his list of contracts (1988) makes no mention of this transaction.

14 TNA WO, 199/3243, TA2 memorandum, 2 November 1940.

15 Shore, 1997, p. 156. The Ministry of Food (Denbighshire) Home Guard were issued 100 Ross rifles between 500 men until the spring of 1941, when they received US M1917 rifles on a scale of one for every two men (Smith, 1945, pp. 32 and 46.)

16 TNA WO 199/3237, Home Guard monthly returns.

17 The 'Ought Three' was actually manufactured by both Springfield Armoury and the Rock Island Arsenal. See: Culver, D., 'The U.S. Rifle, calibre .30, M1917', published on the Civilian Marksmanship Program website, www.odcmp.com/Forms/M1917.pdf (accessed 19/2/2010).

18 TNA CAB 66/11/19, Minister of Supply to War Cabinet, August 1940. 20th Battalion Kent Home Guard, for example, initially received P14 rifles, exchanging them for M1917 rifles at an unrecorded date during late 1940. Brown and Peek, 1944, p. 4.

19 TNA WO 199/3237: HOFORS signal, 8–9 July 1940.

20 Although these are amongst the last 1903 rifles to be manufactured from new, Remington had taken over the tooling previously used by the Rock Island Arsenal before America's entry into the First World War, hence initial production examples (before the tooling wore out, and wartime makeshifts were introduced) are 'time capsule' early 1903s. The United States relentlessly remanufactured its service rifles, so most surviving 1903s (plus 1903A1s, A3s, A4s and M1917s and M1s) are 'mixed master', i.e. rebuilt from a hotchpotch of renovated parts of different dates, finishes and manufacturers. Hence, the 'as produced' ex-Home Guard 'Red Star' 1903s are valuable collectors' pieces – preferably unfired and with cosmoline and straw packing adhering (see reference below.)

21 Hansen, W.R., *The Red Star Remington 03 Rifles*, Remington Society of America Journal, 2007. Available online at www.remingtonsociety.com/rsa/journals/RedStar/?na=5 (accessed 23/2/2010).

22 The red band was introduced for all arms not accepting standard British service ammunition in Army Council Instruction (ACI) No. 1571.

23 Unhelpfully, Home Guard returns simply specify '.300 Rifles'.

24 Having been converted from a rimmed design, the magazine of the M1917 could accommodate six rounds of rimless .30-06, although the Home Guard does not seem to have spotted this (being used to the P14). The Americans did give some thought to introducing a six-round loading charger during the First World War. See: Culver, *Op. Cit.*

25 *Home Guard Instruction No. 38-1941, Winter Training 1941–1942,* War Office, September 1941, p. 2. Regarding 'Small mark' ammunition, Mr Mark Hodgins of the Historical Breechloading Smallarms Association says: 'I can remember buying boxes of small mark ammunition from the NRA. It was thus called because the cases and bullets had small blemishes, scratches or stains: nothing to affect performance but enough to fail the final cosmetic inspection for passing into Govt service.' (Email to author, 30/11/2010.)

26 The rifles concerned might have been types of long Lee-Enfield, rather than the Lee-Metford, which had rifling optimised for use with black powder .303 ammunition, and the differing sights could have been due to some being sighted for Mk VI, rather than Mk VII smokeless .303 ammunition, but the point remains the same.

27 TNA WO 199/3237 *Home Guard Instruction No. 14*, GHQ Home Forces, September 1940, p. 3.

28 In December 1941, in a speech on the Home Guard, Churchill had insisted that every volunteer must be armed, 'if only with a pike or mace'. See: MacKenzie, 196, p. 97.

29 http://hansard.millbanksystems.com/lords/1942/feb/04/the-home-guard (accessed 14/3/2010).

30 See: Fleming, 1957, pp. 201–2. MacKenzie places their arrival later, in early 1942. MacKenzie, 1996, p. 97.

31 Croft was Under Secretary of State for War.

32 TNA WO 199/3237, Home Guard monthly returns.

33 The first edition of October 1940 had featured the P14, with a reference to the 'P.17 Lee-Enfield' as being in use with 'a number of Units of the Home Guard'. Southworth, 1940, p. 5.

34 In fairness to the No. 4 rifle, when the worst of the wartime makeshifts had been swept away, it proved to be a worthy successor to the SMLE, indeed a better and more

accurate service rifle. The pre-war production No. 4 rifles were used as the basis of the No. 4 (T) sniper's rifle, which remained in service, albeit re-barrelled to 7.62 NATO calibre, until 1992.

Chapter 4

1 See: *Home Guard Instruction No. 30: Collective Training*, War Office, May 1941, p. 3.
2 Ibid.
3 TNA WO 199/3247, Home Guard returns.
4 Dineley Scrapbook: WWII/Home Front, Bapty Archive.
5 Major General Peter Pellereau, MA, Ceng, FIMechE, FIMgt, RE (Retd). Major General Pellereau died in February 2014.
6 Ightham, Kent, Maj. Gen. P. Pellereau, Telephone interview with author, October 2000.
7 TNA WO 199/3238, TA2 circular, *Notes for Guidance in Examining 12 bore Guns*, 15 June 1940.
8 *Home Guard Instruction No. 51, Battlecraft and Battle Drill for the Home Guard, Part IV: The Organisation of Home Guard Defences*, GHQ Home Forces, November 1943, p. 14.
9 'The Germans were invoking a passage in the Hague Decrees (the predecessor of the Geneva Convention), which stated: "It is especially forbidden to employ arms, projectiles or materials calculated to cause unnecessary suffering."' See: Canfield, 1991, pp. 100–1.
10 TNA WO 199/3247, Home Guard returns.
11 As originally designed, the Greener riot shotgun used a non-standard 14-bore cartridge (to prevent it being turned on the authorities). However, a 16-bore cartridge could be chambered if wrapped in thick paper. Subsequently a special bottle-necked cartridge was developed and, in its final version, the gun was fitted with lugs on the breech block, which engaged a groove in the base of the cartridge, preventing the use of any off-the-shelf ammunition. See: www.martinihenry.com/faq.htm (accessed 9/12/10). Greener shotguns remained in use with British troops in Cyprus during the late 1950s. See: http://history.farmersboys.com/Postings/Cyprus/cyprus_rberks.htm for an illustration (accessed 9/12/10).
12 *Home Guard Instruction No. 51, Battlecraft and Battle Drill for the Home Guard, Part II: Battle Drill*, GHQ Home Forces, September 1942, pp. 3–4.
13 Ightham, Kent, Telephone interview with author, October 2000.
14 Department of the Army Technical Manual TM 31-200-1, *Unconventional Warfare Devices and Techniques: References* (Department of the Army, Washington, USA, April 1966). This manual contains much information derived from Second World War British, German and Japanese experience.
15 *Military Training Pamphlet No. 42: Tank Hunting and Destruction*, War Office, 1940, pp. 23–4.
16 Harding, T., 'Soldiers tell how torrent of burning petrol poured into their Warrior', *Daily Telegraph*, 21 September 2005.
17 *Military Training Pamphlet No. 42: Tank Hunting and Destruction*, p. 19; Rigden, 2001, p. 267; Longmate, 1974, p. 69.
18 See: Langdon-Davies, 1941, p. 38, for an account of the involvement of Spanish quarrymen and Asturian miners in anti-tank operations.

19 Wintringham, T., 'We Make Our Own Mortar for 38/6', *Picture Post*, 26 July 1941, reprinted in *Daily Telegraph* magazine, No. 496, 10 May 1974, pp. 14–5.
20 Ibid.
21 Wintringham, *Op. Cit.*, p. 15.
22 Early versions of the AFV smoke grenade discharger used a Martini-style falling block firing mechanism, later versions used a Lee bolt action.
23 Via Chris Henry, Curator of the museum of naval firepower, Priddy's Hard, Hants, UK, formerly curator of the Royal Artillery Museum, and an authority on the Spanish Civil War, conversation with author: July 2001.
24 In its final version the 2in mortar became the '51mm' mortar, and remained in British Army service in Afghanistan although officially superseded by the underslung grenade launcher (UGL). It was eventually replaced by a more powerful 60mm mortar.

Chapter 5

1 The engraved Colt government model 1911 automatic pistol carried by Mark Dineley during the Second World War is in the Bapty collection.
2 *Home Guard Instruction No. 51, Battlecraft and Battle Drill for the Home Guard, Part IV: The organization of the Home Guard Defence*, GHQ Home Forces, November 1943, p. 14.
3 Ibid.
4 See Chapter 9 for a scale of issue to Auxiliary Unit personnel in Bath (Auxunit.org, with thanks to former Auxilier Robert Millard). See also: Angell (1996), p. 65.
5 TNA WO 199/3247, Home Guard monthly returns.
6 Extracted from TNA WO 199/3247, Home Guard monthly returns.
7 US Army revolvers, Models 1889, 1892, 1894, 1895, 1896, 1901, 1903, were all in .38 'Long Colt' calibre. Smith & Wesson produced the Model 1899 and 1902 in the same calibre. The .38 Special round was introduced with the Marine Corps M1905 and the army M1908. The US Army reverted to .45 with the M1909 and adopted .45 ACP with the M1911 automatic pistol. See Hogg and Weeks (1973), pp. 1.38–1.39.
8 The oft quoted example being the lack of stopping power of .38 rounds fired against the Moro in the Philippines campaigns of 1898–1900. See Hogg and Weeks (1973), p. 1.38.
9 The author, as a film armourer, encountered an adult male actor who was nearly incapable of firing a Webley Mk IV .455 revolver; due to the small size of his hand, when gripping the pistol, the web of his thumb prevented the hammer fully cocking. It is the sort of problem that led to the adoption of the functionally similar but smaller Enfield .380 revolver in 1929.
10 TNA WO 199/3237, War Office memorandum, Home Guard ammunition scales, 28 July 1940.
11 One full magazine on the weapon and one full spare continues to be British doctrine. When the author was serving in the coalition headquarters in Baghdad in 2006, he was issued a 9mm Browning pistol and two magazines, one on the weapon, one off, enabling him to load twenty-six rounds of ammunition – much to the derision of his US colleagues, who considered that amount hopelessly inadequate, should the pistol actually need to be used.
12 A tall tripod was available, but it was an anti-aircraft mount.

13 A late dated American-produced Hotchkiss M1914 tripod in the Bapty collection may
    have come to the UK in 1940 as part of a redirected French order.

14 TNA WO 199/3247, Home Guard monthly returns.

15 The Hotchkiss machine gun is emphasised as an alternative to the Lewis in *Home
    Guard Instruction No. 50, Winter Training for 1942–1943* (War Office, 25 September
    1942). This, and the increasing numbers in returns towards the end of 1942, suggests
    that .303-calibre Hotchkiss guns were being released by the army for Home Guard
    use: '[the semi-trained man] will also be trained in the use of the light machine guns
    issued to his unit. These may be the Lewis Machine Gun and/or Hotchkiss Machine
    Gun.' (*Op. Cit.*, p. 7.)

16 Also known as the 'VGO', or the 'Vickers K' from its commercial designation (Wallace,
    1972, p. 71).

17 The Mk II was the first purpose-built Lewis aircraft machine gun, and featured a slim
    jacket around the barrel but no radiator assembly.

18 TNA CAB 66/11/19.

19 After a brief dalliance looking at .50in calibre weapons, the RAF settled for multiple
    rifle-calibre mounts, pending the arrival of a reliable and effective 20mm cannon
    (Wallace, 1972, p. 36).

20 *Notes on Gunnery for Defensively Equipped Merchant Ships*, Admiralty (Gunnery),
    London, October 1939, p. 90.

21 Ibid.

22 TNA WO 199/3237: Memorandum from War Office department MT7, dated
    7 July 1940.

23 'An Instructor', *The Complete Lewis Gunner* (Gale & Polden, Aldershot, 1940).

24 TNA WO 199/3247, Home Guard Monthly returns.

25 TNA WO 199/3247, Home Guard Monthly returns. The .303-calibre guns may have
    been British aircraft or ground-role guns, ex-Canadian Savage-Lewis ground-role
    guns, or ex-US .303-calibre ground-role guns from the 353 ordered from Savage
    during 1916 for militia use on the southern US border (Easterly, 1998, p. 123) – or, in
    all probability, a mixture of all of the above.

26 The Webley .38 Mk IV revolver was only approved on 20 September 1945, despite
    some 55,000 having been delivered since April 1940. See: Stamps and Skennerton
    (1993), p. 87.

27 Any Lewis gun could accept either the forty-seven- or ninety-seven-round magazines,
    but an extension had to be fitted to the magazine post to hold the taller aircraft drum.

28 *Home Guard Instruction No. 51: Battlecraft and Battle Drill for the Home Guard, Part II
    Battle Drill*, War Office, 1942, p. 4.

29 TNA WO 199/3247, Home Guard monthly returns.

30 *Instructional Notes on the .300-inch Browning Automatic Rifle (Provisional)*
    (War Office, 1940).

31 TNA WO 199/3247, Home Guard monthly returns. A US Ordnance Report of
    12 September 1945 (*Project Supporting Paper Caliber .30 Browning Automatic Rifle 1917
    to 1945*, prepared by Captain Charles E. Schroder) gave a total of 25,000 M1918
    Browning Automatic Rifles supplied to the UK for Home Guard use (Schroder, 1945,
    cited in: Ballou, 2000, p. 368). Some of these may have been lost in U-boat sinkings.

32 *The Bren Light Machine Gun: Description Use and Mechanism* (undated, *c.* 1941,
    Aldershot), sections 6–9.

33 Sevenoaks, Kent, telephone interview with author, July 2001. See: Fleming, 1957, p. 254.

34 TNA WO 199/3247, Home Guard monthly returns. Small numbers of Brens are reported as early as February 1941 under 'other machine guns', and the Dorking gun probably came into this category.

35 *Home Guard Instruction No. 51: Battlecraft and Battle Drill for the Home Guard, Part II Battle Drill*, War Office, 1942, p. 4.

36 Ibid.

37 The gun purchased was the Model 1928A. The military Thompson went through a series of modifications and simplifications resulting in the M1 and M1A1 – the latter being a second generation, fixed firing pin, simple blowback SMG, that only really resembled the original gun in its outline. It was the M1928A and 1928AC (with Cutt's compensator muzzle brake) that were the weapons of the Home Guard.

38 A US Army ordnance officer, General Thompson had been involved with the production of the M1917 rifle, and sought to introduce a delayed-blowback self-loading rifle based around the 'Blish Piece', a sliding 'H'-shaped bronze component that locked the bolt at the moment of firing. This failed to work reliably (as so many automatic systems had) with the .30-06 cartridge, but did work with the other US government cartridge, the .45ACP. Subsequently it emerged that the Blish Piece was not required with such a low-velocity cartridge, and the mass of the bolt was enough to delay the opening of the breech until safe pressure had been reached. The Blish Piece was therefore omitted from the M1 and M1A1 Thompsons.

39 The original rendering was 'Thompson Submachine Gun'. See *Handbook of the Thompson Submachine Gun, Model of 1928* (Auto-Ordnance Corporation, Bridgeport, 1940).

40 See: TNA WO 199/3247, Home Guard monthly returns.

41 TNA WO 199/3247, Home Guard monthly returns.

42 *Home Guard Instruction No. 51, Battlecraft and Battle Drill for the Home Guard, Part IV: The organization of the Home Guard Defence,* GHQ Home Forces, November 1943, p. 14.

43 As originally built, the M1917 Browning machine gun was fitted with sights graduated to 2,600yd, similar to those on the M1915 Vickers, which was also in Home Guard service. Adoption of lower velocity, but longer range, 'boat-tailed' M1 .30 ammunition in the 1920s resulted in the production of a new sight leaf, calibrated to 3,300yd. Guns supplied to Britain in 1940 came with both types of sights. M1 .30 ammunition fired from a gun fitted with .30-06 sights was inaccurate at ranges over 800yd, and vice versa. Measures were put in place to fit M1 sights to all M1917 Brownings (*Instructional Notes on the .300-inch Browning Machine Gun (Model 1917), 1940, PROVISIONAL,* War Office, September 1940, p. 2).

44 For issue of forty-three wireless sets to Workington battalion Home Guard see: www.users.globalnet.co.uk/~rwbarnes/defence/hg2.htm (accessed 11/02/2006).

45 See: *Home Guard Instruction No. 51 Battlecraft and Battle Drill for the Home Guard, Part II, Battle Drill*, also *Part III, Patrolling*, in the same series (War Office, 1942 and 1943 respectively), where the key support weapon for all minor tactics is the BAR. Also, from *Home Guard Instruction No. 14, Winter Training*, September 1940, p. 5: Vickers Machine Gun: Instructions in this weapon will be given for direct firing only. Indirect fire and night firing will not be taught until proficiency is reached in direct fire and until the necessary instruments are available. Units armed with the M.G. should form M.G. sections.

46 The M1919A4 Browning has been highly successful – but largely as a vehicle weapon.

47 TNA WO 199/3247, Home Guard monthly returns.

48 The firing mechanism or 'lock' is a self-contained package, as is the feed mechanism.

49 The contract lies between the two dates given, but is recorded as 'No date'.

50 British machine gunners developed a slick drill for deploying the Vickers/Maxim tripod which was passed on to American troops. Holding the 'crosshead' (cradle), the front legs were allowed to swing forward and fall to the ground, finding their own level, at which point they were securely clamped and the gun placed in the crosshead. While the original M1917 Browning tripod was functionally identical to the Vickers/Maxim tripod, the M1918 was an over-sophisticated response to the challenge of providing accurate supporting fire at long range with a machine gun. The slightly modified M1917A1 tripod, and the utilitarian M2 tripod, subsequently proved quite sufficient for battlefield use.

51 *Instructional Notes on the .300-inch Browning Machine Gun (Model 1917), 1940, PROVISIONAL* (War Office 1940) p. 55.

52 11/7/43. Exercise. Attack and Defence of a Road Junction ... memorable as the first exercise in which the B.M.G. team took part.

53 TNA WO 199/3247, Home Guard monthly returns.

54 *Instructional Notes on the Browning Heavy Machine Gun, .300 calibre (Model 1917) (Provisional)* (War Office, 1940, 1941) p. 3.

55 Sevenoaks, Kent, telephone interview with author, July 2001. That efforts were in hand to ensure that all British BMGs were fitted with the correct sight leaf for 'M1' (confusingly termed 'MI' in British literature), indicates that this machine-gun ammunition was being supplied independently of the standard .30-06 ammunition. See *Instructional Notes on the .300-inch Browning Machine Gun (Model 1917), 1940, PROVISIONAL*, p. 2.

56 Early in the Second World War the term 'heavy' was applied to tripod-mounted rifle-calibre machine guns, but these were subsequently retitled 'medium' machine guns, the term 'heavy' being reserved for large calibre machine guns, such as the Browning M2 .50-calibre and Soviet 12.7mm DShK.

57 The US Army bought around 2,800 'Potato-diggers' for training at the start of the First World War, and the Canadian Army was equipped with Colt M1895s until they were replaced by Lewis guns. The Russians and Italians used them in significant quantities, and it was these two big contracts that Colt handed over to Marlin-Rockwell.

58 The 1904 Madsen was a Danish light machine gun which used a unique Peabody-Martini-style falling block system with a mechanical extractor and rammer. Although not adopted by any major nation, they were tested or used in small quantities by most armies. It is usually stated that some Madsen LMGs were purchased by Great Britain in .303-calibre during the First World War, and that these were used by the Home Guard during the Second World War. Whilst this is entirely plausible, the Home Guard returns do not anywhere mention Madsen machine guns, although small numbers of Colts, Brens, and so forth do get identified (see: Chamberlain and Gander, 1974, p. 8, and Hogg and Weeks, 1973, p. 5.08).

59 TNA WO 199/3247, Home Guard monthly returns show thirteen Colt machine guns at 1 June 1941. That these were Model 1895 and purchased from 'dead stock' at Browning was confirmed by Browning *doyen* Dolf Goldsmith (email to author, 7–9/9/2010).

60 TNA WO 199/3247, Home Guard monthly returns.

61 It is possible that some of the later 'Colts' may have been Colt Commercial models – effectively minor variations of the M1917 US government model, manufactured Browning, but with a very high quality of build and finish (email correspondence with Dolf Goldsmith, 7–9/9/2010).

62 TNA CAB 66/11/19.

63 TNA WO 199/3247, Home Guard monthly returns.

64 Extracted from TNA WO 199/3247, Home Guard monthly returns. February 1941 is the first month for which this style of detailed breakdown is given, November 1942 the last.

Chapter 6

1 TNA WO 199/3247, Home Guard monthly returns.

2 Ibid.

3 Trials were also undertaken using the Melville Johnson, Czech ZH29 and YSC automatic rifles in a 'machine carbine' role, as well as the stripped Lewis light machine gun, Soley-Lewis (a stripped Lewis modified to feed from a top-mounted Bren magazine), and the Bren light machine gun fired from the hip (Hobart, 1973, p. 71).

4 The MP 38 was developed by an unknown designer working for Berthold Geipel at Erma Werke, based on designs by Heinrich Vollmer (Hobart, 1973, p. 122). 'Schmeisser', like 'Spandau' (a machine-gun factory), became soldier's shorthand for a type of weapon.

5 A photograph of the Sevenoaks Spigot Mortar crew *c.* 1943–44, shows two of them equipped with Mk I Stens (Carol, 1999, p. 72). The Sten Mk IV was a shortened, folding stock airborne version that did not enter production, the Sten Mk V was an improved-quality wooden stock version that only saw limited wartime service (Hogg and Weeks, 1973, pp. 2.42, 2.43).

6 *Military Training Pamphlet No. 42, Tank Hunting and Destruction*, War Office, 29 August 1940, p. 19.

7 Armishaw, A., 'Flame Fougasse', *Loopholes No. 42*, available online at www.pilbox-study-group.org.uk/poyningsflametrappage.htm (accessed 3/3/2008).

8 www.staffshomeguard.co.uk/DotherReminiscences10staffshg.htm (accessed 3/3/2008).

9 *Military Training Pamphlet No. 42, Tank Hunting and Destruction*, War Office, 29 August 1940, p. 35.

10 TNA WO 199/3247, Home Guard monthly returns.

11 TNA WO 199/3262, Endicott Report.

12 TNA WO 199/3247, Home Guard monthly returns.

13 *Home Guard Instruction No. 26 – 1941, Miscellaneous Notes*, War Office, March 1941, p. 1.

14 TNA Air 2/6262/Finch. *Home Guard Information Circular No. 53*, War Office, 9 August 1944 lists four Home Guards receiving bravery awards. Three are for training incidents involving hand grenades.

15 Longmate (1974, p. 77). Opinions differ, vigorously, concerning the origins of the term 'EY'. It is either a contraction of 'Emergency' – the original EY rifles having been reject-quality SMLEs pressed into service during the First World War – or the inventor's name – Edwin Yule. Skennerton (1993, p. 356) is unable to provide a

conclusive explanation of the term, but on balance, the former is probably the most likely. Close examination of an EY rifle in the author's collection suggests that it was salvaged from the battlefield and returned to service, despite rust pitting, as an emergency measure. Converting such rifles to grenade launchers makes excellent sense, as they were already 'spoiled', but serviceable. The term came to mean any grenade-launching rifle reinforced with wire or string binding. In August 1942 an adaptor was accepted into service, which allowed the No. 1 cup to be fitted to the SMLE, P14 and M1917 without modification.

16 See: *Small Arms Training Vol. I, pamphlet No. 13, Grenade,* War Office, 15 July 1942, p. 3.
17 *Military Training Pamphlet No. 42, Tank Hunting and Destruction,* War Office, 29 August 1940, p. 7.
18 *Military Training Pamphlet No. 42, Tank Hunting and Destruction,* War Office, 29 August 1940, p. 25.
19 TM 31-200-1: *Unconventional Warfare Devices and Techniques,* DOD, Washington, 1966, p. 21.
20 *Small Arms Training, Vol. 1 Pamphlet No. 13, Supplement No. 2, No. 73 Anti-tank Grenade, the ST Grenade (Hand), the Hand Incendiary Bomb,* War Office, London, 27 August 1941, p. 1.
21 MacKenzie, *Home Guard,* p. 93.
22 *Small Arms Training, Vol. 1 Pamphlet No. 13, Supplement No. 2, No. 73 Anti-tank Grenade, the ST Grenade (Hand), the Hand Incendiary Bomb,* War Office, London, 27 August 1941.
23 *Military Training Pamphlet No. 42, Tank Hunting and Destruction,* War Office, 29 August 1940, p. 31.
24 *Small Arms Training Volume I, Pamphlet No. 13, 1937, SUPPLEMENT No. 2, No. 73 Anti-Tank Grenade (Hand), The S.T. Grenade (Hand), The Hand Incendiary Bomb,* War Office, 27 August 1942, p. 3.
25 www.bbc.co.uk/ww2peopleswar/stories/12/a2159912.shtml (accessed 14/7/2007).
26 Cody, J.F., *The Official History of New Zealand in the Second World War 1939–1945,* Historical Publications Department, Wellington, 1953. Online resource, www.nzetc.org/tm/scholarly/tei-WH2-21Ba-c7.html, p. 175 (accessed 25/12/2007).
27 Penetration figures, Hogg, 1979. Boys details contained in *Small Arms Training Volume I, Pamphlet No. 5 Anti-Tank Rifle,* War Office, 25 April 1942, which superseded the 1937 and 1939 editions, with data based on operational experience.
28 In British doctrine, the No. 36M was 'an H.E. (High Explosive) grenade'. See: *Small Arms Training, Volume I, Pamphlet No. 13, Grenades,* War Office, 15 July 1942, p. 24.
29 *Home Guard Circular, No. 41,* War Office, 14 December 1943.
30 *Home Guard Instruction, No. 51, Battlecraft and Battle Drill for the Home Guard, Part III, Patrolling,* GHQ Home Forces, January 1943, p. 34.

Chapter 7

1 The closure of Osterley Park was officially notified on 25 November 1940. The notification stressed that the Chief Instructors from Osterley would be moving to a new school at Denbeis, near Dorking. See: TNA, WO 199/3237/468, *Admin Instruction, Home Guard School.*
2 *Military Training Pamphlet No. 42, Tank Hunting and Destruction,* War Office, 29 August 1940, p. 38.

3 *Handbook for the Projectors, 2½ inch Marks I and II on mountings, 2½ inch Marks I and II*, Chief Inspector of Armaments, 1941.

4 The barrel assembly weighed 60lb, the Mk I mount 74lb. The Mk II mount was slightly heavier. *Handbook for the Projectors, 2½ inch Marks I and II on mountings, 2½ inch Marks I and II*, Chief Inspector of Armaments, 1941, p. 1.

5 Ashworth, 1998, p. 46. By 1943 'best ranges had been reduced to 50 yd for the No. 68 grenade and 70yd for the SIP, 150–200yd for the No. 36, depending on the type of fuse'. Thus the range of the Northover Projector was the same as that of the EY rifle. See: *Home Guard Instruction No. 51*, Part IV, *The Organization of Home Guard Defence* (GHQ Home Forces, November 1943), p. 15.

6 *Home Guard Instruction No. 51*, Part IV, *The Organization of Home Guard Defence* (GHQ Home Forces, November 1943), p. 15.

7 Initial production was of 10,000 projectors by Bisley Clay Target, with subsequent orders for a further 3,000. These were the Mk I version. Another 8,000 Mk IIs were produced by Selection Manufacturing. See: Skennerton, 1988, p. 75 for contract details.

8 Ibid.

9 *Home Guard Instruction No. 51*, Part IV, *The Organization of Home Guard Defence* (GHQ Home Forces, November 1943), p. 15.

10 See: Forum discussion at http:/tank-net.org/forums/lofiversion/index.php/t16747. html (accessed 21/07/2007). The international input on this forum strand uses an alternative spelling, *Ampulemjot*. Contributors report that the '176th Ampule Thrower Company was attached to Sixth Guards Army on the Voronezh Front at Kursk'.

11 *Handbook for the Projectors, 2½ inch Marks I and II on mountings, 2½ inch Marks I and II* (Chief Inspector of Armaments, 1941), p. 27.

12 See: TNA WO 199/3248, *Home Guard Instructions No. 40: The Northover Projector*, November 1941.

13 *Home Guard Instruction No. 51*, Part IV, *The Organization of Home Guard Defence* (GHQ Home Forces, November 1943), p. 15.

14 *Home Guard Information Circular No. 53* (War Office, 9 August 1944), p. 3.

15 TNA WO 199/3262, Endicott report.

16 *Tank Hunting and Destruction, Military Training Pamphlet No. 42* (The War Office, August 1940), p. 38.

17 Holman Bros was a Cornish engineering company specialising in equipment such as compressors and drills for the mining industry.

18 http://www.naval-history.net/WW2Memoir-RussianConvoyCoxwain03.htm (accessed 21/7/2007).

19 http://www.raf.mod.uk/bob1940/august2.html. Addendum to 1 August report (accessed 21/7/2007). Another version of this story has the *Highlander* sailing into harbour with a Heinkel 'draped across her stern', having been damaged by machine-gun fire, losing height and striking the ship's boat with its port wing. This may reflect newspaper coverage, which would not, at that period, mention a 'secret weapon'. The official log is certainly quite specific in crediting the 'kill' to the Holman Projector. For the 'collision' version see: http://www.bpears.org.uk/NE-Diary/Inc/ ISeq_05.html (accessed 03/10/2008).

20 See: *Home Guard Instruction No. 30 – 1941* (War Office, May 1941), p. 4 – 'Northover Projectors and other secret weapons'.

21 The rule of thumb is that, all other conditions being optimum, a hollow charge warhead will penetrate 2.5 times its diameter of armoured plate.

22 Penetration of the No. 68 grenade is given as 50mm of armour, under ideal conditions. It was improved by replacing the original hemispherical void with one of cylindro-conoidal form. Hogg, 1979, p. 160–1.

23 Bombards are fifteenth-century muzzle-loading guns, having a calibre greater than 30cm and a barrel of five–six calibres length. See: Smith and Rhynas Brown, 1989, *passim*.

24 The Tiger I on display at the Royal Armoured Corps Museum, Bovington, was famously incapacitated by a 6pr round from a Churchill tank, which supposedly jammed the turret, causing the crew to abandon the vehicle. During restoration it became evident that the round had struck the underside of the main armament and deflected downwards, damaging both the armoured roof above the driver and the driver's hatch. This suggests that the tank was abandoned because the driver was incapacitated by the strike, and illustrates the vulnerability of even the heaviest tanks' top attack. See the restoration website www.tiger-tank.com/secure/journal36.htm (accessed 22/8/2010) for discussion.

25 www.portsdown-tunnels.org.uk/invasion_defences/spigot_mortar.html (accessed 12/8/2007).

26 *29mm Spigot Mortar (Blacker Bombard) Training Instruction (Provisional)* (War Office, 1941), p. 7.

27 Blacker family, via Mr Clive Hughes, Hughes Fabrication Ltd (specialist restorers, Firepower and Royal Armouries), 1999.

28 TNA WO 199/3248, *Home Guard Instruction No. 48* (War Office, July 1942), p. 3.

29 Scale of ammunition as at September 1942. See: Gulvin, 1980, p. 16.

30 TNA WO 199/191-1913.

31 TNA AVIA 22/576.

32 For discussion, see: Clifford, P., 'Love, Hate and the Spigot Mortar', *Loopholes No. 14*. Available online at www.pillbox-study-group.org.uk/spigotmortarpage.htm.

33 TNA AVIA 22/576, MOS, Blacker Bombard requirement.

34 In May 1939 Dineley had sought to establish manufacture in the UK of the Király SMG, a conventional and effective design, which later performed well in the hands of Hungarian troops on the Eastern Front in WW2. He was also involved in assessing and repairing examples of 'rubbishy' (his words) SMGs captured in the Spanish Civil War, which influenced the design of the Lanchester SMG. See Clarke D.M., PhD thesis: *Arming the British Home Guard, 1940–44*, Cranfield University, 2010.

35 TNA WO 199/1912, Blacker Bombard, Southern Command papers.

36 TNA AVIA 22/576, MOS, Blacker Bombard requirement.

37 TNA CAB 66/28/47, Fulfilment of Moscow Protocol.

38 TNA AVIA 22/576, MOS, Blacker Bombard requirement.

39 TNA, WO 199/324, *Home Guard Instruction No. 51*.

40 *Home Guard Information Circular No. 27* (War Office, 12 May 1943), p. 2.

41 www.feldgrau.net/phpBB2/viewtopic.php?p=185882&sid=7e54fa385e2e7b260e34 64e0e4f4 (accessed 20/1/2008).

42 http://www.nzetc.org/tm/scholarly/tei-WH2Egyp-c12.html (accessed 20/01/2008).

43 Rawlinson, correspondence with author, 2/9/2002.

44 TNA WO 203/540, Blacker Bombard.

45 *Small Arms Training Volume I, Pamphlet No. 23, The 29-mm Spigot Mortar,* War Office, 1942, p. 6.

46 Ranges: the manual of November 1942 gives 450yd maximum, 75–100 best. *Home Guard Instruction No. 51,* Part IV, *The Organization of Home Guard Defence,* GHQ Home Forces, November 1943, gives A–Tk 200yd maximum, 100yd best, and A–Pers, 750yd maximum, 400yd best.

47 TNA AVIA 22/1520, Smith lightweight gun.

48 TNA AVIA 22/1520, Smith lightweight gun.

49 *Home Guard Instruction No. 51: Part IV: The Organization of Home Guard Defence,* p. 80.

50 *The 3-inch O.S.B. Gun,* War Office, 1942, p. 11.

51 Performance of the 2pr on introduction was given as 42mm of homogenous armour at 1,000yd, at a 30 degree angle of attack (see: Hogg, *Allied Artillery of World War Two,* p. 137). Because it relied on kinetic impact, performance could be improved by using the gun at close range, hence the shortening of the weapon's effective range as tank armour improved and thickened.

52 *Home Guard Instruction No. 51,* Part IV, *The Organization of Home Guard Defence* (GHQ Home Forces, November 1943), pp. 16–17.

53 Smith Guns and limbers survive in the collection of the National Army Museum and the Royal Armouries, and in the historical collection of the RAF Regiment.

54 Brown and Peek, 1944, pp. 22–3.

55 See: http://www.rafregiment.net/smith_Gun.jpg (accessed 14/11/2009).

56 See: *Operations, Military Training Pamphlet No. 23, Part II. – The Infantry Division in the Defence* (War Office, March 1942), p. 29.

57 *The 3-inch O.S.B. Gun,* War Office, 1942, p. 2.

58 *Home Guard Instruction No. 51,* Part IV, *The Organization of Home Guard Defence* (GHQ Home Forces, November 1943), p. 87.

59 *Home Guard Instruction No. 51,* Part IV, *The Organization of Home Guard Defence* (GHQ Home Forces, November 1943) p. 11.

60 *Home Guard Instruction No. 51,* Part IV, *The Organization of Home Guard Defence* (GHQ Home Forces, November 1943), p. 15.

61 *Home Guard Instruction No. 51,* Part IV, *The Organization of Home Guard Defence* (GHQ Home Forces, November 1943), p. 16.

62 *Home Guard Instruction No. 51,* Part IV, *The Organization of Home Guard Defence* (GHQ Home Forces, November 1943), p. 17.

63 *The 3-inch O.S.B. Gun* (War Office, 1942), p. 5.

64 Chamberlain and Gander, 1975a, p. 49.

65 Ashworth, 1998, p. 51.

66 TNA, AIR 2/8177,78 and 83, amongst others in the same series.

67 First World War trench mortars had no role in mobile warfare and were left behind when the situation became fluid. See Clarke, 2004, p. 16.

Chapter 8

1 TNA WO 199/3247.

2 The Army Council accepted the possibility of employing Home Guard in limited roles in coast batteries in response to an enquiry from Home Forces, dated 2 July 1941 (TNA WO 32/9757).

3 On 18 September 1941 Brooke, C-in-C Home Forces, met Viscount Bridgeman, Director General Home Guard, to discuss the use of Home Guard in coast artillery (Danchev and Todman, 2001, p. 184). The following day General H.C. Loyd, Chief of the General Staff, issued a memorandum to Home Forces commands, regarding employment of Home Guard in coast artillery explicitly stating that this is necessary 'in order to provide manpower, within the ceiling allotted to Home Forces, to form additional armoured units ... Home Guard [are to] be used as higher gun numbers, wherever possible' (CGS to HF commands, H.F. 4022/9/G. (S.D.),19 September 1941, TNA WO 32/9757).

4 The gun commander was 'Number 1', with the remainder of the crew numbered in declining order of importance, the higher numbers being responsible for providing and readying the ammunition, the lower numbers for laying and operating the gun.

5 Casualties from Corbett, J., *The Official History of the War, Naval Operations Vol. II*, quoted at www.historyofwar.org/articles/raid_hartlepool1914.html (accessed 8/5/2010).

6 The Coastal Artillery was disbanded in February 1956.

7 Email correspondence with Russell Barnes, May 2010. See: www.users.globalnet. co.uk/~rwbarnes/defence/hgcb.htm#home, *passim* (accessed 8/5/2010).

8 The 4in gun was replaced as the secondary armament of choice by the QF 6in from 1914, but remained available in large numbers as pre-First World War Dreadnoughts had carried batteries of up to sixteen 4in guns. See Moore, 2001, p. 38, regarding armament of the *King George V* class and *Orion* class.

9 *Handbook for the 4 inch Mark VII and VIII BL*, Admiralty Gunnery Branch, 1913.

10 www.users.globalnet.co.uk/~rwbarnes/defence/hgcb.htm#home (accessed 8/5/2010).

11 Extracted from the War Diary, 561 Coast Regiment RA, are to be found at www. users.globalnet.co.uk/~rwbarnes/defence/hg_/battery_/wardiary.htm (accessed 8/5/2010).

12 *Notes on Gunnery for Defensively Equipped Merchant Ships*, Admiralty SW (Gunnery Branch, 1939), p. 39–62.

13 www.users.globalnet.co.uk/~rwbarnes/defence/hgcb.htm#home (accessed 8/5/2010).

14 The press announcement was issued on 2 December 1941 (TNA WO 32/9757), and was a response to the 'most disappointing' numbers of Home Guard being recruited to coast batteries. A memorandum issued by CGS to Home Forces commands on 16 December instructed Regimental Commanders to inform Home Guard commanders that Home Guards joining the coast artillery would not merely be ammunition numbers, but would 'be able to carry out practice with all the weapons ... That on becoming proficient, they can be trained in all Coast Artillery duties, e.g. as range finders, gun layers, signallers and lamp and engine room attendants.' (CGS to HF Commands, H.F. 4022/9/G(SD), 16 December 1941. TNA WO 32/9757).

15 www.users.globalnet.co.uk/~rwbarnes/defence/hgcb.htm#home (accessed 8/5/2010).

16 F. Lewthwaite, via R. Barnes, a transcript of the war diary can be viewed at www. users.globalnet.co.uk/~rwbarnes/defence/hg_/battery_/wardiary.htm (accessed 25/8/2010).

17 www.users.globalnet.co.uk/~rwbarnes/defence/hgcb.htm#home (accessed 8/5/2010).

18 War Diary, 561 Coast Regiment RA. www.users.globalnet.co.uk/~rwbarnes/defence/ hg_/battery_/wardiary.htm (accessed 25/8/2010).

19 The 1910 *Courbet* class of Dreadnoughts consisted of the *Courbet, Jean Bart, Paris* and *France*. Moore, 2001, p. 184, also Preston, 2001, p. 120.

20 www.users.globalnet.co.uk/~rwbarnes/defence/copeland/whiteha_/sketch-.htm3 (accessed 22/11/10). The French designation was *Cuirassés de 1er rang.*

21 The 4in guns were sent to the Port Talbot battery, and later sent on to the Mumbles. Whitehaven battery ceased operations on 1 June 1945. www.users.globalnet. co.uk/~rwbarnes/defence/whitehav.htm (accessed 22/11/2010).

22 www.users.globalnet.co.uk/~rwbarnes/defence/hg_/battery_/wardiary.htm. The reference actually states '2nd 4in Gun dismantled. 6pdr 6cwt Mobile Gun arrived'. (accessed 25/8/2010).

23 A (now) extremely rare First World War Mk IV 'Presentation Tank' survived the Second World War scrap drive at Ashford in Kent, as it had been used to house an electricity sub-station. An excellent article on Presentation Tanks can be found on the Ashford Borough Council website: www.ashford.gov.uk/about_the_borough/ history_and_heritage/the_tank.aspx (accessed 4/6/2010).

24 The well-preserved and presented type-28 pillbox which survives in the grounds of Bodiam Castle in Sussex was examined by the author, who concluded from the remains of the mounting ('holdfast') that a 6pdr 6cwt was emplaced *vice* a 2pdr anti-tank gun. The recorded testimonial of a local Home Guard who manned the pillbox states that there was no gun fitted and that the embrasure was covered with a piece of wood. This suggests that the gun was either fitted and subsequently removed, before the Home Guard took over guard duties from the army, or was never actually fitted.

25 TNA WO 199/3247, Home Guard monthly returns.

26 See: Headlam, 1937, pp. 338–40 for the introduction of modern movable armament to defend the land fronts of coast artillery in the first decade of the twentieth century, and its relationship to the development of heavy field artillery.

27 www.users.globalnet.co.uk/~rwbarnes/defence/hgcb.htm#cons (accessed 22/11/2010).

28 The original Mk I gun was fitted with a modified recuperator system to become the Mk I*. New-build guns to the modified design were Mk IIs. The Mk III design never entered service; a few Mk IV guns saw action in the last weeks of the First World War. Clarke, 2004, pp. 33 and 39.

29 *Handbook for the Q.F. 18-pr. Mark IV Gun on Marks III, III*, IV and V field carriages* (War Office, 1924), p. 75.

30 The 'Mk IV' designation referred to the gun (i.e. the barrel and breech mechanism). The box trail carriage (shaped like a 'U', with the arms attaching to the axle of the gun carriage, allowing the gun to elevate so that the breech was below the level of the trail, which was not possible with a pole trail), was named the Carriage, 18pr, Mks III, III*, IIIT and IV. The split trail carriage (which opened to form the shape of an inverted 'V') was the Carriage, 18pr Mk V. *Handbook for the Q.F. 18-pr Gun on Marks III, III*, IIIT and V Field Carriages, Land Service, 1924* (War Office, 1924), *passim.*

31 The converted guns were a mixture of box and split trail types (Henry, 2002, pp. 6–7).

32 The 18pdr shell actually weighed 18.5lb – 8.4kg, the German 77mm 6.85kg and the French 75mm, as used by the United States, 6.2kg (Clarke, 2004), p. 34.

33 In a War Cabinet memorandum dated 29 August 1940, Minister of Supply, Herbert Morrison, reported that 820 75mm guns have been sent from the United States (TNA CAB 66/11/19).

34 http://208.84.116.223/forums/index.php?showtopic=18739&st=20 (accessed 9/5/2010). Also see: http://www.historykb.com/Uwe/Forum.aspx/world-war-ii/3536/Psych-War-Tank-Destroyer-and-Jagdpanzer (accessed 11/6/2010 [below]):

War sales for cash during 1940 totalled 1,095 75mm guns broken down as:

200 M1917 to Finland
395 M1917 to the UK
500 M1897 to the UK

Lend-Leased 75mm totalled 230 guns, all M1916, 170 to the UK and sixty to other minor nations.

In addition, one of the Field Artillery regiments of the Hawaiian division was equipped with forty-eight M1917 and forty-eight had been shipped to the Philippine Army.

Now total production of M1917 was 724 and the above accounts for 691 of them, some twenty-three years after they were built, so I have a feeling we can assume the other thirty-three were used up inter-war.

The state of the M1897 is a bit harder to find. A total of 918 were modernised on the M2 carriage from June 1940 through November 1941 and 2,202 were utilised in the T12 SP carriage, for a total of 3,120. But, see below, it appears that at least some (c. 395?) of the M1897 on carriage M2 may have been later utilised for the SP conversion?

So we have possible inventory totals c. mid-1940 of:

M1897 3,120 + 500 = 3,620
M1917 = 691
M1916 = 230

For a total of 4,631 or 395 more than the 4,236 reported in inventory as of June 1940. But production of the M1916 totalled 810, the Lend-Lease only accounts for 230 of those, leaving 580. However, the bulk of those may all have been used up or converted to the M1, M2, M3 and M4 sub-caliber mounts for the Coast Artillery? Faint evidence for that is that in June 1940 when the debate over drawing from reserve stocks to fill the British requests were raging, the Chief of Field Artillery basically said something to the order of 'please give them the 200 M1916, they aren't much good anyway'. Plus of course the notional inventory totals above indicate that there was not many more M1916 available. That may indicate that the 230 Lend-Leased were about all that remained on field carriages by 1940.

35 TNA CAB 66/11/19, MOS to War Cabinet, memorandum 29 August 1940.
36 Ibid.
37 Ibid.
38 See IWM photograph H9522 for a picture of Polish field gunners using a QF 75mm Mk 1* towed by a Morris Commercial Quad gun tractor, on exercise in Scotland, May 1941.
39 TNA WO 32/9757.
40 62mm AP (1931), 42mm APHE (1916) www.miniatures.de/shells-british.html (accessed 14/12/2010).
41 TNA WO 199/3247, Home Guard monthly returns.

42 www.bunwellhistory.co.uk/bunwell_home_guard.htm (accessed 20/5/2010).

43 Being a relatively low-velocity, high-trajectory weapon, the 4.5in howitzer was less suitable for anti-tank use.

44 TNA AVIA 38/340. The 75mm gun on halftrack T12 was urgently pursued by the British, in December 1941, pending arrival of Valentine tank-based Bishop self-propelled 25pr guns. Some 170 units were eventually delivered, seeing service in North Africa and Italy.

45 Not to be confused with the Mk I Churchill tank, which mounted a low-velocity 3in howitzer in the front hull for firing HE and a 2pdr AT gun in the turret.

46 www.wwiivehicles.com/unitedkingdom/infantry/churchill.asp (accessed 3/8/2010).

47 The prototype was built by Vauxhall motors; the production of gun carriers was undertaken by railway locomotive builders Beyer, Peacock and Co., in Gorton, Manchester. The sides of the fixed casemate fighting compartment were formed as an upward extension of the tank's side armour, so the Gun Carrier was not simply a gun tank with the turret removed. The vehicle's enduring popularity with model makers and wargamers, out of all proportion to its military significance, is due largely to an excellently researched 1970s article. See Woodhall, 1974, p. 11.

48 Most sources simply state that the Churchill 3in Gun Carrier was used 'for training' or describe the vehicle as 'experimental'. Its brief service use has emerged from Canadian sources (see reference below).

49 The 'Heavy Support Squadron' … was a temporary change to the brigade's organisation which took place in June 1942, when the brigade headquarters was expanded to include a heavy support squadron having a strength of five officers and ninety-two other ranks. It was equipped with nine Churchills, each mounting a 3" 20cwt Mk I gun which fired a projectile at a speed of 2,000ft per second and could penetrate armour 100mm thick at 200yd. It was to be used against what were being referred to as enemy super-heavy tanks until the 17-pounder anti-tank gun came into full production. These tanks were called Churchill Gun Carriers and could be assigned when required to individual tank battalions (Re: PAC, RG 24 Volume 14062). This squadron was disbanded in March 1943 (Source: DRAGOONS OF STEEL, Canadian Armour in Two World Wars). www.mapleleafup.org/forums/showthread.php?s=&threadid=2847&highlight=Churchill (accessed 3/8/2010).

50 Subsequently used operationally on a Valentine tank hull.

51 Research into this equipment is on-going, but it appears likely that the 3in Gun Carriers, once replaced by the 17pdr AT gun, were immediately obsolete and expended as targets. It should be noted that DGHG specifically stated in 1943 that the Home Guard 'possess neither tanks, heavy artillery nor aircraft' (TNA 199/3247). That said, the Home Guard most certainly did possess armoured cars, and two 60pdr guns, so there is every possibility of a Home Guard Churchill 3in Gun Carrier emerging from the archives.

52 Figures given are those given for the tank mounted 3in 16cwt gun.

53 TNA WO 199/3247, Home Guard monthly returns.

54 TNA WO 199/3247, Home Guard monthly returns.

55 www.users.globalnet.co.uk/~rwbarnes/defence/hg1.htm (accessed 22/5/2010).

56 www.users.globalnet.co.uk/~rwbarnes/defence/hg1.htm (accessed 20/5/2010).

57 George Forty describes the Boys anti-tank rifle as 'cumbersome' and 'ineffective', 'virtually useless after 1940, being not much better than a large calibre infantry rifle'.

He is slightly kinder to the 2pdr, admitting that it 'did well in 1940', but describing it as having a 'relatively poor performance – it could only penetrate 53mm of armour at 500 yd'. Forty, 1998, pp. 210 and 213.

58   Penetration figures 1,000yd, Hogg, 2002, p. 75, 500yd, Forty, 1998, p. 213.

59   The PzKpfw VI Tiger entered service in September 1942, the PzKpfw V Panther entered service in February 1943.

60   *Home Guard Instruction No. 51, Part IV, The Organization of the Home Guard in Defence* (War Office, November 1943), p. 15.

61   The Coventry Mk I armoured car, which was accepted for service in late 1944, was armed with a 2pdr gun (the Mk II was equipped with a 75mm gun). Most were eventually sold to France and saw action in French Indochina (see Foss, C. et al., *The Encyclopedia of Tanks and Armored Fighting Vehicles*, Staplehurst, 2003, p. 153–4).

62   *Home Guard Instruction No. 51, Part IV, The Organization of the Home Guard in Defence* (War Office, November 1943), p. 17.

63   The ferocity of the Boys anti-tank rifle is often commented on. The reader can form their own judgement, as there is footage of the rifle in action with original service ammunition on YouTube.

64   *Small Arms Training Volume I, Pamphlet No. 5, Anti-Tank Rifle* (War Office, April 1942), p. 1.

65   *Small Arms Training Volume I, Pamphlet No. 5, Anti-Tank Rifle* (War Office, April 1942), p. 11. The SdKfz 251 halftrack had armour of between 7mm and 12mm, the SdKfz armoured car had armour of 5mm to 30mm. See: Foss, 1981, p. 106.

66   Hogg, 1979, pp. 148–9. 'Undoubtedly the most famous incident involving the PIAT was the action in Italy in which Fusilier Jefferson dashed into the open and fired it from the hip, stopping two Tiger tanks at close range. He was awarded the Victoria Cross for this remarkable feat, and the general opinion in the ranks was that he deserved it for firing the thing from the hip, let alone killing two tanks with it.'

67   *Home Guard Instruction No. 51, Part IV, The Organization of the Home Guard in Defence* (War Office, November 1943), p. 18.

68   Ralph T. Walker, a noted US gunsmith, re-chambered a quantity of Boys anti-tank rifles to .50 BMG, while on assignment as a small-arms expert to the Chinese Nationalist Army in Formosa (Taiwan) during the Korean War. The guns were fitted with 20 x tank telescope sights and were successfully used for harassing fire between Nationalist and Communist-held islands. Gilbert, 1997, p. 139.

69   The 3in AA gun had been adopted under Royal Navy auspices in March 1914. Hogg, 2002, p. 104.

70   There was considerable demand for 40mm Bofors guns from the Admiralty, from the RAF for airfield defence and from the Field Army. Production was initially very slow. Pile, 1949, p. 131.

71   GOC-in-C Anti-Aircraft Command, Gen. Sir Frederick Pile, declared himself both 'astonished and pleased' that the BEF actually opted to take the 3in gun in preference to the 3.7in, as a result of which, AA Command GB lost far fewer of the urgently needed modern guns than would have otherwise been the case. Pile, 1949, p. 112. 3in guns lost earlier in the war were absorbed into German service as the 7.5cm *Flugabwehrkanone Vickers(e)*. Captured 3.7in guns were gratefully received by the Germans, who even manufactured ammunition for the 9.4cm *Flugabwehrkanone Vickers M39(e)*. See: Gander and Chamberlain, 1978, pp. 163 and 169.

72   The 3in 20cwt gun was declared obsolete in 1946 (Hogg, 2002, p. 104).

73 www.kenthistoryforum.co.uk/index.php?topic=3890.0 (accessed 15/8/2010).
74 MOI, *c.* 1943, pp. 293–303. In the British Army, the rule that 'there should never be a female finger on the trigger' was a political imposition that only passed in the 1990s. As COC-in-C Anti-Aircraft Command, Gen. Pile had the highest regard for the ATS under his command (more so than for the Home Guard), and was well aware that they could operate AAA, probably better than the increasingly poor male recruits he was forced to employ. However, to do so crossed some societal line that was far deeper and more visceral than simple national survival and military logic. ATS on all-female searchlight positions could not, therefore, return fire when a German aircraft shot at their light, as a male or mixed position would, and ATS sentries were only permitted to carry a pick helve, despite the isolation and vulnerability of some of their locations. The fact that a single male was initially located on each all-female position, because male muscle was required to swing the starter on the generator, was a closely guarded secret, to prevent exposure in the more prurient press, and in Parliament. The manner in which Anti-Aircraft Command used media operations to contain and pre-empt damaging publicity, in order to preserve military capability, is a case study in the utility of military media operations. See Pile, 1949, p. 193 and *passim.*
75 Brophy, 1945, p. 41. The Dornier Do 17 downed by an unnamed Home Counties Home Guard unit 'with 180 rounds of rapid fire' was recorded by British Pathé in a newsreel released on 22 August 1940 (Film ID 1053.48). The sequence, which also includes good footage of an early 3.7in AAA site in action, can be viewed at www.britishpathe.com/record.php?id=25884.
76 *Home Guard Instruction No. 45* (War Office, March 1942), p. 3.
77 Home Guard AA personnel are first differentiated from General Service Home Guard in the HG returns for 30 April 1942, which show 1,451,881 GS Home Guard and 2,593 AA Home Guard (TNA WO 199/3247, Home Guard monthly returns).
78 General Pile states that although AA Command had the same number of guns in action in 1945 as 1940, army manpower in the command had been reduced by 60 per cent.
79 TNA WO/199/3247, Home Guard returns.
80 The ratio improved through the course of the war, it stood at 2,668 'per bird' in June 1941. Pile, 1949, p. 216.
81 TNA WO/199/3247, Home Guard returns.
82 The 3.7in gun was replaced by the Thunderbird missile in British Army service in 1959.
83 TNA WO/199/3247, Home Guard returns.
84 www.users.globalnet.co.uk/~rwbarnes/defence/hg2.htm (accessed 24/8/2010).
85 Unlike the blow-back system of the Oerlikon, the Hispano was a gas-operated gun firing from a locked bolt.
86 The senior civilian engineer in the Gun Section of the Ministry of Aircraft Production, Wallace was personally involved in the provision of guns for RAF aircraft.
87 The diameter of the drum meant that a large bulge was required in the aircraft's wing to accommodate the gun. This could be diminished somewhat by mounting the gun on its side, but this resulted in feed and ejection difficulties. Wallace, 1972, p. 87.
88 More difficult than the relatively small amount of ammunition was the problem of quality. The UK manufacturers of the drums, Austin Motors, lacked the specialist machinery that Hispano had used to manufacture magazines, resulting in misfeeds and

stoppages which limited the utility of the Hispano gun during the Battle of Britain. Development of a belt-feed system was started before the fall of France by French military engineers at Châtellerault, based on a captured Soviet 20mm aircraft gun supplied by Spanish Nationalists. The work was completed in the UK by the Molins Machine Co., manufacturers of cigarette-making and packing machinery, who proved to have a remarkable aptitude for weapon automation. Wallace, 1972, pp. 85 and 187.

89 Hawkinge airfield (Kent) was struck by an air raid on 12 August 1940. According to the station Operations Record Book: 'The ground defences were surprised and no guns, except two Hispano, were fired.' www.kbobm.org/events.htm (accessed 5/9/2010).

90 On one raid on Deal, Kent, anti-aircraft gunners expended 350 rounds of 40mm and 2,000 rounds of 20mm in a quarter of an hour. Pile, 1972, p. 242.

91 TNA WO 199/3247, Home Guard monthly returns. In April 1943, AA Command GB was deploying 424 20mm guns, but it is not clear what proportion of those were Hispanos. Pile, *Ack-Ack*, p. 243.

92 *Home Guard Instruction No. 60, Miscellaneous Notes – Weapon Training* (GHQ Home Forces, December 1943), p. 10.

93 Whilst impressed by the quality of 'old-school' Home Guard volunteers, General Pile had little time for 'Directed Men', who he described as: 'those men who were doing nothing else, and in most cases were determined to continue to do nothing else. Disciplinary action against them was almost impossible. Many were, anyway, mentally or physically useless.' Pile, 1949, p. 258.

94 TNA WO/199/3247, Home Guard returns.

Chapter 9

1 Talent, P., '*The Countryman's Diary 1939*' (Coleshill, 1943), p. 13.

2 '… almost certainly the nearest that the official name of the British Resistance organization ever came to being set up in type and printed on paper until after the official stand-down order had been given.' Lampe, 2007, p. 139.

3 See: Commander Langley's memoir published in Turner, 2006, p. 18.

4 See also Turner, 2006, p. 159 for a description of hollowing lumps of real coal and subsequent use of black-dyed PE.

5 See Angell, 1996, p. 68 for a reference to the 'Aux Unit Mk II'. Oxenden states that a modified 'Aux Unit Mk I' was being delivered 'by the summer of 1941' (Oxenden, 1998, p. 12).

6 Ex-Bathampton auxilier Robert 'Bob' Millard to author, e-mail, 13/2/2008.

7 Ibid.

8 Page 6 of the November 1940 issue of American Rifleman carried the following appeal: 'SEND A GUN TO DEFEND A BRITISH HOME: British civilians, faced with threat of invasion, desperately need arms for defense of their homes. THE AMERICAN COMMITTEE FOR DEFENSE OF BRITISH HOMES has organised to collect gifts of pistols, rifles, revolvers, shotguns, binoculars from American civilians who wish to answer the call and aide in defense of British homes. The arms are being shipped, with the consent of the British Government, to CIVILIAN COMMITTEE FOR PROTECTION OF HOMES, BIRMINGHAM, ENGLAND.'

http://www.fa-ir.org/ai/second_amend.htm (accessed 14/2/2008).

9 See: Turner, 2006, p. 164. 'We received boxes and boxes of arms. There were all kinds of rifles, revolvers, pistols, automatics, sub-machine guns, and a Colt machine gun that had last seen action in the Cuban/American War. Alf and I had to unpack them all and of course try them out!'

10 Letter from ex-auxilier Bob Bennet to David Waller, available online at www.btinternet.com/~david.waller/bobmillardadmiraltynotes.htm (accessed 14/2/2008).

11 Richard Ashley, BRO Museum. To author, e-mail, 15/2/2008.

12 Ibid.

13 Auxilier Fred Simpson in Dorset. The knife is now in the Museum of the BRO at Parham. See: Warwicker, 2004, p. 30.

14 http://gotavapen.se/gota/artiklar/fs/shanghai/shanghaiknife.htm (accessed 6/2/2008).

15 Ibid.

16 Cassidy, W.L., 'A Brief History of the Fairbairn Sykes Fighting Knife'. Available online at http://www.888knivesrus.com/category/allbrands/.allbrands.sheffield_knives.sfstory/ (accessed 9/2/2008).

17 http://bpl.blogger.com/_CWr1WAB3VK4/R2JKumJHo31/AAAAAAAAAIA/15Fvpue8cAI/s1600-h/Contractdetail-1.jpg (accessed 6/2/2008).

18 http://wilkinson-fs-knife.blogspot.com/ (accessed 6/2/2008).

19 Founded as volunteer, mounted, battlefield first aiders in 1907, during the Second World War the Field Auxiliary Nursing Yeomanry (FANY) provided a military parent unit for female personnel engaged in special operations duties, as well as numerous other support roles requiring discretion and intelligence. See http://www.fany.org.uk/our-history/index.html (accessed 28/12/2015).

20 Delivery addresses from the Wilkinson contract book are Knebworth, Brockhall-Weedon, Weedon, Room 55a or collect, and Station 6 (WD). See R. Wilkinson-Latham, Op. Cit., passim. Credit for inventing the cover title 'Station 6 (WD)' rests with its former OC, Major (subsequently Colonel) L.J.C. Wood. See: Turner, 2006, p. 6.

21 Cassidy, W.L., 'A Brief History of the Fairbairn Sykes Fighting Knife'. Available online at http://www.888knivesrus.com/category/allbrands/.allbrands.sheffield_knives.sfstory/ (accessed 9/2/2008).

22 See: Turner, 2006, p. 136 – Colin Meek, Scientific Officer, Station XII: 'Aston House then became responsible for Design, Testing, Production, Inspection, Packing and Despatch of Stores and Administration.'

23 'I was given another fascinating job, the collecting and batching of all the 23, explosives etc. in caches for the secret army of Great Britain.' Recorded interview with Colonel Wood, Turner, 2006, p. 97.

24 Cassidy, W.L., 'A Brief History of the Fairbairn Sykes Fighting Knife.' Available online at http://www.888knivesrus.com/category/allbrands/.allbrands.sheffield_knives.sfstory/ (accessed 9/2/2008).

25 Total Auxiliary Unit numbers in late 1941, given by Brigadier Major from his own records in 1967, were 3,524. Lampe, 2007, p. 161.

26 http://gotavapen.se/gota/artiklar/fs/fs_knife 1.htm (accessed 7/2/2008).

27 Cassidy, W.L., 'A Brief History of the Fairbairn Sykes Fighting Knife.' Available online at http://www.888knivesrus.com/category/allbrands/.allbrands.sheffield_knives.sfstory/ (accessed 9/2/2008).

28 Bob Millard to author, e-mail, 17/2/2008. Mr Millard goes on to say that he believes

the 3rd pattern knives were most common. This has been questioned by Richard Ashley, on the grounds that these knives came into use rather late in the Auxiliary Unit's history, and he believes 2nd pattern knives are more likely to have been used by Auxiliers (email communication with author 18/2/2008).

29 http://gotavapen.se/gota/artiklar/fs/fs_knife 1.htm (accessed 7/2/2008).

30 Work in progress by Richard Ashley at the BRO Museum, Parham (email correspondence 13/2/2008).

31 See: Angell, 1996, p. 66, and http://www.auxunit.org.uk passim. Ex-Auxilier Bob Millard has listed the 'Monk' wire garrotte ('supplied in a pouch for ease of carrying', made up from 24in of high tensile piano wire joining 2½in handles. The garrotte was used 'cross armed' to form a loop, which was dropped over the victim's head. Also brass knuckledusters and 14in weighted rubber truncheons (email, 13/2/2008).

32 Fairbairn, W.E., *Get Tough* (New York, 1943).

33 http://www.gutterfighting.org/smatchet.html (accessed 7/2/2008).

34 The National Archives, WO 199/3237: HOFORS signal 8–9 July 1940.

35 See: Rigden, 2001, p. 377 – 'The tendency is to compare the Sten unfavourably with the Thompson. This is wrong, as the Sten is really the better weapon for the type of work with which we are concerned, as it fires Standard Continental Ammunition, it is lighter, more easily concealed and has a much more simple mechanism than the Thompson.'

36 In 1953 Salter & Varge were involved in the disposal of surplus and obsolete military firearms from Eire, so they clearly had some interest in military small arms. Dáil Éireann, oral answers, 29 April 1953. Available online at http://historical-debates. oireachtas.ie/D/0138/D.0138.195304290020.html (accessed 15/2/2008).

37 There is an order for a batch of 100 of various models of Iver Johnson and Stevens rifles from Messrs R.J. Adgey, dated 24 July 1941, which may be the first part of the Auxiliary Unit order, but telescopic sights are not specified (Skennerton, 1988, p. 21).

38 UK NRA historical resource at www.rifleman.org.uk.

39 For a discussion of the No. 42 scope and including confirmation that these were set up on silenced Winchester Model 74s at 'Welwyn and Bletchly', see Laidler, 1993, p. 65.

40 Discussion with Messrs Richard Ashley and Bob Millard at MBRO have confirmed that only standard military or club .22 ammunition was used by Auxiliary Units (e-mail correspondence 18/2/2008).

41 Bob Millard recalls it was so marked during the Second World War, and remained so into the 1980s.

42 'Maxim's Gun Proves that it's Noiseless', *New York Times*, 9 February 1909. Available online at http://query.nytimes.com/mem/archive (accessed 10/2/2008).

43 Muzzle velocity for Eley rifle ammunition, including 'Club' and 'Trainer'.

44 Home Office Circular 176/72 of 1972. Available online at www.amstevens.fsnet.fsnet. co.uk/the%20Home%20Office20Choice.htm (accessed 14/2/2008).

45 Instructions for the Third Home Guard Patrol Competition, issued on 4 July 1943, stated: 'Event 3. Miniature Rifle Practise. – Grouping. Lying with wrist or forearm supported. 10 rounds per man. Range approximately 20yd (probably by artificial light). Rifles will be without telescopic sights and for Semi Finals and Final will be supplied by Coleshill. Scoring will be for group of best NINE shots. i.e. one wide will be allowed. 0.5 …5pts. 1 … 3pts. 2 … 1pt.' (Angell, 1996, p. 13).

46 The author served in Territorial Army Surveillance and Target Acquisition patrols in

the 1980s, when stay-behind patrols, expected to operate as forward artillery observers behind Soviet lines in the event of war, were issued with a single L34A1 silenced Sterling SMG carried by one trooper. The other members of the 'sabre' patrol being equipped with the standard issue un-silenced L2A3 Sterling sub-machine gun and L1A1 Self-Loading Rifle – a weapon as unsuited to life in an underground hide as the BAR had been forty years previously. Following the issue of the SA80A1 'Individual weapon' in the mid-1990s, the silenced SMG was withdrawn without replacement.

47 There were two versions of the Welrod, the Mk II in .32in and the Mk I in 9mm. The Mk II appears to have come into service first, during 1943, the Mk I arrived later, mid-1944. See: www.timelapse.dk/production.php (accessed 11/2/2008).

48 'The first year had been a blaze of wild priority; then in 1941 and 1942 had followed a period of organised power, guarded by a security that nobody could get past, however much they might resent it, and now, in 1943 there was, throughout the areas, a realisation that the soundest attitude was unobtrusiveness.' Oxenden, 1998, p. 21.

49 Reproduced at http://timelapse.dk/mk.I.php (accessed 11/2/2008).

50 Angell, 1996, p. 69.

51 Equipment covered in the first Auxiliary Unit handbook included the paraffin incendiary, SIP grenade, time pencil and the Sticky bomb.

52 *Tank Hunting and Destruction, Military Training Pamphlet No. 42* (War Office, 29 August 1940).

53 *Small Arms Training, Volume I, Pamphlet No. 13, Grenade, 1942* (War Office, 1942), p. 35.

54 Aston House production figures, reproduced in Turner, *Aston House Station 12*, appendix A.

55 Colonel L.J.C. Wood, interview. Turner, 2006, p. 65.

56 Talent, P., '*The Countryman's Diary 1939*' (Coleshill, 1943), p. 41.

Chapter 10

1 Alanbrooke (ed. Danchev and Todman), *War Diaries 1939–1945*, p. 98.

2 Pile, *Ack-Ack*, p. 244.

3 Fairfax, *Calling All Arms*, p. 45.

4 See: www.neam.co.uk/usworth.html, for example.

5 Fairfax, E., *Calling All Arms* (London, 1945), pp. 94–5.

6 It is not entirely clear why Admiral Evans should have been visiting a factory in Birmingham, as he was London Regional Commissioner for Civil Defence 1939–45. See: List of RN officers at www.unithistories.com/officers/RN_officersE.html (accessed 7/9/10).

7 www.walberswickww2.co.uk/academic-research.

8 www.users.globalnet.co.uk/~rwbarnes/index.htm.

9 See: Beckett, 1991, p. 269. Also: 'Is it a Family Record? Three Generations in Home Guard at Dunton Green,' *Sevenoaks Chronicle*, 4 July 1941.

BIBLIOGRAPHY

References

Agar, J. *Britain Alone: June 1940–June 1941* (Bodley Head: London, 1972)

Angell, Stewart *Secret Sussex Resistance: 1940–1944* (Middleton Press: Midhurst, 1996)

Archer, F. *When Village Bells were Silent* (Hodder & Stoughton: London, 1975)

Ashworth, E.W. 'Dad's Army against the Panzers', *Military Illustrated*, No. 120, May 1998

Ballou, James L., ed. Stevens R. Blake *Rock in a Hard Place: The Browning Automatic Rifle* (Collector Grade Publications: Ontario, 2000)

Banks, Lieutenant, A.G. *'A.G.'s' Book of the Rifle*, 4th edition (Jordan and Sons: London, 1950)

Barlow, Lieutenant Colonel, J.A. *The Elements of Rifle Shooting,* 3rd edition (Gale & Polden: Aldershot, 1942)

Baxley, Major Brian T. *9 April 1940 German Invasion of Norway – The Dawn of Decisive Airpower During Joint Military Operations.* (The Research Department, Air Command and Staff College: US, 1997)

Baxter, Ian 'Hitler's Last Defenders' *Military Illustrated*, No. 156, May 2001

Beckett, Ian F.W. *The Amateur Military Tradition 1558–1945* (Manchester University Press: Manchester, 1991)

Breer, A. *American Acquisition of French Field Artillery in the Great War.* (Western Front Association: USA Phi Alpha Theta prize-winning essay, 2007)

Briggs, Asa *The Channel Islands: Occupation and Liberation 1940–45* (B.T. Batsford, Imperial War Museum: London, 1995)

Brophy, John, ill. Kennington, Eric *Britain's Home Guard: A Character Study* (George G. Harrap: London, 1945)

Brophy, John *Home Guard: A Handbook for the L.D.V.*, 6th impression (Hodder & Stoughton: London, 1941)

Brophy, John *Advanced Training for the Home Guard, with Ten Specimen Field Exercises* (Hodder & Stoughton: London, 1941)

Brophy, John *A Home Guard Handbook. Revised.* ed., 2nd impression (Hodder & Stoughton: London, 1942)

Brown, G.L. and Peek, A.W. *1940–44, Being a Diary of 'D' Company 20th Bn. Kent H.G.* (Sevenoaks: private circulation only, 1944)

Cambs. and Isle of Ely TAA – The Cambridgeshire and Isle of Ely Territorial Army Association. *'We Also Served' – The Story of the Home Guard in Cambridgeshire and the Isle of Ely* (W. Heffer and Sons: Cambridge, 1944)

Canfield, Bruce N. *A Collector's Guide to Winchester in the Service* (Andrew Mowbray: Rhode Island, 1991)

Carrol, David *The Home Guard* (Sutton Publishing: Stroud, 1999)

Chamberlain, Peter and Gander, Terry *WW2 Fact File Series: Allied Pistols, Rifles and Grenades* (Macdonald and Jane's Publishers: London, 1976)

Chamberlain, Peter and Gander, Terry *WW2 Fact File Series: Infantry, Mountain and Airborne Guns* (Macdonald and Jane's Publishers: London, 1975)

Chamberlain, Peter and Gander, Terry *WW2 Fact File Series: Light and Medium Field Artillery* (Macdonald and Jane's Publishers: London, 1975)

Chamberlain, Peter and Gander, Terry *WW2 Fact File Series: Machine Guns* (Macdonald and Jane's Publishers: London, 1974)

Chamberlain, Peter and Gander, Terry *WW2 Fact File Series: Mortars and Rockets* (Macdonald and Jane's Publishers: London, 1975)

Churchill, Winston S. *The Second World War: Volume One: The Gathering Storm*, 8th impression (Reprint Society: London, 1954)

Churchill, Winston S. *The Second World War: Volume Two: Their Finest Hour*, 8th impression (Reprint Society: London, 1955)

Churchill, Winston S. *The Second World War: Volume Four: The Hinge of Fate*, 8th impression (Reprint Society, London, 1954)

Clarke, Dale, ill. Delf. Brian. *British Artillery 1914–19: Field Artillery* (Osprey Publishing: Oxford, 2004)

Cole, Howard and Fulton, Robin *The Story of Bisley* (Biddles: Guildford, 1990)

Cornish, P. *Clandestine Weapons and the Welwyn Connection* (lecture notes, 2003) Report (Quarterly Bulletin of the Historical Breech Loading Smallarms Association), London, July 2003, p. 35.

Danchev, A. and Todman, D. (eds.) *Alanbrooke War Diaries 1939–1945: Field Marshall Lord Alanbrooke* (Weidenfeld & Nicholson: London, 2001)

Delaney, J. *The Blitzkrieg Campaigns* (Arms and Armour Press, London, 1996)

Dowling, Christopher 'The Campaign of Hate' *Purnell's History of the First World War*, Vol. 2, No. 13 (London, 1970)

Easterly, William M., ed. Stevens, R. Blake. *The Belgian Rattlesnake: The Lewis Automatic Machine Gun, a Social and Technical Biography of the Gun and its Inventors* (Collector Grade Publications: Ontario, 1998)

Ellis, J. *The Sharp End: The Fighting Man in World War II*, 2nd edition (Pimlico: London, 1990)

Fairfax, Ernest *Calling All Arms* (Hutchinson: London, 1945)

Featherstone, Donald, ill. John Mollo *Weapons and Equipment of the Victorian Soldier* (Arms and Armour Press: London, 1996)

Fleischer, Wolfgang *Panzerfaust and Other German Infantry Anti-Tank Weapons* (Schiffer Publishing: Atglen, 1994)

Fleming, Peter *Invasion 1940* (Rupert Hart-Davis: London, 1957)

Forty, George *British Army Handbook 1939–1945* (Sutton Publishing: Stroud, 1998)

Foss C.F. (ed.) *Tanks and Armoured Fighting Vehicles*, 5th impression (Salamander Books: London, 1981)

Foss, Christopher (ed.) *The Encyclopaedia of Tanks and Armoured Fighting Vehicles* (Spelmount: Staplehurst, 2002)

French, David *Raising Churchill's Army: The British Army and the War against Germany 1919–1945* (Oxford University Press: Oxford, 2000)

Gander, T. 'Desperate Measures: The Smith Gun' *Journal of the Ordnance Society*, Vol. 17, July 2005, p. 60.

Gander, Terry and Chamberlain, Peter *Small Arms, Artillery and Special Weapons of the Third Reich, an Encyclopaedic Survey* (Macdonald and Jane's Publishers: London, 1978)

Gilbert, Adrian *Stalk and Kill, the Sniper Experience* (Sidgwick and Jackson: London, 1997)

Goldsmith, Dolf L., ed. Stevens, R. Blake *The Browning Machine Gun, Volume II: Rifle Calibre Brownings Abroad* (Collector Grade Publications: Ontario, 2006)

——. *The Grand Old Lady of No Man's Land: The Vickers Machine Gun.* (Collector Grade Publications: Ontario, 1994)

Greene, Graham *The Last Word and Other Stories* (Penguin Books: New York, 1999)

Guderian, General Heinz, trans. Fitzgibbon, Constantine *Panzer Leader* (Michael Joseph: London, 1952)

Gulvin, K.R. *Kent Home Guard: A History* (North Kent Books: Gillingham, 1980)

Henry, Chris, ill. Fuller, Mike *The 25-pounder Field Gun 1939–72* (Osprey Publishing: Oxford, 2002)

Hobart, Major F.W.A. (Retd) *Pictorial History of the Sub-Machine Gun* (Ian Allen: Shepperton, 1973)

Hogg, Ian and Weeks, John. *Military Smallarms of the Twentieth Century* (Arms and Armour Press: London, 1973)

Hogg, Ian V. *Allied Artillery of World War Two* (Crowood Press: Marlborough, 1998)

Hogg, Ian V. *British & American Artillery of World War Two*, revised edition (Greenhill Books: London, 2002)

Hogg, Ian V. *The Encyclopedia of Infantry Weapons of World War II*, 4th impression (Arms and Armour Press: London, 1979)

Hogg, Ian V. *The Guinness Encyclopaedia of Weaponry* (Quarto Publishing: London, 1992)

Hunt, Richard *Uniforms of the Home Guard* (Historic Military Press: Pulborough, 2002)

Jowitt, The Earl *Some Were Spies* (Hodder & Stoughton: London, 1954)

Klee, Karl. *Dokumente zum Unternehmen ,,Seelöwe: Die geplante deutsche Landung in England 1940.* (Musterschmidt-Verlag: Gottingen, Berlin, 1959)

Ladd, James, Melton, Keith and Mason, Captain Peter *Clandestine Warfare: Weapons and Equipment of the SOE and OSS* (Blandford Press, London, 1988)

Laidler, P. and Howroyd, D. *The Guns of Dagenham* (Collector Grade Publications, Ontario, 1995)

Laidler, Peter *Telescope Sighting No. 32, Mk 1 – OS 466A, Mk 2 – OS 1650A, Mk 3 – OS 2039A, including the No. 42, 53 & L1 A1: An inside view of the Snipers rifle telescope.* Reprint of 3rd edition. (IDSA Books: Piqua, 1993)

Lampe, David int. Sheffield, Gary *The Last Ditch*, reprint with new introduction.(Greenhill Books: London, 2007)

Langdon-Davies, John *Home Guard Warfare* (George Routledge and Sons: London, 1941)

Langdon-Davies, Major John *The Home Guard Fieldcraft Manual* 2nd edition. (John Murray and the Pilot Press: London, 1942)

Langdon-Davies, Major John *The Home Guard Training Manual.* Facsimile reprint of 6th edition. (R.J. Leach: Ditton, 1942)

Longmate, Norman *The Real Dad's Army: The Story of the Home Guard* (Arrow Books: London, 1974)

Lyall, W. 'Some Memories of Bapty's Gunshop' *Guns Review,* June 1976, p. 309.

Mace, Martin F. *Vehicles of the Home Guard* (Historic Military Press: Pulborough, 2001)

MacKenzie, S.P. *The Home Guard.* Paperback edition. (Oxford University Press: Oxford, 1996)

Manders, Lieutenant E.W. Grenades, *EY Rifle and Cup Discharger, for the Home Guard* (Practical Press: London, undated)

Marks, Leo *Between Silk and Cynanide: A Codemaker's War 1941–1945.* Corrected paperback edition. (Harper Collins: London, 2000)

Mazower, Mark *Inside Hitler's Greece: The Experience of Occupation, 1941–44.* 2nd paperback edition. (Yale University Press: New Haven, 1998)

Mendenhall, Captain M. 'The MP28,II, Successor to the MP18,I' *Small Arms Review,* March 2004

MOI – Ministry of Information. *Britain's Modern Army* (Odhams Press: London, *c.* 1943)

MOI – Ministry of Information *Roof Over Britain: The Official Story of Britain's Anti-Aircraft Defences 1939–1942* (HMSO: London, 1943)

Mondey, David *The Concise Guide to Axis Aircraft of World War II.* Reprint, 2nd edition (Chancellor Press: London, 1997)

Moore, Captain John (ed.) *Jane's Fighting Ships of World War I* (facsimile reprint of *Jane's All the World's Ships,* 1919, with additional material from the 1914 edition) (Random House Group: London, 2001)

Oxenden, Major N.V. *Auxiliary Units: History and Achievement 1940–1944.* Reprint of 1944 War Office report. (390th Group Memorial Air Museum: Parham, 1998)

Perret, B. *Panzerkampfwagen III Medium Tank.* Revised edition. (Osprey Publishing: Oxford, 1999)

Perret, B. *Panzerkampfwagen IV Medium Tank* (Osprey Publishing: Oxford, 1999)

Pile, Gen. Sir Frederick *Ack-Ack: Britain's Defence against Air Attack during the Second World War* (George G. Harrap: London, 1949)

Ponting, Clive *1940: Myth and Reality* (Hamish Hamilton: London, 1990)

Preston, Anthony (ed.) *Jane's Fighting Ships of World War II* (reformatted reprint of *Jane's Fighting Ships 1946/47,* with additional material) (Random House Group: London, 2001)

RAI – Royal Artillery Institution. *Growth and Development of the Royal Artillery During the War* (Royal Artillery Institution: Woolwich, 1919)

Rawlinson, J.G. *My War Years, 1939–1946* (Temple Sowerby: private circulation only, 2002)

Rigden, Denis *SOE Syllabus: Lessons in ungentlemanly warfare, World War II* (PRO: Richmond, 2001)

Robinson, Captain Ernest H. and King, Gordon R. *Rifle Training for War*. 3rd edition. (Cassell & Company: London, 1940)

Robinson, Derek *Invasion 1940*, 2nd edition. (Constable and Robinson: London, 2006)

Schellenberg, SS General Walter, int. Erickson, John *Invasion 1940*. 2nd edition. (St Ermin's Press & Little, Brown and Company: London, 2000)

Schenk, P. 'Sealion – The Invasion that Never Was', *After the Battle*, No. 69, 1990.

Seaman, Mark (Intro) *Secret Agent's Handbook of Special Devices*. Reprint of the *SOE Descriptive Catalogue of Special Devices and Supplies* (1944), with introduction. (PRO: Richmond, 2000)

Shirer, William L. The Rise and Fall of the Third Reich. 3rd ed. (Reprint Society: London, 1962)

Shore, Captain C. *With British Snipers to the Reich*. Facsimile reprint of 1948 first edition. (Greenhill Books: London, 1997)

Sims, D. *Defence Against Invasion: The Suffolk Coastline, Aldeburgh to Walberswick, 1939–34*. (MA dissertation, University of East Anglia, 2008)

Skennerton, Ian *British Small Arms of World War 2: The Complete Reference Guide to Weapons Codes and Contracts, 1936–1946*. (Greenhill Books: London, 1988)

Skennerton, Ian *The British Sniper: British and Commonwealth Sniping and Equipments, 1915–1983* (Ian Skennerton/Arms and Armour Press: London, 1984)

Skennerton, Ian *The Lee-Enfield Story: The Lee-Metford, Lee-Enfield S.M.L.E. and No. 4 Series Rifles and Carbines, 1880 to the Present* (Greenhill Books: London, 1993)

Slater, Hugh *Home Guard for Victory*. 4th edition. (Victor Gollancz: London, 1941)

Smith, Henry *Bureaucrats in Battledress: A History of the Ministry of Food Home Guard* (R.E. Jones & Bros: Conway, 1945)

Smith, Robert D., and Rhynas Brown, Ruth *Bombards: Mons Meg and Her Sisters* (Royal Armouries: London, 1989)

Southworth, A. *The Home Guard Pocket Manual* (The Ruberoid Company: Stonehouse, 1940)

Southworth, A. *The Home Guard Pocket Manual*. 10th edition. (The Ruberoid Company: Stonehouse, 1944)

Stamps, Mark and Skennerton, Ian *.380 Enfield No. 2 Revolver* (Greenhill Books: London, 1993)

Steppler, Glenn A. *Britons To Arms! The Story of the British Volunteer Soldier*. 2nd edition. (Budding Books: Stroud, 1997)

Stroud, A., et al., *Salisbury. Intelligence Section Home Guard*. (Salisbury, private circulation only, Bapty archive, 1944)

Summerfield, Penny and Peniston-Bird, Corinna *Contesting Home Defence: Men, Women and the Home Guard in the Second World War* (Manchester University Press: Manchester, 2007)

Talent, P. *The Countryman's Diary, 1939* (War Office/Coleshill House: Highworth, 1943)

Turner, Des. Aston House, Station 12: SOE's Secret Centre (Sutton Publishing: Stroud, 2006)

Wade, Col G.A. *The Defence of Bloodford Village* (War Office/HMSO: London, 1940)

Wallace, G.F. *The Guns of the Royal Air Force* (William Kimber: London, 1972)

Ward, Arthur *Resisting the Nazi Invader* (Constable: London, 1997)

Warwicker, John *With Britain in Mortal Danger: Britain's Most Secret Army of WWII*. 2nd edition. (Cerberus Publishing: Whitchurch, 2004)

Whiting, C. *Skorzeny: The Most Dangerous Man in Europe*. 2nd edition. (Leo Cooper: Trowbridge)

Wills, Henry. *Pillboxes: A Study of U.K. Defences 1940* (Leo Cooper/Secker and Warburg: London, 1985)

Woodhall, M. 'Modelling the Churchill 3-inch gun carrier' *Airfix Magazine Annual* 1974, Cambridge.

PRIMARY SOURCES

National Archives

AVIA 22/576	Blacker Bombard weapon requirements Ministry of Supply
AVIA 22/1520	Smith 3" lightweight gun and equipment
AVIA 22/2921	Manufacture of Mortar, Spigot, 29mm
AVIA 38/340	Self-propelled 75mm gun
CAB 66/11/19	Minister of Supply's report to the War Cabinet, August 1940
CAB 66/28/47	Fulfilment of the Moscow Protocol
CAB 66/36/9	Munitions production, 1942
HO 186/838	Vehicle requisitioning
Prem 3/428/10	Northover Projector
WO 199/191–1913	Blacker Bombard
WO 199/1912	Blacker Bombard, Southern Command papers
WO 199/3237	Home Guard administration and Policy
WO 199/3243	History of formation and organization Home Guard
WO 199/3247	Monthly strength returns and arms Home Guard
WO 199/3248	Home Guard Instruction
WO 199/3262	Endicott (USA) report on the British Home Guard
WO 199/3264	Anti-aircraft Battalions
WO 199/9757	Employment of Home Guard in Coast Artillery
WO 203/540	Blacker Bombard

Imperial War Museum
Photographic archive.

Bapty (2000) Ltd, Archives and Collection
Archives: 'Home Guard' folio, comprising miscellaneous letters, official ephemera, photographs and cuttings, chiefly relating to Home Guard in Wiltshire.

Official Ephemera
LDV Instruction/Home Guard Instruction series
(Note, the author worked largely from his own collection of Home Guard Instructions and Home Guard Information Circulars. However, sets of both may be viewed at The National Archives.)

No. 8 Chief of the Imperial General Staff (CIGS) – July 1940, *Tanks and Tank Destruction* (War Office/HMSO: London)

No. 11 Chief of the Imperial General Staff (CIGS) – August 1940,*Miscellaneous Notes*. (William Clowes & Sons: London, for War Office HMSO)

No. 14 CIGS – 18 September 1940, *Winter Training*. (War Office/ HMSO: London)

No. 23 CIGS – 16 January 1941, *Night Training*. (War Office/HMSO: London)

No. 26 CIGS – March 1941, *Miscellaneous Notes*. (William Clowes & Sons: London, for War Office/HMSO)

No. 30 CIGS – 8 May 1941, *Collective Training*. (War Office/HMSO: London)

No. 38 CIGS – September 1941, *Winter Training 1941–1942*. (War Office/ HMSO: London)

No. 45 CIGS – 10 March 1942, *Miscellaneous Notes*. (War Office/ HMSO: London)

No. 47 C-in-C Home Forces – 3 May 1942, *Miscellaneous Notes*. (War Office/ HMSO: London)

No. 50 C-in-C Home Forces – 25 September 1942, *Winter Training for 1942– 1943*. (War Office: London)

No. 51 C-in-C Home Forces – September 1942, *Battlecraft and Battle Drill for the Home Guard, Part I: Introduction and Battlecraft* (War Office/ HMSO: London)

No. 51 C-in-C Home Forces – September 1942, *Battlecraft and Battle Drill for the Home Guard, Part II: Battle Drill* (War Office/HMSO: London)

No. 51 C-in-C Home Forces – January 1943, *Battlecraft and Battle Drill for the Home Guard, Part III: Patrolling* (War Office/HMSO, London)

No. 51 C-in-C Home Forces – November 1943, *Battlecraft and Battle Drill for the Home Guard, Part IV: The organization of the Home Guard Defence* (War Office/HMSO: London)

No. 56 C-in-C Home Forces – 20 February 1943, *Summer Training for 1943* (War Office/HMSO: London)

No. 58 C-in-C Home Forces – 20 July 1943, *Miscellaneous Notes from Other Theatres of War*. (War Office/HMSO: London)

No. 59 C-in-C Home Forces – September 1943, *Winter Training for 1943– 1944*. (War Office/HMSO: London)

No. 60 C-in-C Home Forces – December 1943, *Miscellaneous Notes – Weapon Training*. (War Office/HMSO: London)

No. 62 C-in-C Home Forces – 6 December 1943, *Miscellaneous Notes: Notes from North Africa, November 1942–May 1943* (War Office/HMSO: London)

No. 64 C-in-C Home Forces – March 1944, *Notes on Summer Training, 1944 and Revised Range Courses.* (War Office/HMSO: London)

Home Guard Information Circular series

No. 19 Army Council, 2 December 1942. (The Whitefriars Press: London, for HMSO)

No. 27 Army Council, 12 May 1943. (The Whitefriars Press: London, for HMSO)

No. 30 Army Council, 16 June 1943. (The Whitefriars Press: London, for HMSO)

No. 37 Army Council, 10 November 1943. (The Whitefriars Press: London, for HMSO)

No. 53 Army Council, 9 August 1944. (The Whitefriars Press: London, for HMSO)

Home Guard Training Posters and Notice Board Information

.300-inch Browning Automatic Rifle Instruction Sheet (Fosh and Cross, London, for HMSO, Undated, *c.* 1940)

Notice Board Information No. 87. *Injuries and Damage Caused By Accidents with Ammunition and Explosives* (War Office/HMSO: London, March 1944)

Misc. Provisional Training and Instructional Notes (date order)

Chief of the Imperial General Staff (CIGS), *Instructional Notes on the .300-inch Browning Machine Gun (Model 1917) 1940, PROVISIONAL.* (War Office/HMSO: London, 28 August 1940)

CIGS, *Instructional Notes on the .300-inch Browning Machine Gun (Model 1917) 1940, PROVISIONAL.* (War Office: London, September 1940, October 1941 impression)

Chief Inspector of Armaments *Handbook for the Projectors, 2½-inch Marks I & II on Mountings, 2 ½-inch Projector Marks I & II.* (Military Library Research Services: Smalldale, September 1941, 2006: facsimile reprint)

CIGS, *29mm. Spigot Mortar (Blacker Bombard), Training Instruction PROVISIONAL.* (Military Library Research Services: Smalldale, 11 November 1941: undated facsimile reprint)

CIGS, *Instructional Notes on the .300-inch Lewis Machine Gun (Ground Action), 1940, PROVISIONAL*, amended reprint. (War Office: London, April 1942)

CIGS, *The 3-Inch O.S.B. Gun (Smith Gun)*. (Military Library Research Services: Smalldale, 23 July 1942, 2006, facsimile reprint)

Small Arms Training (SAT), Vol. I Pamphlet Series (In Pamphlet Number Order)

SAT, Vol. I, Pam. 3. Army Council. *Small Arms Training, Volume I, Pamphlet No. 3: Mortar (2-inch)*. (War Office/HMSO: London, 18 October 1939)

SAT, Vol. I, Pam 5. Army Council. *Small Arms Training, Volume I, Pamphlet No. 5: Anti-Tank Rifle*. (War Office/HMSO: London, 25 April 1942)

SAT, Vol. I, Pam. 6. Army Council. *Small Arms Training, Volume I, Pamphlet No. 6: Anti-Aircraft*. (War Office/HMSO: London, 14 January 1942)

SAT, Vol. I, Pam. 13. Army Council. *Small Arms Training, Volume I, Pamphlet No. 13: Grenade*. (War Office/HMSO: London, 15 July 1942)

SAT, Vol. I, Pam. 13, Sup. 1. Army Council. *Small Arms Training, Volume I, Pamphlet No. 13, SUPPLEMENT No. 1: No. 68 Anti-tank Grenade (Rifle), No. 69 Bakelite Grenade (Hand)*. (War Office/HMSO: London, 8 February 1941)

SAT, Vol. I, Pam. 13, Sup. 2. Army Council. *Small Arms Training, Volume I, Pamphlet No. 13, SUPPLEMENT No. 2: No. 73 Anti-Tank Grenade (Hand), The S.T. Grenade, The Hand Incendiary Bomb*. (War Office/HMSO: London, 27 August 1941)

SAT, Vol. I, Pam. 23.

Army Council. *Small Arms Training, Volume I, Pamphlet No. 23: The 29-mm Spigot Mortar*. (War Office/HMSO: London, 7 November 1942)

SAT, Vol. I, Pam 27. Army Council. *Small Arms Training, Volume I, Pamphlet No. 27: 6-pr., 7-cwt. Anti-Tank Gun*. (War Office/HMSO: London, 5 February 1944)

Miscellaneous War Office Manuals

CIGS *Military Training Pamphlet No. 23 Part II – The Infantry Division in the Defence*. (War Office: London, 23 March 1942)

CIGS *Military Training Pamphlet No. 23 Part IX – The Infantry Division in the Attack*. (War Office: London, 21 July 1941)

CIGS *Military Training Pamphlet No. 23 Part VI – Withdrawal*. (War Office: London, May 1940)

CIGS *Military Training Pamphlet No. 23 Part X – The Infantry Division in the Advance*. (War Office: London, 22 September 1941)

CIGS *Military Training Pamphlet No. 42, Tank Hunting and Destruction.* (War Office: London, 29 August 1940)

Talent, P. *The Countryman's Diary, 1939.* (War Office/Coleshill House: Highworth, 1943)

Wade, Col G.A. *The Defence of Bloodford Village.* (War Office/HMSO, London, 1940)

War Office, *Handbook for the Q.F. 18-pr Gun on Marks III, III*, IIIT and V Field Carriages, Land Service, 1924.* (War Office/HMSO: London, February 1924)

War Office Intelligence Publications on the German Army

Periodical Notes on the German Army, No. 24. (General Staff, War Office: London, July 1940)

Periodical Notes on the German Army, No. 28. (General Staff, War Office: London, June 1940)

Periodical Notes on the German Army, No. 30. (General Staff, War Office: London, August 1940)

Popular Guide to the German Army, No. 3. (General Staff, War Office: London, June 1941)

The German Army in Pictures. (General Staff, War Office, London, January 1941)

The German Forces in the Field. (General Staff, War Office: London, July 1940)

Admiralty Publications

Admiralty Gunnery Branch. *Handbook for the 4-inch Mark VII and VIII BL.* (Admiralty: London, 1913)

Admiralty Gunnery Branch. *Notes on Gunnery for Defensively Equipped Merchant Ships.* (Admiralty: London, 1939)

Home Office Publications

Home Office, Air Raid Precautions Department. *Air Raid Precautions Handbook No. 1, Personal Protection Against Gas.* (HMSO: London, 1937)

Regional Commissioner for Civil Defence. *Consolidated Instructions to Invasion Committees in England and Wales.* (HMSO: London, 1942)

US Official Publications

TM 31-200-1: Unconventional Warfare Devices and Techniques. (Department of Defense, Washington, 1966)

Non-official Home Guard Ephemera
Commercially Produced Weapon Manuals

.300 Lewis Machine Gun for the Home Guard, 3rd edition. (The Bravon
 Ledger Company: Bradford-on-Avon, 1941)

'An Instructor' *The Complete Lewis Gunner*. Reprint of 1918 edition.(Gale &
 Polden: Aldershot, 1940)

Handbook of the Thompson Submachine Gun, Model of 1928 (Auto-Ordnance
 Corporation, Bridgeport, 1940)

Lewis Gun Mechanism Made Easy, 6th edition, 20th impression. (Gale & Polden:
 Aldershot, 1941)

Manders, Lieut. E.W. Grenades, *EY Rifle and Cup Discharger, for the Home Guard*
 (Practical Press: London, undated)

Manual of Modern Automatic Guns (Anonymous reprint of Bernards'
 original, undated)

Sten Machine Carbine, 9mm. Mk. II and Mk. III, 4th edition. (The Bravon
 Ledger Company: Bradford-on-Avon, 1942)

The Bren Light Machine Gun, Description, Use and Mechanism (Gale & Polden:
 Aldershot, undated)

The Browning Automatic Rifle (Gale & Polden: Aldershot, undated)

*The Browning Heavy Machine Gun, .300 Calibre model 1917 (water-cooled)
 Mechanism Made Easy.* (Gale & Polden: Aldershot, 1942)

The Thompson Submachine Gun Mechanism Made Easy (Gale & Polden:
 Aldershot, undated)

Commercially Produced Home Guard Training Manuals, Strategy and Tactics

Brophy, John. *Advanced Training for the Home Guard, with Ten Specimen Field
 Exercises.* (Hodder & Stoughton: London, 1941)

Brophy, John. *A Home Guard Handbook*. Revised edition, 2nd impression.
 (Hodder & Stoughton: London, 1942)

Brophy, John. Home Guard: A Handbook for the L.D.V. 6th impression.
 (Hodder & Stoughton: London, 1941)

Elliot, Andrew G., with 'J.B.' and Scientist. *The Home Guard Encyclopaedia.*
 (Thorsons: London, undated)

Langdon-Davies, John. *Home Guard Warfare.* (George Routledge and Sons:
 London, 1941)

Langdon-Davies, Major John. *The Home Guard Fieldcraft Manual.* 2nd edition. (John Murray and the Pilot Press: London, 1942)

Langdon-Davies, Major John. *The Home Guard Training Manual.* Facsimile reprint of 6th edition, 1942. (R.J. Leach: Ditton, 1998)

Levey, Lieut.-Colonel J.H. *Home Guard Training.* 3rd impression. (Eyre and Spottiswoode: London, 1940)

Marques, Capt. C.A. *Training Course for Home Guard Instructors.* 3rd edition. (Privately Published: Gt. Amwell, 1942)

Robinson, Captain Ernest H. and King, Gordon R. *Rifle Training for War.* 3rd edition. (Cassell & Company: London, 1940)

Slater, Hugh. *Home Guard for Victory!* 4th impression. (Victor Gollancz: London, 1941)

Southworth, A. *The Home Guard Pocket Manual.* (The Ruberoid Company: Stonehouse, 1940)

Southworth, Capt. A. *The Home Guard Pocket Manual.* 10th edition. (The Ruberoid Company: Stonehouse, 1944)

Thompson, Major Paul W. *Modern Battle.* Penguin edition. (Penguin Books: Hamondsworth, 1942)

INDEX

You may also be interested in …

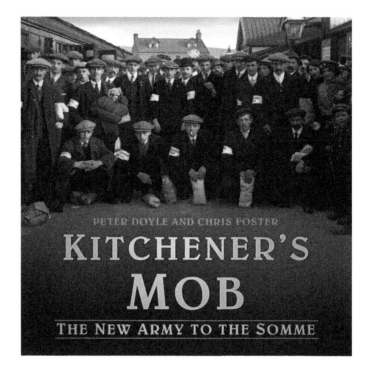

978 0 7509 6495 1

This book tells the amazing story of 'Kitchener's Army' and its volunteer soldiers, the men of the 'First Hundred Thousand' and the many Pals' battalions that were later raised across Britain, in its industrial heartlands and leafy shires alike. Through artefacts and original documents, this moving tribute bears witness to the indelible imprint this memorable 'mob' made on British history.